The Third Rose

By John Malcolm Brinnin
DYLAN THOMAS IN AMERICA

The Third Rose

GERTRUDE STEIN AND HER WORLD

by
JOHN MALCOLM BRINNIN

WEIDENFELD & NICOLSON
20 NEW BOND STREET LONDON W1

COPYRIGHT © 1958 BY JOHN MALCOLM BRINNIN

First Published in Great Britain 1960

PRINTED IN GREAT BRITAIN BY
LOWE AND BRYDONE (PRINTERS) LIMITED, LONDON, N.W.10

R.6124

this book is
for Frances and Bill and Rosalie T.

Civilization began with a rose. A rose is a rose is a rose is a rose.

— GERTRUDE STEIN

What after all is so natural as to assume that one object, called by one name, should be known by one affection of the mind?

— WILLIAM JAMES

Sometimes I think that there will be place in the future for a literature the nature of which will singularly resemble that of a sport.

Let us subtract, from literary possibilities, everything which today, by the direct expression of things and the direct stimulation of the sensibility by new means — motion pictures, omnipresent music, etc., — is being rendered useless or ineffective for the art of language.

Let us also subtract a whole category of subjects — psychological, sociological, etc. — which the growing precision of the sciences will render it difficult to treat freely. There will remain to letters a private domain: that of symbolic expression and of imaginative values due to the free combination of the elements of language.

— PAUL VALÉRY

Man is timid and apologetic; he is no longer upright; he dares not say "I think," or "I am," but quotes some saint or sage. He is ashamed before the blade of grass or the blowing rose. These roses under my window make no reference to former roses or to better ones; they are for what they are; they exist for God today. There is no time to them. There is simply the rose; it is perfect in every moment of its existence.

— RALPH WALDO EMERSON

Author's Note

WHEN in the course of a conversation I told him that I was writing a book about Gertrude Stein, my friend Erv Harmon, one of the last great comics on the dwindling stages of the burlesque circuit, seemed suddenly thoughtful. "Well —" he said finally — "I can go along with those first two roses of hers all right . . . but when she gets to that third rose she loses me." Erv Harmon's response to Gertrude Stein's most famous utterance is of course a familiar one. "A rose is a rose" does not seriously disturb the equilibrium of most people and, like "business is business," may even strike some people as simple good sense made clear and final. But for considerations that must include the indeterminate reaches of semantics and metaphysics, "Rose is a rose is a rose is a rose" opens up a literary avenue upon which few people have the temerity or the desire to step. In these pages I have attempted to trace the intentions of Gertrude Stein in terms of "that third rose" (the fourth, fifth and sometimes sixth roses, as well) and, in the process, to document the life and show the development of an artist who for a few years in her late middle age was at the same time the most obscure and the most famous writer in the English language.

If Gertrude Stein had never lived, sooner or later works very much like those she produced would have been written by someone else.

Once a particular set of conditions was present, her arrival was inevitable — like an event in chemistry.

She told the story of her life and work more completely and more obsessively than any other writer of her time. But her purview was subjective to the point of myopia and she was as self-satisfied and as full of contented whimsies as a cat on a hob. The task of the biographer, in her case, is threefold: to strip away the undergrowth of subjectivity that hedged expressions of her true personality; to relate her creative life to aesthetic standards and movements which she regarded with indifference or altogether ignored; to place in temporal order events which in her scattered telling she runs together, juxtaposes wrongly, or magnifies out of proportion to their significance. Since, more than most human beings, she tended to see everything as concentric to herself, the task is also to view intellectual or anecdotal events in patterns that give them meanings sometimes greater than those she assigned to them, sometimes lesser, but in any case, in patterns that relate them to the general history of a time she tended to domesticate and make her own.

Gertrude Stein belongs in the last phase of the governance of reason; she is one of the last daughters of the Enlightenment. While she spent a lifetime trying to escape the nineteenth century, her career belongs to its sunset phase — to the era of William James and John Dewey, George Bernard Shaw and the science of economic reform, of the "Boston marriage" and votes for women, of the incandescent lamp and the Michelson-Morley experiment.

She believed exclusively in the power and efficacy of the rational mind when all of her major contemporaries in art and literature were examining with fascination the power of the non-rational as a source of aesthetic communication. She believed in consciousness as a positive glory when the temper of her time ran toward intimations that an understanding of the unconscious might be a major source of wisdom.

In her lifetime a general public would not take her seriously at all, while an intellectual public took her all too seriously. Americans obsessively driven somehow to understand what they could not anyhow experience made her the Sacred Cow of modern letters and all but succeeded in separating the figure from her work. Yet behind the romance of her reputation she was simply a writer who produced something confoundingly new, something based in the lively vision of a knowledgeable personality and an erudite mind. She may not endure, as James Joyce or Picasso may not endure. But our history would be poorer and narrower without her, and generations to follow may not knowingly deny themselves the pleasure of her company. She can delight as often as she can mystify or intrigue, and no one who has browsed for long in the marvelous meadows of her monotone has failed to come back with a daisy.

If it is difficult to be passionate about her work, it is equally difficult to be passionate about a Brancusi bird or a Mondrian canvas. But it is easy and perhaps necessary to be passionate about her devoted practice of the art of language without reference to utility. Since her time, oily tides of *Kitsch* have continued, in the name of literature, to wash in pulpy masses of sensationalism and the soggy detritus of adolescent minds. Beyond the luster that poets continue to give to this literary age, the excitements of books written thirty, forty and fifty years ago are, sad to say, still the only excitements. As the century grows older, criticism becomes nostalgic as our representative literature seems to be more and more uncomfortably symptomatic, or diagnostic and efficient, and — except for the saving grace of a handful of writers in love with their language — as safe, aseptic and as undisturbing to the five senses as an A & P supermarket or the lobby of the local Hilton. In any case, a passion for Gertrude Stein's valiant explorations has been the history of her admirers who tend, almost unanimously, to praise her methods at the expense of the writings that document them, and to regard her less as a subject to be examined than as an object to be accounted for, or simply acclaimed.

Her influence — in the verifiable sense that Whitman and Henry James, Flaubert or Proust, Rilke and Hopkins have been influences — has been all but nil. Her small, easily recognized effect on the careers of Ernest Hemingway and Sherwood Anderson has been vastly overemphasized and subsequently accepted as something significant mainly by critics who deal most congenially in the secondhand. She has always had well-wishers, even among those who did not care to pay more than passing attention to her actual work. For the most part, literary historians, critics and compilers of textbooks have written of her putative influence in a transparent bewilderment as to the means of accounting for her fame and inescapable presence in any other way. She has always needed less of elaborate, often embarrassed defense and more of simple unworried understanding.

The way in which she maintained integrity of life — the artist's life — was her real and resonant influence. And yet, in the last years of her life, when much of her writing seemed guided by the compromises of the literary marketplace, some aspects of her conduct as a public figure shook the faith of even those friends and admirers who had always regarded her integrity as unassailable.

In a writing career that lasted more than forty years, Gertrude Stein separated literature from history, from sociology, from psychology and anthropology, even from knowledge itself. As a poet, she destroyed the connecting tissues that hold observed realities together and, as a writer of novels, she attempted to remove from the body of literature the very sinew and bone of narrative. She preached that literature was an art not necessarily dependent upon any of these, and she practiced what she preached. While she believed that most writers failed to allow writing to express all that it could, in her own practice she scrupulously saw to it that writing expressed less than it would.

Among writers driven in one way or another to find the limits of language, she had forebears in the poets of Alexandria, in the translators of the King James Bible, in John Lyly, in Góngora, in Marivaux; and on the continent of Europe she had active contemporaries in the figures of Max Jacob and Pierre Reverdy in France, Carl Einstein in Germany, for a time Pär Lagerkvist in Sweden, and Ramón Gomez de la Serna in Spain. If there is going to be a continuing life of literature, it seems reasonable to assume that in the ghost that sings in the underwood of her forty books — or in the flesh of someone who, like her, wants words to rise like Alhambras carved in air — she will come again.

Illustrations

Acknowledgments

We are grateful to the following for kind permission to reproduce the photographs in this book: The Baltimore Museum of Art, Cone Collection, for the photograph facing page 178; Julian P. Graham, page 307; Man Ray, page 275; The Metropolitan Museum of Art, Bequest of Gertrude Stein, 1946, page 179; Carl Van Vechten, page 306; and The Yale University Library, American Literature Collection, pages 146, 147 and 274.

The Third Rose

CHAPTER 1

Once upon a time when Poland had a capital
and Washington was the capital of the United
States there was born in Allegheny in the state
of Pennsylvania the seventh child of a father and
a mother. The father had many a brother, the
mother was as a mother what would be reasonably certain to necessitate kindling not only religion but traveling. And so they traveled to what
was then a capital kingdom which had in it no
relation to eliminate any education unaccompa-
nied by intoxication.

— GERTRUDE STEIN

ON the eve of the birth of Gertrude Stein
in 1874 a great storm broke upon the length of the Eastern states to
spoil the mildest winter in thirty years. With snow piled knee-
deep in the streets of Manhattan, the *New York Times* raised an angry voice to demand that underground railroads replace the horse-
drawn streetcars that had foundered in heavy drifts, causing "many
feeble women and children, all exhausted by the labors of the day,
to make their way to distant homes on foot as best they might
through the blinding snowstorm." With new transportation, promised the *Times*, "nearly all the vexations incidental to the traffic of
the Metropolis will disappear."

Snow was the big news next morning, but the world was harried
by other troubles, too. In Paris, barely recovered from the terrors of
the Commune, no less than nine hundred Communists were awaiting trial; and at 168 Bleecker Street, New York, one M. Désiré
Debuchy, a maker of artificial flowers who had been apprehended by

3

the police for having in his possession thirty-one hand grenades, was released only after Justice Sherwood had "satisfied himself of the respectability of M. Debuchy," who "had nothing whatever to do with the Communists." Harper and Brothers announced the publication of *The Parisian*, a novel by Edward Bulwer (Lord Lytton), who, "conscious of the lapse of time, is consciously writing for posterity"; and at the Union Square Theater, Dion Boucicault's *Led Astray* was continuing with "undiminished success." Two young women had run into trouble: Mary O'Brien, arriving alone from Philadelphia on the midnight train, was tricked by a hackman who carried her off to a rendezvous where "a brutal outrage" took place; and Ellen Washburn was arrested and locked up for having relieved George Burroughs of Hoboken of a diamond ring "while he was in her company at a house of ill-fame in Thompson Street." In Boston, a new temperance movement which sponsored visits to barrooms by bands of praying men and women was started by a group of clergymen; and in Philadelphia the bodies of Chang and Eng, the celebrated Siamese twins, were awaiting autopsy "to set at rest that very debatable question as to their physical and metaphysical relationship." The nineteenth century with all its melodramas and pomposities, its dreadful suspicions and moral earnestness, lowered over the bed where Gertrude Stein came into life. Though she would point to her intellectual distance from it as an indication of her personal emancipation from its toils, her character was inevitably formed by her century and her achievement was more limited by its horizons than she would ever suspect.

Her parents, Daniel and Amelia Keyser Stein, both of German-Jewish extraction, had at the time of their marriage in 1864 agreed to have five children. With nice spacing and variety they had achieved this full complement within seven years. Still they had not produced the offspring that would bring to the name of Stein a lasting resonance and the makings of a twentieth-century legend. But when two of the first five children died early in life, the sad circumstance permitted first, the arrival of Leo, followed within two years by that of the sister under whose ample, constant and finally engulfing shadow he was to live and die. She was born at eight

4

o'clock in the morning of February 3, "a perfect baby," in the words of her father who expected nothing less. When Gertrude came to the stages of measles and whooping cough, he took every opportunity to remind her of the unblemished condition in which she had made her first appearance.

She was the last of the Stein children and for many years the pampered baby of the family, circumstances of birth having already determined, and perhaps partially excused, a lifelong and unapologetic self-indulgence. If, she said, you come into the world as she had, "it is not lost all the rest of one's life, there you are you are privileged, nobody can do anything but take care of you, that is the way I was and that is the way I still am, and any one who is like that necessarily liked it. I did and I do." It did not take her long, she confessed, to learn "that there was a way of winning by being winsome."

The Steins lived on Western Avenue in Allegheny, Pennsylvania, an upper-middle-class street in a suburb which was later to be absorbed by Pittsburgh. Their house was the twin of another in which lived the family of Daniel Stein's brother and business partner, Solomon, and his wife, Pauline. But the proximity was purely physical; the twin houses were sorely divided. Shortly before Gertrude's birth, the brothers' wives had brought years of intermittent wrangling to a showdown by severing ties for good. Now they were no longer on speaking terms. Things were nearly as bad for the brothers in the wholesale woolen business they ran at the corner of Wood and Fourth Streets in downtown Pittsburgh. Daniel Stein's bad temper drove customers away so often that Solomon had begun to spend much of his business day figuring out ways to win them back. Under the strain of disagreement at home and continual dissension at business, the brothers finally agreed to part. Solomon settled in New York, where he went into banking and, on his own, quickly became successful.

Daniel, taking advantage of ancestral connections in Austria, sighted an opportunity "in wool" there and set out for Vienna. A few months later, accompanied by Rachel Keyser, one of Amelia's spinster sisters, the family followed, for what turned out to be an absence from America of nearly three years. As a result of this early uprooting, Gertrude Stein's first memories had the flavor of scenes from a Victor Herbert operetta. In later years, recalling pictures and sensations, she remembered the Volksgarten through which the bewhiskered Emperor Franz Josef strolled while the band played patriotic strains; the miniature Theseus temple, and the kiosk where she got glasses of milk; the cold frightening feeling of the dark salt caves; birds, butterflies, lizards, little green tree-frogs she kept at home in a jar; and the sight of her mother and older brothers handsomely riding on horseback through the Vienna woods. The hedges in the gardens of the Belvedere remained strong in her memory because "in a kind of way a formal garden pleases a child's fancy more than a natural garden. It is more like a garden you would make up yourself." And, most clearly, she remembered her first delvings into books, picture books to be sure, but "books all the same since pictures in picture books are narrative."

The Steins had just begun to feel settled in Vienna when Daniel had to return to America on a business assignment. In his absence, letters sent to Baltimore assured him of his youngest child's good progress: "Our little Gertie is a little Schnatterer. She talks all day long and so plainly. *She outdoes them all.* She's such a round little pudding, toddles around the whole day & repeats everything that is said or done." All of the children were continually beguiled in their marvelous foreign playground, which extended to the Tyrol on the River Traun in the summers, but their mother was not happy. Even with the companionship of her sister and her brother Ephraim, who came on visits from Germany where he was studying sculpture, and the help of a governess and a Hungarian tutor — Herr Krajoletz, a medical student from Budapest who turned the Stein children into collectors of everything in nature they could waylay or snare — Milly Stein was burdened and lonely as she watched over the routines of five active children and longed to be back in America. Returning at this time was out of the question because of Daniel's unsettled situation, but one day homesickness led her suddenly to dismiss the tutor and governess, pack up the family's belongings and escort her brood to Paris.

6

She leased a house in Passy and they settled down for another period, adventurous for the children, but for their mother only a time of waiting for the day when finally they would all go home. In Paris Gertrude had her first taste of formal schooling, played about the Arc de Triomphe where there were chains to swing on, picked up a child's smattering of the French language, and learned to get used to soup for early breakfast, leg of mutton and spinach for lunch. In less than a year, Daniel joined them in Paris. Life became brighter and more active for everyone under the restless drive of paterfamilias, but soon the family was homeward bound. With trunks full of Parisian finery — skin coats, caps, muffs, dozens of gloves, fancy plumed hats, riding costumes, plus an expensive microscope and a many-volumed history of zoology for the junior naturalists — the prodigal family went to London in the summer of 1878, and from there sailed for America.

En route to Baltimore, they stayed over in New York just long enough for hopeful relatives to try to bring Milly and her sister-in-law Pauline together again. But Milly Stein, "a gentle pleasant little woman with a quick temper," could be as intransigent as her husband. She refused every peacemaking offer paving the way toward a renewed partnership that would have allowed Daniel's family to share in the great prosperity Solomon was enjoying. Her stubbornness had long-range effects: Gertrude's branch of the Steins would have to settle for being "reasonably poor" instead of becoming as rich as the family of Solomon Stein. Gertrude had some rueful thoughts about the lost chance of fortune, but ultimately she was glad that her mother and aunt had not patched up their differences. Otherwise, she might not have escaped "the horrors" of being brought up in New York City.

In Baltimore, where her father's brothers, Meyer and Samuel, were well known as the original firm of Stein Bros., she stayed in the house of her kindly religious grandfather Keyser. The household was large and opulent, and the favored youngest child was petted and fussed over by a bevy of good-natured aunts and uncles. Hardly five years old, Gertrude had already undergone the influences of three vastly different environments, an advantage of which she

7

later wrote: "So I was five years old when we came back to America having known Austrian German and French French, and now American English, a nice world if there is enough of it, and more or less there always is." A cosmopolitan youngster, she had previously expressed herself in odds and ends of German and French. Now her emotions began "to feel themselves in English." The bustling atmosphere of a family even larger and more complicated than her own was something of an enchantment to her. Already she was absorbing the rhythms, observing the personalities and undergoing the familial experiences she would store up until she was ready to give them full and fond expression as the substance of her magnum opus, *The Making of Americans*.

Daniel Stein, uncertain of his business future, was again restless and anxious to remove himself from Baltimore and the frustrations of working and living with relatives. In her description of the family's attitude toward her father, Gertrude notes tendencies that kept their life in continual instability: they "came then more and more to know it about the father of them that he had a great bigness in him, that he was strong in beginning, that he would then push everything away from him or go away and leave it and soon then there would be in him a new beginning and he would then be to every one who saw him as big as all the world around him." California became Daniel Stein's next goal. After a reconnaissance trip during which he lived briefly in Los Angeles and then in San Jose, he returned to Baltimore and, with the large family in tow, set out by train, this time for San Francisco. The only thing Gertrude remembered about the long train journey across the continent was that one day her sister's ostrich-plumed hat blew out the window. Her father quickly pulled an emergency cord that stopped the train in the middle of nowhere. He then stepped out, retrieved the hat and, while the stunned conductor and passengers looked on, calmly returned to the train and resumed his seat.

In California, after living at Tubb's Hotel in Oakland for a year while Daniel investigated the best business possibilities San Francisco had to offer, they settled down in sparsely populated East Oakland, at Thirteenth Avenue and Twenty-fifth Street. Their new home, known to the community as the "old Stratton house," stood on a rise in the center of ten acres fenced in by a wooden railing. An avenue of eucalyptus and blue gum led from the house to the gate; and a flower garden, a hayfield and an orchard covered the rest of the property. "It was wonderful there in the summer with the dry heat," Gertrude wrote, "and the sun burning, and the hot earth for sleeping; and then in the winter with the rain, and the north wind blowing that would bend the trees and often break them, and the owls in the walls scaring you with their tumbling . . . In the summer it was good for generous sweating to help the men make the hay into bales for its preserving and it was well for one's growing to eat radishes pulled with the black earth sticking to them and to chew the mustard and find roots with all kinds of funny flavors in them, and to fill one's hat with fruit and sit on the dry ploughed ground and eat and think and sleep and read and dream and never hear them when they would all be calling; and then when the quail came it was fun to go shooting, and then when the wind and the rain and the ground were ready to help seeds in their growing, it was good fun to help plant them, and the wind would be so strong it would blow the leaves and branches of trees down around them and you could shout and work and get wet and be all soaking and run out full into the strong wind and let it dry you, in between the gusts of rain that left you soaking. It was fun all the things that happened all the year then."

The Stein children went to the Sweet School in Oakland, but by this time marked differences in age and vast differences in temperament allowed them few other activities in common. Gertrude and Leo tended to keep to themselves, sharing precocious intellectual interests and continually hoarding up feelings of sullen animosity toward their father. Their mother, ill of cancer, had been confined to her bed not long after their migration from the East. Invalidism prevented her from arbitrating family disputes and perhaps modifying their intensity. Daniel Stein was continually making up strict new rules of deportment and his authoritarian sense of family order had already turned his youngest children into rebels. In Vienna, at one point, he decided that the children must eat everything that was put before them. The rule was in force one Sunday when visitors came for dinner. Leo was served boiled turnips and carrots. These particular vegetables nauseated Leo and he was usually granted permission to refuse them. However, in front of the visitors, Daniel was prompted to exercise his Prussian notions of discipline. Leo, forced to eat the turnips and carrots, was violently sick all through the rest of the day. Through similar experiences, Gertrude and Leo came to resent their father with unmitigated passion and to remain vividly unsentimental about him for the rest of their lives. Even as a child Gertrude felt that her father was, in the most comprehensive meaning of the word, "depressing." Later she applied the term so broadly as to include *all* fathers. Whatever filial emotions she felt in childhood were directed toward her brother Leo. The time was still far off when he too would become paternal and, inevitably, "depressing."

She always regarded her oldest brother, Michael, with deep and simple affection. But she thought that Simon and Bertha were rather simple-minded, as indeed they were, and remained indifferent to them from the beginning. In the East Oakland years she had to sleep in the same room with Bertha who "was not a pleasant person, she naturally did not like anything," and worse, was always grinding her teeth while she slept. Simon struck her as clownishly funny, but not really amusing. He had an obsession with eating which no one could curb; he could devour a family-sized pudding at one fell swoop. Gertrude was careful to point out that he had an obsession amounting to gluttony, as distinct from a nicer obsession with food in itself, and seems to have regarded the distinction as imperative: her own love for food was an emotion as profound as any other by which her life was shaped, and no amount of trouble, travel and expense was ever too much to undertake in order to satisfy it. She even came to resent stories in which characters "sat down to a hearty meal" without the author's having taken the trouble to give a soup-to-nuts account of the menu. Simon was also funny because no one, not even bookish Leo and Gertrude, could begin to educate him: about the discovery of America he could remember neither Columbus nor 1492.

When Daniel Stein was appointed vice-president of the Omnibus Cable Company, Mike became first assistant superintendent. When Simon came of age, he joined his father and brother in the street railway business in the capacity of gripman. This job, in which he acted as a kind of human clutch, regulating the car movements according to bell signals from the conductor, was dull and repetitive but it suited his retarded personality, according to Gertrude, and accommodated his best abilities. He liked contact with all sorts of people, always had candy in his pockets for the children and cigars for the men, and led the happy life of a local "character" until within a few years he retired and, in the phrase of Gertrude's sisterly epitaph, soon died "fat and fishing."

Her own career showed its first dim outlines when, at the age of eight, she attempted to write a drama "in the manner of Shakespeare." Things were going along nicely in this bravura undertaking until she put down a stage direction which read: "The courtiers make witty remarks." Unable to think of even one witty remark, she abandoned drama on the classic scale in favor of less trying effort on a melodrama that was finished without a hitch and entitled *Snatched from Death, or The Sundered Sisters*. For the time at least, Shakespearean avenues to fame were closed. Many years later, Leo insisted that this composition was undertaken when Gertrude was closer to fourteen than to eight and that her memory had flattered her. In his version of her first attempts at writing, Gertrude never got beyond the scenario of a project he had suggested, which involved writing imitations of Elizabethan plays. He, on the other hand, completed with dispatch the greater part of an opus about Attila the Hun replete with "blood-and-thunder Marlovian speeches." If Leo's account is the more dependable, their childhood attempts at authorship show a reversal of their later careers when Leo, hindered by a series of psychological blocks, wasted his creative forces in obsessive talk while Gertrude turned out one volume after another.

At some point in these pre-puberty years, Gertrude intensely read the Bible. In Revelation, she hoped she would find some illumination of the problems of immortal life and eternity that had begun

11

to trouble her thinking. But Revelation cast no light. The voice of God was heard surprisingly often, she observed, but eternity was just not one of His topics. The omission puzzled and frightened her, but eventually she became resigned: there must be a God, she decided, but there is no such thing as eternity.

Her reading had begun with whatever she could lay hands on around the house, and soon branched out to include all that she was allowed to draw out or carry away from the Free Library of Oakland and, in San Francisco, the Mercantile and Mechanics Library and the Marine Institute Library, where for days at a time she sat in a window seat reading Swift, Burke and Defoe, and all of Elizabethan literature, including the prose. Part of the fun of visiting libraries across the Bay was the ferryboat ride, especially when the kindly captain would allow her and Leo to take turns at the helm. Books in their house were mostly Victorian novels, illustrated travel books, gilt-edged and beribboned volumes of Wordsworth and Scott and Burns, and *Pilgrim's Progress*, Shakespeare with annotations in minuscule print, and a file of the *Congressional Record*. From her eighth year or thereabouts, when she absorbed Shakespeare and tried to emulate him, to her fifteenth year, when she had arrived at Fielding and Smollett, she "lived continually with the rhythms of the English language." Her appetite for anything in print extended to the most opaque and snail-paced treatises. She "had a passion . . . for the long dull poems of Wordsworth and Crabbe," and she was probably the only female west of the Mississippi who, having read every word of Carlyle's *Frederick the Great*, could still confront with zest Lecky's forbidding *Constitutional History of England*.

Of contemporary ideas, the one to which she was most often exposed was evolution. Darwin, Huxley and Agassiz were still alive and articulate, and the controversies they had evoked were in the forefront of intellectual and religious concern. "The world was full of evolution, with music as a background for emotion and books as a reality and a great deal of fresh air as a necessity, and a great deal of eating as an excitement and as an orgy," she later recalled. "Evolution was as exciting as the discovery of America, by Columbus quite as exciting, and quite as much an opening up and a limiting, quite as much. By that I mean that discovering America, by reasoning and then finding, opened up a new world and at the same time closed the circle, there was no longer any beyond. Evolution did the same thing, it opened up the history of all animals vegetables and minerals, and man, and at the same time it made them all confined, confined within· a circle, no excitement of creation any more. It is funny all this and this was my childhood and youth and beginning of existence."

A shared fascination with natural history often took her and Leo on excursions along the dusty California roads. They would carry a basket of bread crusts to munch on as they walked at a laggard pace, discoursing like infant Aristotelians, stopping now and then for close inspection of some surprising new aspect of flora or fauna. In the midst of wild life, Gertrude tended to think often of death. Great issues were beginning to trouble her and Leo, but their talks on these sorties, according to Leo, were entirely objective. "I wondered so much about everything," said Gertrude, "that I was almost alone and if you are almost alone well all that there is is almost alone." Their companionship was close and constant, and while they shared some thoughts about the universe, they did not share intimate thoughts about themselves. Gertrude wrote hers down in a secret prose raddled with exclamation marks; Leo kept his to himself.

Sometimes they went, on a tandem bicycle, to San Leandor and sometimes they went with a group of youngsters to Dimond's Cañon, not far from East Oakland, where Leo's interests, at least, were not wholly centered in picnic treats of sarsaparilla and potato salad. Already a precocious observer and amateur of aesthetic theory, at Dimond's Cañon he first became aware of composition in nature — of the particular arrangement of a group of live oaks at the bend of a road that made the landscape take on a character more memorable than any other landscape around. This led him, some years later, to make one of his first definitions of art: "nature seen in the light of its significance." When he recognized that the significance he had in mind was concerned with forms, he amended the definition to read: "nature seen in the light of its formal significance." He had arrived, he believed, at a definition of art as Significant Form — thus anticipating the English critic Roger Fry by many years, just as later he was to make sweeping claims of having anticipated the theories of Benedetto Croce, and of Sigmund Freud and, before he was done, of almost every other important thinker of the century.

Etna Springs, where Gertrude and Leo could swim in cold mineral water and go down into quicksilver mines worked by Chinese coolies, was another favorite spot for excursions. In a theme she wrote a few years later as a schoolwork assignment, Gertrude tells of one of these trips:

The porter woke us early in the morning and we started out bravely. We carried a shotgun and a small satchel with refreshment. It was a delicious summer morning. The air, fragrant with pine, had that crispness and clearness that I think is peculiar to California mountains. . . . We soon covered the level ground, and struck up the heavy mountain grade. As we were passing a pond in a canon, we saw a bird that was new to us, resting on what seemed a little island near the bank. My brother raised his gun and fired. The bird fell over dead. We were heartless youngsters then, and were so fond of our shooting that we had no sympathy for our victims. . . . Our hunting became more successful and we had added two heavy rabbits and a wood-pecker to our baggage. To make progress easier we hung all our goods and chattels on the gun, each taking an end of it, and thus we managed to get along. We were now about five miles on the road. Before this we had refused several offers of a "lift," from sympathetic farmers, but now our weary little souls began to yearn for the repetition of offers, that we had hitherto so indignantly refused.

We had not got much farther on our journey when we were overtaken by a jolly farmer, who of course urged us to have a ride. We made a feeble protest, as a sop to our pride and then, only too happy to yield to his urgency, we scrambled in. . . . As we mounted higher and higher into the hills we could see the whole broad Napa Valley below us with the slight haze of the summer's heat hanging over it. . . . Our farmer was very much amused at our project of walking to the Springs. Every few miles he would ask us jocularly, whether we did not want to get out and walk, but our ardor had been so thoroughly dusted, that we were perfectly willing to let him joke while we rode, rather than to be proud and walk. He finally deposited us within a mile of our destination and we gave him a squirrel that we had shot. . . . We once more loaded our gun with our spoils and started. When we had walked about a quarter of a mile, those rabbits began to grow painfully heavy. We decided finally that rabbits were not much good anyhow, they were so common, so we dropped just one and then the other by the side of the road. We arrived at last foot-sore and weary and covered with dust a little after one o'clock. As soon as the people heard that we had started to walk without waiting for the rest, they dubbed us the infant prodigies and hurried us into dinner.

We never lost that reputation in spite of all disclaimers. Many years after when we went back to the old place, we heard the legend told, of a tiny boy and girl, who had walked twenty miles up the mountain in half a day. Thus shall we figure in the future folk-lore of California.

Nearly fifty years later, the legend of her childhood had not quite become part of the general folklore of California, but such adventures remained still vivid for Gertrude. "When my brother and I walked and walked up into the mountains on the dusty roads," she recalled, "and we left and we came and everything and nothing came in between, we were a legend then, just then. When we went camping and dragged a little wagon and slept closely huddled together and any little boy or any little girl could have been what any little girl or any little boy was, we were a legend then, we were legendary then."

Gertrude and Leo were one another's best friend when having a best friend was all-important. Had they known it, they might have found close attachments in a family of remarkable youngsters living nearby — the Duncans, including Isadora and Raymond and Elizabeth, whose father sold exotic Chinese shawls in San Francisco. But it was not until many years later that Gertrude learned from Raymond Duncan — then in the Omar Khayyam phase preceding his conquest of Greece — that he was one of the young vandals who used to steal apples from the Stein orchard.

Since the illustrious Duncans and Steins did not come together until they were all wearing sandals in Paris, Gertrude and Leo endured their brooding years without competition from contemporaries who were equally driven to self-expression. The most awful moment in her early intellectual life, Gertrude felt, was when she realized that there were civilizations that had completely disap-

15

peared from this earth. As for death, when she thought about it on her long walks, she found the idea of ending less upsetting than the fear of dissolution, the loss of identity in total blankness. But her broodings, she came to feel, were but necessary preparations for fulfillment of her destiny. "Between babyhood and fourteen," she said, "I was there to begin to kill what was not dead, the nineteenth century which was so sure of evolution and prayers, and esperanto and their ideas." Fifteen was the turning point of her life, she believed, because it was then that less lugubrious observations not only made life tolerable but offered the promise of continuing interest. For the first time, she saw a girl taller than she was and wondered if she was beautiful. She milked a goat. She began to understand boredom. "You would spend all day intending to go somewhere and nothing happens and you wonder if you will be revenged." At fifteen, it wasn't so much that time passed slowly, but simply that there was nothing to do except stand around. At this adolescent impasse, with adult conceptions and childish notions manifesting themselves with equal force, she became aware that neither could be expressed in ways that were quite "proper." Like the hero of *Yes Is for a Very Young Man*, "she liked to smoke and she still liked chocolates." Everything important seemed to be beginning all at once — the understanding of money, of possessions, the idea of eternity, the suspicion that some people were enemies. In this welter of undifferentiated experience, she tried to objectify her feelings by writing them down. Once she had given them written expression, she found that she could often confront them calmly and put them away.

In their bookish privacy with its secret signs and secret language, Gertrude and Leo remained strangers to the other children, who were already "out in the world." To their continually troubled parents they remained officially congenial but emotionally distant. In 1885 the family had moved from their big house to a smaller one on Tenth Avenue. Amelia Stein was too ill to manage a household and when Daniel was not at business his time was taken up in waiting upon her. The intimacy of the youngest and most introverted members of the family was further strengthened by their

16

having to depend mostly on each other. Their indifference to their invalid mother made them feel guilty now and then, but in general they were not conscious of their neglect or of their abnormal household situation. They had come to accept the fact that they could do without her long before her death in 1888, when Gertrude was fourteen. Then Daniel Stein presided over the motherless ménage as best he could, a useful provider and guardian but a bothersome person of little affectionate interest to his already coolly intellectual youngest children. According to Leo, Daniel Stein was "a stocky, positive, dominant aggressive person, with no book learning whatever." In spite of his never having been known to read a book, he had a passion for the education of his children and his mind was active and argumentative. But matters he was concerned with were alien to Gertrude and Leo, and they took few pains to disguise their boredom and embarrassment when he expounded his opinions or made a monologue of his arguments.

An intellectual bent gave the young Steins reservations about most people, and removed them from generally accepted ideas and customs; but they were gregarious, too, always part of the good times any situation might afford. Many years later, Grace Davis Street, one of their adolescent friends, recalled an occasion probably typical of many innocent merriments: "One afternoon, a few of us girls met at your home. We found everything packed up to move and already in huge packing boxes. . . . Suddenly I proposed a *party*, meaning ice cream. Bertha was there, and Leo, Mary Cook and some others. I had just learned to make cake and Bertha took me right up, when I said I would make a banana layer cake. Our Chinese cook was cross, so Bertha said for me to make it at your house. So I *did* — in the afternoon. We then pooled our dimes and nickels and ordered a gallon of ice cream. Came the night, my mother would not let me go to the party unless my two little brothers, Sumner and Reeve, went along. I was against it for they were devils and I knew what would happen — John Cook, Simon and my brothers would simply raise hell, in some way. Now our idea was a Bohemian party — sitting around on packing cases and eating and drinking with absolute careless abandon. But

17

— enter the picture right here — Mike Stein, home from Harvard and held in awe by us little girls. Now Mike had no such Bohemian ideas as we did — No sir — Mike made us — Yes he *made us* — drag out of those packing boxes linen and dishes and we had (I can hear Bertha protesting now) to sit down, absolutely against our desires — to a set-table. All the joy was gone, for me, but I remember Mike dished up the ice cream from the freezer on your back porch and Leo passed it around. We were sort of stiff and not happy but were getting on and were ready for the second round of ice cream when — well — Mike found the freezer *gone!!* No more ice cream but plenty of cake. Our worst fears were true — those four devils of brothers had stolen the ice cream and run off with it. We found the freezer in a vacant lot, next day."

They went to the Oakland High School as a matter of course, finding it dull, resigned to its necessity, looking with detachment upon activities normal children are expected to take up with enthusiasm. Gertrude summed up their attitude in this way: "Look right and not left look up and not down look forward and not back and lend a hand. That used to be called a Lend a Hand Society when I went to school and all the children had to write once a week when the society inside the school met, how they had lent a hand, most of them had an easy time, they could mind the baby or watch the cow or cut wood or help their mother. Nobody wanted us to do these things and I and my brother who spent our time at home mostly eating fruit and reading books never could remember how we had lent a hand."

To classmates they offered little but signs of their own superiority. One day during "rhetorical period," a Miss Tillie E. Brown gave an "inspirational" talk entitled "Lighten the Ship," which was concluded with these lines:

If safe on the billows you fain would ride —
Cast over for ever thy burden of pride
Lighten thy heart of its fatal weight,
Ere voices shall whisper, "too late, too late"
For the heavily laden shall never see
The blessed port of Eternity —

When Tillie took her seat, Gertrude handed her a note. " 'Luna, lunae, feminine,' " it read, "Who do you think you are a preacher?"

The one thing that Gertrude found really exciting in her school-work was diagramming sentences. "I suppose other things may be more exciting to others," she said, "but to me undoubtedly when I was at school the really completely exciting thing was diagramming sentences and that has been to me . . . the one thing that has been completely exciting and completely completing. I like the feeling the everlasting feeling of sentences as they diagram themselves." But there was little else to engage her interest or Leo's, and to compensate for the tiresome routine and for association only with people they considered earnest and dull, they turned to readings not included on secondary school lists, took up arguments the Debating Society would never have countenanced, and explored problems of post-puberty philosophy that had no classroom sanction.

There were but few Jewish families in East Oakland. Daniel Stein sometimes attended synagogue services, and the children for a time went regularly to Sabbath school. But in the public school, the young Steins were a very small Jewish minority. Reviewing his early years, Leo could remember no instance of anything like persecution, but rigid self-consciousness allowed him no security and drove him toward imagining slights and insults when none had occurred. His "Jewish complex," he felt, was part of his "pariah complex," and it plagued him throughout his lifetime. The pariah, as Leo defined him, "is one from whom love and participation are not desired. The pariah complex is the fantastic belief that such is the case." These feelings led him to a lack of interest in people, and into a state of insularity where his greatest need was emotional privacy. One of the consequences of his removal from all social relations was the development of an obsession with historical facts. Satisfied to know, as he said later, he was not concerned with the trouble to understand. He loved Gibbon whom he read assiduously, and soon felt that he himself would become a historian. As a beginning in this direction, he made listings of the dynasties of Assyria and Egypt, memorized the English and French kings and the emperors of Germany, and added hundreds of historical dates to his already encyclopedic memory. While he showed no conspicuous talent for its practice he had an early love for graphic art manifest in continual attempts to draw, and in his custom of scissoring out and carefully mounting engravings from the *Century* magazine. He and Gertrude were taken by their father to see enormous cycloramas of the battles of Waterloo and Gettysburg which, with great and profitable showmanship, were exhibited in San Francisco; and one of his earliest memories of a painting that deeply impressed him was that of the newly famous *Man with a Hoe* by Millet.

Like Gertrude's, his world was rich by his own devising. In this self-concerned cast of mind and self-centered view of circumstance, neither he nor his sister was prepared for the consequences of their father's sudden death in 1891. One morning Daniel Stein failed to come down for breakfast at his usual time. Thinking that their father had overslept, the children tried his door but found it locked. When they had shouted to him and got no response, Leo was delegated to go out of doors and climb into his father's room through a window at the side of the house. Daniel Stein had died in his sleep. Their immediate shock was natural, yet Gertrude and Leo did not grieve or worry about having suddenly become orphans. Their real dismay lay in the fact that they would no longer exist in the dreamy isolation they had become used to, but would have to assume a responsible part in family life.

As new master of the household, Michael, nine years older than Gertrude, continued to earn its keep in the same street railway offices where his father had worked. In the judgment of Leo and Gertrude, he was a far more lenient and lovable mentor than their father had ever been. They had to go to court to consent officially to his guardianship, and shortly afterwards the family moved to San Francisco, where for about a year they lived in a small ornate frame house on Turk Street. Joyless Bertha served as general housekeeper, but when there were plans and decisions to make, Gertrude and Leo were Mike's confidants. Their father's estate contained, along with holdings in a number of mining and railroad enterprises, the deed to nearly five hundred acres of land in Shasta

County. But Daniel Stein had left many debts. It became apparent that the residue of the estate would amount to little more than a stake to build upon. Still, poverty was no immediate threat. Mike's position promised advancement, and the clang of trolley bells on the booming Barbary Coast grew louder every day.

As orphans, Gertrude and Leo, to their great relief, were still left pretty much to their own pursuits. But they were fond of Mike as they had never been of their father and sought his company often. To call for Mike at his office was always a happy occasion, even though he took a short view of their extravagance in the bookstores and print shops they visited en route. But he was quick to forgive, and once they had shown him the books and etchings they had bought, and allowed him time to deliver his routine scolding, they would all make up. Then they would go to dinner in a fancy restaurant and afterwards perhaps to the Tivoli Opera House or Baldwin's Academy of Music or the Bush Street Theater, where they might see *Othello*, or *Uncle Tom's Cabin* or *Richelieu* or *Dr. Jekyll and Mr. Hyde*. San Francisco was a lively show town during the period of Gertrude's adolescence. Actors liked to go out to the Coast and because of the expense of the trip were apt to stay a while when they got there. At times Gertrude and her brothers could choose their evening's entertainment among such great names as Edwin Booth, whose *Hamlet* Gertrude remembered "enormously," Tommaso Salvini, James O'Neill — father of the playwright, who performed Edmond Dantes in *The Count of Monte Cristo* more than six thousand times — David Belasco, Otis Skinner, Modjeska, William Gillette, whose *Secret Service* she considered the best melodrama of all, and the child actress, Maude Adams. Yet drama in itself held but secondary appeal for Gertrude; she was more impressed by the feeling of being grownup in public. She had seen her first theatrical performance, *Pinafore*, when she was in London as a very young child, and while she had no memory of what happened on the stage, she remembered being excited by the feeling of the audience and the glitter. Things moved too fast in plays, she felt; your eyes and ears were assaulted by everything at once. When you got emotional about something, something else was always

21

getting in the way. Your feelings lagged behind the action and you could never quite catch up.

For years Gertrude had harbored an intermittent "fear of madness" and some of the melodramas she saw worried her to a critical pitch. When Richard Mansfield played *Dr. Jekyll and Mr. Hyde*, her "own fear was so completely expressed and so terribly portrayed" that she had to beg to be taken out at the end of the second act. The following nights were sleepless, irritated further by her sister's grinding teeth. As "dreadful possibilities of dark deeds" (not altogether directed at Bertha) crowded upon her, she prayed, like Faustus, for relief.

When she saw *Uncle Tom's Cabin*, all she could remember were the blocks of ice moving up and down. But when she was twelve, Buffalo Bill, long retired from his service as Army scout and his pursuit of the Sioux, came to San Francisco in *The Prairie Waif*. In the acting company were several real Indian chiefs borrowed from the government. Gertrude loved everything about Buffalo Bill and was devoted to Indians in particular. Sarah Bernhardt, on a world tour that kept her away from France for two and a half years, came to town in April, 1891, to play *La Tosca, La Dame aux Camélias, Cléopâtre* and *Jeanne d'Arc* before packed houses. Watching her, Gertrude found that the curious nervous reaction she experienced at most plays was entirely absent. "It was all so foreign and her voice being so varied and it all being so french I could rest in it untroubled. And I did . . . It was better than the opera because it went on. It was better than the theatre because you did not have to get acquainted. . . ."

Her taste for melodrama spent itself quickly. When she had had all she wanted of plays like *The Heart of Maryland*, "in which the heroine, to save the life of her lover, climbs to the belfry of a church and grasps the clapper of the bell to prevent its ringing an alarm"; *The Great Diamond Robbery* and *Lover on Crutches*; and more than enough of Secret Service men, bat-infested manor houses, footling English butlers and pussyfooted Chinese, she found new interest in opera. But this enthusiasm was also short-lived, not to be renewed until she was at college. "I came not to care at all for

22

music and so having concluded that music was made for adolescents and not for adults and having just left adolescence behind me and besides I knew all the operas anyway by that time I did not care any more for opera."

Mike's clever management of the Stein estate soon made the family better off than ever. An early supporter of plans for consolidation, Daniel Stein had worked out a system for bringing all of the street railways together. But when he presented his ideas to the companies involved in the proposed merger, his impatient single-mindedness spoiled his case and he had to settle for the vice-presidency of the Mission Line, a small branch of the general system. Mike was blessed with a more patient nature and a more resourceful sense of business diplomacy. He persuaded Collis P. Huntington of Central Pacific Railroads to take on the Mission Line, and eventually he was appointed manager, at a large salary, of the whole system. To Gertrude and Leo, who tended to take a casebook view of those around them, his marked progress in the business world was something of a puzzle. When the Mission Line was expanded, they asked Mike where he got his new workers. He said he merely leaned on a wall and waited; someone would come along, and then someone else. His only obvious skill, as far as they could see, was an ability to make up timetables. As for his arithmetic, when he called on Gertrude and Leo to check his division and addition and subtraction, they always found them to be full of errors. But his genius for scheduling apparently transcended such details. He served as general manager for two years, and invested his money in various projects, among them San Francisco's first apartment house, to the great advantage of all of his charges. The children were told that, provided they lived modestly, they would have enough money to keep them for the rest of their lives. Gertrude's share of the small fortune brought an ample, dependable income throughout her earlier years. Had she not decided to leave America, however, it would have been entirely inadequate to cope with the continually rising standard of living. Individually independent, the family was dispersed in 1892. Gertrude and Bertha were sent to live with their mother's sister, Fannie Bachrach, "and a whole group of lively little aunts who had to know everything" in Baltimore; Leo went to Harvard to continue with college work begun at Berkeley; Simon and Mike stayed on in San Francisco, where Simon was to live out his short life and Mike was to marry, in 1895, a young student of painting, Sarah Samuels, who bore, in 1896, his only child Allan.

In spite of the resourceful ways in which the Stein ménage had got on, Gertrude had often remained deep in the loneliness of adolescence. According to her own account of emotional stresses, expressed in an early college theme in which she called herself "Hortense," the breakup of the family came as a blessing: "Circumstances had forced Hortense Sänger to live much alone. For many years this had suited her completely. With her intense and imaginative temperament, books and her own visions had been sufficient company. She had been early inured to heavy responsibilities, and had handled them firmly . . . though a dreamer by nature she had a strong practical sense. She had now come to a period of her life, when she could no longer content herself with her own nature. She fairly lived in her favorite library. She was . . . motherless . . . and so at liberty to come and go at her own pleasure. Now the time had come when her old well-beloved companions began to pall. One could not live on books, she felt that she must have some human sympathy. Her passionate yearnings made her fear for the endurance of her own reason. Vague fears began to crowd on her. Her longings and desires had become morbid. She felt that she must have an outlet. Some change must come into her life, or she would no longer be able to struggle with the wild moods that now so often possessed her.

"Just at this critical time her father died and thus the only tie that bound her to her old home was snapped. Not long after she accepted the invitation of some relatives and left her old haunts and, she hoped, her old fears, to lead an entirely new life in a large family circle."

In Baltimore, Gertrude was happy because she had no chance to feel lonely. Life was complicated and busy in the bosom of the Bachrach family. Her grandparents, uncles and aunts lived in opulent and clannish warmth, among possessions representing "good

24

solid riches." There was "a parlor full of ornate marbles placed on yellow onyx stands, chairs gold and white of various size and shape, a delicate blue silk brocaded covering on the walls and a ceiling painted pink with angels and cupids all about, a dining room all dark and gold, a living room all rich and gold and red with built-in couches, glass-covered bookcases and paintings of well washed peasants of the German school, and large and dressed up bedrooms all light and blue and white. Marbles and bronzes and crystal chandeliers and gas logs finished out each room. And always everywhere there were complicated ways to wash, and dressing tables filled full of brushes, sponges, instruments, and ways to make one clean. . . ." But more than the solid material comfort of the Baltimore house, the variety of life within its walls charmed and fascinated her. She felt that, after having lived for years an "inner" life which, in spite of Leo's nominal companionship, was essentially lonely, she was entering into a phase of "outer" life in which everybody knew and accepted her. During the winter, she went to visit Leo in Cambridge, and there took steps leading toward her own formal education.

CHAPTER 2

I can often remember to be surprised
By what I see and saw.
— GERTRUDE STEIN

BY the time she was nineteen years old, Gertrude Stein had decided that "all knowledge" was not "her province." This magnanimous concession did not prevent her from seeking entrance to Radcliffe College, then known as the Harvard Annex, in the autumn of 1893. Since she was not interested in working toward a degree, her case was somewhat unusual, and she had to convince the Academic Board of her serious interest in doing "independent" college work. The letter she addressed to the authorities disappeared from the files of Radcliffe College as early as 1915, but it must have been a persuasive appeal; she was allowed to enter in good standing after passing only a part of the required entrance examination.

Officially a member of the Radcliffe class of '98 while actually studying with the class of '97, she took a course under George Santayana in philosophy and a course in metaphysics under Josiah Royce; studied the morphology of animals, the embryology of vertebrates, and cryptogramic botany; became part of a boarding-house coterie; took a course in cloud formation for the fun of it; joined the Idler Club (a dramatics society that produced playlets followed by discussion periods with cake and lemonade); served for two years as secretary of the Philosophy Club and, as a student in William Vaughn Moody's English 22, wrote a number of passionately jejune themes which have been preserved.

When she arrived to begin her college career she brought with her trunks packed with English classics — poetry and history — that filled the wall of her room to the ceiling. Her wardrobe, a far more modest collection, contained few garments that struck her classmates as stylish. The only item for which Gertrude showed obvious affection was a sailor hat of misshapen straw, with faded ribbons whose original color no one could any longer guess. She wore this until a classmate secretly removed it from her room and buried it in an ash barrel. "She was a heavy-set, ungainly young woman," according to one of her Cambridge friends, Arthur Lachman, "very mannish in her appearance. Her hair was cut short at a time when this was by no means the fashion among the fair sex. She always wore black, and her somewhat ample figure was never corseted."

She had come to Cambridge partly because Leo was there, but once her studies were under way she was absorbed into the life of Radcliffe and the congenial daily affairs of the young people who lived in her boardinghouse. She saw Leo frequently, but he had his friends as she had hers, and only now and then did groups of them join up for picnics, trips to the South Shore or, sometimes, theological discussions over tea and cake on Sunday nights. Leo spent all of his free time looking at paintings in the museums of Boston and Baltimore and New York. Gertrude was not as dedicated to this pursuit, but she did frequently go to museums. One of her particular friends was Thomas Whittemore, then at the Boston Museum of Fine Arts, who would later become famous as the man who uncovered the mosaics in Sancta Sophia in Constantinople. On occasion, Whittemore would invite Gertrude to join him in unpacking shipments of paintings from the Orient that were about to become part of the Museum's great collection.

B*

She followed the fortunes of the Harvard football team with passing interest, but her real passion was playgoing and she made countless trips into Boston to see the traveling companies of Henry Irving and Ellen Terry and other theatrical giants of the time. In the year intervening between East Oakland and Radcliffe, she had lost the adolescent self-consciousness that had made going to the opera and the theater such a trial and now went to them sometimes twice in the same day. But she had not lost her talent for self-sufficiency. She rode a bicycle about the streets of Cambridge and made a pastime of taking long solitary walks around the Fresh Pond reservoir which, not yet overtaken by the expanding city, still possessed pastoral charms. "She had none of the girl crushes," according to one of her classmates, "so common of girls then and now. She spent much of her time reading the French psychologists . . . wasn't interested in clothes or suffrage or politics . . . was jolly, natural and simple. She wasn't easy to know, but once you knew her, you found her to be charming."

The predominant interest of her college years was the mind and person of William James. In this devotion she was emulating her brother, who for a time was also a pupil of James. With the deep self-appreciation that seldom deserted him, Leo wrote to a friend: "James goes to my most innards in Philosophy as Shakespeare and Keats do in poetry . . . my own thinking goes so absolutely on all fours with his." Gertrude had hardly made James's acquaintance before she was writing of him in superlatives: "Is life worth living? Yes, a thousand times yes when the world still holds such spirits as Professor James. He is truly a man among men; a scientist of force and originality embodying all that is strongest and worthiest in the scientific spirit; a metaphysician skilled in abstract thought, clear and vigorous and yet too great to worship logic as his God, and narrow himself to a belief merely in the reason of man.

"A man he is who has lived sympathetically not alone all thought but all life. He stands firmly, nobly for the dignity of man. His faith is not that of a cringing coward before an all-powerful master, but of a strong man willing to fight, to suffer and endure. He has not accepted faith because it is easy and pleasing. He has thought and lived many years and at last says with a voice of authority, if life does not mean this, I don't know what it means.

"What can one say more? His is a strong sane noble personality reacting truly on all experience that life has given him. He is a man take him for all in all."

Gertrude's philosophical relationship with William James was to be lifelong, even though she tended to shy from acknowledging it as an obvious factor in her development. From their first association, James must have been arrested by some promising aspect of her personality. Since she was a mere undergraduate, his particular request that she be admitted to his graduate seminar was an honor in itself. The work leading to her being singled out by James had been undertaken in a course with young Hugo Münsterberg, recently from Berlin, whose teaching interests in the experimental phases of the subject led James to regard him as "the Rudyard Kipling of psychology." In Münsterberg's estimation, Gertrude stood out among all the types and kinds of student with whom he had worked and was the model of what a young scholar should be; when he came to write his impressions of American students for publication in Europe, he told her, "I hope you will pardon me if you recognize some features of my ideal student as your own."

Gertrude thought the other students in James's seminar were a "funny bunch." But since she always thought people in groups were absurd, the description is not especially informative. One of the students was working on the psychology of religious conversion, a major interest of James himself; another was observing the incubation and growth of chickens; another, Leon Solomons, was working on problems of consciousness. From their first meeting in the seminar until his early death in 1900, Solomons and Gertrude were very close friends. She did experimental work with him which resulted in the published report, "Normal Motor Automatism," in the *Psychological Review*, September, 1896.

In their joint experimental projects on such problems as "The Place of Repetition in Memory," "Fluctuations of the Attention" and "The Saturation of Colors," Solomons and Stein were their own subjects, in spite of the hazard of Gertrude's singularly dim responses.

She had announced at the beginning of her laboratory work that she had no subconscious reaction at all, and no one was able to disprove her. Even her conscious reactions were unrewarding. One of her classmates devised an experiment in which an individual was suddenly confronted with a table covered by a cloth under which lay a pistol. His idea was to observe reactions when the cloth was suddenly whisked away. When the experiment was tried on Gertrude, she was neither surprised nor alarmed, and not very much amused. She thought the whole thing was silly and said so.

The first problem set up for Gertrude and Leon Solomons when they began to work as a team involved a tuning fork. When they discovered they were both almost tone deaf, the project had to be abandoned. Then they attempted a study of fatigue. Using themselves as subjects, they set out to observe the limits of pure motor automatism in the normal human being. They sought to find the exact point at which the personality may be said to be "split," thereby releasing a second personality operating without discernible reference to the first. At William James's suggestion, they began with a planchette of the sort used with ouija boards, but as soon as they found that it was possible, in spite of distractions, to produce spontaneous writing movements, they changed to ordinary pencil and paper. In one experiment, while the subject wrote the same single letter over and over again, he also read a story. This resulted in involuntary recordings of words or parts of words from the story, and usually these were immediately noticed by the subject. But in repeated experiments they eventually found that many words would be recorded with no break in the subject's attention.

Some of her experiences in the laboratory were not pleasant, as Gertrude made clear in a report written in 1894: ". . . this vehement individual is requested to make herself a perfect blank while someone practices on her as an automaton.

"Next she finds herself with a complicated apparatus strapped across her breast to register her breathing, her finger imprisoned in a steel machine and her arm thrust immovably into a big glass tube. She is surrounded by a group of earnest youths who carefully watch the silent record of the automatic pen on the slowly revolving drum.

"Strange fancies begin to crowd upon her, she feels that the silent pen is writing on and on forever. Her record is there she cannot escape it and the group about her begin to assume the shape of mocking fiends gloating over her imprisoned misery. Suddenly she starts, they have suddenly loosed a metronome directly behind her, to observe the effect, so now the morning's work is over."

In a variant experiment, a subject read a story while he put down words dictated to him. At first these always disrupted the reading, but then the experimenters discovered that the subject would sometimes write down five or six of the dictated words without being conscious of their sounds or of the movements of his arm. Finally they decided to explore the possibilities of wholly spontaneous automatic writing. Distractions by reading were by this time no longer necessary. Gertrude found that she could write unconsciously and go on writing distracted only by words *behind* the movement of her pencil. She and her partner noticed that words and phrases came often in grammatical sequences, but found that evidences of logical thought were rare. Complete unconsciousness of the movement of the pencil was unattainable, yet the experiment at least offered evidence that words in sequence could sometimes be achieved in passages of considerable length.

Branching out on her own, Gertrude worked with students outside the field of psychology. By having them submit to an experiment just before and just after taking examinations, she hoped to test the validity of the earlier work with Solomons by enlarging the scope of the conditions under which it was conducted. Yet she found nothing that might pass for automatic writing. There were circles at times, now and then a vaguely discernible letter; but after operations of this sort by more than forty students, nothing had appeared that could be called writing, automatic or otherwise. More interested in observing the personalities of her subjects than in their experimental recordings, she began to study the speed or laxity of their aptitude, the emotional penumbra surrounding them on their excursions into scientific research, the specific devices that held their attention and devices that relaxed it. Keeping notes, she made comparisons and correlations. When she was finished she

31

believed that she could make diagrams and charts that would accommodate every possible span of attention.

Combining his comments and notes with hers, Leon Solomons wrote up the earlier joint experiments and published them. In this way Gertrude made her first appearance in print. "It is very interesting to read," she wrote of this report, "because the method of writing to be afterwards developed in *Three Lives* and *Making of Americans* already shows itself." Gertrude did not participate in the ultimate formulation of the published paper. Though she could vouch for the authenticity of the methods reported, she did not agree with the article insofar as it attempted to prove the possibilities of automatic writing. Her own summation of the work was succinct: ". . . one of the things I did was testing reaction of the average college student in a state of normal activity and in the state of fatigue induced by their examinations. I was supposed to be interested in their reactions but I· soon found that I was not but instead that I was enormously interested in the types of their characters that is what I even then thought of as the bottom nature of them, and when in May 1896 I wrote my half of the report of these experiments I expressed these results as follows: In these descriptions it will be readily observed that habits of attention are reflexes of the complete character of the individual."

Her brief contribution to the science of psychology remained in a not altogether undeserved oblivion for nearly forty years. When she became famous it was hauled out of its archives in order to be used against her. The phrase "automatic writing," as it was represented by Professor B. F. Skinner in an article entitled "Has Gertrude Stein a Secret?" and published in the *Atlantic Monthly* in 1934, came to be the handiest and most glib way in which to account for her more difficult works, or to dismiss them. For thousands who were puzzled by her, yet who were unable or unwilling to conclude that she was insane, feeble-minded or inaccessibly cerebral, "automatic writing" became a necessity. The question put forth by Professor Skinner was intriguing, but the answer he supplied, which suggested that her most famous writings were products of the same sort of experiment she had made in the laboratory and could only be explained in terms of their resemblance to automatic writing, was, as any full account of the course of Gertrude Stein's progress would show, picturesque, perhaps inevitable, yet entirely wrong. There was no reason to accept the report of the experiments in "normal motor automatism" in any other terms than those in which Gertrude herself regarded them — a minor scientific encounter from which she struck off in directions of her own.

As she approached the end of her career at Radcliffe, William James, curious about her future plans, asked her what she had in mind. When she expressed uncertainty, he suggested that she continue in philosophy. In her understanding, this meant that she would have to prepare in mathematics, and that she would have to enter the field of psychology wholeheartedly. According to Leo, her report that James had recommended mathematics in order to prepare for philosophy was patently absurd. In his recollection, the real *fons et origo* of the matter was Josiah Royce, who had told her that she would have to occupy herself deeply with logic before she could seriously entertain a career in philosophy. Since philosophy had no appeal for her unless it were removed from the sphere of pure speculation, she decided to follow James's second recommendation and to go into psychology. To do this she would have to acquire a background in medicine. But in order to pursue further the work she had already done in biology and chemistry, she was faced with the necessity of obtaining an academic degree. She would finally have to pass customary entrance examinations, she learned, even though her actual course work entitling her to an A.B. was by then completely accomplished and in order. As soon as she passed the entrance examination in advanced Latin, she was told, she could have her degree *magna cum laude*. It was clear to Gertrude that there was nothing to do but conquer the Latin problem, but at the same time Leo was beckoning her to Europe, promising her the pleasures of traveling in the Low Countries, a steamer trip up the Rhine and a long visit to Paris where, as he put it, "the opportunities are infinite."

"In her approach to the problem of learning Latin," said one of her classmates, "may be found one of the keys to her life. She

33

was always doing what was most significant for her at the time. To know Latin was not significant for her, but she had to pass Latin to do what was significant — study at Johns Hopkins. She put off the real study of Latin until the last moment, carrying a Latin grammar under her arm and apparently hoping she might absorb it through her pores. One of her anxious friends taught her that *isieme esiumibus* were the endings of the third declension, but it is doubtful that she knew where the dividing lines came. She wrote a Caesar examination that she said was very consistent, either all right or all wrong. Then in fun she used the Bible as oracle to see if she had passed, and found her finger on a passage in *Lamentations*. The prophecy was true. *E* would have meant a failure, but her mark was *F*. She spent the summer gaily in Europe and the next year learned and passed Latin."

The last notable incident of her Radcliffe career was a now-famous exchange with her favorite teacher. On the day of final examinations, she came into the room, perused the questions along with the rest of her classmates, and calmly wrote across the top of her examination book: "Dear Professor James, I am so sorry but really I do not feel like an examination paper in philosophy today." Before the eyes of her curious classmates, she then picked up her things and departed. On the next day, her mail brought a post-card from Professor James: "Dear Miss Stein, I understand perfectly how you feel. I often feel like that myself." Affixed to the blithe message was her mark for the course, a higher grade than any received by those who had stuck with the questions to the weary end of the examination period.

Gertrude departed from Cambridge with a feeling of having lived fully and richly among stimulating people, but without regret or nostalgia either for college haunts or personal friends. In Cambridge, some thirty-five years later, she had few memories to arouse sentiment, and had difficulty even in recognizing the most familiar streets and the most famous buildings. As for Radcliffe itself, she tended to be crotchety about the publications and notices that continually came to her as an alumna. "They are foolish at Radcliffe," she said, "at least it seems so when they send me their printed any-thing."

Toward Baltimore, her new home town, she had become deeply sentimental. "Baltimore, sunny Baltimore," she had written as a fresh-man, "where no one is in a hurry and the voices of the negroes singing as their carts go lazily by, lull you into drowsy reveries. It is a strangely silent city, even its busiest thoroughfares seem still and the clanging car-bells only blend with the peaceful silence and do but increase it. To lie on the porch, to listen to the weird strains of Grieg's spring-song, to hear the negro voices in the distance and to let your mind wander idly as it listeth, that is happiness. The lotus-eaters knew not the joys of calm more completely than a Baltimorean. Let us alone for we have the essence of contentment, quiet dream, slothful ease in the full sensuous sunshine."

When she returned to Baltimore in the fall of 1897, she was not looking for a retreat but for an arena in which she could begin to realize her large ambitions. When a Radcliffe friend, Margaret Sterling Snyder, heard of her decision to follow a career in medicine, she offered Gertrude the possible benefit of her own sad experience. "I now see," she wrote, "that I was one of the most deluded and pitiable of all these many young women who are aspiring after what is beyond them in our day. . . . A sheltered life, domestic tastes, maternity, and faith are all I could ask for myself or you or the great mass of womankind." Bent on becoming "a useful member of society," Gertrude was not dissuaded by this or other warnings about the limitations of women in a man's society. Against the advice of her brother Mike and his wife, who were doubtful that Gertrude was capable of running a household, she settled down in an establishment of her own, first shared with Leo while he was studying biology at Johns Hopkins, and later with a fellow student Emma Lootz, and a servant named Lena — "the gentle Lena" of *Three Lives* — and began to attend Johns Hopkins Medical School. The fairly large house, situated in an unfashionable neighborhood, was within walking distance of the Medical School. Leo's collection of Japanese prints gave a certain individuality to its interior, but outside, it was, as Gertrude described it, just another typical Baltimore dwelling "of all the same kind that made a close pile like a row of dominoes that a child knocks over." Occupied with laboratory work under Doctors Llewellys Barker and Franklin Mall, she found the first two years productive and satisfying. She had become particularly absorbed in her study of brain tracts, a study which, she later said, "attracted the attention of [Sir William] Osler and [William Stewart] Halstead," and provided the beginnings of a comparative study eventually published by Barker.

Disputing this version of her work at Johns Hopkins, Leo attributes her later false recollection to a loss of a sense of humor in regard to her student days. At the time, he said, she used to make fun of her work. While she knew it was absurd to make models of brain tracts, "she didn't mind doing it as it was purely mechanic work and rather restful." Furthermore, she agreed with the German anatomist who said "it was an excellent occupation for women and Chinamen." Whether she was serious about this work or not, during the first two years at Johns Hopkins she was "bored, frankly openly bored." Absorbed by little struggles and intrigues, she followed currents of gossip that ran through the school, but the practice and theory of medicine had become dull and tiresome.

As a member of the medical school, she assisted in the delivery of infants, particularly in the Negro districts of the city. Her observations in the course of this duty provided firsthand experience for her first celebrated work, *Melanctha*, and allowed her experience of a segment of life in Baltimore from which, on the basis of her picaresque impressions of the city recorded in her Radcliffe theme, she had long been protected.

During summer vacations from her medical studies, except for two occasions, one on which she braved the troubles of the Pullman strike to go back to California to visit Mike just after his marriage, and one on which, as a devoted aunt, she attended the christening of her brother's first-born, Allan, she joined Leo in Europe. Florence, "an eminently serious-minded city," in Leo's view, where "a limited range of activity is almost insisted on," was usually their headquarters. Having given up his studies in history at Harvard (by the time he was twenty-two, history had become for him "a mare's nest of illusory knowledge") and his studies in biology at Johns Hopkins, Leo had set himself up as a painter and student of aesthetics. He had originally gone to Europe to write a book on Mantegna, but soon realized that his interest in art was aesthetic rather than historical. Giving up the project, he concentrated his attention on *quattrocento* paintings, particularly the works of Piero della Francesca, Paolo Ucello, Domenico Veneziano, Andrea del Castagno and the early Sienese.

One of the best descriptions of Gertrude at this period was written by the author-journalist Hutchins Hapgood, an old friend of Leo's. They had met during the course of the round-the-world voyage which Leo had taken in the company of his cousin, Fred Stein, early in 1896. Leo and Gertrude were in Heidelberg on one of their frequent excursions away from Florence when Hapgood encountered them: ". . . an extraordinary person: powerful, a beautiful head, a sense of something granite. I felt in Gertrude Stein something wholly intense, not the sort of mental activity I had seen in Bertrand Russell . . . but a deep temperamental quality, which was also inspiring . . . but in the case of Gertrude Stein, even at that moment of her youth, with a kind of almost unfeminine beauty, with a brilliant academic past behind her, the ego was apparent. She . . . was by an inner necessity compelled to be conscious of her essential superiority, but at that time her extraordinary life-quality and her beauty were what struck the eye and the imagination."

In following summers, when Hapgood saw them at Bernard Berenson's elegant eighteenth-century forty-room villa, *I Tatti*, in Vallombrosa, not far from Florence, he felt that Leo and Gertrude seemed out of place. Life at *I Tatti* with its great paintings and its library of forty thousand volumes was graceful and easy, dominated by a host whose disposition was sophisticated and ritualistic, whereas the Steins were "weighty and stalwart," arriving like prophets in their monkish gowns and sandals. "They frequently attempted to be light," Hapgood wrote, "in harmony with the general background of place and time; but it was the lightness, in Leo's case,

37

of a self-conscious heavyweight who often had the gift of wit and of contemptuous criticism. And, in Gertrude's case, with plenty of physical weight (she weighed then something over two hundred pounds), but with amiability and easy pregnant silence, she was quite agreeable, and still devoted to her brother, whose qualities and gifts she felt and heralded." Hapgood's opinion was shared by Berenson himself, according to Aline B. Saarinen, who remarked in her book, *The Proud Possessors:* "The Steins were not Berenson's type. Gertrude offended the aesthetic sensibilities which Berenson had been refining for so many years, and he found Leo a tiresome bore. But he could not resist a man who lived in his mind (even when he considered the mind mediocre), and so he was willing to rescue Leo from his intellectual funk."

Gertrude's far-flung summers when she entered into the life of Leo and his cosmopolitan friends had already put wanderlust in her blood. Indolent in her studies at home, she neglected fundamentals in the preparation of classwork and became desultory in recitation. As final examinations approached in her last year, some of her professors were outspoken in their irritation with her careless-ness. Others, apparently charmed in the same way that William James had been before them, were impressed with her reputation for original work as a result of laboratory researches under Llewellys Barker, and tended to be lenient. The eminent doctors Halstead and Osler made examinations a mere matter of formality, but the professor of her course in obstetrics decided she should be taught a lesson and threatened to flunk her outright. Undaunted, Gertrude remained, in the memoir of a classmate, her "own vigorous self, traipsing across town or into the country swinging down the corridors full of life and sanity and humour." Upset in the prospect of Gertrude's disgrace, her close friend, Marion Walker, tried a feminist appeal to impress the gravity of her situation upon her. "The cause of women" was deeply involved, she felt, in Ger-trude's success or failure. But Gertrude remained indifferent. She did not mind the cause of women, she decided, or any other cause; she was bored beyond her own salvation. Hearing of her academic difficulties in Florence, Leo became mildly alarmed. "What is all this nonmedicated rumble that issues from your quarter?" he wrote. "Is it representative of a phase or a general condition? It would be too bad if the first person in the family who had gone so far as to get the adequate preparation for anything should go back on it. Well I suppose you won't, especially as there's nothing else to be done. If you had my very superior talents for loafing it might do, but you haven't, so it won't."

After repeated threats from her professor and exhortations from her friends, she flunked the crucial examination, but was offered the chance of making up the work in summer school. This offer in itself represented a severe check to her airy progress and struck at her pride. Summer school as an alternative was humiliating. Worse than that, it would cancel the opportunity to spend another few months in Europe. She dismissed the notion and, with it, the whole idea of a career in medicine. Minor in itself, this academic failure allowed her to assess the true state of things. She knew finally that she had resisted the study of medicine from the beginning and came to feel that her ambition for a career, plus the warm expectations of William James, had misled her. She had entered upon a road that would never take her where she wanted to go. Now that she understood her position, she made a point of thanking the adamant professor who had blocked her graduation and was shortly on her way to join her brother in Italy.

In the Umbrian valley they lived for a time in a pension in Perugia and then moved on to Assisi. Excursions into the neighboring countryside for sightseeing, gallery tours and swimming in Lake Trasimeno occupied their days pleasantly, and in late August they went to London. After a brief tour of the Lake District, they signed the lease for a flat at 20 Bloomsbury Square, intending to spend the winter. Before they had time to settle down in Bloomsbury, they were asked for a week end with Bernard Berenson and his wife at their place in Haslemere. Charmed with the region which, in Leo's words, was "so absolutely lovely, so rich and brilliant in its deep sun-washed color and so beautiful in its contours and composition," they decided to take a nearby cottage, "Greenhill," for a few weeks. They continued to spend their leisure with the Berensons and with their

39

friends, the ailing novelist and playwright Israel Zangwill, and "a young mathematician of genius," Bertrand Russell, whose wife was Mrs. Berenson's sister. Conversation among them had a way of turning irresistibly toward comparisons of English and American character. In the course of one of these discussions, Gertrude argued against Russell with a vehemence that was to be repeated on her second and last meeting with him many years later. Russell felt that the American mind was closed to new political ideas. On patriotic principle — certainly not in any real conviction or knowledge — Gertrude disagreed. Her own mind, as time would tell, was closed to new political ideas and, particularly at this period, hardly aware that there were such things.

In 1902, the Steins had little notion that they would become permanent exiles from America and spoke often, if vaguely, of the life they were about to resume when in a matter of months they would return to the States. Their English friends and their expatriate friends could not understand why people of their taste and disposition would think of returning to America. But the Steins remained keen patriots through a long series of Anglo-American disputes. Gertrude's position may be attributed to the intense loyalty she always felt toward anything that was hers by natural right or by appropriation. As for Leo, the grievances he held against America boiled down to two: the fact that it was always so far away from the center of his aesthetic and spiritual interests, and the fact that the few American cities where he might even think of living were so cold. Yet he still felt that some day not too far off he and Gertrude would settle down to a placid contemplative life, in Connecticut, perhaps, or in Massachusetts.

They took up residence in Bloomsbury Square in October. There Leo blazed his way "through the aesthetic wilderness," while Gertrude became a daily habituée of the British Museum Reading Room, rediscovering old loves in literature and coming upon new ones. Long years of "living continuously with the rhythms of the English language" had brought her reading tastes beyond maturity to sophistication; now, for the first time since East Oakland, she had the leisure to browse at will. She found the works of Robert Greene arresting and, reading for the first time the novels of Trollope, became engrossed for days on end. She began to collect volumes of eighteenth-century memoirs in the nearby bookshops, bought Walpole and the Creevy papers, and began to read everything with a notebook beside her. Recording phrases which pleased her, she enjoyed a series of little shocks of recognition as she came again upon passages that had pleased her as a child. In this she was simply pursuing a lifelong predilection: the satisfaction of "caressing" words and phrases.

But beyond the walls and windows of the British Museum, London was dismal and depressing. It reminded her of the London of Dickens with its frightening dark backgrounds and poverty-stricken streets and byways. Overcome with the bleakness of it all, she booked passage for America and "the white snow line of New York harbor . . . the clean sky and the white snow and the straight plain ungainly buildings all in a cold and brilliant air without spot or stain." When she had made her wintry voyage, she joined three friends, Mabel Weeks, Estelle Rumbold and Harriet Clark, and spent the remainder of the winter with them in Manhattan, in "The White House"— a wooden apartment building situated at the west end of 100th Street, with a garden that overlooked the Hudson River. Here she began to write a novel, a psychological study of young women, of precisely the same educational background and social status as the friends with whom she lived. This work occupied her on and off for nearly a year after which, as it turned out, the novel was to "disappear" for almost thirty years.

While Gertrude was in America, Leo left London on Christmas Eve, intending to go to Florence by way of Paris, and then later to join her in Baltimore. But in Paris a new impetus came with the force of an annunciation. One evening, as he was dining with the young cellist Pablo Casals, he was suddenly aware that "the leaven of pictorial vision was working." Telling Casals that he felt himself growing into an artist, he went to his hotel, took off his clothes and began to draw (apparently in the nude) from his own mirrored image. In the Louvre during the following week he began drawing from statues. Fate, he decided, had meant him to stay in Paris; he could only accede. The problem of living quarters was easily solved. His cousin Eph Keyser, the sculptor, after a long search had recently found a suitable apartment and studio for himself. Loathing the idea of having to look for a place on his own, Leo asked his cousin whether in the course of his apartment hunting he had perhaps found some other suitable dwelling that might serve as a combined home and studio. His cousin recommended the vacancy at 27 Rue de Fleurus.

CHAPTER 3

What is poetry, history is poetry when you get
used to the french.

— GERTRUDE STEIN

THE man with the face of a gentle Hebraic
ram and his stout imperious sister, Mlle. Gertrude, became in 1903
the new tenants of the ground-floor flat at 27 Rue de Fleurus, a quiet
little street connecting the Boulevard Raspail, which was "cut
through" in 1907, with the west side of the Luxembourg Gardens.
Their new home was located in what was then considered the suburb
of Montparnasse, a somewhat dingy area where a few English and
American painters had already settled, but which otherwise offered
no challenge to Montmartre as the world's most famous artists' quarter. The celebrated landmarks of Montparnasse, and the notorious
ones — the Rotonde, the Sélect, the Bal Nègre and the Boule
Blanche — came into existence during the Steins' years of residence,
and the Café du Dôme, then a modest little establishment named
simply Le Dôme, was soon to be transformed into unofficial headquarters of the American expatriates. But as far as Gertrude and her
brother were concerned, their choice of 27 Rue de Fleurus was based

43

simply on its convenience to everything they considered important in Paris. As their first real and permanent home since East Oakland, it promised to serve them well.

Their nomadic years of random scholarship and dilettantism were behind them. Wanderlust had taken Leo westward around the world on a trip he found largely boring, and later sent him on forays into Italy, Germany and England in search of that elusive ideal center for a career he meant to dedicate to the study and, he doggedly hoped, the practice of art. Gertrude's formal education had been accomplished by way of Oakland, Cambridge and Baltimore, she had become acquainted with the Low Countries and Germany, had made her *Italienische Reise*, had tasted at leisure English country life, and had become an independent scholar in London and finally a neophyte author in New York. Her progress was not so clearly in the nature of a quest as was Leo's, yet it showed her restlessness as well as her developing taste for life abroad. She still cherished family connections in America and was confident that she would always be welcomed in Baltimore, but Continental ways to which Leo had introduced her finally turned her mind against living in her native country. Like him, she blew "the American trumpet as though it was the whole of Sousa's band," but now — with the important proviso of an annual visit to America — she was eager to settle into the life of Paris. Leo, for a while at least, had fixed on the idea that his natural talents would bring him success as a painter. When a man has become educated to pictorial seeing, he said, "The beauty of the world is immensely increased; it becomes all, potentially, beautiful. Every man, woman and child is beautiful, and any group of them. The superabundant beauty becomes at times exasperating; one feels a need to do something about it; one is almost forced to try being an artist, not only in seeing but in doing; one tries to paint." Gertrude, candidly hungry for celebrity, was not yet certain of her creative direction, but at least she was not going to continue the pursuit of "*la gloire*" in the field of psychology.

As a tentative exercise of her first impulses toward writing, she continued to work on the short novel she had begun on her return to New York from London. When she finished this narrative on October

44

24, 1903, she put aside the two notebooks which it filled. These remained "forgotten" for almost thirty years, coming to light apparently quite by accident one evening in 1932. As she was reminiscing of early days in Paris during a visit by French critic Bernard Faÿ and novelist Louis Bromfield, she had occasion to rummage through some old papers and, seeking something else, turned up the lost manuscript. "The most exciting thing really the most exciting thing," she wrote at the time, "was finding the first thing that had been written and was it hidden with intention." When Gertrude later told the circumstances of this mislaid novel, Leo answered her question in the affirmative. The manuscript had been deliberately kept out of view because, he recalled, Gertrude shared his feeling that it was worthless. In his opinion, the work was impossibly bad in terms of style, and only feeble as a piece of objective writing. "The stuff was interesting —" he wrote, "it was the original material of Melanctha and had nothing to do with Negroes — the writing was impossible. There was no objectification." This opinion of Leo's, expressed long before the lost novel actually appeared in print, gains but scant support from the work itself. One of his friends believes that Leo never read the manuscript and feels that his criticism must apply to some other fragment of Gertrude's with which he had confused it. In any case, the novel was eventually published under the title *Things As They Are* (it was originally called *Q.E.D.*), four years after Gertrude's death. The very first of her imaginative writings, it was preceded by some thirty-odd volumes before coming into the hands of readers.

Perhaps the most pertinent thing about this first piece of Steinian literature, written when its author was twenty-nine, is its excellence as an example of conventional fiction. To those who hold to the argument that Gertrude Stein's troublesome and idiosyncratic later works were proof of her desperate inability to handle the King's English, the book gives firm denial. It is a youthful work, earnest in spirit, and naïvely colored by touches of Henry James, including an overt reference to Kate Croy, a leading character in *The Wings of the Dove*. Yet there is authority in its manner, and in its control of delicate subject matter — emotional relations among three highly

45

educated young women — there are signs of a talent of the first order.

Her method in *Q.E.D.* is one of continual, relentless analysis. The facts of a situation are given and their meanings are constantly qualified and elaborated. Like her master, Henry James, she was far less interested in events or situations in themselves than she was in the endless resources of the mind when it is moved to make interpretations of events or to register the climates of emotional situations. Unlike all of her following works, in which the presence of the author as controlling agent and arbiter is almost always dissolved, she maintains the conventional distance between subject and observer. Her story is "framed," told from a point where author and reader share more or less the same view. But it is also pressing toward abstraction and the geometry suggested by the original title. She deals with passion as if she were exhuming it, charting its variations and racking them up for discrete study.

The most surprising aspect of this work is perhaps its luminous charm. A geometrical necessity may control the narrative, but verbal grace and an easy, mature delight in people and things give it substance. As a period piece, it is neither weighty nor tasseled, but shines with an intellectual light close to that found in the works of James where meticulous concentration upon manners, fashion, protocol is but one way of humanizing ethical problems and giving them romantic interest. The young American women in *Things As They Are* are starched, correct, somewhat breathless about their release into the era of the New Woman; they are also pathetic, embroiled in emotions which the usual period piece only renders laughable. The fact that these emotions are of a nature rarely hinted at in the literature of the time gives the book one kind of singularity, but its deeper distinction lies in Gertrude Stein's ability to keep the forbidden subject muted while she examines it with geometrical precision and from many points of view as her story moves crisply toward the final satisfaction and resolution of *Quod Erat Demonstrandum*.

Written in Paris about American persons and places seen from the point of vantage that life in Paris afforded, the mislaid novel was the first tangible accomplishment in that long period of Gertrude's

46

career of which she said: "I have lived half my life in Paris, not the half that made me but the half in which I made what I made." While some Americans looked upon Paris as the world's greatest market and rag fair of culture and of license, to Gertrude it was simply a place where the spiritual and intellectual atmosphere was salubrious. "Paris was the place that suited those of us that were to create the twentieth century art and literature, naturally enough. . . . France could be civilized without having progress on her mind, she could believe in civilization in and for itself, and so she was the natural background for this period."

Gertrude believed that the creative individual had a fundamental need of the experience of another civilization after his own. She pointed to the need of Renaissance artists for the civilization of Greece, of the English romantic poets for Italy, of modern painters for influences from the diverse civilizations of Africa. The creative process, she felt, is quickened and enriched by distance; at a remove from his first sources the artist can more quickly isolate his particularity and shape his own sense of craft. In his native civilization the creative man is apt to be confused, retarded by unimportant influences and crosscurrents, and tyrannized by immediate realities. Just as any creator needs two civilizations, she believed that a writer should have more than one occupation. After reading and writing, which for herself she considered synonymous with existing, her occupation was looking at paintings. Paris, in the words of Paul Valéry, "the political, literary, scientific, financial, commercial, voluptuary, and sumptuary capital of a great country," admirably satisfied all of these needs.

Yet in the long run, she felt, it was not what Paris gave to her and to other artists that was most to be cherished, but what Paris did not take away. She chose Paris for the calm and peace necessary to her mode of life and work, and loved the French because they were cordial yet not obtrusive. She was happy, too, with the elegance of her adopted city — "the men wearing their silk hats on the side of their head and leaning heavily on their cane toward the other side making a balance, the heavy head the heavy hand on the cane were the elegance of Paris." Above all, she felt that Paris was most fertile for the twentieth-century artist because it has "scientific methods, machines, and electricity, but does not really believe that these things have anything to do with the real business of living. . . ."

Her appreciation of Parisian virtues is made largely on a basis of ease — physical ease, to a great degree, but more importantly, intellectual and spiritual ease. Gertrude Stein was never moved by the necessity of the visionary to be subsumed or immolated in mystical reaches; her vision, clear as it was, encompassed no prospect in which her own place was not comfortably and importantly defined. Great good fortune had brought her to Paris when the excitements of a fiercely creative period were being lived as life, not as legendary events in aesthetic and social history. In 1900, the background that everybody needed was, she felt, "the background of tradition of profound conviction that men and women and children do not change, that science is interesting but does not change anything, that democracy is real but that governments unless they tax you too much or get you defeated by the enemy are of no importance." Looking backward, we know that she had moved in upon a revolution that would float her own career and carry it along, and for which she would become a stubborn spokesman and valuable press agent. In Paris she had found an ancient, enlightened city, alive in the deepest meaning of sophistication. The milieu she entered was one to permit the release of sensibility, and the exercise of talent, thwarted or curbed in America where culture was still more of a social ornament than a creative force. Often unknowingly supported by scientists, Parisian artists in all fields had become explorers into realms beyond those by which, in the conventional and common sense, reality was considered to be bound. It was time and occasion for the miraculous meetings of theories and imaginative signs. Individual works that artists were writing or painting or composing would soon emerge as living illustrations of what seemed then to be the far-removed theories and investigations pursued by such men as Albert Einstein, Henri Bergson, Sigmund Freud. In this climate of crucible heat the twentieth century found its identity in art. Gertrude Stein would appear in many ways to be the purest example of the artist in this revolution; yet in other ways she would seem not to

48

be an artist at all, but a scientist elaborately constructing metaphors in a laboratory of words. Yet for herself as a candidate for glory she had found the right place at the right moment. To her unexpected advantage — an advantage not without its peculiar irony — she would achieve great fame beyond the confines of avant-garde literature only when she would step out of the laboratory and become the anecdotal historian of a movement continually swirling about her and, sometimes, quite over and beyond her.

As new householders in their adopted city, Leo and Gertrude set about furnishing their quarters with a number of Renaissance pieces they had picked up in Italy. All at once the small flat seemed as full of stuff as a warehouse. But the old pieces provided a combination of elements they liked: severity and elegance. They soon became used to grand proportions within their acutely limited space. Besides, their real concern was not where to put furniture, but where to hang paintings. Buying with acumen and timeliness, they had already founded a collection that would in a few years become a Left Bank institution and, in its minor way, a private landmark of contemporary culture.

Leo guided the picture buying, and there is little question that in the early years the collection reflected his particular tastes. He sometimes consulted Gertrude when a new purchase was contemplated but, in the making of final decisions, usually operated alone. Gertrude's independence as a collector was not established until years later when, on her own decision and with her own money, she bought her first cubist Picasso. Before coming to Paris, she had acquired a number of etchings and had paid six hundred dollars for a painting by the American Alexander Schilling. But she soon disposed of this. "It's too bad the Schilling is so out of it," her friend Mabel Weeks wrote in a letter of 1905. "You did have a real enthusiasm for it once, but that's not to the point. I'd hate to be confronted by all my past enthusiasms, and I fancy Paris makes one grow very fast. . . ." Leo's first purchases were made in a desultory way, not because he lacked means or the desire, but because very little of what he saw in the galleries of Paris caught his eye. His first acquisition, made in London just before his removal to Paris, was a Wilson Steer. Soon after taking up residence in the Rue de

49

Fleurus he bought another — a little picture by DuGardier of a woman dressed in white with a white dog on a green lawn. But this purchase was also made with only mild enthusiasm. He had spent so much time talking and looking without acting that he finally decided to buy the DuGardier as his entrance fee into the collectors' world, hoping that thereafter he would be *persona grata* in the galleries where he spent so much time.

When he complained to Bernard Berenson of the poverty of choice in Paris, his friend suggested that he investigate the works of one Paul Cézanne currently on view at the shop of Ambroise Vollard on the Rue Lafitte. On his first visit to Vollard's, Leo bought a landscape. But he was not really seriously taken with Cézanne until the following summer in Florence. There, in the drafty palace of Charles Loeser, a middle-aged art critic and connoisseur, he found a plethora of Cézannes. Loeser, son of a Brooklyn department store magnate, had made his Florentine place of exile into a private museum filled with paintings and vast collections of bronzes, faïence, antique furniture and ivory-headed canes. Leo spent all summer looking at Cézannes — Provençal landscapes, still lifes and nudes. As one of his first collectors, Loeser had already come into possession of some of the finest works of Cézanne ever painted and had built a music room in which to house them. In that setting they could be viewed while the Lener Quartet — a group Loeser kept in courtly fashion before they became famous concert artists — played Haydn and Mozart through the afternoons.

In the succeeding years, the crucial beginnings of one of the world's great periods of painting, Leo and Gertrude made purchases — Renoirs, Gauguins, a Valloton, a Manguin and more Cézannes — frequently and at prices which, though modest in comparison with the sums the pictures eventually commanded, soon came to be a serious drain on their joint income. Fortunately, Michael Stein and his wife had moved from San Francisco to Paris and had decided to make a permanent home there even before Gertrude and Leo had come to the Rue de Fleurus. Under Leo's influence, they had themselves developed collectors' passions. On occasion, Mike was able to advance money to his brother and sister for paintings they could not have otherwise afforded. The Stein flat soon began to assume the atmosphere of a small and very crowded museum; Gertrude was its curator, Leo its guide.

People from all over began coming to see both the pictures and the Steins, commonly supposed to be eccentric millionaires always dressed in corduroy who lived in a pavilion — a little detached house in a court — in order to be different. Those who came were sometimes openly appreciative, sometimes snobbishly pleased merely to be on hand, sometimes simply and quietly amused. Leo gave substance to the evenings with zestful and opinionated lectures which, he hoped, would go off as impromptu performances. The talks were important to him — someone remarked that all he wanted in life was an Ear — as a substitute for the writing for which he believed himself not yet prepared, or the painting toward which he was at the moment psychologically indisposed. "People came," he said, "and so I explained, because it was my nature to explain. Many wanted to know why I didn't write. I said I couldn't write. This was before I knew of Freud, so I could not tell them about inhibitions. . . ." Most of the paintings tended to puzzle even persons of broad culture, and sometimes left them with a sense of frustrated antagonism. Visitors could remember evenings when, upon leaving, someone who had contained himself and kept a straight face indoors, broke into laughter or got off snide remarks as soon as the Steins were out of hearing. But on his home ground and in his own sanctuary, Leo blossomed as, aggressively and proudly, he silenced any voice lifted against his defense of a new acquisition. Intent upon conveying every nuance of his own acute appreciation, he assumed a proprietary attitude that put many listeners off. Some of them felt he had confused his purchase of the pictures with the painting of them.

His approach was always messianic: "Someone had to 'discover' it if it is a new kind," he said, "and then propaganda, which propagates appreciation, is required to make others come to scratch. I've done some discovering and some propaganda, and know how it happens. One man who came to my place in Paris told me that the only Cézannes he cared for were those he saw there. Certainly they were not the best Cézannes, but the place was charged with the atmosphere of propaganda, and he succumbed."

Leo's own efforts to become a painter foundered through many prolonged attempts, yet he was obsessively committed to finding some place for himself in the new movement. Dominated by his belief that "Every action having as its purpose to give satisfaction to one's interest in forms is art," he had begun to assume the critical regency which, in his own eyes, he maintained without peer for the greater part of his life. "Often when a painter cannot find the last word," he said, "I can find it for him. . . . A French painter whom I knew slightly asked me to look at his work. As I did not know how he would take it, I made conventional remarks, but at last could not keep from pointing to a hole and suggesting how it could be filled. He was pleased, and asked whether I had noticed anything else. I said I had noted many things; so we went all over the pictures again, and he learned a lot about composition."

His pose of authority was not confined to painting. Bored by brief readings in Henry James's *The Wings of the Dove* and *The Golden Bowl*, he was generous enough to give them another perusal, another chance, because "My one reading assured me that they are candidates for classical honors. My next reading will tell whether or not they have passed." In the field of aesthetics, his self-announced eminence was sweeping. "One day I got an idea that seemed fruitful for aesthetics — something like that Croce turned out a few years later, and which he as a philosopher considered permanently important, but which I, with an interest in art and not in philosophy, soon came to regard as of little importance." In later years, having cast a cold eye upon the essays of T. S. Eliot which had become central directives in modern letters, he remarked on ". . . the extraordinary commonplaceness of Eliot. He is at some pains to phrase his things meticulously, but really never goes beyond the commonplace — which is perhaps really inevitable in this *via media* kind of thing. It is, as I said before, essentially a bore — not interesting." He concluded: "We have passed beyond the time where naïveté in judgment, like Eliot's, is admissible." Nor was he, at least in his family circle, surpassed in culinary art. "Everything Gertrude tried to cook turned out badly," he said, whereas he made such difficult things as bread and apfelstrudel and invented new pies and pancakes which were actually eaten. His terpsichorean talents were not, as a rule, open to public inspection. But on one occasion, when he was a little drunk, Leo was accompanied on the concertina by Georges Braque as he danced, à la Isadora Duncan, an extemporaneous composition, "The Young Girl and Death." One of the spectators, Leo reported, felt that his performance was too beautiful to be burlesque, and was otherwise so moved that she went home and wrote a poem about it. But these were minor accomplishments for a man who could claim "I am not a productive scientist because I haven't the aptitude for that kind of work, especially I have not that kind of patience. But I simply spill over with scientific ideas which serve *my* practical end, but which I do not study for their own sakes and therefore never insist upon. In this respect I think that I am both more intelligent and more conscientious than Freud and all the other analysts." He had independently discovered the pragmatism of James, Peirce and Dewey, he later asserted and, quite by himself, had anticipated by years the whole theory of cubism.

To many people Leo seemed merely self-centered, aggressive and fatuous. Not the least annoying of his habits was his repeated attempts to tell people who said they completely agreed with him that, really, they didn't agree with him at all. "But at a distance," wrote Hutchins Hapgood, who had known him intimately from the time of their meeting in Japan during the course of Leo's world voyage, "Leo always seems sympathetic; for one is impressed by his intense effort to be, and tell, the truth. He is limited only by the shadow of himself, the dignity of which he felt the need of sustaining under all circumstances. But he genuinely desired the well-being of everybody, and cared only for the highest. To be sure he associated the highest overmuch with himself, but that is better than not caring for it. His mental activity indeed was constant; too constant and intense for the undifferentiated parts of his nature. There wasn't enough volume of the unconscious instinct to give his mind a fair chance to work on, so it worked largely on itself."

Since he was "a Columbus setting sail for a world beyond the

53

world," or, in the view of Bernard Berenson, a man "who was always inventing the umbrella," the floor was exclusively Leo's in the early days of the atelier. Gertrude remained habitually in the background, quietly listening, perhaps often as puzzled and unsure and resistant as were many of the visitors about what it was they were being exhorted to accept. Alfred Stieglitz, the American photographer and painter who was a frequent caller at "27," was impressed by her unwavering silence under the force of such provocations. He said he had never known a woman who could sit still for so long without having to speak up. Gertrude explained: ". . . by that time I was writing and arguing was no longer to me really interesting. Nothing needed defending and if it did it was no use defending it. Anyway that was the beginning of my writing and by that time my brother had gotten to be very hard of hearing."

Turning to writing at this early stage appears to have been her most natural means of breaking away from Leo's paternalistic domination. Their relationship, still no more sentimental or personally intimate than it had been when they were children, was based on common pursuits and, to a degree, on shared ideas. But the intellectual initiative continued to be Leo's, and his aggressive self-assertions often silenced her and left her resentful. Somewhere along the line Gertrude apparently realized that only when she became an artist in her own right and on her own terms might she escape her brother's overzealous control. By producing something while he remained creatively inchoate, she might establish a superiority she must have begun to feel. ". . . my brother needed to be talking and he was painting but he needed to talk about painting in order to be painting, he needed to understand painting in order to be painting." Her creative life, the privacy of which she took pains to insure, was something Leo would not accommodate. His consequent frustration at being silently shut out could lead only to jealousy. Since he showed no overt interest in what she was doing, and since his mind was restlessly interested in everything else, his deliberate neglect suggests that he regarded her efforts as acts of personal defiance and disloyalty.

With evenings given over to the entertainment and the uninterrupted instruction of friends and casual callers, Gertrude adopted a practice of writing only late at night. She would begin about eleven, or at any time when she felt reasonably sure that no one else would ring the bell, and work until just before daybreak. When bird-noises in the trees and rooftops signaled it was time to put aside her pen, she would then sleep until late morning. When she would review by daylight the results of the long night's labor, few revisions occurred to her. The major part of her work was composed and final, she felt, before it was set down.

CHAPTER 4

Nobody knows what I am trying to do but I do
and I know when I succeed.
                                        — GERTRUDE STEIN

WITH the "lost" novel, *Q.E.D.*, behind her
and its aseptic Americanism and Jamesian finesse out of her system,
Gertrude Stein's long controversial career properly began with her
translation into English of Gustave Flaubert's *Trois Contes* (1877),
upon which she now quietly worked through the length of every
night. Translation was a unique undertaking for her and she was as
likely directed to it by her brother's enthusiasm for the French
master as by anything else. What she learned in the process can be
read in the genuine if tentative affinities between her very first
works and the stories which were among Flaubert's very last. In any
case, her labor of translation was germinal; once she had joined influences from Flaubert with influences from Cézanne as equally fertile sources of inspiration and method, she had made the first step
involving the relations of painting and literature upon which the
greater part of her career depends.

Leo, a devoted reader of Flaubert, had read no one else during the first few months he and Gertrude lived on the Rue de Fleurus and must have intrigued his sister by his exegeses of the novelist's technique, whether or not she was a willing listener. Even without Leo's pointed instruction, her reading of Flaubert would immediately have shown her that the French writer's passion for exactitude, compositional balances and analytical adjustments embodied ambitions of her own. Of the three tales of Flaubert — *Un Coeur Simple, La Légende de Saint Julien l'Hospitalier, Hérodias* — actually but one, *Un Coeur Simple*, is remotely akin to the triumvirate of stories Gertrude eventually published under the title *Three Lives*. The story on which she modeled her experiments was that of Félicité, "the simple heart" whose life was but a long series of attachments to the lives of others, whose deepest loves were borrowed or stolen. A more full-blown grotesque than Emma Bovary, Félicité like her is a character caught between a mundane world her temperament does not allow her to see and a world of fantasy sustained by her passionate romanticism. Finally approaching insanity — or, it could be equally well argued, sainthood — she comes to believe that her precious stuffed parrot is the Holy Ghost Himself. This heroine of Flaubert's whose pitiful silent suffering brings her to the brink of madness was a sister of many other illiterate drudges Gertrude had known. At a point where her fictional materials were ready, but where the form they might take was still hazy and undefined, Gertrude found in Flaubert's character a catalyst that clarified the picture and allowed her to explore her own resources. At the same time, she found in the words of the symbolist poet, Jules Laforgue, just the chord to introduce the gray proletarian stories she wanted to tell — "*Donc je suis un malheureux et ce n'est ni ma faute ni celle de la vie.*" Inarticulate humanity had always fascinated her; she now saw ways to record the whole sound and sense of the unlettered yet massively human type of servant she knew. No further observation was necessary; for years, in many households, including her own, she had studied such women with a natural human curiosity as well as with her scientifically informed eye. But to record the matter was one thing; to make the proper music was another. Gertrude's problem was twofold, yet one answer would serve.

57

In the late phase when he made his last refinements of naturalism, Flaubert had related the life history of Félicité with an astringent, almost clinical irony. With similar servant types in mind, Gertrude set about to encompass the meanings of the lives of *The Gentle Lena* and *The Good Anna* and *Melanctha* not with irony, but with a magnified, slow-moving and sympathetic realism. The basis of her style was rhythmic iteration of thought and speech which, she hoped, would match the precise colorful details that give visual sharpness to Flaubert's story. The vitality of her stories would lie in the degree of deftness with which she might catch the illusion of speech and thought as they were directly perceived. She had observed, under laboratory conditions, the ways in which repeated rhythms of an individual's speech identify him, indicate his attitude toward reality and his approach to experience. She had a strong feeling that character was revealed less in psychological chartings than in the casual, half-conscious, spoken phrases and rhythms by which individuals articulate their feelings. Things said might make a conventional narrative but more important, she felt, was the *manner* in which things were said; the meaning of a really interesting story was not something imbedded in the conclusion but something alive in every moment of the telling. By recreating modes of speech she felt she could express character with a clarity and force no compilation of biographical details could match.

When the respective methods of *Three Lives* and *Un Coeur Simple* are compared, only a few stylistic correspondences suggest that she had any thought of directly imitating Flaubert. She sought from the outset to create character by means of several modes of the vernacular in which her heroines thought and spoke. In the course of his *conte*, Flaubert maintains the position of the free, removed and omniscient author. He tells us that Félicité was saddened by certain events and made happy by others — a simple narrative method following a suggestion he made in a sketch depicting the household where his living prototype for Félicité was employed: "Monotony of their existence — little facts." Gertrude Stein, on the other hand — most particularly in *Melanctha* — tells us very little about her heroines. Instead, she shows them to us as the rhythms in which they speak and think are quickened or relaxed or endlessly repeated. She seldom dwells at any length on details of domestic existence; when such matters are called for, they simply crop up in the minds of the servants whose world they delimit with a naturalness wholly appropriate to the flow of vernacular.

The Good Anna and The Gentle Lena remain largely within the naturalist mode of storytelling. Still, their differences from naturalist conventions are significant. The simple, homely, almost litany-like movement of narrative in each of them represents a sharp departure from the typical rhetorical style of the nineteenth century. Immediacy is one of the results, a continual sense of hearing and over-hearing the particular quality of consciousness that belongs to each subject. Her situations are devised less for dramatic action and eventful continuity than for opportunities to observe character as a type of consciousness. The world Gertrude Stein's characters inhabit is strictly limited to the range of their personalities and their intellectual capacities. It is not extended, as in the case of Flaubert, by the all-seeing eye of the author and thus demands unusually intimate reader-participation. The meaning of the story depends upon the way in which characters are seemingly allowed to fulfill themselves in their own semiliterate terms rather than by the telling irony and ingenious plot manipulations of the narrator. It is a fiction technique without provision for a middle distance — that space between the reader and the abstract narrative where information and opinion may qualify the movement of the plot. In Flaubert, there is the documentation of a simple life by a wealth of appropriate homely or exotic detail, and constant reminders of the sophistication and acerbity of the storyteller himself. In Gertrude Stein detail and documentation are omitted in favor of a rendering so abstract that the sense of a narrator is all but effaced. The illuminating reality, she felt, would not be achieved by catalogues of her servant woman's possessions, or summary accounts of their past experiences, or diagnoses of their emotional states, but through the self-revealing perception of their emotions as they struggle to articulate their thoughts.

This technique inevitably leads to literary distortion far beyond hitherto acceptable notions of the storyteller's prerogative. To understand the true source of the method Gertrude Stein elaborated in *Three Lives* and carried to further development in *The Making of Americans*, we must look not to Flaubert or any other strictly literary source but, first to science — the science of William James and the naïve science of Gertrude Stein in the laboratory — and then to Cézanne. She had come to a resonant new motion: instead of narration in the honored convention of beginning, middle and end, she would make a composition where the story would be presented as an all-at-once revelation, like something painted on a wall, rather than by the accumulated disclosures of page after page. Like Cézanne, she would emphasize the vivid solid physical presence of her objects — in her case, characters. Yet she would neither forget nor ignore the fact that fundamental demands of the narrative medium would not allow her to deal entirely with lyrical impressions. Like Cézanne, in even his most advanced phase, she stopped short of the inevitable leap to abstraction. She was about to make the beginnings of a new kind of fiction in which conceptual aspects dominated the perceptual, in which scientific formulations gave way to imaginative suggestions. Yet she was still not ready to forego the force of human nature observed in the raw in favor of entirely cerebral projections or, as would soon be her practice, to allow the subject to be dispersed in the polyhedral vision of the observer.

Scientific training and day-to-day awareness had convinced her that in the twentieth century the old sense of narrative time had become transformed into an awareness of the present moment. William James had said that the utmost of rationality was the "feeling of sufficiency of the present moment," and her own experience had confirmed his observation. Immediacy, then, would be the first and final thing to achieve. To experience her meaning one would not depend on following tensions of plot development or on absorbing details highlighting aspects of dress, deportment or *décor*. Meaning would come by participation in the struggle within character that gives character its peculiar force. She would attempt to create a continuous present, demanding from the reader a continual arrest of attention, a prolonged dwelling on ideas that could otherwise be stated in a moment. For readers accustomed to the beguilements and tricks of suspense employed by ordinary writers, this would naturally be a challenge, if not an affront. Yet, with her version of the continuous present, she was in some ways only hearkening back to the methods of Samuel Richardson, one of her first loves among English writers. "Shakespeare, *Clarissa Harlowe* and detective stories" remained her preferences in reading all through her lifetime. She never expressed in words her indebtedness to Richardson's heroine, yet she was clearly, and perhaps unconsciously, emulating the process of direct rendering and immediate recording of feeling and thought that makes *Clarissa* memorable.

Through the first ten or twelve years of her writing, two equally strong forces in Gertrude Stein's nature contended for control. One of these was bent on making her an artist; the other would have her remain a scientist. Her first work, *Quod Erat Demonstrandum*, suggested by its very title an attempt to work out a human problem with mathematical precision; and the conception of works immediately following it was strongly biased by what she had learned through chartings of character and type in her laboratory work at Harvard. The mellowing and relaxation of her scientific approach gradually came about through her interest in painting. Submitting to the influence of Cézanne, she tried to reject the scientific bent that had previously directed all of her inquiries into human behavior. While science had provided the behavioristic conception of character underlying the design of *Three Lives*, her intentions were now those of an artist for whom the potentiality of the medium suggests the form of expression. In following the example of Cézanne, she was aligning herself in creative endeavors with one of the first of the great modern painters to regard nature as something to reshape, distort or otherwise arrange according to the dictation of his own feelings.

In her own words, *Three Lives* was conceived in this way: ". . . there was a constant recurring and beginning there was a marked direction in the direction of being in the present although naturally I had been accustomed to past present and future, and why, because the conception forming around me was a prolonged present . . . naturally I knew nothing of continuous present but it came naturally to me to make one, it was simple it was clear to me and nobody knew why it was done like that, I did not myself although naturally to me it was natural."

Beyond science and Cézanne, an event remembered from her childhood predisposed her to the kind of literary composition toward which her new conviction ran. In her statement, "the composition forming around me was a prolonged present," she is, perhaps unconsciously, recalling an impression she got when, at the age of eight or thereabouts, she saw the first oil painting that meant anything to her — a cyclorama of the Battle of Waterloo. Even as a child she already knew about the events depicted in the painting, and while she found it exciting to be reminded of them, her real delight came in realizing that the whole circle of interest was an oil painting, a "surrounding reality that had nothing to do with the Battle of Waterloo." So it is with *Three Lives*: the important thing is the "surrounding reality," the penumbra of feeling emanating from each completed composition and containing its "message" above and apart from the personalities and events of which each composition is made.

With a literalness and naïveté which she was never to outgrow, she confessed that she composed these works as she sat beneath Cézanne's portrait of his wife in which the subject is seated in a red chair and wearing a blue dress. This odd approach smacked of laboratory procedure, yet Gertrude Stein understood herself and she understood the essentially new character of the painting. She knew that deliberation and independence were propelling her toward a departure from convention in fiction as complete as Cézanne's departure from Delacroix in painting. By a ceaseless flow of half-articulated thoughts, worn phrases of speech and homely inflections from domestic life, she would match Cézanne's iterations of the qualities of light. She would recreate the dumb animal power of human nature and the coarse reality of human relations with the same solid geometry with which Cézanne had invested his peasants, his landscapes, his apples. With little concern for ingenious highlighting of detail, assignment of symbolic overtones, or picaresque charm, she aimed for an over-all presentation — a whole segment of life illuminated and given substance by its own inner power. Disregarding plot sequence and conventional maneuvers by which fictional character is developed, she hoped to create and to order a bolus of reality in which "everything was there, really there . . ." Her people and places would resemble their living counterparts but would not be reduced to "realistic" size by the employment of the tags and turns by which conventional writers achieve verisimilitude. By rendering the "essential nature" of individuals through exposure of their binding habits of speech and thought, she assumed, perhaps too hopefully, that conventional dramatic elements would not be missed. The important thing would be the creation of an immediate reality, an impact so strong and a substance so pure that academic questions of exposition, motivation, character and plot would have no meaning. "I came to Cézanne and there you were," she said, "at least there I was, not all at once but as soon as I got used to it. The landscape looked like a landscape that is to say what is yellow in the landscape looked yellow in the oil painting, and what was blue in the landscape looked blue in the oil painting and if it did not there was still the oil painting, the oil painting by Cézanne. The same thing was true of the people there was no reason why it should be but it was, the same thing was true of the chairs, the same thing was true of the apples. The apples looked like apples the chairs looked like chairs and it all had nothing to do with anything because if they did not look like apples or chairs or landscape or people they were apples and chairs and landscape and people. They were so entirely these things that they were not an oil painting and yet that is just what the Cézannes were they were an oil painting. They were so entirely an oil painting that it was all there whether they were finished, the paintings, or whether they were not finished. Finished or unfinished it always was what it looked like the very essence of an oil painting because everything was there, really there . . . This then was a great relief to me and I began my writing."

If Cézanne hung before her as a model, William James whispered behind her as a guide — James who said that, although the same fixed ideas may dominate a situation, consciousness of some kind goes on as "states of mind" succeed each other. When she had learned

63

his lesson, the significant thing for Gertrude Stein as a writer became the perception of relationships within a fixed situation. And if she listened further she could have found reason to justify her slow, stammering recordings of thinking-as-thought. It was James who also said: "There is not a conjunction or a preposition, and hardly an adverbial phrase, syntactic form, or inflection of voice, in human speech, that does not express some shading or other of relation which we at some moment actually feel to exist between the larger objects of our thought. . . . So inveterate has our habit become of recognizing the existence of the substantive parts [of speech] alone, that language almost refuses to lend itself to other uses."

With such evocative echoes behind her, and with the closer echoes of her brother's nightly harangues and soliloquies about her, the shape she gave to *Three Lives* was not a matter of whimsy, as many bewildered or shocked critics felt, but the logical development of an ambitious and already highly resourceful talent.

As an alert receptor, and an adroit investigator of the operations of the rational mind, Gertrude Stein had grasped for herself the dominating impressionism which had already initiated the greatest change in art expression in four hundred years. She had become a practicing artist in a movement so new that it had neither theory nor vocabulary. Others would explore that revolutionary movement for generations and the terms they devised to name it and account for it would soon come tumbling onto the pages of textbooks and of the daily press: relativism, antisystemism, subjectivism, psychologism, cubism, expressionism. In her grand simplicity, Gertrude Stein used none of them. Yet they are terms denoting the relative or perspective nature of truth dominating nearly every significant endeavor of art and science in the twentieth century. A new world of mind had been constituted. Gertrude Stein had come to its threshold, folded her umbrella, and crossed over as easily and naturally as if it led into a house she knew.

CHAPTER 5

Mama loves you best because you are Spanish.
— GERTRUDE STEIN

It's hard to be so smart that the next minute
can't fool you.
— LEO STEIN

IN the world of art — a semicelestial area
horizontally and vertically subdivided by the famous, often-painted
streets of Montmartre — discovery and innovation had long been the
rule. Yet each marvelous new incident was cause for celebration and,
sooner or later, for pitched battles. Parisians had become quite used
to the rapid-fire explosions that continually resounded from the slopes
of La Butte. But in the buoyant winter of 1905, even jaded observers of the scene had something new to talk about — the emergence, at the age of thirty-five, of Henri Matisse as the particular
genius of a brash, brilliant group of painters no one could ignore.
From his obscure position as a copyist of paintings in the Louvre,
Matisse was suddenly the recognized leader of a startling congrega-
tion of artists shortly to be known as *Les Fauves*, or "The Wild
Beasts." This group, famous for its loud, flat colors swabbed on canvas with only incidental regard for plastic form and composition, was
most clearly influenced by the tortured impressionism of Van Gogh

and by the large decorative works of Gauguin that seemed to call for the space of a wall rather than the nice proportions of an easel. *Les Fauves* rose to prominence in the waning of impressionism, hastened the demise of the older movement and, for a time, all but obliterated it from public attention.

As a consequence of having acquired Matisse's *La Femme au Chapeau* — a painting which had evoked squalls of wrath and resentment upon its first being shown at the Petit Palais in the second *Salon d'Automne* — Gertrude and Leo had already made the new painter's acquaintance. Gertrude had been slow in coming to appreciate many of Leo's discoveries, but she surprised her brother by admiring *La Femme au Chapeau* on first sight. According to her report — later disputed by Leo and their sister-in-law, Sarah Samuels Stein, Michael's wife — she immediately offered four hundred francs for the painting. When the secretary of the gallery told her that Matisse could not accept a fee so modest, she went home, only to return the next day for a second viewing of the painting. When she found gallery visitors scoffing at it (one inflamed soul was apparently bent on scratching the thick paint from the canvas) she met Matisse's price of five hundred francs — in those days, one hundred dollars — without further quibbling. The Matisse purchase, she later explained, was actually prompted more clearly by her feeling for the artist's aesthetic bravado than by her pleasure in the picture itself. The derision it evoked in the *cage des fauves* — as the exhibition room of the new "wild beast" painters had been dubbed — "bothered her and angered her because she did not understand why because to her it was so alright, just as later she did not understand why since the writing was all so clear and natural they mocked at and were enraged by her work."

Leo took issue with Gertrude's story of the purchase. The painting had caught his attention, he said, because it signaled Matisse's emergence from the period of neoimpressionism when, in faltering imitations of Seurat, he applied his pigment in pointillist dots — a method which Leo abhorred. But he could not get used to the picture; he thought it was brilliant and powerful, but that it was also "the nastiest smear of paint" he had ever seen. He had to let his mind play about the work for a few days before deciding in its favor. Sufficiently gallery-wise to know that no one ever offered the catalogue price — in this case five hundred francs — he then made the offer of a price amounting to around two thirds of the asking price. Matisse countered with a compromise proposal and Leo bought the painting. Sarah Stein modified Leo's story when she recalled that her interest in *La Femme au Chapeau* was arrested not only by "the unprecedented magnificence of its color" but by the close resemblance of the portrait to her mother. This sentimental consideration led her to urge Leo to buy it "for the family." When all stories are taken into account, it becomes apparent that the decision to buy the work was a family affair in which Leo's voice was simply the most persuasive; the painting was purchased for something in the neighborhood of five hundred francs. In the early 1950's, *La Femme au Chapeau* was sold to Mr. and Mrs. Walter A. Haas of San Francisco for twenty thousand dollars.

Shortly afterwards Leo and Gertrude were introduced to the painter and his wife, the model for *La Femme au Chapeau*, when the artist Henri Manguin escorted them to Matisse's immaculately well-ordered atelier. There they saw for the first time a painting — a landmark in Matisse's early career — which was to become a central fixture in the gallery at 27 Rue de Fleurus: the large *Le Bonheur de Vivre*. They found Matisse convivial and kindly — Leo described him as "bearded, but with propriety; spectacled neatly; intelligent; freely spoken, but a little shy"— yet sensed that he did not assume a too easy intimacy. From the first it was Leo's opinion that Matisse was the most intelligent of the new painters, one of the few capable of saying precisely what he meant when talking about art. Just as important in gaining Leo's warm opinion was the fact that Matisse would listen to him and, according to Leo, even allow the course of his work to be influenced by what he said. He believed Matisse had the temper of the eternal pupil and continued for many years to regard him as a willing — though eventually errant — pupil. Ideal as this relationship must have been for Leo, it was comparatively short-lived. After having discovered and celebrated Matisse and, through the good offices of the picture dealer M. Vollard, having enormously helped the sales of his work, Leo came to the conclusion that Matisse was "insufficient" in rhythm. Before this feeling took root, many purchases of Matisses, not only by Leo and Gertrude, but also those by Mike and Sarah, made the Stein family the most active of his collectors, save one. The Muscovite businessman, Sergei I. Shchukin, whose purchases had preceded the Steins' by two years, was Matisse's greatest supporter; his vast private collection later became the basis of Moscow's Museum of Modern Art. The advanced taste of the Michael Steins, who had come to Paris in 1902 when, at home, labor troubles and their expanding fortune seemed to make the move propitious, is reflected in their acquisition for their salon in the Rue Madame of, among many others, the *Young Sailor, No. 1*, the *Blue Still Life* and the *Pink Onions*. In 1907, Sarah Stein helped to organize a painting class for Matisse in which she herself was an enthusiastic pupil. She and her husband became notable collectors not only of Matisse but of many other moderns; their solid commitment to radically new art led them, many years later, to give the architect Le Corbusier one of his first commissions when he built the villa Les Terrasses, their home at Garches.

Leo's conviction of Matisse's rhythmic inadequacy and the subsequent loss of interest in his progress led to his selling all of his collection of the artist's paintings in 1914. Since he had come to the conclusion that "so-called modern art" was "only very occasionally good enough," his waning interest as a collector was turned elsewhere until after the First World War. By that time, Leo felt Matisse had overcome, or compensated for, failings that were evident as early as 1907. He did not name these new virtues but felt that they showed more clearly in Matisse's drawings than in his paintings; he was convinced they were leading Matisse into a phase in which his destiny would be fulfilled in paintings that were "completely satisfying."

Gertrude was deeply impressed by *Le Bonheur de Vivre* — later regarded as the ultimate masterpiece of the Fauve movement — and fascinated by its strangeness and vast simplicity. When Leo parted company with her some years afterwards, it was to be the one Matisse she would not consider giving up, even though her brother coveted it as the most important painting composed in modern times.

68

For Gertrude the painting represented a moment of victory in Matisse's continual struggle. She saw in it an example of the creative wrestling in which her most abiding interest was centered. His distorted drawing, for all its violence, was a constant effort in the direction of clarification and simplicity, she felt, and she admired its naked ugliness. Cézanne, she believed, had come to the point of unfinishedness and distortion by an inevitable development of his way of seeing once he had been disabused of the necessity for traditional forms; Matisse had come to the same point by deliberation, by a knowledgeable reapplication of what Cézanne had discovered.

Immersed in the creative experience and meanings of Cézanne and Matisse and, in her own parallel way, involved in the aesthetic revolution they represented, Gertrude was at the point of meeting one of the major influences of her creative life and, for many years, one of her dearest friends.

In his unceasing ruminations through the obscurer galleries of the Rue Lafitte, *"la rue des tableux,"* Leo had come upon paintings by Pablo Picasso — or, as he sometimes signed his works, Pablo Picasso y Ruiz — in an establishment, a former pharmacy in which many stale medicines were still stored, owned by an ex-circus clown, Clovis Sagot. While Picasso was still all but unknown in the crowded art world his work, like Matisse's, had already been spotted by the incredibly acute Sergei Shchukin of Moscow who had become his first substantial collector. Leo's first purchase was a work of the Blue Period — a mountebank with a woman and child and an ape in which, according to Leo, "the ape looked at the child so lovingly that Sagot was sure this scene was derived from life; but I knew more about apes than Sagot did, and was sure that no such baboon-like creature belonged in such a scene. Picasso told me later that the ape was his invention, and it was a proof that he was more talented as a painter than as a naturalist." When the painting was hung in "27," it was noticed and identified by a good friend of the Steins, Henri-Pierre Roché. A tall, red-headed journalist, painter and art expert, Roché was later to figure importantly in choosing paintings for the great John Quinn Collection in New York. But at the time he was regarded as a man of little originality and much general curiosity who, like Leo himself, "always had many irons in the fire but the fire went out before the forging." Roché's curiosity about people was his career; he knew nearly everyone of interest in the art world, and it was he who provided Leo with an introduction to Picasso. Gertrude did not accompany him on the occasion of their first meeting, which took place in Picasso's Rue Ravignan studio. Leo was impressed with his "extraordinary seeing eyes"; his gaze was so intense, Leo reported, that after Picasso had looked at a drawing or a print one felt, literally, that his eyes had absorbed everything on the paper. But as a personality he found him wanting as compared with Matisse. Besides a lively intuition that would match Picasso's, Matisse had an enormous capacity for concentration. Unlike Picasso, who lived in a domestic circus of squalor, Matisse was orderly; he had "a place for everything and everything in its place, both within his head and out."

Gertrude met Picasso in 1905 at Sagot's, when she went there to inspect *Jeune Fille aux Fleurs*, which Leo was thinking of buying. Picasso happened to be in the gallery. When he saw Gertrude, he asked, "Who is the lady?" When Sagot identified her, Picasso said, "Ask her if she will pose for me," and retired to await an answer. When Gertrude accepted the proposal, their first shy meeting had already established a harmony that governed nearly all of their lifelong relations. But, according to Leo, at the very moment when Picasso was demurely awaiting her word of acceptance, Gertrude was vocally expressing total dislike of the painting they had come to see. Her lack of enthusiasm was not dissuasive; a few days later Leo went back to Sagot's and bought it. When he announced his acquisition to Gertrude at the dinner table, she lost her appetite. She hated "that picture with feet like a monkey's," according to Leo, and resented the waste of the hundred and fifty francs it had cost. Not many years later the painting had become a favorite of hers. She refused to sell it for an enormous sum — even when Leo, who had lost enthusiasm for it, insisted that the money they might realize would enable them to buy much better things. Eventually *Jeune Fille aux Fleurs* became the pivotal work around which the continually rearranged works on the walls of "27" were grouped. Now in the possession of the Stein estate, the little canvas that originally cost thirty dollars might, according to authoritative estimates, bring at auction the highest price of any figure painting of the twentieth century.

The truth of Gertrude's first acquaintance with the art of Picasso has been disputed, but her wholehearted response to the man himself remains unquestioned. She may have been slow in coming to acceptance and appreciation of the painter's work, but when its significance did become apparent to her, his impact on her career was resonant for many years. She and Picasso had begun to exchange afternoon studio visits shortly after the meeting at Sagot's. Soon Gertrude was in the habit of going daily to the dilapidated quarters in the Rue Ravignan to which Picasso had moved in 1904. She would walk across the Luxembourg Gardens to the Odéon from where, every half-hour, the famous Batignolles-Clichy-Odéon omnibus, drawn by three dappled gray horses abreast, set off across Paris. Sometimes seated on the imperial, she would travel across the Seine and then uphill to the Place Blanche in Montmartre; from there she had to climb on foot to the little square onto which Picasso's ramshackle tenement faced. For perhaps eighty or ninety days through the winter of 1905-1906, she sat for him in a large broken armchair beside a cast-iron stove held together with wire and around which lay heaps of cinders and other pieces of crippled furniture, dirty palettes and matted brushes. Still fiercely poor, Picasso had at least emerged from the period when he and Max Jacob occupied a room in the Hôtel du Maroc and shared one bed in turns. In those days Picasso would work through the night, scattering drawings across the floor while Jacob slept. When Jacob got up in the morning in order to let Picasso have his turn at sleeping, he would often leave his footprints on drawings some of which, years later, had to be carefully removed by art experts. But poverty was no hindrance to the association of souls as congenial and minds as lively as Picasso's and Gertrude's, and during the long series of sittings for the portrait the foundations of their long, celebrated friendship were laid.

Living with Picasso was Fernande Olivier, a statuesque young woman who had been his neighbor in the tenement house and

71

whom he had first met in one of its shadowy corridors. Among Mlle. Olivier's gifts was a talent for reciting poetry. During the course of Gertrude's sittings, she read aloud all of the fables of La Fontaine. But mostly Gertrude talked and listened, charmed with the vivacity of Picasso's speech, amused by the way he dressed in the blue over-all and pullover that was the conventional outfit for Parisian plumbers, delighted by the ideas and notions that flitted through his head and, sometimes, came to rest in his paintings. According to Jaime Sabartés, an intimate lifelong friend of the painter, with him it was "difficult to make a sustained journey along any one path, and even more difficult to carry on a conversation from a given point of departure about a specific subject. No one can even remotely guess where a discussion with him will lead, partly because of his impatience with itineraries, for his imagination blocks the road and interrupts the initial plan, changing the course of the conversation. . . . His mind moves so rapidly from one thing to another that heaven and earth could not contain him or force him back; in any case, as a rule he makes one forget the very origin of the discourse; he changes the entire character of the theme, as he might a line when he sets about juggling it to shape one of his myriad fantasies."

Gertrude found that she could share with Picasso confidences she would carefully keep from her brother. Problems neither she nor Picasso could discuss with Leo were, between themselves, matters of easy discourse. She had by this time found the beginnings of personal independence, but her deep-rooted need for a mentor, as evidenced by her many years of devotion to Leo, was undoubtedly a salient part of her attraction to Picasso. To make her independence even more complete, she could in Picasso's company often reverse roles and be the dominant one herself.

A naturally powerful painter from the time of his first astonishing compositions as an art student in Spain, Picasso had not come swiftly into a company of peers without showing the influences of a number of artists, notably Toulouse-Lautrec. But random influences had quickly disappeared as he moved into the Blue Period of his first impoverished years in France. The lyrical greens and liquid blues, and the sentimental postures in which his beggars, prostitutes and the

72

other sick, lame and hungry figures of that phase hold themselves were, except for certain decorative moments suggesting Gauguin, largely his own expressions. When Gertrude came into his ken he was in the closely related Rose and Harlequin Periods, when he used a neutral palette in attempts to come upon a less romantic, more objective expression of sentiments no less melodramatic than those portrayed in the Blue Period. With the portrait of Gertrude Stein, his fecund Rose Period came to an end, and the foreshadowings of cubism began to be apparent. During the months Gertrude sat for him, his works began to show less and less preoccupation with the pathos of circus figures especially characteristic of the Harlequin Period, and his light, graceful use of line became heavier as his drawing became more solid. He was beginning to translate into his own portraiture the influence of primitive Iberian sculpture, which he had known all his life, and the African sculpture which had recently come to Paris. When the influences of primitivism began to show, his portraits bore strongly delineated features of an archaic nature, with more obvious concern for facial planes than for character likeness; and his colors tended to be almost monotone, or to borrow earthen, terra-cotta textures and hues reminiscent of Pompeiian frescoes and other Roman wall decorations.

Since he had last worked from a model when he was sixteen (he was now twenty-four), Gertrude was puzzled by his having chosen her. Being an American had something to do with it, she eventually felt, and also the happy accident of meeting him when the inspiration of the Rose Period was exhausted, while that of the transitional Negroid period had not yet begun. One day, just as the portrait seemed finished, Picasso painted out the entire face. He told Gertrude he could no longer "see" her when he looked at her. With Fernande Olivier he went off for the summer to the Pyrenees, staying at Gosol, a little town in the Spanish province of Lérida. Faceless and abandoned, the powerful figure stood against a studio wall for months. But as soon as Picasso returned to Paris, and before Gertrude had come back from her own summer holiday in Fiesole, he painted in the final version of the head. Like the *Autoportrait* he made at the same time, the *Portrait de Gertrude Stein* now showed

73

clearly the style that had emerged in the canvases he had worked on in Gosol, notably his *Peasants from Andorra* and *Woman with Loaves*, and indicated the treatment soon to be employed in the grotesque figures, seemingly hewn with hatchet strokes, of *Les Demoiselles d'Avignon*. Most of the many studies Picasso made for *Les Demoiselles*, some showing the influence of Gauguin, some the influence of Iberian sculpture and some that of African masks, were actually made at the time when he finished the portrait of Gertrude by giving her a masklike and somewhat Negroid face. The solid placid proportions of the rest of the figure seemed finally to serve more as a setting for the head than as its organic base. In the space of time between the comparatively naturalistic working out of the figure proper and the primitivistic delineation of the face, two styles had crept into his canvas. Meeting without conflict in the portrait itself, they add a good measure of historical interest to one of the most "successful" paintings of the twentieth century.

Pleased with what he had done, Picasso called Gertrude in to view the final product. She was delighted, just as she was many years later when she said, "I was and I still am satisfied with my portrait, for me, it is I, and it is the only reproduction of me which is always I, for me." Picasso made her a gift of the work; it was that period when "the difference between a sale and a gift was negligible."

It was still four or five years before Gertrude would herself attempt to do portraits using words rather than pigments. Then it was only natural that Picasso should serve as one of her very first subjects. When her word-portrait of Picasso appeared in the American periodical *Camera Work*, the composition went into history as the first public appreciation of the painter to be published anywhere. In having chosen to paint her, Picasso had implicitly praised her. Gertrude's study of him, as one random excerpt may show, was praise in return: "Some were certainly following and were certain that the one they were then following was one bringing out of himself then something that was coming to be a heavy thing, a solid thing, and a complete thing. . . . Something had been coming out of him, certainly it had been coming out of him, certainly it was something, certainly it had been coming out of him and it had meaning, a charm-

ing meaning, a solid meaning, a struggling meaning, a clear meaning.
. . . This one would be one all his living having something coming
out of him."

While Picasso was spending his creatively eventful summer in
Gosol, Gertrude and Leo were again in Italy, at the Villa Ricci, a
house with elegantly terraced gardens overlooking Florence from the
heights of Fiesole. "Working tremendously," Gertrude began to
write her monumental *The Making of Americans*. Before the summer was out, they had brief visits by the Matisses, by the American
painter Alfred Maurer, and by Etta Cone, a lonely young woman
from Baltimore who had been their intimate friend and correspondent for years. *Three Lives*, at that time still entitled *Three Histories*,
had been completed during the months when Gertrude was daily
posing for her portrait. She had found good employment for Etta
Cone, who was spending the winter in Paris, by setting her to work
typing copy to be submitted to a publisher. Concerned to have a
faithful transcript of the unorthodox work, she was at first worried
that Etta might get involved in the stories and apply to them her
own sense of the language. She was relieved when she found that
her friend was copying the manuscript word for word, letter by letter, faithfully and without question. The typing was soon completed
in good order, thereby furthering Etta Cone's reputation for romantic charities. It was she who, along with her distinguished sister
Claribel, was often called upon to save the day when Picasso and
Fernande found themselves financially embarrassed. When this frequently happened, Gertrude or Leo would lead the Cone sisters to
Picasso's studio and help them to select a drawing for which they
were expected cheerfully to pay twenty American dollars. As with
the Cones, Leo and Gertrude made use of others of their well-to-do
friends in Picasso's behalf during the difficult early years.

Gertrude said that in the period between 1906 and 1909 the Stein
family had their pick of Picasso's new work simply because no one
else was interested in buying it. A long-range importance attaches
to the fact that they heralded the painter's genius from their commanding position in the art world. At the time, their more important
support was in the form of cash when it was immediately needed,

when its absence might have seriously curbed Picasso's creative existence. "In 1910, I bought my last picture from Picasso," Leo wrote, "and that was one that I did not really want, but I had from time to time advanced him sums of money, and this cleared the account. Picasso was amusing sometimes when he was hard up. At one such moment the pictures of Renoir for the first time brought large prices at an auction, and Picasso, who had no coal and no money to buy it, drew glowing pictures of Renoir's house with sacks of coal everywhere and some specially choice hunks on the mantelpiece. Once when I gave him a hundred francs to buy coal, he stopped on the way home and spent sixty of it for Negro sculpture."

Benefactors who, for one reason or another, had been enlisted in Picasso's behalf, lived to see their unpremeditated acts of charity transformed into enormously profitable investments. The most conspicuous example of this occurred in the case of the shy, long-suffering Etta Cone and her dynamic sister Claribel, who had begun her career at Women's Medical College in Baltimore and, after graduate work in medicine at the University of Pennsylvania, became a resident physician at the Bloakley Hospital for the insane. Claribel Cone was an able and strong-minded woman who shared Gertrude's taste for being lionized, and something of her flair for doing as she liked regardless of what others did. A familiar sight in the great cathedrals of Europe, she walked through their stained-glass light under an open umbrella which, supposedly, would protect her from bats. When she and her sister, heiresses to a cotton-mill fortune, came to Europe as they did almost yearly in the continuing pursuit of Claribel's medical researches, the Steins took them into the ever-widening circle of the Saturday evenings. Picasso's blunt speech and behavior often shocked them but, emancipated from the lacy constrictions of genteel Baltimore, they were gradually able to tolerate his Bohemianism and eventually became his good friends. But their deeper friendship was shared with the Matisses, to whom they had also been introduced by the Steins. From Matisse they eventually bought forty-three canvases, along with large folios of his drawings, and some of the most important of his sculptures. At the time of Claribel's death in 1929, the sisters had amassed a collection of

76

Manets, Renoirs, Degas, Bonnards and Cézannes ranking high among the great private collections of their time and, in the case of Matisse, the best over-all representation in the United States. Gertrude was deeply moved to hear of Claribel's death and, by sending to Etta a portrait of Leo Stein that Picasso had done, accomplished three things with one gesture: while the gift was nominally a tribute to Claribel's memory, it also served the purposes of removing her brother's image from her walls and of giving Picasso forceful representation in the Cone Collection. Since Claribel had died still dubious about the degree of acceptance the citizens of Baltimore might be generous enough or enlightened enough to grant their masterpieces, she left her share of the works to Etta, to be maintained in the huge old-fashioned Marlborough Apartments on Eutaw Place where, with their brother Frederic, they lived in three different apartments. Upon Etta's decease, they were to be bequeathed to the Baltimore Museum, together with a $400,000 building fund. The conditions of Dr. Cone's will specified that this be done only if the people of Baltimore gave up the stubborn resistance to modern art they had shown all through her lifetime. During the twenty years she survived her sister, Etta Cone added to the collection materials emphasizing the backgrounds of the new painting, framing a documentary and educational setting for it, and thereby helped to bring about the acceptance for which Claribel had hoped. In 1949, a few months after Etta's death, the Cone Collection, valued at three million dollars, went on view and the Baltimore Museum immediately assumed a ranking of national importance in modern art. The distance from Picasso's grimy Rue Ravignan studio seemed incalculable, and the sisters had in fact stopped buying his works after his cubist period in favor of expenditures upon Matisse. But, as in the case of the Steins themselves, accidents of time and place had thrust strangers into an enormously significant development in art they were wise enough to recognize and had the means and the continuing will to support.

Independent of fashion, indifferent to established custom, the Steins maintained their own preferences in dress, their own rules of

77

deportment with a blithe assurance that set them apart. Leo was markedly apathetic toward people whose distinction lay in conspicuous signs of wealth or titles of royalty, and while Gertrude tended eventually to surround herself with figures from the *haut monde,* in the early days the society they chose was notably free of individuals whose aesthetic pretensions served mainly to ornament their social positions. A congenial and closed company of two, the Steins took little notice of opinion that reported them to be eccentric and theatrical, cranky and messianic, or snobbish and sybaritic. They regarded their celebrity merely as recognition of a singularity they had themselves never questioned.

Leo was hardly "the American Maecenas" and Gertrude was not quite the "sibyl of Montparnasse," yet these epithets contained the seeds of a legend that would blossom and proliferate. Leo *was* a well-to-do, large-mannered patron of the arts; and Gertrude *was* of a Delphic disposition and would play the pythoness whenever she found the opportunity. Since remarks about them contained a little verifiable truth, a little patent falsehood and a great deal of fascinating conjecture, romance was inevitable. Fernande Olivier, whose association with them was for a time comparatively intimate, remembered them in this way: "He, looking like a professor, bald, with gold-rimmed glasses. Long beard with ruddy lights, cunning glance. A big, stiff body, with peculiar poses, with abbreviated gestures. The true type of German-American Jew.

"She, fat, short, massive, beautiful head, strong, with noble features, accentuated regular, intelligent eyes, seeing clearly, spiritually. Her mind was clear and lucid. Masculine, in her voice, in all her walk. . . . Both were dressed in chestnut-colored · corduroy, wearing sandals after the fashion of Raymond Duncan, whose friends they were. Too intelligent to care about ridicule, too sure of themselves to bother about what other people thought, they were rich and he wanted to paint."

While they were a familiar and apparently congenial pair, "the aristocracy almost exclusive of all but two," in the out-of-the-way galleries of Paris, privately at home they were in harmony about almost everything except the respective arts to which they addressed

78

themselves. Gertrude was now spending long hours at her desk every night — a practice to which Leo gave but passing attention, since his interests were centered exclusively in himself and the fabulous ideas that elated him one day and wracked him the next. Interminably fingering his neuroses, he continued to make cantankerous assays into the field of aesthetics, now and then actually tried to paint. In discussions of theory, and the excitement of many discoveries, they had shared much — that is, after Leo's tutelage had provided Gertrude with enough basic knowledge and understanding for her to define her own reactions. But when they pursued their separate careers, all cooperation ceased, and all mutual interest. As Gertrude expressed it, "I was writing in the way I was writing. I did not show what I was doing to my brother, he looked at it and he did not say anything. Why not. Well there was nothing to say about it and really I had nothing to say about it. Slowly we were not saying anything about it that is we never *had* said anything about it . . . Then slowly he began explaining not what I was doing but he was explaining, and explaining well explaining might have been an explanation. Now and then I was not listening. This had never happened to me before up to that time I had always been listening sometimes arguing very often just being interested and interesting and very often it was just that we had always been together as we always were . . . Slowly and in a way it was not astonishing but slowly I was knowing that I was a genius and it was happening and I did not say anything but I was almost ready to begin to say something. My brother began saying something and this is what he said.

"He said that it was not it it was I. If I was not there to be there with what I did then what I did would not be what it was. In other words if no one knew me actually then the things I did would not be what they were."

Time and again, Gertrude would have occasion to remember this particular aspect of her brother's criticism, but she would ignore it later no less completely than she did when she first heard it. But when she refused Leo as a mentor in her creative life, her attitude was neither the result of weakness nor of stubbornness. Leo was as intolerant of experiment in literature as he would soon prove to be intolerant of innovation in painting. A writer, he felt, should aim only at fitting meaning to purpose with the exquisite precision of a jeweler. He believed that "the cheap poet can easily get his effect by using words that pour over their natural confines of meaning — loves and doves, roses and woeses, home and mother, Alabama and Dolores" and that in the hands of good poets words "go into place as though they were jeweled" rather than, as in the case of a bad poet, "slip into place as though they were greased."

Gertrude, already committed to a method, was gradually becoming dedicated to a purpose. In the person of her learned brother she could sense the response of the conventional reader, yet she would nevertheless insist on listening first to her own steady-voiced Muse. She was already writing, as she said, "for myself and strangers." Sibling rivalry cannot be discounted as a factor in her refusal to be further tutored. Leo had never relinquished the sense of his sister's position as both his intellectual ward and his most able adversary. "As a boy at school," he proudly recalled, "I was expected by the others to answer offhand almost any question about anything, and for the years that my sister and I lived together she, who never used a dictionary or an encyclopædia and had no general information, expected me to supply on demand all that kind of knowledge." Gertrude's quiet confidence in herself, in contrast with Leo's uneasy fits and starts as an artist, could not have been easy to tolerate. As early as 1907, Leo had made a series of drawings of an abstract nature, but he was dissatisfied with the results and may very likely have extended his impatience with abstractionist art to include Gertrude's experiments. "I came to the conclusion that nothing complicated was possible," he said, "because intersecting lines and planes bred confusion. When Picasso and Braque began their abstractions I was interested but couldn't see that they succeeded." Whether or not Gertrude "succeeded" in any sense he would recognize, it became apparent that she had found in writing the one means by which she could gain ascendance over Leo and that she would no longer allow her progress to be curbed. "He did not say it to me but he said it so that it would be true for me. And it did not trouble me and as it did not trouble me he knew it was not true. . . . But it destroyed him for me and it destroyed me for him."

Leo's own diagnosis of the causes that set them on different paths to different achievements is succinct: ". . . Gertrude's sort of massive self-admiration, and, in part, self-assurance, enabled her to build something rather effective on her foundations. I, on the other hand, through the upsetting, complicating and stultifying effects of a terrific neurosis, could build nothing substantial on my intelligence, which came through only in fragments and distorted bits."

Their actual separation was still a number of years away, yet Gertrude was coming to a state of mind in which she would welcome a break in their lifelong relations. Reaching for the mantle of genius, she preferred to don it alone. "It is funny this thing of being a genius, there is no reason for it, there is no reason that it should be you and should not have been him, no reason at all that it should have been you, no reason at all." Her sure sense of her abilities had deepened and her creative career expanded as Leo continued to wrestle with his own intimations of genius: "Quite lately I was explaining to Matisse, to Gertrude and to others why I was going to stop painting entirely," he wrote to a friend. "I had an abundance of good reasons. The same night at twelve o'clock I began to do a big composition and have since done much the best thing yet. It's hard to be so smart that the next minute can't fool you."

Most of Gertrude's important new friendships were still shared with her brother, but gradually her creative needs brought her closer to Picasso and his circle and to relationships in which Leo had no part. While Leo continued to maintain good relations with Picasso, there was never any doubt that, in both his critical estimation and his affection, Matisse came first. With his passion for analysis and his continual tendency to make a romance of his intellectual experience, Leo looked suspiciously at anyone who operated principally on the level of intuition. Since Picasso believed that knowledge and intellect were dangerous things for an artist, there was very little common ground on which he and Leo could meet.

Impatience with Picasso as a personality finally led Leo to reject Picasso as an artist. His reasons were unequivocal: "Picasso is a man

81

of the finest sensitiveness, the keenest observation and a strong sense of man in his humors. Goethe said of Byron that he was a child when he thought, but then Pablo is a babe in arms. Both he and Gertrude are using their intellects, which they ain't got, to do what would need the finest critical tact, which they ain't got, neither, and they are . . . turning out the most Godalmighty rubbish that is to be found." The prescience which had led Leo to his remarkable discoveries among the new painters was, as time would tell, fundamentally erratic and limited, in spite of his having been, in the judgment of the critic Alfred H. Barr, Jr., for the two years between 1905 and 1907 perhaps the most discerning connoisseur and collector of twentieth-century painting anywhere in the world.

If the development of modern painting is read in the conventional and roughly successive categories of impressionism, neoimpressionism, Fauvism, cubism, Dadaism, surrealism, and all of their variants and splinter movements, Leo Stein's relation to this history, at least after the advent of cubism, was tenuous and marginal. On the other hand, Gertrude Stein, from the time of her friendship with Picasso, was never far from the center of developments, whether or not she approved of them. She neither embraced nor followed any school after the cubists and, in fact, derided the programs of a number of the somewhat sensational and exhibitionistic movements succeeding it. Personal interest in individual painters kept alive her sources of aesthetic intelligence and, in the long run, she was correctly identified in the public mind as the more knowledgeable mentor and the more forceful influence in the art history of her time. In contrast to Leo's erinaceous insularity, she was always alive to currents in painting, moving with them sometimes and sometimes resisting them. The disparity of outlook that separated her and Leo was based finally not on abstract philosophic or aesthetic ideas, but upon their differing sense of life and of the possible fulfillments of their diverse personal goals. The world and the climate inhabited by Picasso and his friends — where impulse was the lively agent of freedom and iconoclasm, where notions of order existed only to be escaped or broken — were utterly alien to the taste of Leo Stein, and he gave them no quarter or compromise.

CHAPTER 6

History takes time.
One likes to have history illustrated by one's con-
temporaries.
— GERTRUDE STEIN

BY the time Gertrude and Leo Stein had
brought their ambitions to the Rue de Fleurus and had begun to
look on all of Paris as their own preserve, the history of painting in
Europe was about to shift before their eyes from the course it had
followed from the moment — four hundred years before — when
perspective was introduced into the Renaissance. Responding to
thunder over Montmartre and quakings in distant Spanish villages, the lazy swollen stream of "tradition" had suddenly begun to
quicken and to branch off in channels that would cut deep. The
meandering stream of impressionism had already come to the misty
stillness of Monet's lily ponds; Fauvism, turgid with mineral matter
from the brushes of Matisse and Rouault and Derain, had already
overflowed its banks; while pointillism, subjecting even a summer's
day to its minute analyses, had dwindled to a rivulet that went nowhere. Each of these movements had brought new aspects of the terrain into view and reflected colors no one had ever seen. But their

wonderful strangeness still had not essentially altered the face of a landscape that had been the joy of painters as often as it was the object of surveyors. With the force of a raging cataract, a new stream was about to cut a gorge in tradition. Spilling over foothills and plains, it would demolish the landscape of the twentieth century and make it unrecognizable. This stream was cubism.

As early as 1905, the dynamic group of painters who were to make cubism, and the writers who were to be its interpreters and press agents, had assumed a discernible character. They were not predominantly French, but a mixture of young men who had uprooted themselves from many parts of Europe. In defiance of poverty, loneliness and professional anonymity they had come to Paris. Brilliant, dispossessed, loyal to no tradition, they held little reverence for the "common reality" that figured so importantly in the teachings of the academies. Regarding themselves as oppressed victims of "common reality," they felt less impulse to confirm its supposed beauties than to challenge its premises. The most imaginative among them were Spaniards and Jews; their best theoreticians and publicists were Frenchmen. If the group could not then be considered as a "school," at least it had the cohesion and *joie de vivre* of a band. Its members, most of them, lived in or near a big lopsided tenement house situated on a little square — now named the Place Émile Goudeau — where the Rue Ravignan meets the Rue Norvins. This building, the famous Bateau Lavoir, was so named because of its resemblance to the ugly Seine river barges used as washhouses. Another of its names, "The Trapper's Hut," was suggested by the dark labyrinthine hallways that led from one rickety ascent to another throughout its rambling length. Tenants had neither gas nor electricity; water came from a single tap over a sink used by the occupants of some ten or more studios. The austerity of the Bateau Lavoir was matched only by its gritty charm, yet no one could complain of high rent: the cost of the choicest studios came only to four hundred and fifty francs — ninety dollars — annually. Rattling and shaking with every gust of wind, echoing on stormy days with ghoulish noises, the Bateau Lavoir seemed not so much to stand on the side of the Butte Montmartre as to cling to it. The tenement became famous as the common home of a number of artists, yet its tenants had little to share in common but filth and inconvenience. Besides studios, it provided quarters for enterprises, both legitimate and "discreet," that ranged from tailoring shops to the fusty parlors of *filles de joie*.

Here, and in the neighboring coachmen's and bricklayers' hangout, the Restaurant Azon in the Rue des Pyramides, foregathered individuals whose personal odysseys had brought them from many corners of Europe: Guillaume Apollinaire, Max Jacob, André Salmon, Maurice Utrillo, Henri Matisse, Francis Picabia, Amedeo Modigliani, André Derain, Juan Gris, Pierre Reverdy, Georges Braque and "an unrecognized explosive foreign body," Pablo Picasso. The sentimental, murky artists' quarter made famous by Henri Murger's *Scènes de la vie de Bohème* with its raggedly cloaked heroes and gaunt, operatic heroines, was something that belonged to the past. This new Bohemia was as determinedly gay as it was helplessly poor. Its infectious éclat was clearly edged with bitterness, but its creative life was based in the essential warmth of brotherhood. In a book which discusses the most influential figures of this period, *The Banquet Years*, Roger Shattuck asserts: "To a greater extent than at any time since the Renaissance, painters, writers, and musicians lived and worked together and tried their hands at each other's arts in an atmosphere of perpetual collaboration." In love with legend, refusing to wait upon time to make them legendary, they transformed ordinary events into historical occasions, treated anybody's random witticism with the gravity of a pronouncement, and celebrated grim, often childish practical jokes as metaphysical gestures of defiance. "You joined Cubism in the same way as you join a political party," wrote the critic M.C. Lacoste. "And you had to prove your mettle. The test was not the rewards obtained, but in the rebuffs received. The winner was the artist whose works were refused by the greatest number of salons."

By virtue of having sat for Picasso in scores of periods during the months when he was painting her portrait, Gertrude Stein had come to know many of his Bateau Lavoir friends and neighbors. But with few exceptions, they were never to become more than acquaintances. She was bourgeois, after all, thoroughly American bourgeois,

85

with personal standards of living and behavior firmly established long before. "If you are way ahead with your head," she said, "you naturally are old fashioned and regular in your daily life." In the nature of things, the gritty devil-may-care Bohemia of the Butte and its *enfants* was nothing that she could accommodate with ease, much less with intimacy. While she was drawn toward the group by the youthful and obsessive force of their dedication to the artist's life, she was never really drawn into it. This was perhaps unfortunate, since a writer's place in their councils was one of particular respect and influence. Long before the painters had begun to articulate their *"esprit nouveau,"* the writers among them had advertised the group's aims and meanings and had widely publicized the personal exploits of its various members. While their basic interests were undeniably aesthetic, most of them were lighthearted about intellectual matters and some of them professed a sort of mindless anarchy. To many conservative observers, among whom few realized they were falling for a calculated line, the cubists were no more than a bunch of showy iconoclasts and clowns and their personal behavior, as wild and as absurd as the stuff they produced in the name of art, was utterly *de trop.*

In literature, as in life, they delighted in paradox, praising in one breath Baudelaire, Mallarmé and Rimbaud, in the next breath Conan Doyle, the penny-dreadful exploits of Fantômas and Nick Carter, *Les Histoires de Buffalo Bill.* They regularly patronized the Cirque Medrano, as well as the Tuesday soirées given by Paul Fort, editor of the review *Vers et Prose,* at the Closerie des Lilas, a café which had retained the name of a dance hall formerly on the same site at the corner of the Boulevards St. Michel and Montparnasse. Under the leadership of Picasso, Apollinaire, Salmon and Max Jacob, they became a close-knit *bistro* society. But paradox lurked behind their façade of harmony: entrée into the group was best gained by outrageous lies and calumnies. Those most adept in the more imaginative forms of excoriation, backbiting, and betrayal, were apt to be rewarded with full membership. Their association, always informal and buoyed by the comic spirit, was eventually dignified by critics as *"L'École de la rue Ravignan."* But before critics gave them a responsible place in history, the group lived by a philosophy expressed in a remark by a character in André Salmon's novel, *La Négresse du Sacré Coeur:* "There is only one truth, steadfast, healing, salutary, and that is the absurd."

Beloved among the inhabitants of the Bateau Lavoir was the accountant and actuary, Maurice Princet. Everyone thought that Princet's skills would make him rich and that, while he shared with everyone the trials of poverty, his residence among the poor was but temporary. Apollinaire once comforted him with a couplet:

> *Princet, de l'Institut des Actuaires membre,*
> *Ce mois-ci n'a pas pu payer sa pauvre chambre.*
> (Princet, member of the Institute of Actuaries,
> This month could not pay for his poor room.)

A learned man who had studied at the École Polytechnique, Princet made a great contribution to cubism which he had never planned, but which came about simply by his being the one to retail to his artist companions news of the worlds of mathematics and physics — worlds of wonder to his hearers who, in their own way, were about to add the fourth dimension to art and to literature.

While she developed an intimately close relationship with Picasso and, later, with Juan Gris, Gertrude was never more than a peripheral associate of the Rue Ravignan group and, at least inside her own home, entertained but few of its personalities. Georges Braque was a frequent visitor for a year or so, but Gertrude had deep reservations about his work. She believed that "after every great creator there follows a second man who shows how it can be done easily. Picasso struggled and made his new thing and then Braque came along and showed how it could be done without pain." She tended to regard him as a "minor poet with a musical rhythm who was able to put these qualities into paint" rather than as the great and original painter who, with Picasso, has equal claim as the father of cubism. However, like the French painters for whom the new activity in painting was both an influence and a *cause célèbre*, she participated in the spirit of the group, without descending to its burlesquing tactics, and eventually went further than any of the writers among them in translating the lessons of the new painting into literature. The group was heterogeneous and the individuals in it were too independent to have allowed her to appropriate them in any personal sense. Since a measure of appropriation was always necessary to her, she was kept at a distance. Besides, she differed with them fundamentally in regard to their postures as newborn phenomena in the world of art. She felt she could never emphasize strongly enough her conviction that it was essential "to be completely conservative that is particularly traditional in order to be free." In her later years her attitude toward individuals in the group tended to be patronizing and, since she came to regard them as adjuncts to her personal history, somewhat proprietary. While she was of their number as an artist and belongs in the same phase of aesthetic history they dominate, she offended many of them by claiming to have lived with them in terms of an intimacy neither they nor the situation could have allowed.

The dour darling of the early days of the Bateau Lavoir circle was the perverse, brilliant Alfred Jarry. At the Théâtre de l'Oeuvre on December 10, 1896, Jarry's fiercely irreverent dramatic farce, *Ubu Roi*, had jolted Paris and, incidentally, evoked from the visiting young Irish poet, William Butler Yeats, the cry, "After us the Savage God!" Jarry's play, written when its author was fifteen years old, was a kind of literary monument to the sovereignty of ignorance and avarice, and struck its first audience with the force of a manifesto. Responding as if they had at last found a leader, if not a savior, young rebel artists made its author a living symbol. No one had so sharply dramatized their revolt against the pieties of the academies and the constraints of the *petit bourgeois* backgrounds from which most of them had only recently fled. The subject of *Ubu Roi*, who represents in literature a successor to Flaubert's Yuk, God of the Grotesque, is a king of license, lewdness and every other manifestation of foul human instinct. He represents, at the same time, a judgment upon the pretensions of society and a humiliating acknowledgment of the forces by which they are maintained. Catapulted into celebrity, twenty-three-year-old Jarry had soon himself been nicknamed "Père Ubu." In the justice of an irony he may have been

88

the first to perceive, he soon began to develop characteristics of his monstrous creation. Constantly propped up and imaginatively inflated by absinthe, his *herbe sainte*, Jarry maintained a cynical sovereignty over rebel art circles. He carried a pistol with him as he went about Paris and brandished it on any occasion that might serve to reinforce his reputation as a menace. But his real power over his friends was not a matter of firearms. Erudite and keen-witted, brutally insolent, he could hold any gathering for hours with talk that was at once learned and obscene. "Talking about things that are understandable," he said, "only weighs down the mind and falsifies the memory, but the absurd exercises the mind and makes the memory work."

Living in a kind of proud, dedicated poverty, he was guided socially by nothing but whim. Once he turned up at the theater dressed in a dirty white linen suit and a shirt he had made himself out of paper; on the shirt, in India ink, was painted a cravat. In Paris for a time he lived in an apartment which an ingenious landlord, apparently with midget tenants in mind, had divided horizontally in two. The whitewash on the ceiling was continually rubbing off on Jarry's hair as he moved about, but with two owls and a cat for companions, he was not otherwise discomfited. His famous pistol was merely an appurtenance of his cultivated disgust; he used it for taking pot shots at any object within range that piqued him. Once, when he was amusing himself shooting apples from the branch, his gun play came dangerously near to some children playing in the orchard. When the children's attractive mother upbraided him, he is reported to have said, "Do not worry, madame, I will replace them for you." On another occasion, it is told, he reached for his gun and quickly silenced some obstreperous nightingales.

Jarry's poetry, showing signs of fragmentary influences from Mallarmé, combined strains of wild fantasy with perverse eroticism and the *humeur noire* of anarchy. Reality and unreality were mixed to his order. His favorite comment on any noteworthy occasion was "It was as beautiful as literature, wasn't it?" But this was familiar play in the era of *les enfants terribles*. Jarry's special distinction was his role as one among the rebels who had already achieved universal notoriety. Even comparatively sanctified precincts of literary Paris had to admit him or, at least, openly recognize the power of his presence. But by the time Picasso had met Apollinaire in 1905, Jarry's personal participation in the Rue Ravignan circle was over with. He was the hero of the Bohemians, and his *Ubu Roi* was still the most celebrated literary scandal in memory, but he had himself retreated to Corbeil. There he lived like a hermit in a converted stable, continually absorbed in hallucination. He died in 1907, at the age of thirty-four. "Jarry's life seems to have been directed by a philosophical concept," wrote the critic Gabriel Brunet. "He offered himself as a victim to the derision and to the absurdity of the world. His life is a sort of humorous and ironic epic which is carried to the point of the voluntary, farcical and thorough destruction of the self. Jarry's teaching could be summarized thus: every man is capable of showing his contempt for the cruelty and stupidity of the universe by making his own life a poem of incoherence and absurdity."

When the clown-king of the Bohemians was dead, his scepter passed logically to his friend Guillaume Apollinaire. Through him the chimerical presence of the absurd and the anarchic was maintained in the creative life of another generation.

As Picasso's confidante, Gertrude Stein shared his creative excitements and problems, as well as the domestic and romantic disturbances with which he was continually beset. But she was also on the friendliest terms with Matisse and saw him nearly as often. It was not signally clear then, but Matisse and Picasso had begun in their respective ways to lay down the foundations of two entirely different modes in painting. Picasso, supported by Braque, "like two mountaineers roped together," had started to make use of suggestions from primitive art and to express them in the light of certain notions of space-time physics he had picked up, perhaps in random conversations with his neighbor Princet. The immediate results were paintings which, it is now apparent, stand for cubism's nascent period. Matisse, on the other hand, had begun to pursue a direction away from the Fauvism of which he had been master, toward a graceful clarity of line, a new simplicity of design incorporating huge flat areas of pure color. Matisse had already painted *Le Bonheur de*

Vivre; Picasso, in answer to its challenge, some people suspected, had recently produced *Les Demoiselles d'Avignon* which, he told Braque, was "going to cause a big noise." In retrospect, the two paintings, both strongly based on Cézanne's great compositions of bathers in landscapes and seascapes, dramatize the divergence of his most illustrious successors and stand like separate thresholds: beyond the one, in the far distance, looms *Guernica;* beyond the other, in a distance even greater, rise the pink and white simplicities of the little Chapelle du Rosaire in Vence. But while the leadership of painting in Paris had suffered a division, the Stein atelier where, in fact, the two painters had first met, was still a place where they gathered congenially and frequently. Loyalty and betrayal were always acute issues in the seething confines of Montmartre and Montparnasse but, for the time at least, 27 Rue de Fleurus was an untroubled sanctuary. Gertrude and Leo Stein had proved they could make good friends and keep them.

But the times were perilous. Gertrude's close association with two such eminent rivals was bound to lead sooner or later to charges of preference and disloyalty. When they came, it was Matisse who advanced them. In his eyes, Picasso was still an outlander. No one of Gertrude's tastes, he felt, could have a really serious friendship with anyone of his sort. Picasso, in truth, was still but an impoverished newcomer (at one point in the winter of 1902, it was said, he had to burn his sketches to keep himself warm) whose only Parisian friends, until his very recent absorption into the Jarry-Apollinaire circle, were his fellow Catalan artists. None of these had attained any reputation to distinguish them from the thousands of other painters who infested the garrets of the Butte.

Disappointed by Gertrude's growing defection, Matisse tried to rationalize her greater loyalty to the inconsequential Spaniard. He thought that at the bottom of it must be Gertrude's well-known taste for idiosyncrasy and theatrical values — attributes which Picasso possessed in abundance. Matisse may also have been concerned with her tolerance of Picasso's friends, whose *"ubuesque"* behavior was not to his taste and whom he had reason to suspect of mischief. On the walls and fences of Montmartre there had recently appeared chalked scrawlings: "Matisse drives people mad!" and "Matisse has done more harm than alcohol!" In any case, since Gertrude had never given Matisse's work preference over Picasso's, their intimacy remained comparatively low-keyed. When finally Matisse charged her with losing interest in his work altogether, she answered, in terms that must have seemed quite inscrutable to him, "There is nothing within you that fights itself — hitherto you have had the instinct to produce antagonism in others which stimulated you to attack. But now they follow." She had come to feel that Matisse's growing reputation had led to a relaxation of the "important feelings within himself" responsible for his first success; he seemed now to accept and repeat his own conventions as if he had deserted his most vital character. Since he was no longer scoffed at and had become a famous figure in a kind of painting that was beginning to achieve a large measure of public acceptance, he had lost qualities that had led Gertrude to see him as "certainly a great one." His famous credo of 1908 — an "art of balance, of purity, and serenity, devoid of troubling or depressing subject matter, an art which might be like . . . a comfortable armchair" — was hardly one to which she might assent.

Although Gertrude continued to refer to Matisse for many years as *cher maître* and to see him often, the beginnings of an ever-widening estrangement had set in. Her attitude toward his progress and success apparently made its register upon Matisse; while she may never have moved him to any change in practice, he was for years openly concerned to have Gertrude's good opinion of his efforts, and to tell her of his creative wrestling. "Painting is always very hard for me —" he wrote to her in 1912, "always this struggle — is it natural? Yes, but why have so much of it? It's so sweet when it comes of its own accord." Their friendship was not really severed until, in her memoirs of the period, Gertrude wrote that Mme. Matisse "was a very straight dark woman with a long face and a firm large loosely hung mouth like a horse."

Gertrude's friends were already well on their way to becoming the most eminent painters of their time. Through the first years of her acquaintance with them she was deeply engaged in the most sustained effort of her career, *The Making of Americans*. For the life of a literary generation this book would languish unpublished and unread. When, finally, it would be published and republished, it would stand clearly as the enormous cornerstone of a long submerged yet always viable career.

Further, we pardon people more easily for following natural desires, since we pardon them more easily for following such appetites as are common to all men, and in so far as they are common; now anger and bad temper are more natural than the appetites for excess *i.e.* for unnecessary objects. Take for instance the man who defended himself on the charge of striking his father by saying, "*Yes*, but *he* struck *his* father, and *he* struck *his*, and" (pointing to his child) "this boy will strike *me* when he is a man; it runs in the family"; or the man who when he was being dragged along by his son bade him stop at the doorstep, since he himself had dragged his father only as far as that.

This quotation comes from Aristotle's *Nicomachean Ethics*, Book VII, Chapter 6. There is nothing in all of Gertrude Stein's writing about her work or about the range of her reading to suggest conscious application, yet the first passage in *The Making of Americans* reads as follows:

"Once an angry man dragged his father along the ground through his own orchard. 'Stop!' cried the groaning old man at last, 'Stop! I did not drag my father beyond this tree.' "

Echoing Aristotle, fingering scores of charts and diagrams marked out on tall folio paper to indicate types of personality and kinds of consciousness, Gertrude Stein had made a scrawling progress into her longest and most obsessing work. She had the history of her family to tell, and in her telling it would become nothing less than a boundless parable history of America with all its open-sky restlessness and migrations, its riches, ambitions and its enormous middle-class vitality. More than nine hundred pages long, this novel, as Donald Sutherland described it in *Gertrude Stein: A Biography of Her Work*, is "like the Pentagon building, both appalling and magnificent. Gertrude Stein was accurate in calling it a 'monumental' work. As the Escorial is the expression of the nation in its permanent terms, nothingness and glory, and as Versailles expresses the ultimate national equilibrium between concentrated violence and sensuous splendor, so the Pentagon is or was a self-contained labyrinth of simple essential abstractions."

As a scientific demonstration of Gertrude Stein's belief in the final absolutism of human character, *The Making of Americans* carries the weight of its conviction and the conviction of its enormous weight. As a work of literaturé, it is all but swept bare of the felicities of detail, color and anecdote that beguile the attention in great books as well as minor ones. But Gertrude Stein had had enough of the picaresque trappings and sentimental diffusions that recommend novels to the insatiable reader. She wanted to come to essentials — to ideas in action rather than ideas comfortably couched in formulation, and to character as an entity alive rather than character as an identity pinned to the wall like a butterfly. Her conception would test the power of the intellect to usurp the power of the emotions in communicating living experience, yet she was ready to face the challenge.

If one can conceive of *À la Recherche du Temps Perdu* as a series of bleached landscapes with all of its characters reduced to a society of self-insistent theorems, one will have accommodated the range of the book and approached the nature of the characters Gertrude Stein presents. The pages of *The Making of Americans* are as full of rolling and repeated cadences as the Bible, but its more prevalent sound, like that of Oriental ritual, is the music of the continuous present, always going on and always, almost always, but not quite, the same. Its people are less like images from life than they are like defleshed monsters whose bones articulate genus and species. The design of the book, as Donald Sutherland suggests, may be on the scale of the Pentagon building, but it is difficult not to conclude that its contents would be more congenially at home in the halls of the Smithsonian.

Gertrude Stein had come early to a notion that was to dominate her creative life — the notion that the "continuous present and using everything and beginning again" was the final reality in fact and thus the final reality that words could communicate. Escaping from the conventions of beginning, middle, and ending, she simply laid out a space — a space of time as big in its proportions as a canvas of Jackson Pollock — and proceeded to make sure that it would be

94

"always filled with moving." In a monumental abrogation of the barriers that separate literature from painting, she produced a work having the fascination of a symbol that powerfully impresses itself upon the imagination long before the thing it symbolizes is open to scrutiny or subject to understanding.

She made a composition, "covering" time as if it were a flat surface upon which she was free to work. In the tail-swallowing movements of her sentences and paragraphs and chapters, she retained just enough propositional content to remind her reader that she was telling a history, "The History of a Family's Progress," in which actual events actually occur. These events, like the fragmented features of portraits or landscapes in early cubist paintings, served as links between her individual view and the common view. Like the cubist paintings, her composition demanded continuous activity upon the part of the observer. Points of rest — points of information, dramatic turns of circumstance, passages of description — are few and far between as hours of abstraction overwhelm moments of representation.

Using people she knew, she bellwethered them one by one into the collective corrals of her attacking and resisting, dependent-independent and independent-dependent types. There they slowly disappeared as individuals and became less characters than propositions about characters in the mind of Gertrude Stein. In spite of the great length of the book, she is actually concerned to present in full only four characters. Two hundred and eighty-eight pages are devoted to heredity and "the old people in the new world." One hundred and ninety-eight pages are devoted to Martha Hersland who is of "the new people made out of the old" and who was drawn from one of her cousins. Two hundred and forty-four pages are given to Alfred Hersland and Julia Dehning, who are also of the "new" and who are drawn from her brother Michael and from another cousin. One hundred and eighty-four pages are devoted to David Hersland, whose living prototype was her old laboratory partner, Leon Solomons.

One problem dominates the conception of the book — a problem whose solution would seem to bear far more relevantly on laboratory science than upon literary aesthetics. Is the motor impulse a more certain index to character than appearance? In what ways, she asks

95

herself, are the subconscious and essential personality related to consciousness and personality and motor impulses? If other writers "framed" their characters and qualified their speech and their gestures by settings and dressings that placed them in the real world, she would deliberately discard such obfuscating means in her determination to get at the essential "bottom nature" of everyone. Only character in action, she believed, only character resisting, attacking or otherwise being a present participle, could register the truth of personality.

By the time she had combed and honeycombed her charts and diagrams and their human manifestations, the music of her continuous present had become a very special music, pitched so high or so low that it was beyond the hearing range of most humans. Yet her efforts were heroic, and for many years it would be as difficult to damn the gigantic work that produced them as it would be to read the book itself. Like almost everything else Gertrude Stein produced, *The Making of Americans* was supported by creative logic that stood in the form of a guardian angel at its threshold and sanctified its precincts. The fools that would rush in would soon rush out to shout their bewildered and often foolish judgments. The wise, impressed but unhappy, would linger, meditate and, for the most part, hold their tongues. Others, more particularly wise than the wise, would speak with the authority of creative genius. "By this epic of ourselves," wrote Marianne Moore, "we are reminded of certain early German engravings in which Adam, Eve, Cain, and Abel stand with every known animal wild and domestic, under a large tree, by a river. *The Making of Americans* is a kind of living genealogy which is in its branching, unified and vivid. We have here a truly psychological exposition of American living — an account of that happiness and of that unhappiness which is to those experiencing it, as fortuitous as it is to those who have an understanding of heredity and of environment, natural and inevitable." And in 1927 Katherine Anne Porter wrote, that these pages "make a psychological source book and the diary of an aesthetic problem worked out momently under your eyes. . . . I doubt if all the people who should read it will read it for a great while yet . . . and reading it is anyhow a sort of permanent occupation. Yet to shorten it would be to mutilate its vitals, and it is a very necessary book."

Gertrude Stein could not read these statements until nearly twenty years later, yet, as she worked, the intensity of her concentration was so great and her confidence so deep that neither praise nor condemnation could ever after surprise her. Deep in the coils and spirals of a work that seemed to renew itself like some diabolic machine, Gertrude was alone in Paris one day in 1908 when suddenly she killed off her hero. Later in the day, when she went to see her friend Mildred Aldrich, she was in a state of profound agitation. When Miss Aldrich asked her what was wrong, Gertrude said, "My hero — I've killed him!"

"My God, why?" said Miss Aldrich.

"I know all about him," said Gertrude, "and about them and about everybody in that story."

This was her moment of revelation, that point at which she knew that the whole book was "a little description of the winning of so much wisdom." But if she had won wisdom for herself, and had arrived at the decisive point where she could say, "If it can be done why do it," she had also left many of her future readers thoroughly guyed and in the lurch. Among those who tend to see Gertrude Stein as a monstrous sport born out of a "frantic, fumbling, nightmare age," no one has more eloquently expressed the unhappy relation between the artist and her audience than B. L. Reid in his book *Art By Subtraction*. "I have said that her thinking . . . is sophistical," wrote Reid, "but again this is not strictly true. The rationale of her repetitive or 'insistent' style is symptomatic of a deadlier disease than sophistry. It is another manifestation of her schizophrenic divorce of aesthetics and art and offers an extreme instance of the thing that finally damns her as an artist. It is her colossal blind spot, her refusal, or perhaps her real inability, to recognize the inescapable gap between the sensorium of a private, idiosyncratic thinker and writer and the sensorium of an audience that has to make its peace not with the process or the theory, but with the end product. Inevitably, her 'insistence' is our repetition, and the result is not art but anodyne."

97

Embroiled in the long slow vermiculations of her second book, Gertrude had still to wrestle with the onerous and, as it turned out, protracted problem of getting her first one into print. "My book is finished now," she wrote to a friend, "and the worst thing will be to get it published . . . it will certainly make your hair curl with the complications and tintinabulations of its style, but I'm very fond of it." She had first thought to submit *Three Histories* under the pseudonym of "Jane Sands." But when the manuscript was put into the hands of agents and publishers, her own name was affixed to the title page. Hutchins Hapgood, who had read the manuscript in Europe, tried to get it accepted by his own publishers, Duffield and Company. But Mr. Duffield, rejecting the stories on grounds that they were too unconventional and too literary, suggested they be turned over to an agent, Flora M. Holly. Miss Holly, who was dubious about sales possibilities, tried to peddle the stories to magazines, but her efforts came to nothing. She finally sent them to Gertrude's college friend Mabel Weeks, who was then teaching at Barnard. She in turn sent them on to another mutual friend, Georgiana King of Bryn Mawr, and between them they arranged to have the book read by Macmillan. When Macmillan refused the manuscript, it went back to Mabel Weeks, who sent it to Bobbs-Merrill. There it was also rejected, but not without qualification: "Our readers' reports on the manuscript indicate that their attention was arrested and their sympathy engaged by a certain originality in the work, by its sincere simplicity and a general flavor out of the ordinary, but the objections urged seemed to quite outweigh these undeniable merits. While it was conceded that there was present a literary reality — despite the foreignisms of the style — the readers felt that the strain of intensity was too unbroken and that the character studies were too greatly elaborated, that the portraits were over-complete and too infinitesimally detailed. A miniature may be overdone and apparently that is the way our readers felt about The Good Anna and the other people of the author's presentation. . . ."

Someone suggested the Open Court Publishing Company in Chicago, but this led only to another rejection. Finally, Mabel Weeks submitted the book to the literary agent, Mrs. Charles Knoblauch. After a few unrewarded tries, Mrs. Knoblauch suggested to Gertrude that she publish the book herself — that is, that she foot the bill for its printing — under the imprint of the Grafton Press in New York. This company published mainly genealogies and historical works, most of which were printed at cost to the author. The expense of printing *Three Histories*, it was estimated, would come to six hundred and sixty dollars. Gertrude asked Etta Cone if she would share this expense. When Etta replied that her investment in a Renoir painting would take all of her presently available income, Gertrude finally had to assume the whole cost herself. A contract calling for an edition of one thousand copies — half of which were to be bound while the other half were to remain in sheets awaiting demand — was signed on November 16, 1908.

Frederick H. Hitchcock, president of the Grafton Press, felt that some other title would enhance the sales possibilities of the book, and Gertrude agreed to changing it to *Three Lives*. However, when Hitchcock further suggested that "some pretty bad slips in grammar, probably caused in the type-writing" be corrected by an editor in Paris he would be glad to send around to "27," Gertrude was irate. She insisted upon no textual changes whatsoever. Mr. Hitchcock acquiesced, but he could not refrain from having the last word: "I want to say frankly that I think you have written a very peculiar book and it will be a hard thing to make people take it seriously. . . ."

In spite of her dogged insistence that what she had written was inviolable, Gertrude had moments of both doubt and conviction in regard to what she had done and where it would all fit in. "I am afraid that I can never write the great American novel," she wrote to Mabel Weeks. "I don't know how to sell on margin or to do anything with shorts and longs, so I have to content myself with niggers and servant girls and the foreign population generally. Leo he said there wasn't no art in Lovett's book and then he was bad and wouldn't tell me that there was in mine so I went to bed very miserable but I don't care there ain't any Tchaikovsky Pathetique or

Omar Kayam or Wagner or Whistler or White Man's Burden or green burlap in mine at least not in the present ones. Dey is very simple and very vulgar and I don't think they will interest the great American public."

CHAPTER 7

The central theme of the novel is that they were
glad to see each other.

—— GERTRUDE STEIN

AMONG the far-reaching consequences of
the San Francisco earthquake and fire of 1906, not the least was Gertrude Stein's meeting with Miss Alice Babette Toklas, a small, dark,
velvety young woman who was to become famous as her palpa-
ble shadow and satellite. By the time they had shared more than
thirty expatriate years together and Gertrude decided to write her
companion's "autobiography," she quite naturally subsumed in literature an identity she had always quite naturally dominated in life.
Some of the whimsical preferences in food, landscape and literature
recorded in *The Autobiography of Alice B. Toklas* belong to the
book's nominal subject, some of its speech rhythms and most of its
personal peccadilloes. But the impulsive egotism that gives zest to
the book and the four-square glory it celebrates are wholly Gertrude
Stein's, and so are its wise-child style, its self-centered recall and its
maternal murmur.

Shortly after news of the disaster had been flashed around the world, Michael Stein, Gertrude's oldest brother, and his wife Sarah decided they had better return to San Francisco to see for themselves the extent of damage done to the real estate holdings upon which a good part of their income in exile depended. Leaving Paris in considerable haste, they did not neglect to take with them some of the treasures they had acquired as beginning collectors of the astonishing new painting of the twentieth century. Among these were a Matisse drawing and three small oil paintings, including *Portrait à la Raie Verte*, sometimes called simply *The Green Line*. To avoid the American customs tax on paintings then in effect, the Steins cooked up a scheme. When the paintings would be examined on the pier in New York, they told their friends, Michael Stein was going to tell the inspector that Matisse was without question the world's greatest artist and that the value of his works was inestimable. As the bewildered customs man would presumably be thinking this over, Sarah was going to take a position behind her husband, point to his head with a pitying glance, and then meaningfully tap her own forehead. As it turned out, their scheme never went beyond the outlines of a joke, and they encountered no trouble in getting the works — probably the first oil paintings of Matisse's ever to cross the Atlantic — onto American soil.

Their fun as collectors of the mad painters of Montmartre continued when they got to San Francisco. Sarah reported back to Gertrude: ". . . I have had a pretty hot time with some of the artists. . . . You see, Mikey sprang the Matisses on one just for fun, & since the startling news that there was such stuff in town has been communicated, I have been a very popular lady; it has not always been . . . 'pleasant.'

"Oh, Albert Bender has been our most faithful & devoted — as always . . . but his devotion hardly stood the test of the *'femme au nez vert'* ['*Woman with a Green Nose*']. Upon his demand, I assured him that perhaps he'd better spare himself this test, as I knew his belief in my infallibility was something very dear to him. "No," he said, "I shall *never, never, never* say, as others have, that you are crazy." Well — he saw it — for two minutes he was speechless — then he meekly inquired — "But don't *you* think you're crazy?"

"Have been called to the telephone six times during this effort — six more invitations, accepted 'em all — going morning, noon, afternoon, evening, night — it's rather amusing — and I do love to show my clothes; they always create such a sensation!

"And, oh, the slang, Gertrude, it's great — I don't understand most of it; — but when I do, I wonder — as I do at most everything. . . ."

Among the circle of friends and acquaintances who came to welcome Sarah and Mike, to look at their puzzling acquisitions and to hear, firsthand, their reports of life abroad, was a well-bred young woman noted for elegant loveliness of bearing and a penchant for costuming herself in dove-gray, Miss Alice Toklas. Impressionable, intelligent and, at the age of twenty-eight, yearning to know more of the great world than San Francisco could offer, Alice looked, listened and went home to her spinster's household of practical-minded relatives with a marvelous new notion in her mind. Not many days after the reunion at the Steins', she began gently to hint to her father that she might like to go abroad for a while herself. Since he was aware that her prospects for marriage were not noticeably good, and must have sensed that his only daughter's pretty gift for the piano and her taste for the novels of Henry James were ephemeral bases on which to build a professional career, he took the suggestion with sympathy. But money for such an important venture was a problem. Conveniently enough, Alice's grandfather, who owned extensive lands in the San Joaquin Valley, died and left her a modest legacy. She did not hesitate to put her plan into effect. With a close friend, Harriet Levy, as traveling companion, Alice crossed the continent and sailed for Europe before the year was out. Planning on a long winter's stay in Paris, together they leased a small apartment on the Rue Notre Dame des Champs.

The Michael Steins meanwhile, having overseen reconstruction and otherwise put their holdings in order, and having made for Henri Matisse his momentous first sale in America — to the San Francisco painter, George Of — had returned to their home in the Rue Madame. Their Parisian friends gave a party to welcome them back with news of San Francisco, and it was on this occasion that the meeting of Alice Toklas and Gertrude Stein took place. In the *Autobiography*, Alice was made to say that it was precisely then and there she heard for the first time the psychic ringing of bells that announced the indubitable presence of genius. In spite of the fact that she would meet thousands of gifted men and women engaged in every variety of mental and physical endeavor, the bells that acted as her personal sort of radar were to respond on only two other occasions: shortly afterwards, when she met Pablo Picasso, and seven years hence, when she first shook hands with the philosopher Alfred North Whitehead.

Alice Toklas's Polish-Jewish family had settled in California during the Gold Rush days of 1849, and she herself was born in San Francisco. Her younger days were passed largely in upper-middle-class gentility but, through unfortunate family circumstances, also in something bordering on domestic servitude. When her mother died, Alice's father arranged for her to keep house for her grandparents, Mr. and Mrs. Louis Levinson, and the adult sons who lived with them at 922 O'Farrell Street. As housekeeper and provider of food, Alice became the key figure in a largely male household where business matters were the only topics of interest. Life as a "poor relation" tended to be confining and monotonous, but once a year, at least, Alice found a way to escape domestic imprisonment. With money realized from the sale of old clothes and worn-out furniture, she took an annual holiday at the nearby resort town of Monterey. There, putting off the nunlike garb of gray, or black, which was to become her lifelong trademark, she donned brilliant, sometimes Chinese finery, and enjoyed a brief summer's pleasance among the vacationers at the exotic old adobe home, "Sherman's Rose" — so named because of the legend that General Sherman had once planted a rose tree there in tribute to a daughter of the house whom he had courted and lost. Alice became friendly with the erstwhile object of the General's affections, who was by this time an old but very lively lady. "She would throw one of her shawls over my shoulders," Alice recalled, "and say with a devilish glint, Go out and stand under the rose tree and let the tourists from Del Monte take your photograph. They will try to give you four bits but you may continue to turn your back on them." But Alice's excursions into resort life only sharpened her sense of confinement when she had to return to her foster home.

When, years before, her mother's death had sharply disrupted her sheltered and easy life, Alice had gone dutifully along with her father's decisions as to what would be best for both of them. Except for the daily worry of keeping domestic affairs in order, her existence in San Francisco had come to be fairly pleasurable, rather banal, and without prospect of change. She still saw her girlhood friends but, one by one, they were deserting their maiden state, while Alice was forced to devote herself to pleasing her father and to the enrichment of her musical education. Since she lived in an era when serious pursuit in any direction not leading unequivocally to marriage was suspect, she was not encouraged to dwell on professional possibilities that might be open to her. Lacking the confidence, and the means, to proceed on her own toward a musical career, she remained, in the sadly descriptive phrase of the time, simply "at home."

"To a bourgeois mind that has within it a little of the fervor for diversity," Gertrude Stein wrote, "there can be nothing more attractive than a strain of singularity that yet keeps well within the limits of conventional respectability, a singularity that is, so to speak, well dressed and set up." Gertrude's own "strain of singularity" showed little that could not be excused or made acceptable by the carelessly stylish appointments among which she lived. Years of domestic boredom had all but quashed Alice's "fervor for diversity," but in Paris she was released, free to respond wholeheartedly to a kind of life she had previously known only by hearsay and romantic novels. Although she was of that upper circle of San Francisco society which felt itself to be an aristocracy (the vulgarity of New York, she used to say, would make San Franciscans weep with loneliness), Paris offered far more: the cosmopolitan *haute monde* of taste and leisure and the great attraction of life among art and artists. In the advanced state of her spinsterhood, she was not, as it turned out, unresponsive to the tenderness and friendship which, in lieu of marriage, would soon determine the course of her existence.

On Saturday nights, Gertrude and Leo Stein had long been in the custom of holding open house, preceded by dinner parties for a few of their friends, mainly art collectors, painters and, sometimes, writers. When Alice was first invited to their home at 27 Rue de Fleurus to attend one of these evenings, she was told that Pablo Picasso, already a close friend of both of the Steins, and his tall, willowy mistress, Fernande Olivier, would be among those present for dinner. On arrival, Alice proceeded through a little stone-paved courtyard with a round plot of greenery, rang the bell, was greeted by Gertrude and led from the entrance pavillion with its mirrors and umbrella stand and barometer and elaborate sconces to the atelier, reached by an outdoor connecting passageway. In the atelier, which was furnished by heavy groupings of Renaissance pieces, she first noticed a table on which stood a stack of notebooks with covers showing scenes of exploration, erupting volcanoes and earthquakes. These, Gertrude told her, were French children's notebooks. She liked to write in them because they were handy, cheap and portable. Light came from gas fixtures suspended high overhead, falling on whitewashed walls which were covered with a bewildering variety of paintings up to the ceiling. A small cast-iron stove glowed warmly at one end of the room, and in a corner was a table piled high with little masses of debris: horseshoe nails, pebbles, pipe-type cigarette holders, seashells, pieces of bone, buttons and matchboxes. These turned out to be odds and ends put there by Gertrude and Picasso, who had by this time reached a point of intimacy where not only the detritus of their minds was mutually examined, but also the accumulations of their pockets.

Only a few of the many guests expected that evening had been favored with dinner invitations and during the meal the others began to crowd into the little gallery across the courtyard. Alice was meanwhile entertained by Picasso, for whom her genius-divining bells were already clearly ringing. He was unexpectedly small, she thought, quick-moving, yet did not give the impression of restlessness. His eyes, "always in ambush for surprises," had, Alice noted, a strange faculty of opening wide, like a bird's, and drinking in those things he particularly wanted to see. There was a proud sense of isolation about him, she thought, a carriage of the head suggesting that of a bullfighter as he marched in the van of a procession. Dark-eyed Fernande Olivier, swathed in draperies, seemed to her extraordinarily beautiful. Making conversation, Picasso asked Alice if she thought it was really true, as many people had remarked to him, that he looked like Abraham Lincoln. She made a quick survey of his face and said she did not think so at all. Picasso was unhappy; he had even arranged his hair by studying photographs of Lincoln.

When they retired to the atelier after dinner, she found it crowded, threaded by tentative trills of conversation as everyone waited for Leo to be offered some gambit that would start him on an evening's discourse, or challenge him to some extended argument. As chatelaine of the establishment, Gertrude was kept moving back and forth from the door to her warm chair close to the small black stove. When strangers came, they were asked — merely as a matter of form, since anyone interested was free to come without reference — "De la part de qui venez-vous?" ("By whose invitation do you come?") Whether or not they could supply verbal credentials they were usually admitted. Henri Matisse and his wife were among the company, but their presence in the Stein household was familiar. The unusual thing that night was the number of foreigners. This particular period of the Stein salon was dominated by Hungarians, as a consequence of a young painter's having returned to Budapest with exciting accounts of evenings he had spent at "27." But there were also Germans, a number of Frenchmen and a sprinkling of Americans, of whom Picasso liked to say "Ils sont pas des hommes, ils sont pas des femmes, ils sont des Américains" ("They are not men, they are not women, they are Americans").

Soon after this evening Alice began to visit picture galleries with Gertrude, and sometimes with Leo, to attend concerts and the theater with them, and gradually to make the acquaintance of the wide circle of their friends. While the old-fashioned Bohemia of the novelists was but a minor part of the buoyant Paris to which Alice was introduced, she could not avoid seeing that poverty among artists was the rule and that marriage was a convenience few could afford or even cared to investigate. If she could not accept the easy morality of Montparnasse quite as naturally as Leo and Gertrude accepted it, the difficulty was simply the difference between their background of youthful iconoclasm and her own background of sheltered gentility. She soon learned that to share the Steins' friends was to become involved in the freespoken climate of confidence and romantic dissension in which they seemed continually to live. Fernande Olivier had walked out on Picasso shortly after the Steins' dinner party, and now had to be visited in her own separate quarters. Alice had proposed to study French with her and a price of fifty cents a lesson had been agreed upon. To make sure that the first lesson would come off gracefully, Gertrude went along. They stopped at Picasso's studio on the way to Fernande's, and there Alice saw the strange and violent *Les Demoiselles d'Avignon*, a painting which Picasso's friends had christened "the philosophic brothel," and which would find its place in the history of art as the first masterpiece of cubism.

Leo had already expressed his judgment on this work by calling it "a horrible mess" and Picasso's first collector, the Russian businessman Shchukin, had been so overwhelmed by its ugliness that he said it could only mean the end of modern French art. Alice found the painting painful and also beautiful; she felt it had the power of something oppressive and imprisoned. When she was left alone to study the work, Gertrude and Picasso carried on one of their customary knee-to-knee conversations, punctuating their talk with long silences and monosyllabic utterances in a trilingual argot of French and Spanish and English. When it was time to go, Gertrude presented Picasso with the Sunday supplement of a Baltimore newspaper containing comic strips of *Little Jimmy* and the *Katzenjammer Kids*.

Fernande served them tea as a warm-up for the first French lesson, but since she was unhappy and distracted in the turmoil of her break with Picasso, tea-table conversation was not easy. The long shadow of the absent Pablo limited exchanges of gossip that would sooner or later be bound to include him. When they finally came around to the lesson, Alice was dismayed: Fernande's only topics of conversation, it seemed, were hats, perfumes and furs. Their efforts to develop a discussion had all but foundered when, to make matters worse, Fernande suddenly realized that the week's funny papers from Baltimore had gone to Picasso. She became sullen and resentful, said that she had been betrayed, and forced Gertrude to promise that the next installment would be brought directly to her. Happily for everyone, when the next episodes of the comic strips arrived, Fernande and Pablo were back together. The delicate domestic situation was no longer a matter for diplomacy on Alice's part but it became apparent that her first French lesson with Fernande was also her last.

Alice's role as amanuensis and secretary began with the correcting of proofs of Gertrude's collection of stories, *Three Lives,* as they came from the Grafton Press in New York. At the same time, having taught herself to use Gertrude's battered old typewriter, she began to transcribe the formidable manuscript, running to more than a thousand pages, of *The Making of Americans.* When summer came, she and Harriet Levy accompanied the Steins to Italy, where they took rooms in Fiesole at the Casa Ricci, while Gertrude and Leo took a larger place, the Villa Bardi, nearby. Situated on a cliffside, the Casa Ricci looked westward over the Arno valley and the whole city of Florence. From this pleasant eyrie which had minutely terraced hanging gardens, orange trees planted in wooden tubs, and a lily pond where goldfish swam, Gertrude introduced Alice to those places in Italy she already knew well. They made excursions to Rome, Siena, Perugia and to Assisi where, in deference to one of Gertrude's three favorite saints, the humble Francis, they came on foot. Near the end of the summer, Alice had a telegram from Harriet Levy, who had meanwhile returned to Paris. Michael and Sarah, she said, were going back to San Francisco for another visit and she was going with them. Alice was faced with a great decision. She knew that she did not want to go back to America, and she certainly did not want to return alone to her small apartment in the Rue Notre Dame des Champs. With Leo's agreement, Gertrude offered her a home with them at 27 Rue de Fleurus. She accepted the proposal and thus became the third member of the Stein household.

While Alice Toklas regarded herself as a personality who is acted upon rather than as one who acts, she was never the clinging, dependent character that legend had made of her. Intellectually acute, full of acerbities and strong opinions, she *chose* her role with Gertrude Stein and, for nearly forty years, played it with utter success. The fact that she chose, defined and never deviated from a carefully considered role, rather than came by default to a position she could not escape, is of the first importance. It is obvious to anyone who has known her that her own gifts are substantial and her ability to make an interesting career for herself unquestioned. In contrast to Gertrude's large-mannered ease and broad embrace of people and ideas, Alice Toklas was salt and spice, brevity and incisiveness. She was in a way Gertrude's natural complement as well as her "sieve and buckler," and only by the grace of Alice's faithful companionship and meticulous attendance could Gertrude have afforded the enormous personal indulgence that characterized every phase of her life.

Alice's father, a lonely and, according to reports from San Francisco, a wistful old man, had patiently awaited his daughter's homecoming. While he expressed disappointment in the new turn of events, he made no demands upon Alice to tell him when, if ever, she might be expected to return. Within a short time it became apparent that he had accepted permanent separation. Resigned to his daughter's absence, he even came to appear genial about his role as financial contributor to the Stein *ménage à trois* in distant Paris. But Alice's friends were still reluctant to admit that she would not return. Photographs sent home so horrified Harriet Levy (Alice had apparently lost a great deal of weight) that she threatened to publish them in the hope that solicitous friends might order her back to San Francisco at once. At the same time, Harriet began to perceive through Alice's letters the happy change in her life, and knew that San Francisco was far from her thoughts and had no place in her future. She kept Alice supplied with a calendar of marriages and other social events in the home town and, later, when she felt that writings of Gertrude's which Alice had forwarded would only cause lifted eyebrows, took it upon herself to keep them from Mr. Toklas and the "profane gaze" of Alice's old acquaintances. Not all gazes in San Francisco were profane, apparently. Harriet told of one occasion when she recited an opus of Gertrude's to a women's luncheon party. "The audience," she reported inscrutably, "roared its appreciation."

Since she was easily disposed to accept the unorthodox in life and art and was naturally tolerant of eccentricity, Gertrude Stein had already accommodated, without personally following, the tendency of her Parisian contemporaries to spend half of their time and talent in looking for new ways to *épater le[s] bourgeois*. But to Alice Toklas the goings-on in the embattled lives of artists were deplorable and a little frightening. Genteel by birth and fastidious by nature, she suddenly found herself a member, at least in honorary terms, of a society committed to the systematic outraging of every rule of morality and refinement her upbringing had conditioned her to maintain. Picasso's famous dinner party for the *douanier* Rousseau was an eye-opening event in her initiation, and considerably hastened her understanding, if not her acceptance, of the world she had barely entered.

The "banquet Rousseau," one of the most notable social events of the twentieth century, was neither an orgiastic occasion nor even an opulent one. Its subsequent fame grew from the fact that it was a colorful happening within a revolutionary art movement at a point of that movement's earliest success, and from the fact that it was attended by individuals whose separate influences radiated like spokes of creative light across the art world for generations. Many years later, when time had made the event illustrious, the French writer André Salmon recalled the setting of the banquet — Picasso's ramshackle studio in the Bateau Lavoir — in all of its significance: "Here the nights of the Blue Period passed . . . here the days of the Rose Period flowered . . . here the Demoiselles d'Avignon halted in their dance to re-group themselves in accordance with the golden number and the secret of the fourth dimension . . . here fraternized the poets elevated by serious criticism into the School of the Rue Ravignan . . . here in these shadowy corridors lived the true worshippers of fire . . . here one evening in the year 1908 unrolled the pageantry of the first and last banquet offered by his admirers to the painter Henri Rousseau called the Douanier."

The works of Rousseau, an unlettered little man of no artistic pretense beyond a belief in his own native talent, had been discovered by Alfred Jarry at a time when some of his paintings were hung in the *Salon des Indépendants*. Jarry introduced him to the *bistro* society of writers and painters, some of whom came to regard Rousseau as the absurd master of *"le style concierge,"* while others made much of him as a rare symbol of childlike uncorrupted vision. To Guillaume Apollinaire, Rousseau was "the sentimental Herod, the splendid childlike old man, whom love brought to the outskirts of intellectualism, where the angels came to distract his grief, and prevent him from entering the frightful kingdom of which he had become the Douanier; finally, they admitted the old man to their company, and fitted him with heavy wings." But even Rousseau's champions were ambivalent in their regard for him, tending to patronize his oddities one minute and praise his innocent creations the next. They found him profoundly touching and amusing as a person, but they were not beyond taking advantage of him. When they celebrated his naïve works with extravagant claims, it was apparent they were merely making one more protest against the academic banalities they abhorred.

Leo Stein considered himself initially responsible for bringing about the dinner party, the story of which has been distorted, magnified and made epochal by nearly everyone present. According to Leo, he was visiting Picasso and Fernande one day when, carrying his violin, Rousseau dropped by their studio. Since his retirement after working for fifteen years at his job as a minor employee of the city of Paris toll service, Rousseau had set himself up as a professor of "Diction, Music, Painting, Solfeggio," and, in particular, as teacher of the violin. Leo asked the little old man to play, but Rousseau said he was too weary to lift his bow; whereupon Fernande asked him to come to dinner soon to play for her and Picasso and their friends. A date was set and a guest list made out. But when the appointed evening arrived, a horde of the uninvited were also on hand, almost doubling the number Picasso had counted on.

Before going up the Butte of Montmartre to Picasso's studio, guests and assorted gate-crashers assembled in Fauvet's neighborhood café for *apéritifs*. By the time Alice and the Steins arrived, they had to press through a milling crowd. In the midst of the multitude a tall slim woman, the painter Marie Laurencin, was making bacchantic movements to the pelting music of a nickelodeon. Mlle. Laurencin's romantic intimacy with the idol of Bohemian Paris, the poet Guillaume Apollinaire, had but recently been terminated with unhappiness and widely published recriminations on both sides. Since Apollinaire was expected to join the party, Marie was apparently not only fortifying herself with wine but submitting to a sort of self-hypnosis as she whirled and turned quite by herself.

Fernande entered Fauvet's with cries of consternation: Félix Potin, the caterer, had forgotten to send his part of the dinner and now his shop was closed. Alice, well trained to meet domestic crises, rose to the occasion. With Fernande in loud lamentation at her heels, she set out on a round of grocers to select substitutes for the menu, and returned with adequate supplies. Most of the company had by this time started to climb the hill. The two women followed the disorderly herd and soon caught up with Gertrude and Leo, who were trying to keep the distraught Mlle. Laurencin from falling backwards. Marie, refusing to walk, had insisted on dancing up the hill and on accompanying herself with song as she ascended. Furious with "Coco," as Marie was nicknamed, Fernande nudged Alice ahead. As soon as they were inside the labyrinthine tenement, they heated up great pots of Fernande's specialty, *arroz a la valenciana* — chicken, fish, lobster, sausage, pimiento, in rice, with artichokes and green peas — in a kitchen commandeered from the poet Max Jacob, who lived on the floor below Picasso's. Max was an old friend, but he had recently quarreled with Picasso and had not been invited to the party. Ignoring the estrangement, Fernande had imperiously decided that his quarters would do "for the rice and for the men's overcoats."

Upstairs, meanwhile, the company had begun to assemble around a huge table hastily put together with carpenters' trestles. At the head of it a large canvas, *Portrait de Mme. M.* — painted by Rousseau in tribute to his Polish schoolteacher mistress — was ceremoniously hung in the place of honor. Picasso, walking on the Rue des Martyrs one day, had spotted this painting in the shop of the

113

junk dealer Père Soulier. When he asked the price of it, the dealer said, "Five francs. [One dollar.] You can paint over it!" Retrieved from these ignominious surroundings, the painting, which Picasso regarded as "one of the most revealing French psychological portraits," was now festooned with flags and flowers, while anonymous statues were grouped about it to add a note of academic dignity. When Rousseau arrived, escorted by Apollinaire, there was a moment of silence as, touched by the simple smiling pleasure of the old man, they watched him being led to his special chair mounted on a box. There he was enthroned under a banner reading *"Honneur à Rousseau."* As he sat among his shoddy trappings, Rousseau at one point beckoned to Picasso. "After all," he whispered into Picasso's ear, "you and I are both great painters; myself in the modern style, and you in the Egyptian."

Stacks of crockery for the banquet had been borrowed from Azon, the neighborhood café; but there were not enough glasses to go around and wine finally had to be poured into old mustard pots. When dinner was announced, Fernande's specialty came steaming up the stairs. Just as the meal was about to begin, the festive air became troubled: Apollinaire took his place at the table alongside Marie who, a few minutes before, had fallen into a row of tarts *glacés* placed temporarily on a divan. She still bore treacly evidence of her fall, as did a dozen other people whom she had meanwhile embraced. The close company of her estranged lover proved too much for her to cope with now, and the first few mouthfuls of *arroz a la valenciana* were halted by a burst of hysteria. As she shouted and wept, Apollinaire extricated her from her chair and took her into an adjoining room. When they returned shortly, Marie showed definite marks of violence, but she was at last chastened, seemed sober, and the dinner proceeded in a happy hum. When Frédé, the proprietor of the famous café, the Lapin Agile, came in with his donkey Lolo, for a visit *en passant*, he was welcomed; but when a band of Italian street singers joined the crowd, Fernande ordered them out immediately. Background music for the diners continued to be supplied by the painter Georges Braque, who played tunes on his accordion.

114

Quite overcome with emotion, age and wine, Rousseau had fallen asleep early in the meal, and then could give his attention to the proceedings only in fits and starts. Wax dripping from a string of Chinese lanterns overhead fell onto his hair, forming a sort of clown's cap. Fernande remarked that he looked like a candle about to be lit. But songs and poems had been prepared, and no one cared whether or not Rousseau himself could hear them. To give official *panache* to the gathering, a pompous white-bearded man who lived nearby and whose work was restoring old paintings was solemnly introduced to the semicomatose Rousseau as the Minister of Fine Arts. Then Apollinaire proceeded to the heart of the program with the tribute of an improvised ode, written in doggerel, which retold some of Rousseau's history, including his adventures in Mexico. Rousseau had never been to Mexico, but Apollinaire was above such minor details as he recited:

> Rousseau, you can recall the Aztec skies —
> The pineapple and mango flowered there
> Where monkeys dripped the melon's blood on trees
> Shaking from guns of a blond emperor.
>
> In Mexico you saw your pictures swarm;
> Over banana trees a red sun ran.
> Yet, valorous, you doffed your uniform
> For the blue blouse of humble customs-man.
>
> Misfortune, lonely, found out who you were:
> She took your darling children and your wives.
> You married Painting, then, and found the cure
> To wring from grief new pictures and new lives.
>
> We come today to celebrate your story
> In wine poured for your honor by Picasso —
> We drink at this fond hour of your glory,
> Shouting with all our hearts, "Long Live Rousseau!"
>
> O glorious painter of our republican might,
> The Independents fly your flag sublime.
> Your face, in pure Pentelic marble white,
> Will always be the great pride of our time.

E

Rousseau listened in sleepy contentment, but André Salmon rose to protest: Apollinaire's eulogy was far too modest for the magnificence of its subject. Jumping on the table, he recited a litany of praise full of rhetoric and nonsense. As his shouts became louder and his claims grander, he seemed suddenly to have been overtaken by delirium tremens. Foaming at the mouth, he was strong-armed off the table and carried babbling to the front atelier where he was locked in. There, it was discovered later, he chewed up a box of matches, shredded and ate papers, including a telegram, and finished off his goat's meal by devouring the trimmings on Alice Toklas's new hat.

Things were quiet around the banquet table then as Marie Laurencin sang some sad Norman songs in a sweet voice. Through it all, according to Fernande Olivier, Alice, along with Leo and Gertrude, looked on quietly appalled, trying without success to drop her natural gravity, and giving the appearance of having somehow been stranded.

As little old Rousseau woke up now and then, he gazed dimly over the heads of the celebrants, mumbled his thanks for everything, and dropped back into sleep. Once he remained conscious long enough to play some tunes of his own composition on his violin, "The Little Bells" and a waltz entitled "Clemency," and to lead a chorus of his favorite song, "Aïe, aïe, aïe, que j'ai mal aux dents . . ." ("Ow, ow, ow, I've got a toothache . . .") Someone suggested it was Alice's turn to contribute to the floorshow. Since she came from the great American West, they wanted her to give them Indian songs. But she had to demur and, sometime after three in the morning, Rousseau and his violin having been packed up and sent home in the care of an old coachman, the gathering broke up. As the remains of the crowd straggled through the darkness down the long slope, the night air was rent by the shrieks of a madman. André Salmon, liberated, shot past them like a comet and disappeared.

Years later, after Gertrude had published Alice's version of the banquet, Salmon disputed her recollections. As far as he was concerned, her impressions of the evening only confirmed the naïveté of which he had always suspected them. His actions, he insisted, were but part and parcel of the relentless burlesque he, Apollinaire, Jacob and others of his friends played every day of their lives. A good part of the performance at the banquet was just another put-up job designed to frighten "the American ladies present." His foaming at the mouth, he said, came not from delirium tremens, but from soap.

CHAPTER 8

How do you do I forgive you everything and there
is nothing to forgive.

— GERTRUDE STEIN

THREE LIVES, a little book without cre-
dentials or sponsors, and issuing from that vague subterranean area
known as the "vanity press" where publishers were obscure and
sometimes fly-by-night, was finally an item on the shelves of a few
bookstores in 1910. Nothing about its inauspicious debut suggested
that this book would mark "the beginning of modern American
literature," not only in the opinion of Gertrude herself but in the
judgment of a critic as little given to nonsense as Carl Van Doren.
Yet in the general critical estimate, the modest volume for many
years represented the high point of innovation and achievement
in the career upon which Gertrude Stein had but recently embarked.

Except in Baltimore, where its advertisement by Gutman & Co.
attracted a modest number of home-town readers, the general public did not buy the book or even hear of it. Etta Cone, who had
in Paris typed the stories without thinking about them, was back
home by this time. In some circles, she reported to Gertrude, the

book had hit the sleepy town like a bomb. The unorthodox stories won the outright admiration of a few readers, and Etta herself was deeply impressed by them. She felt they were to literature what Matisse's paintings and sculptures were to art. But most people, she had to admit, were distinctly disappointed in their lack of style, their easy dispensation with all rules of rhetoric, and their "dreadful immorality." She had even heard some readers criticize Gertrude for allowing the little dog in the care of the Good Anna to manifest its "natural desires." They all thought she dwelt too much on "unpleasant things."

There was a smattering of brief notices across the country in the year following publication but, with the exception of one perceptive review in the *Kansas City Star*, none offered Gertrude the minimal encouragement of being understood. In the retrospect of fifty years, that one review seems just as remarkable as she thought it was. The piece was unsigned, and the name of the reviewer has never been uncovered. The following excerpt represents the most of it:

Three Lives by Gertrude Stein, is fiction which no one who reads it can ever forget, but a book for a strictly limited audience. . . . In this remarkable book one watches humanity groping in the mists of existence. As character study one can speak of it only in superlatives. The originality of its narrative form is notable. As these human lives are groping in bewilderment, so does the story telling itself. Not written in the vernacular, it yet gives that impression. At first one fancies the author using repetition as the refrain is used in poetry. But it is something more subtle still, something involved, something turning back, for a new beginning; for a lost strand in the spinning. It makes of the book a very masterpiece of realism, for the reader never escapes from the atmosphere of these lives, so subtly is the incantation wrought into these simple pages. Here is a literary artist of such originality that it is not easy to conjecture what special influences have gone into the making of her. But the indwelling spirit of it all is a sweet enlightened sympathy, an unsleeping sense of humor and an exquisite carefulness in detail. . . .

Reviews were not generally unfavorable, yet Gertrude was disappointed by their sparseness and the fact that no one of eminence (she had sent copies of the book to H. G. Wells, George Bernard

Shaw, John Galsworthy and Arnold Bennett) had come forth to "discover" her. This regret was tempered when H. G. Wells sent a note saying that while he had at first been repelled by the extraordinary style, he had finally read the book with "deepening pleasure and admiration," and that he would look for her future works "very curiously and eagerly." But William James's response was disheartening. "I have a bad conscience about 'Three Lives,'" he wrote from Germany, just three months before his death. "You know (?) how hard it is for me to read novels. Well, I read 30 or 40 pages, and said 'this is a fine new kind of realism — Gertrude Stein is great! I will go at it carefully when just the right mood comes.' But apparently the right mood never came. I thought I had put the book in my trunk, to finish it over here, but I don't find it on unpacking. I promise you that it shall be read *some* time! You see what a swine I am to have pearls cast before him! As a rule reading fiction is as hard to me as trying to hit a target by hurling feathers at it. I need *resistance*, to cerebrate!"

Three Lives did little to carry her name abroad in the terms she had hoped for, yet its appearance was nevertheless a salutary event in literary history. Slowly it edged its way into American literature, a work about which few people were enthusiastic, yet which none could ignore. Gradually it became famous. Since Gertrude broke all rules of literary deportment in the very next works to follow, *Three Lives* became, comparatively, the pillar of convention toward which puzzled readers of her later works might turn for some assurance that they were not being confronted by a series of literary hoaxes.

The most expertly handled of its three stories, *Melanctha*, became the anthology piece, partly because of its stylistic originality and partly because of its uncommon assumption that Negro characters and themes associated with Negro life were matters as naturally available for imaginative fiction as for sociological tract. In many reviews the book was praised as much for its refreshing non-patronizing attitude toward Negroes as it was recommended for its stylistic innovations. Richard Wright, the novelist, who had not yet been born when the book was written, considered *Melanctha* one of the most important influences on the beginnings of his career. Years before he had become a close friend of Gertrude's, he published in the New York newspaper, *PM*, a recollection of his first delighted encounter with the story. "But in the midst of my delight," Wright recalled, "I was jolted. A left-wing literary critic, whose judgment I had been led to respect, condemned Miss Stein in a sharply-worded newspaper article, implying that she spent her days reclining upon a silken couch in Paris smoking hashish, that she was a hopeless prey to hallucinations and that her tortured verbalisms were throttling the Revolution. I was disturbed. Had I duped myself into worshiping decadence?

"Believing in direct action, I contrived a method to gauge the degree to which Miss Stein's prose was tainted with the spirit of counter-revolution. I gathered a group of semi-literate Negro stockyard workers — 'basic proletarians with the instinct for revolution' . . . — into a Black Belt basement and read *Melanctha* aloud to them. They understood every word. Enthralled, they slapped their thighs, howled, laughed, stomped, and interrupted me constantly to comment upon the characters.

"My fondness for Steinian prose never distressed me after that."

James Weldon Johnson felt in *Melanctha* that Gertrude Stein was "the first . . . white writer to write a story of love between a Negro man and woman and deal with them as normal members of the human family," and the novelist Nella Larsen wrote a letter to Gertrude in which she said, "I never cease to wonder how you came to write it and just why you and not some one of us should so accurately have caught the spirit of this race of mine." But not all Negro writers were in agreement. "In the telling of the story," wrote Claude McKay, "I found nothing striking and informative about Negro life. Melanctha, the mulattress, might have been a Jewess. And the mulatto, Jeff Campbell — he is not typical of mulattoes I have known everywhere. He reminds me more of a type of white lover described by a colored woman. Melanctha seemed more like a brief American paraphrase of Esther Waters than a story of Negro life. The original Esther Waters is more important to me."

The most irate and damning critique of *Three Lives* did not appear until the persistence of what Carl Van Vechten has called the book's "striking underground reputation" had made it a *cause célèbre* as Gertrude's progress took her into realms ever more rarefied. This attack came from the English painter and man of letters, Wyndham Lewis, the gifted bête noire who had often set his horns against Picasso, Proust, Joyce and other modern masters of painting and literature. "It is in a thick, monotonous prose-song that Miss Stein characteristically expresses her fatigue, her energy, and the bitter fatalism of her nature. . . ." wrote Lewis. "In the end the most wearisome dirge it is possible to imagine results, as slab after slab of this heavy, insensitive, common prose-song churns and lumbers by. . . . What is the matter with it is, probably, that it is so *dead*. Gertrude Stein's prose-song is a cold, black suet-pudding. We can represent it as a cold suet-roll of fabulously reptilian length. Cut it at any point, it is the same thing; the same heavy, sticky, opaque mass all through, and all along . . . It is mournful and monstrous, composed of dead and inanimate material. It is all fat, without nerve . . . Its life is a low-grade, if tenacious, one; of the sausage, by-the-yard, variety . . . in adopting the simplicity, the illiterateness, of the mass-average of the Melancthas and Annas, Miss Stein gives proof of all the false 'revolutionary' propagandist *plainmanism* of her time. The monstrous, desperate soggy *lengths* of primitive mass-life . . . are undoubtedly intended as an epic contribution to the present mass-democracy. The texture of the language has to be jumbled, cheap, slangy, and thick to suit . . . Only the metre of an obsessing *time* has to be put into it. It has to be rhythmatized; and this proclivity both of Miss Stein, and of all the characteristic fashions of those for whom she writes, destroys the 'reality' at least, giving to the life it patronises the mechanical bias of its creator."

A sort of aristocratic impatience apparently led Lewis to regard Gertrude Stein as the Emma Goldman of the new fiction. In assigning various obsessions to her, he typified irritated critics who greeted her work as an abominable kind of sport, and who neither investigated nor showed any interest in her serious apprenticeship to the available schools of Flaubert, Cézanne and William James. Lewis's fear of a lava flow of proletarian sympathy, and the literary revolution that might be carried along with it, indicated his confusion about the work and invalidated all of his feelings except his furious anger. To have said that the language of *Three Lives* belongs with works that are "jumbled, cheap, slangy" was to be guilty of patent misrepresentation, as any other reader could have learned for himself by the perusal of a single page. Lewis was more successful with his elaborated reptilian. analogy. The image he details was sharply relevant to a method that might wrap almost any reader in its coils and might at times get a grip on even the most sympathetic one. But this was unlikely if the reader were disposed to take the stories in the terms of their conception and to accept their repetitions and re-beginnings in a way suggested by the *Kansas City Star* reviewer, as searchings for "a lost strand in the spinning." When Lewis said, "Cut it at any point, it is the same thing," he maliciously paraphrased Gertrude Stein's own sense of her method without, of course, crediting the reasons that made her intentions valid. *Three Lives* was never meant to make progressions of incident, or developments of situations, but to make iterations of states of mind sustaining themselves through a long progress of days and years and human encounters which are by nature essentially unchanging. The Stein style may challenge a reader's patience, but it is the result of deliberation on a high plane of creative thinking and in no case an attempt to cater to proletarian tastes or to exploit illiteracy.

It was the usual thing through Gertrude Stein's career that even as critics fulminated over the audacity of a recently published work, she was well advanced into a new, unclassifiable opus. When she could finally read the reviews of *Three Lives*, she had finished and put aside *The Making of Americans*, and had moved on to a period which was to bring her unending censure, ridicule and notoriety of such unprecedented proportions that, for good or ill, she had come into literature and social history to stay. The Frankenstein monster created by her critics and, in some cases, by her friends, was already a figure that would stomp its way through several generations. Meanwhile, Gertrude Stein herself quietly studied and meditated, engrossed in the pursuit of a career so serious and intense that, in any other age, its meaning would perhaps have attracted only literary scholars and philosophers.

Three Lives and *The Making of Americans* are as a rule grouped together as products of the "intelligible" part of her writing. Actually, they can be accommodated in the same breath only when viewed from the broadest perspective. The works are separated technically by a great gap which, in turn, becomes narrow when the tremendous development toward *Tender Buttons* is accounted for. *Three Lives* belongs to the literary area marked out by French naturalism, and can still be placed comfortably in the American grass-roots company of works by Willa Cather, Frank Norris and Stephen Crane. American character, its discovery and assessment, was one of Gertrude Stein's lifelong preoccupations. In pursuit of it, she exhibits, like her contemporaries, a national consciousness that is but an extension of her deep self-consciousness. In spite of her emphasis on rhythm and speech-patterns and her microscopic attention to matters other writers would regard as mere lacunae, the characters of *Three Lives* are more or less of the substance with which all writers of fiction deal. They are in no case constructions pieced together out of signs and echoes as her fictional characters were soon to become. *The Making of Americans,* for all its attenuations and repetitions and vermiculations, can still be regarded as a novel having a discernible relation to many other chronicles of family history which appeared in the late nineteenth and early twentieth centuries. But by the time she had completed the next arc of development — the curve leading out from *The Making of Americans* and rounded off in *Tender Buttons* — she had reached a stage where there was no longer anything in the English language with which her work might be compared, or to which it might even be referred in the quest for ancestral influences. In the space of a mere seven years she had developed so swiftly that she had already stepped beyond the pull of literary gravity. In the years to come, as she floated in the stratosphere, a few observers kept her in sight and knew she had to be reckoned with. Yet to the general public she was as remote as a planet. While, characteristically, she would say, "Here I am. Where is everybody else?" her question was rhetorical. She did not want followers, and she was not interested in "everybody else."

She was about to become the literary representative of a movement among artists in whose final public success she would be conspicuously not included. For more than twenty years she would have to face the fact that she had a vast number of spectators and a pitifully small audience. Finally, the pull of her own history and the excitements of a second world war would bring her down from the upper air, and her descent would be cheered by thousands. She would have the great audience she had always wanted, and she would beguile them and herself by recounting where she had been and how she got there.

CHAPTER 9

You would find it ridiculous if, when you asked someone his name, he replied, "My name is whatever you like to call it."

You would find such an answer ridiculous. And if he were to add, "I have whatever name you care to give me, and it is my real name," you would consider him mad. And yet that is what we must perhaps get accustomed to; indeterminacy become a positive fact, a positive element of knowledge.

— PAUL VALÉRY

CUBIST is the most obvious label for what Gertrude Stein had become, but in those days the term was commonly regarded as symptomatic of a condition rather than as descriptive of an accomplishment. Speaking about herself, she made in the course of her lifetime only a few remarks — almost like conversational asides — to the effect that she was doing in writing just what Picasso was doing in painting. In general she avoided the word cubism, and paid no attention to the theorists who, as early as 1910, had begun to realize just what it was that Picasso and Braque had stumbled upon and to establish a critical canon to account for it. While she herself did not advertise her role as literary cubist, she did not seem to mind having others designate her by the term. Yet she never saw herself as dependent upon the newly famous formulations of the movement's principles, and never indicated her work might or should be read as their literary manifestations.

A few of her early critics sensed, and insisted upon, the connection between her work and that of the new painters. But most of these men tended to use the word cubist as if it supplied total explanation of what she was up to or, in some cases, as if it were vaguely a kind of definition, but mainly an apology. To invoke the contentious word was the easiest way to remove the work under discussion from serious interest and to place it somewhere on the eccentric margins of art history. Like the daily press and even the reasonably art-conscious public, these men had only recently become accustomed to the idea of "impressionism." When the new painting lifted its many-faceted head and stared at them with a hundred eyes, they wanted to banish it like a horrid dream. "Cubism," they thought, was the word to do the trick. Used as a term to designate everything ridiculous and beyond ordinary comprehension, "cubism" became a success.

The scandals of criticism during the emergent period of cubism — the pusillanimous withdrawals of some critics and the *nouveaux* and ignorant enthusiasms of others — are a matter of history. Certain of Gertrude Stein's early critics were antagonistic and full of misconception about cubism, but they were right in assigning her a place in the cubist camp, even when they felt this was but the most convenient way in which to dismiss her. They understood, perhaps hazily, what was soon emphatically clear: that Gertrude Stein's intention at this period was not to create a literature that would merely partake of the vaguely iconoclastic spirit of cubism — or of postimpressionism, as the general sense of the new was popularly designated — but to represent an essential product of cubism itself. As he had for the painters, Cézanne supplied her first with a spirit and a mode, and then with a method that invited the full play of her ingenuity. When Picasso and Braque, the joint creators of cubism, had begun to construct visual objects never possible before Cézanne's inventions, Gertrude Stein was abreast of them in her search for means by which to construct a new kind of literature. Once the break with visual, narrative, common-sense reality had been initiated, this progress would not be curbed.

In general, the cubists were lighthearted men who dealt in surprise. But behind the impulses that led them to surprise themselves no less than the public was the seriousness of a quest. They were pioneers in an early phase of the era which, in the words of the American poet Wallace Stevens, was "experiencing essential poverty in spite of fortune," an era when "the unities, the relations, to be summarized as paramount" were "the projection of reality beyond reality, the determination to cover the ground, whatever it may be, the determination not to be confined, the recapture of excitement at every time, in every way. . . ." Stevens felt that most poets and painters understood the nature of their quest, yet he believed that, as in the case of many of the cubists who clowned their way to aesthetic sainthood, "it is possible to be subjected to a lofty purpose and not to know it." No one can measure the degree of awareness possessed by any of the cubists, yet their history makes it clear that they were determined to uncover signs of the fundamental substance of reality lying behind façades of convention, and that they were determined to uphold the belief that "the only possible error in art is imitation." In her own terms, but not as exclusively in her own preserve as she seemed to think she was, Gertrude Stein was equally determined. Reproduction, imitation of nature was no longer her concern, or theirs; her constructions, like theirs, violated nature, and her methods were the result of an inexplicable mixture of intuition and calculation. The purpose of painting, according to Braque, was not "to try and *reconstitute* an anecdotal fact, but to *constitute* a pictorial fact." Photography and reportage, the dominant graphic and literary means of mass communication, could give more or less accurate accounts of any object or any event. Their work was not the work of the imagination. The work of the creative imagination was not to reflect the world but to invent it: Proceeding like blind explorers, the painters invaded the world, so to speak, broke down appearances, and brought to light hidden versions of reality. At first, intuition alone seemed to sanction what they had found. But suddenly on the threshold of the twentieth century and its investigations of space-time physics, they were comforted to learn that they had the full support of intellect. The beginnings of cubism came to represent an exciting pictorial preview of the space-time continuum that was soon a commonplace matter in science and in metaphysics.

Like the young painters who conceived of their work as independent of exterior reality — as, in the words of Apollinaire, "drifting towards an entirely new art which will stand in relation to painting, as hitherto regarded, just as music stands in relation to literature" — Gertrude Stein now began to conceive of words as independent of exterior reality, which is to say, of fixed meanings, and to regard them as being as "pure" as notes in music.

Perhaps never in all the long association of poets and painters in the same creative climate has a writer attempted with such unabashed literalness to adopt methods springing from the theory and practice of painting. Indeed, seldom before had circumstances allowed a writer or painter to think of composing under rules borrowed piecemeal from an art other than his own. In most previous associations of poets and painters, and in all previous comparisons of their works, identifications and congruencies had for the most part hinged upon similarities in subject matter and attitude. Such comparisons are, perforce, wholly "literary." The subjects and images of paintings, and the philosophies of painters, are discussed in relation to the subjects and images of poems and the philosophies of poets. When the cubists jettisoned subject matter, liaisons between poetry and painting on the old basis were no longer possible. The only course open to literature that would emulate painting was that of contemplating its own structure and image. When the literary content of painting was omitted in favor of the freely conceived mathematical or intuitive exercise of purely plastic values, Gertrude Stein also attempted to drop subject matter in order to concentrate freely upon the "plastic" potentialities of language itself.

On their way toward abstraction, the painters could lean for support upon a rich tradition of Arabic tilework, Persian textiles, Romanesque architectural ornamentation and a hundred other forerunners. If she had to, Gertrude Stein might have leaned upon the poets of Alexandria, upon John Lyly in England and upon Góngora — Picasso's favorite poet — in Spain, and even upon the later Henry James. While she would admit no forebears, except James, of whose methods she felt her own work was a continuation, Gertrude Stein was nevertheless a writer in a long and old succession. She had come to the conclusion that the twentieth century was interested neither in impressions nor emotions, but only in conceptions. Her work began to be more cerebral, abstract, and, paradoxically, more lyrical.

She was now aiming to create something not concerned with visual resemblances, something that would illuminate nuances in human character and behavior that evade case-book documentation. She wanted to break up the data of documentation into resonant parts and to give it a new sequence and order. What led her to portrait writing was a conviction that "as I wrote the movement of the words spoken by some one who lately I have been hearing sound like my writing feels to me as I am writing." These portraits were not analytical studies, but poems made out of suggestions, both verbal and visual, and organized into patterns with as much care, including the care to admit accident, as Picasso would take with the cubist construction of visual elements in paintings such as the series *Ma Jolie*. Like him, she attempted to portray in words "not what you see but what you know is there."

She was not, as has been commonly supposed by her American readers, alone in this attempt. Nor was she unique in that her creative impetus came directly from painting and only indirectly from that development in literature, focused most importantly in Mallarmé, to which it bears a close relationship. Mallarmé had long anticipated the cubist approach to the possibilities of form in his insistence on the plastic value of words apart from connotations and emotional suggestions. The cubists manipulated volumes and shapes without consideration for the objects these volumes and shapes represented. Caring only for their innate power of evocation, they were unwittingly emulating Mallarmé's concern for the sheer power of syllables. But no theory of cubism arrived until the painters had made their discoveries. When cubist writing emerged, it was influenced directly by painting and only indirectly by Mallarmé. By that time certain writers had become the champions of cubism and its only articulate theorists. Painters arrived at cubism in the natural process of exploration. Writers came to it only when cubism had been defined sufficiently to allow its practices to be formulated in terms indicating that literary emulation was possible.

As an intimate of the cubist group, Guillaume Apollinaire had sat with the painters through the long hours of horseplay and serious discussion at Le Lapin Agile and Aux Enfants de la Butte and he had listened with them in bewilderment and excitement as Maurice Princet, the accountant who lived in the Bateau Lavoir, talked about infinities and fourth dimensions and otherwise tried to expound the confounding wonders of new mathematical formulations. Apollinaire had caroused with them up and down the slopes of Montmartre, given them the dispensations of his avuncular wisdom, the example of his methodical madness, and had finally become apologist for their aims and ambitions. His first associations with them had been based merely on natural sympathy for artists attempting something new, rather than upon any real conviction of their individual worth. But Apollinaire gradually began to see what was happening around him and to understand its enormous significance. By the time he was able to say, *"L'art des peintres nouveaux prend l'univers infini comme idéal,"* random discussion and private meditation had brought him to a position as champion of the whole cubist venture. In ensuing years he became its foremost publicist. To pay mock homage to Apollinaire's eminence, Picasso made a drawing of him as pope of cubism, with a miter on his head, a pipe in his mouth and a watch on his wrist.

In his own work, Apollinaire applied, partly, the new methods about which he wrote as a critic of art and, partly, those which had obtained widely in France ever since Mallarmé had followed Baudelaire in positing a theory of poetry in which the subject was secondary to its expression. When Baudelaire said of Edgar Allan Poe, *"Il croyait, en vrai poète qu'il était, que le but de la poésie est de même nature que son principe, et qu'elle ne doit pas avoir en autre chose qu'elle-même,"* he had given words to a notion upon which the whole epoch of symbolist poetry was founded. In a letter to Henri Cazalis, in 1864, Mallarmé had anticipated not impressionism, as many critics have believed, but cubism: "At last I have begun my Hérodiade; with terror, for I am inventing a language which must spring out of my very new poetic conception, which I can define in a few words: to describe not the thing itself but the effect it produces. Therefore the verse must be composed not just out of words but of intentions, and the language must yield before the sensations."

Apollinaire's poems, particularly in the volume entitled *Alcools*, show the cubist attempt in French literature perhaps more specifically than does the work of his friends, Max Jacob and Pierre Reverdy, both of whom went through extensive periods when, quite naturally, poetry and painting in the same place sought to realize more or less the same objectives. No one had yet surpassed Mallarmé in testing the power of the word as an instrument of spiritual and mystical revelation, but Apollinaire was now following the true path laid out by the master. His methods, heavily weighted on the side of intuition, were quite different from those of Mallarmé and quite different from those of Gertrude Stein.

In a poem by Mallarmé there is a compact, many-faceted, ordering of ideas which may be recognized on repeated reading and the plumbing of successive levels of understanding. In a "poem" by Gertrude Stein there is process — the "poem" means only what the reader feels during the successive instants in which he reads it. In a poem by Apollinaire there is a radiation of ideas which leads the reader away from the written poem and into the free imagination, into the poetry of all natural or created things. Apollinaire wanted for the poet the new universe of scientific, microscopic, telescopic, radiographic vision, and in practice developed the means of capturing that ambitious vision by assuming that, for observing and measuring, the imagination is the equal of any of the instruments of science. His particular creativity was in the nature of a release of the subconscious — a gathering of expressive power through incantatory sentences that unrolled freely, beyond conscious control.

In this practice he worked much more closely with the possibilities of automatic writing than Gertrude Stein ever did. His aim, in fact, was quite the same as that which Leon Solomons and Gertrude had sought to realize in some of their experiments at Harvard — the release of a "second" personality which, overwhelming the conscious, controlled, "first" personality, would articulate sensations and feelings either suppressed or conventionalized in the normal course of written expression. He was already tending toward surrealism and away from cubism which, in all of its early manifestations, was not an art of the subconscious but of the hyperconscious intellect.

Apollinaire's tendency to use an amalgamation of painting effects and poetic effects is best illustrated in his later composition of pictorial poems, published in his volume *Calligrammes*. Here, again, he carries forward an innovation of Mallarmé who said, "Let us have no more of those successive, incessant, back and forth motions of our eyes, traveling from one line to the next and beginning over again." In his famous poem, *Un Coup de Dés*, Mallarmé attempted to bring to the page the quality of a musical score, separating primary and secondary motifs typographically and, at the same time, establishing emphases and substitutions for conventional punctuation by calculated placement: the whiteness of an empty page becomes the visual equivalent of silence, the distribution of calligraphy on other pages is entirely consonant with the intended arrest or movement of the particular passage in the poem.

In a number of Apollinaire's picture-poems — modern versions of the conceits of the cruciform, flower-shaped, wing-shaped figured verse of the Renaissance, or of *technopaegnia*, as they were called by ancient Greek poets, which appeared in the shapes of an altar, an egg, an ax or a shepherd's pipe — he played with bicycles, neckties and harps and automobiles and rain falling on umbrellas. Of significant modern poets in English, except for a single instance in the work of Dylan Thomas, *Vision and Prayer*, E. E. Cummings is the only one to have indulged in such experiments. In the case of Cummings, the typographical unorthodoxy is meant to supply emphasis or punctuation, rather than to elaborate pictorial conceit. This phase of Apollinaire's work was brief but, as an attempt, in the fundamental cubist sense, to overcome the staleness of words worn by usage and to break a poem "out of its frame," it was both legitimate and necessary. Gertrude Stein's dramatic swerving into the cubist channel of expression was not opportunistic, nor was it the way toward an alliance to which she had no right. When she adopted the cubist "way of seeing" she had already experienced in literary terms what others had experienced in the terms of painting. Cubism was, in part, an outgrowth of a progress in painting first dimly discerned in the later works of Cézanne. Gertrude Stein's particular cubism was an outgrowth of a personal progress which, when closely read, moves through several searching, tentative phases toward its final resolutions. Manifestations of cubism in painting served mainly to organize and direct her own independent thinking. To assume that she simply reached out for the new method and, without literary warrant, used it for her own purposes, would be to accuse her of a poverty of resourcefulness and imagination denied by both the pre-cubist and post-cubist phases of her writing career.

Had her earliest appearances as a cubist writer been accompanied by such forceful — if not always clearly defined — principles as those which buttressed the positions of the cubist painters, the roar of criticism in which they were received might have been in some measure tempered. By virtue of its plastic freedom, painting tends, especially in our time, to stay well in the vanguard of writing; and when, in this instance, even painting was open to the widest misinterpretation and disapproval, the chances that Gertrude Stein might have had the advantage of an informed audience were highly unlikely.

Of the two modes of cubism — the analytic, in which the intellectual, geometrical, conceptual aspect of things was emphasized, and the synthetic, in which imagination, surprise, composition and lyricism were predominant — Gertrude Stein worked in the analytic in the period growing out of *The Making of Americans* and prior to *Tender Buttons*, when she moved into the synthetic phase.

By the time she had exhausted the continual present of *The Making of Americans* or, as one might better say, by the time the continual present of that slow-spiraling chronicle had exhausted her, Gertrude Stein had begun to produce the peculiar incantatory catalogues and infinitesimally modified repetitions that represent in literature the early, comparatively hermetic period of cubism. The painters who worked in analytical cubism had broken up natural objects and made their canvases into fields of visual geometry. Gertrude Stein likewise broke up natural sequences of thought and made compositions of their basic verbal elements.

When, finally, she could say of *The Making of Americans*, "If it can be done why do it," she was ready to do something that could not be done. As she later reported of this transition, "So then I said I would begin again. I would not know what I knew about everything what I knew about anything. . . . And so it was necessary to let come what would happen to come. . . ." With *A Long Gay Book*, an account of all possible relations between two persons, *Many Many Women*, and *G.M.P.* ("Matisse Picasso and Gertrude Stein"), all written between 1909 and 1912, she proceeded wholeheartedly into cubism. It was a step that meant that she had abandoned history, memory, science and the cursive thought by which the written word ordinarily registers intelligence. Like other contemporaries of the highest aesthetic sophistication, among them Erik Satie, Apollinaire and the French cubist poet Max Jacob, she had deliberately given over her learning and her understanding as if they were intolerable burdens under whose weight the creator was stultified and unable to move. If relief from these burdens would not result in primitivism, at least the creator could feel something approximating the freedom of the primitive, join hands with him over the dead corpus of academic art, and thus support an idea expressed by Vico: "In civilized epochs poetry can only be written by those who have the capacity to suspend the operation of the intellect, to put the mind in fetters and return to the unreflecting mode of thought characteristic of the childhood of the race."

Like Picasso, who had continually to be rid of the confinements of his success and to be challenged always by a new vision and a new kind of solution, Gertrude Stein, privately and without any comparable "success," also had to be moving on.

135

CHAPTER 10

> Einstein was the creative philosophic mind of
> the century and I have been the creative literary
> mind of the century. . . .
>
> — GERTRUDE STEIN

GERTRUDE STEIN's close observation of
a single work of Cézanne's had been directly responsible for the
shape and texture of *Three Lives*. The succeeding phase of her work
was a direct outgrowth of her observations in the psychological laboratory combined with her observations as a member of the third
generation of an American family with a broad history to recapitulate.
Whether she then deliberately turned to painting or whether she
found the impact of painting was irresistible, the next phase of her
work was closely related to a crucial development in the career of
Picasso during the years when she was his frequent companion and
confidante.

The unparalleled bravado with which Picasso had painted his first
cubist pictures had accomplished nothing less than a break through
the barriers of space and time within which the art of painting had
for centuries been less and less comfortably confined. What this
would ultimately mean for painting in general has been amply

recorded in the amazing history of the art during the first half of the twentieth century. Critics who were hard put to accept the notion of any development in art not springing logically from forerunners and traditions were naturally confounded by Picasso's feat; and a vast library of explanatory literature, along with many vulgarizations of his method in commercial design and advertising layouts, has still failed to educate the larger part of the general public to view it as anything but, at best, a sport, and at worst, an aberration. The problem that seems to defy solution and which remains forever new is but the old one of the cart before the horse: before the works of cubism can be analyzed or "understood," they have to be looked at with eyes purified of expectation, or with eyes trained to forget all the other paintings they have ever seen. Since the educated and tradition-biased eye of the critic is, in a sense, the least pure, the least prone to erase its memories, it is little wonder that in the furies of aesthetic polemics the paintings themselves were at times all but forgotten. When Picasso leaped through the mirror of art and picked himself up reflected in a thousand shivers, the only way one could appreciate what he had done was to leap after him. The dilemma of the man who relied merely upon his experience and his intelligence became acute.

"We have to realize," wrote Herbert Read, "that we are now concerned, not with a logical development of the art of painting in Europe, not even with a development for which there is any historical parallel, but with an abrupt break with all traditions, with all preconception of what the art of painting should be . . . all links with the objective world are broken . . . that love of the concrete which has characterized the art of Europe for centuries . . . is deliberately renounced." If the works of Picasso at this period are accepted in the terms assigned to them by one of the leading aestheticians of modern art, they may serve as a starting point in a review of Gertrude Stein's fairly similar development. Her intention was daring, her progress courageous; and yet it was here that she made the great and resonant error which no literary artist of note has been brave enough, or foolhardy enough, to repeat. Ironically, it was the error which established her fame in her own time and curtailed forever her specific influence. In the historical view it must be regarded as an eloquent mistake — a mistake of which only a great and original talent is capable. While her widely read contemporaries were filling the bookstalls with artificial romances, Graustarkian fantasies and journalistic exposures of the rotten underpinnings of society, all in the name of art, she persisted alone in the attempt to give a new dimension to the English language, to find means by which language might express a picture of the observed world where projections of the subjective imagination had come to seem like fading photographs beside the grotesque and urgent facts of the Einsteinian universe.

The years 1908 to 1910 were the ground-breaking or, as it was later called, the "heroic" period of cubism and, whether or not the painters had any clear idea of what the scientists were saying, their intuitions had already directed them to produce works that could serve as graphic illustrations for the theories of science. Herman Minkowski, in *Time and Space* (1908), had announced: "Henceforth space by itself, and time by itself, are doomed to fade away into mere shadows, and only a kind of union of the two will preserve an independent reality." Minkowski's statement keynoted a series of explorations in mathematics, chemistry and psychology which were soon to lead to a new version of the structure of the universe, man, and his experience. The notion of material substance had been dissolved; phenomena were reconstituted as an hitherto unrevealed grouping of complexes and relationships; new discoveries about the nature of the mind led to a conviction of the arbitrary nature of standards and absolutes which had long remained unquestioned. The solid world was transformed into a world of flux and, at any moment, new experiments and explorations might further atomize or rearrange or otherwise disturb the simple comforts of reality. Artists who understood only marginally the basis of these transformations were nevertheless exhilarated by their reports. It was one of those periods of history when a communicable temper results in parallel discoveries as far apart as painting and nuclear physics. The relationship was intuitive — yet in the space of a few years it was possible to delineate the most remarkable points of congruency between the pure scientist and the artist.

Among writers, few were more accustomed to the disciplines of scientific thought than Gertrude Stein, or more naturally receptive to new thresholds and the sight of new vistas. She would have seemed to possess the enormous advantage of a background which afforded her an understanding of the letter as well as the spirit of the new sense of things, and yet she failed in that she interpreted literally, and used literally, what other artists were able to translate into their own terms without limiting effects. Other poets, ever since Baudelaire, had written poems in which the vision was dissociated from the subject. They had maintained, like the cubists, the logic, if not the appearance, of nature, but none of them had treated language as if it had nothing to do with thought.

Language is plastic, but its plasticity must be informed and determined by the philosophy or, at least, by the information it conveys. In her earlier works, Gertrude Stein operated under this injunction naturally; but as she continued, her attraction to painting led her to wish for the same plastic freedom for literature, and eventually to write as though literature *were* endowed with such freedom. "The painter," said Georges Braque, "knows things by sight; the writer, who knows them by name, profits by a prejudice in his favor." This was the profit Gertrude Stein threw away.

Cubism is, first of all, concerned with space. It rejects, or transcends, the sense of perspective which, since the Renaissance, had dominated Western painting. Just as the physical theorist had, since the early nineteenth century, overcome the tendency to "see" only in three dimensions, the cubists attempted a new representation of space in which the objects would be viewed from several points at once. They sought to achieve simultaneity, that quality which inheres in a painting when "time" has been added. Precisely when the freedom of a new dispensation in painting was causing a number of individuals to move toward the beginnings of cubism in 1905, Albert Einstein introduced his *Elektrodynamik bewegter Körper* with a careful definition of simultaneity.

Technically, cubism achieves the disarrangement and recombination of three-dimensional vision in such a way as to add the quality

139

of "time" that introduces the fourth dimension. Yet the cubists themselves were less openly concerned with the technical aspects of what they were doing than with its spiritual aspects. To Guillaume Apollinaire, whose writings on the subject became dogma for half a century, cubism was "the art of painting new structures borrowed not from the reality of sight, but from the reality of insight." To other theorists, such as the painters Albert Gleizes and Jean Metzinger, a cubist was "a realist [who] will fashion the real in the image of his mind, for there is only one truth, and this is our own, when we impose it on others. And it is faith in Beauty which supplies the necessary strength." The true cubist, they believed, sought "the essential, but we seek it in our personality and not in a sort of eternity, laboriously divided by mathematicians and philosophers."

For the cubist painter, the vision determines the means, and he can proceed to realize his vision by new methods but without any essential violation of the materials of his medium. What, in this pursuit, can the cubist writer do? Since painting is a space art, what "happens" in a painting is communicated by the manner in which space is filled, divided, or otherwise dramatized by highlights and figurations. Writing is not a space art but, like music, a time art. "Space," in writing, is an illusion which can be created only by the presentation of successive images, ideas, situations, composed and read in sequence, in time. The rules of prosody and versification have never admitted the notion of space, just as the vocabulary of painting before the cubists, with the exceptions of such naïve storytelling sequences as Masaccio's *The Tribute Money* or Botticelli's *Life and Miracles of Saint Zenobias,* had never accommodated the notion of time.

Gertrude Stein set out to overcome this omission. She would bring space into the vocabulary of an art whose aesthetic was concentrated in its manipulations of time. She would follow the pictorial cubists, moving around an object to seize several successive appearances, which, fused in a single image, reconstitute it in time. As a result, the works attempting to bring this new dimension to writing are, for all but those readers who no longer demand what literature has always offered, impossible to read. In looking at a painting in which the fourth dimension is a factor, the viewer sees it "all at once" and may contemplate the work for as little or as long as his interest is engaged. But the contemplation of a work of literature which has been "spatialized" demands attention to such a protracted degree of endurance that a reader's response is apt to be reduced to doggedness. The untrained mind, however sympathetic, is unable to hold the picture because the time necessary to "read" it is so long and so barren of interest. While Gertrude Stein does achieve duration, she does this at the expense of making it seemingly absolute; arrest of imagination — even of expectation — creates a void in which nothing happens except the unpleasant sensation of being forced to work at a problem the rewards of which are continually beyond reach, if not altogether withheld. Her method, in the view of Malcolm Cowley, "eludes and irritates us and sets us off on a vain search as if through a pile of dusty newspapers for an item we are sure must be there, but which we are equally sure we can never find."

Leo Stein shared the feelings of many of Gertrude's early readers, and spoke for them. "When once you know that a nose is not a nose is not a nose," he wrote, "you can go on to discover what all the other things are not, and arrive at the conclusion that the way to build up 'real' things is out of the broken fragments of a once glorious union, of states dissevered, discordant. But when the analysis is only a kind of funny business, the synthesis will be only another kind of funny business."

The easiest and most obvious thing in denying Gertrude Stein's attempt to approximate poetry with painting is to point out that the materials of painting — color, line, space — cannot be equated with the materials of poetry — sound, rhythm, verbal density — except on a plastic level. The materials of painting, or of music, may evoke delight in themselves, even when they are separated from an organizing concept. They communicate, sometimes delightfully, nothing but what they are. Words, however, communicate something beyond themselves the very moment their sounds are apprehended. Not even the most exclusive attention to their plastic qualities of texture, duration or density can relieve the listener of the burdens of their individual connotations. And as soon as a word communicates, as soon as it is recognized, it becomes to a degree anarchical, simply because the writer cannot entirely control associations of ideas and memories in the mind of the individual who has heard it or read it.

Gertrude Stein had embarked on a path along which no other writer in English would follow. By deliberately limiting her writer's equipment, by destroying the connotative vitality of words, she had thrown away those properties of language which give the literary artist the advantage of definiteness in color, tone, gravity, and the opportunity for precision. While her attempt to get away from the conventional definitions of words in order to touch more evocative seams of interest was valid, her attempt to reduce the materials of literature to the strictness of musical notes and chords was bound to result in a dead end. A composer who strikes a note does not limit himself because the sound that results is "controlled" by the mechanics of his instrument; but an author who writes a noun or a verb cannot control the differing associations these words will summon up in the minds of any two readers. As a consequence, his reduction of words from the status of symbols or simple signs to mere units of verbal stress becomes a denial of the common function of words. Such a writer stands so far outside of any known tradition that it is impossible to make comparative judgments involving his work simply because there is nothing with which he can be contrasted. Since he has chosen to work with only a part of the resources of his medium, his highest flights can represent but partial success. In the long run, he takes the risk of denying the artistry he may possess by confining its exercise to but one aspect of its expression — as if Rembrandt had confined himself to working in wallpaper designs or Shakespeare to basic English.

Gertrude Stein ignored this danger, and proceeded to use words as if they were unencumbered plastic entities of such and such texture, weight and resilience. Like the cubists who wanted to achieve a "pure" art, she set for herself the goal of a "pure" literature and won for herself a language inscrutable to inquiry on both logical and semantic levels. For the language of literature to be "pure" it would obviously have to be divorced from thought. For a time, she seems to have arrived at this conclusion — when her abstractionist experiments brought her to the point of making up words of a new and private language. But while she felt at first that this was a logical and perhaps inevitable step, she soon changed her mind. "It takes a tremendous amount of inner necessity to invent even one word," she said, "one can invent imitating movements and emotions in sounds, and in the poetical language of some languages you have that, the German language as a language suffers from this what the words mean sound too much like what they do, and children do these things by one sort or another of invention but this has really nothing to do with language. Language as a real thing is not imitation either of sounds or colors or emotions it is an intellectual recreation and there is no possible doubt about it and it is going to go on being that as long as humanity is anything. So every one must stay with the language their language that has come to be spoken and written and which has in it all the history of its intellectual recreation."

When she rejected this last logical step, she turned to various forms of post-cubist literature without having recognized, or without caring to admit, her initial error. She may very well have succeeded in purifying her vision, in verbalizing images to a point where their conventional connotations are no longer present, but the vision is one thing and its expression another. Words, since they are accepted as symbols of human discourse, must sit like refugees surrounded by the little baggage of their past and block her way. When she uses words as if they had no history, her vision remains private, unshared; her reader is left with only sparse clues to its meaning, since his only evidence is the record of an echo.

Her experiment was valuable as reconnaissance over areas that sooner or later had to be mapped, if only to warn others away. She may have believed, with other cubists, that "the artist who concedes nothing, who does not explain himself and relates nothing, accumulated an internal strength whose radiance shines on every hand." But it is difficult not to conclude that she had crossed the boundary line from writing to painting only to return equipped with means not proper to her subject. If such considerations moved her at all, they were less important than the endless possibilities that continued to arrive in the process of her lifelong game of solitaire with words.

A Long Gay Book may be regarded as her literary contribution to "disintegrating" or analytical cubism — the early phase in which the painters sought to displace conventional perspective with the simultaneity of a composite view. As in *The Making of Americans,* she is again concerned with the conviction that "Everyone has in them a fundamental nature to them with a kind of way of thinking that goes with this nature in them all the many millions made of that kind of them." However, representationalism has by this time become almost nonexistent. Characters are given names, but that is the extent of their identifications. As Gertrude states in the opening pages of *A Long Gay Book,* "there will be discussion of pairs of people and their relations, short sketches of innumerable ones, Ollie, Paul; Paul, Fernande; Larr and me, Jane and me, Hallie and Ollie, Margaret and Philip, Claudel and Mrs. Claudel, Claudel and Martin, Martin and Jane, Helen and John, everybody I know . . . everybody I can think of ever, narrative after narrative pairs of people. . . ." While her attempt to get down pairs of people resulted in little more than pairs of names, in her own mind Gertrude had much specifically to account for in her ambitious tabulations. In notations she makes for herself as a kind of guide, and which are included in the text itself, she records: "Start afresh with Grace's group, practical pseudo masculine. Then start afresh with Fanny and Helen and business women, earthy type, and kind of intellect. Enlarge on this and go back to flavor, pseudo flavor, Mildred's group, and then to the concentrated groups. From then on complicate and complete giving all kinds of pictures and start in again with the men. Here begin with Victor Herbert group and ramify from that. Simon is bottom of Alden and Bremer and the rest. Go on then to how one would love and be loved as a man or as a woman by each kind that could or would love any one." But the careful distinctions that mark her conception are obliterated in her practice and the work becomes an abstract exercise in recording a process, and only incidentally a work of character analysis. However, toward the end of the book, after the reader has been through an experience that would be akin to having lived in a house built out of IBM cards for days, something new begins to happen. A few rays of common light begin to shine through the punched holes, a few rhythms like the songs of children playing games in the street are heard, and a few images appear to break the statistical nightmare in which he has been trapped.

In the close reading of Gertrude Stein, a reader participates in the stages of her development, and comes to her discoveries exactly when she arrives at them. In the case of *A Long Gay Book*, the reader, like the author, anticipates a departure which was very soon abundantly documented. This development was the new notion of portrait writing. The first works she wrote in this form are almost indistinguishable in manner and content from the abstract categories that fill the earlier part of *A Long Gay Book*, and her later portraits, as well as the method of *Tender Buttons*, grow directly out of the latter part. If she had cared to, she might have augmented her portrait gallery simply by excerpting scores of individual pages from the book and affixing titles to them. In any case, the long period of intermittent portrait writing was about to begin, a period promoted by a variation of the particular interests that had carried her all the way through *The Making of Americans* and *A Long Gay Book*. Commenting upon the special turn of interest that produced the portraits, she said, "I had to find out what it was inside any one, and by any one I mean every one. I had to find out inside every one what was in them that was intrinsically exciting and I had to find out not by what they said not by what they did not by how much or how little they resembled any other one but I had to find out by the intensity of movement that there was inside any one of them."

By the time literary cubism in France had developed its two diverse tendencies — one moving toward an abstract architecture of names, objects, facts, the other toward a more "poetic" enumeration of the associations and essences of names, objects and facts — Gertrude Stein had already dwelt at length upon the first and was about to explore the second. In painting, analytical cubism, for all its confident new freedom, was still a representational mode in which the painters' congeries of facets presented objects as observed simultaneously from several points of view. The work of art as an act of total creation did not arrive until synthetic cubism allowed the painter to abandon the analysis of forms in order to combine visual aspects in terms of their compositional possibilities. In the cubism of the painters this difference can be made clear by comparison of, for instance Picasso's *L'Accordéoniste* (1911) and his *Carte à jouer, compotier, verve* (1914). The paraphernalia of the café had become the iconography of a pure and infinitely pliable visual poetry. There was a reason for "the women playing guitars or the simple chessboards and musical instruments in the paintings by all the friends of cubism," André Chastel has commented. "These were its essential symbols. For a few years their work, with its touching attempt to make the curve of a violin, the base of a glass and a clay pipe the sufficient and necessary actors in a delightful ballet, was the chastest the world had ever known."

In a parallel sense, it was as though Gertrude Stein's scientific preoccupation had worked itself to exhaustion; the poet in her was now ready to take over. Her power as an artist would now be called to full exercise. She had proved beyond doubt that she had the gift of the scientist in her grand catalogues and minute classifications; she had still to prove that she possessed that angelic familiarity with words and rhythms that identifies the poet.

The subject of her first portrait, as might have been expected, was Alice B. Toklas. For reasons of her own, Gertrude entitled the work *Ada*. This portrait was written on a Sunday evening when their cook was out and when, by custom, Alice was preparing an American meal as a relief from the French and Italian dishes they were used to. In a small block-pad notebook, Gertrude swiftly and deftly "painted in" the first strokes of a kind of portraiture that was to be uniquely hers. Since Gertrude did not like to see work being done, particularly domestic work, she had remained out of range of pots and pans while Alice was preoccupied in the kitchen. But when the portrait was finished, she hurried into the kitchen: "You'll just have to take whatever you're cooking off the stove . . ." she said, "or stop cooking entirely . . . you must read this." When Gertrude

146

Gertrude Stein as a
child in Paris

With friends at Johns Hopkins Medical School

The young career
woman

With her nephew Allan
only child of Sarah and
Michael Stein

began to read the work aloud, Alice thought it was meant as a joke to tease her. But in a few moments she recognized the peculiarly personal content of the sinuously woven phrases. Perhaps no other single item in all of Gertrude's work more tenderly expresses the deep attachment uniting the two women. Beyond its meaning as a statement of affection, it shows Gertrude at her most felicitous in the use of simple language, subtle but easy rhythms, and perhaps demonstrates as well as any other example the best qualities of her early portraits. The following excerpt is its conclusion:

She came to be happier than anybody else who was living then. It is easy to believe this thing. She was telling some one, who was loving every story that was charming. Some one who was living was almost always listening. That one who was loving was telling about being one then listening. That one being loving was then telling stories having a beginning and a middle and an ending. Ada was then one and all her living then one completely telling stories that were charming, completely listening to stories having a beginning and a middle and an ending. Trembling was all living, living was all loving, some one was then the other one. Certainly this one was loving this Ada then. And certainly Ada all her living then was happier in loving than any one else who ever could, who was, who is, who ever will be living.

Portraits of Matisse and Picasso soon followed this first effort, and these were brought to the attention of Alfred Stieglitz, then at the most influential phase of his career as dean of the most advanced art life in New York. Stieglitz said at the time that Gertrude had "undoubtedly expressed Matisse and Picasso in words," but he later confessed that he found the portraits inscrutable, in spite of the curious excitement they generated. In any case, he decided to publish the pieces in a special number of his magazine *Camera Work*, in August, 1912. This appearance was Gertrude's first publication in a periodical anywhere. Beyond the few copies of *Three Lives* in circulation, it was as well her introduction to the American reading public. *Camera Work*, in spite of its small circulation, was read with care by people of influence in the art world. Her appearance there provided a dignified, if comparatively quiet, entrance to the American literary scene.

F

147

In these portraits, written halfway between *The Making of Americans* and *Tender Buttons,* Gertrude was not only writing as a cubist, but also availing herself of another new development, the twentieth-century art of the cinema. The changes in picture-space wrought by the cubists and the fantastic new uses of movement in the space of a movie screen both sprang from the interpenetration of space and time. Before long, spectators to either art would be as familiar with the painters' collage as with the moviemakers' montage. In Gertrude's early portraits, she used a method that is parallel to that of the film strip as the vehicle of a narrative sequence in time. When the process of the motion picture is compared with the process of one of her typical early portraits, the connection is unmistakable. Just as in the cinema each picture on the film strip looks like the picture preceding it and yet is slightly different, so are Gertrude Stein's successive sentences; each has been changed ever so slightly in the recording. The movement of a figure on the screen is apprehended as one flowing gesture when, actually, it is composed of a series of static movements following one another at great speed. In a Stein portrait the movement of figures has been slowed down to such an extent that it is as if the reader were looking at a film strip rolled out on a flat surface. A figure is not seen as moving in time, but as many static moments presented in succession. Yet the meaning of the movement is intended to be communicated summarily and at once.

In her conception, the significant thing upon which to base a portrait was not the words spoken, or the attitudes expressed, but the "sense of sound" produced. Like the painters, she had given up models per se. "It is strange," she said, "when you remember models were everything until the beginning of the twentieth century and now hardly any painter who interests anybody really has any realization that everybody used to have a model." She preferred not to imitate nature or to make a likeness, but to find the rhythm and the verbal color that would create a new thing rather than reproduce a familiar one. The sound sense served her as a parallel for the painters' color sense: "I take the conversational side of a number of people," she said, "almost everyone sooner or later has a perfectly determined rhythm in everything they do. It is not so much the words they speak, as the sense of the sound that they produce. That impression is what I have tried to set down. . . ."

In the nature of the case, each portrait is ultimately a partial portrait of Gertrude Stein herself. They exhibit her feelings when she thinks she is most successfully disguising them, and often show her reactions when she means to shed all traces of literal response. They provide angles of vision, or wave lengths, by which subjects are constituted in colors, images and sounds, yet they never present a picture that has anything but accidental objectivity. The fact that her portraits have names affixed to them is unimportant. Except in the cases of Matisse and Picasso and a few others when the subject is clearly related to an interpretive statement or, in some cases, where the subject is made obvious by references, she attempted to record a type rather than to indicate a personality. Impressions rather than portraits would seem to be the more exact term for these writings but, perhaps in revolt against impressionism as an outmoded style in painting and in literature, she found that term unacceptable. An impression suggests a subjective record of a remembered moment of perception; it was her attempt to *provide* the moment of perception, quite unrelated to a place in time and quite free of the information of memory. The justification of this moment of recognition would be that condition described by Apollinaire in *Les Peintres Cubistes*: "The picture will exist ineluctably. The vision will be entire, complete and its infinity, instead of indicating some imperfection, will simply express the relation between a newly created thing and a new creator, nothing more."

Ingenious analogies between the uses of language and those of painting or the cinema might give her one kind of support; fiat releasing the artist from the need to obey all rules and traditions in favor of his own sense of aesthetic necessity might give her another. In any case, Gertrude Stein had allied herself with a movement among artists that would not come to full definition until the many products of that movement would be viewed and assessed by minds less involved in its flights and postures than that of Apollinaire. Since the cubists addressed themselves to the world in utterances that were earnest, flowery, anarchic, insistent and often deliberately and self-assertively obscure, critics and art historians would spend decades separating their finespun theories from their actual practice. But one thing was clear from the beginning, and the practice of Gertrude Stein illustrates it with finality. Like many other poets and painters, she had attempted to create "a model of confusion," a metaphor for that modern state of mind in which the focus of interest is upon the simultaneity of the contents of consciousness; a state of mind in which the demands of present reality make memory and history inadmissible; a state of mind in which the sense of time becomes a perception of process, and experience is objectified in half-articulated fancies and amorphous fragments.

But no explanation, from her or from others, went far in pacifying even those readers who had remained devoted to her through the comparatively slight obliquities of her first two books. Pierre Roché, who had introduced her and Leo to Picasso, and who himself had literary ambitions, expressed himself in a somewhat Gallic version of the bewilderment that was now becoming the rule for all of her readers. "I reread that writing, I altogether sometimes love it," he wrote to Gertrude, "and things in it . . . it is a diamond mine? . . . but all the work of digging, finding, cleaning, polishing the stone remains to be done . . . too much sand is left. I get angry with you to spoil it for me by those d—— repetitions, by so many words duplicate. Many repetitions have great purpose and efficiency, but they have a sea of sisters which, I think, have perceivable meanings for nobody but you. I start reading your style only when I feel very strong and want in a way to suffer. After a few minutes I am giddy, then sea-sick, though there are islands to be seen — it is no river, no sea, *c'est une inondation, l'hiver dans la campagne.* More and more your style gets solitary — the vision remains great, and the glory of some occasional pages — Rhythm? Oh yes. But that sort of rhythm is intoxicating for you. . . . Quantity! Quantity! Is thy name woman? Of course it is very enjoyable to let oneself go and write heaps but . . . why don't you finish, correct, rewrite ten times the same chaotic material till it has its very shape worthy of its fullness? A condensation of 60 to 90% would often do? Do you know any one (human not literary) who, without knowing you, or the models of your portraits, or both, has understood something in them? Melanctha is great in my memory. I was quite at home with her, though I already had some toil. I thought your style would concentrate, it has enormously expanded. The last things stand upon the strength of your personality. Far from your eyes, they fall to pieces. Your own right faith in yourself shakes other people's doubts about your ways of expression — they probably do not tell them in front of you? Are you not after all very lazy? With frankness, humility and perhaps huge stupidity. Yours very sincerely, H. P. Roché."

In one document, this letter introduces nearly all the objections and reproaches the new work was soon to encounter. Gertrude was upset and offended. Roché had been among those who previously had praised, and only praised; she ignored his criticism and took refuge in a feminine and most uncharacteristic reply, telling Roché that he would never have written to a man in such a way, that he had taken advantage of her position as a woman. In his reply, Roché seemed somewhat chastened, but still firm: "I have spoken to you as to a man friend *et même comme à un camerade à une table de café.* . . . I thoroughly respect your work and your mind. I agree with you upon the quality of your art . . . (though not upon the inevitable character of *the whole* of its form today)."

Their exchange of letters put a temporary strain on the friendship, but Roché eventually withdrew the sharpest of his criticisms and, many years later, he and Gertrude were still on warm terms. He translated many of her shorter pieces into French and was instrumental in bringing her work to the attention of Jean Cocteau, one of the few French writers who had any idea of what she was about as an artist and one of the very few who not only looked upon her work with respect but held her personally in affection.

CHAPTER 11

Toasted Susie is my ice cream.
— GERTRUDE STEIN

    IN the spring of 1912, Gertrude went to Spain with Alice and there began to write a series of stark, lively and, to the general mind, ineluctably opaque literary exercises that were in many ways equivalents of the inside-out still lifes of the cubist painters. Two years later, when these were gathered into a volume and published under the collective title *Tender Buttons*, they appalled the world of letters, sent readers into fits of unamused laughter, and finally provoked the most exasperated reaction to greet any book of the twentieth century.

  Ancient Ávila, which they reached leisurely by way of Burgos, was their first important stopping place. Enchanted by a town held in medieval sanctuary by curving, deep-shadowed walls, Alice said she was prepared to settle in Ávila for the rest of her life. Gertrude felt this was nonsense; within ten days they proceeded on schedule to Valladolid and then went on to Madrid. Yet the brief visit had made an impression on Gertrude that was deep and would prove resonant.

Since she could adopt with proprietary finality even a saint, St. Teresa, the illustrious daughter of Ávila, to whom she had been devoted even as a child, was soon to become her very own. St. Teresa, Ávila, the surrounding landscape and the pigeons that seemed to hang flat against the sky — the very soul and substance of *Four Saints in Three Acts* — would before long enter the annals of the modern American theater.

The two ladies cut a fancy if not very wide figure in the capital city and, in their subsequent excursions into Andalusia, were greeted by the provincial Spaniards as curiosities. Gertrude customarily wore a brown corduroy skirt and a loose-pocketed jacket, a straw cap woven by a Florentine craftswoman, sandals (some of which had toes turned up like the prow of a gondola), and brandished an amber-headed cane. Except for one giddy note of contrast, Alice's "Spanish disguise," as she termed it, gave her a solemn and sacerdotal air: a long black silk pelisse, black gloves and a black hat. But the bright cluster of flowers that sprouted from her head made her look like a nun on a spree. Some of the peasants, believing them to be noblewomen, regarded them with unabashed awe and treated them with great shows of respect. In Cuença, Gertrude added to her costume an enormous turtle brooch made of rhinestones. When the interest of the local population got out of hand (under the impression, this time, that she was a bishop en route to a ceremony, part of a crowd pressed forward to kiss the ring on Gertrude's hand) the provincial governor offered to detail a policeman to accompany them. Such histrionic responses to their appearance unsettled them a bit at first, but soon they learned to turn their singularity into an asset. Later on, when they were staying at hotels in France, whenever anything was wrong with their food or living quarters, or Gertrude's inveterate need for maximum comfort was inadequately prepared for, Alice would proceed to the manager. "*La Baronne*," she would announce darkly, "*n'est pas satisfaite!*"

In Madrid they joined their friend Georgiana King of Bryn Mawr and during their visit discovered the dancer Argentina, and attended all of her recitals. Alice, whose geniuses ran in threes, considered herself particularly expert as a judge of dancing. In her triumvirate of "really great dancers," Argentina joined Isadora Duncan and Nijinsky. She was less delighted when Gertrude insisted on taking her to bullfights, but soon found she was able to endure, if not enjoy, the often fairly brutal spectacle. Moving on to Granada, they took rooms at the Washington Irving Hotel, familiar to Gertrude from an earlier visit with Leo just after the Spanish-American War. From there they would descend daily into the city, passing beside the glowing pink walls of the Alhambra in the long shadow of its towers. Granada, provincial, shrunken, bristling with proud grandees who ruled over vestiges of Roman and Moorish conquest, was a lively and sophisticated city, but the attritions of time that had reduced its influence to the very margins of Spanish history could not be disguised. To live in history and yet be no part of it was always the happiest creative situation for Gertrude. Like the cyclorama of Waterloo that she never forgot, Granada was "all there," a surrounding reality, and yet one could take absolute leave of it at any moment. As she wandered through its streets, her eyes might have sometime lighted on the slightly limping figure of the schoolboy Federico Garcia Lorca. But while the greatest of modern Spanish poets was to grow up and come to his tragic death during her lifetime, her devotion to Spain and Spaniards was never to include Lorca or, in fact, to be touched by any awareness of his contribution to literature.

She was now in the habit of working every day, settled in the hotel whose windows gave out on groves of whispering cypresses or, at times, sitting "in the court of the Alhambra watching the swallows fly in and out of the crevices of the walls, bathing in the soft air filled with the fragrance of myrtle and oleander and letting the hot sun burn her face and the palms of her hands." In the course of the sojourn at Granada the significance of her new departure in technique struck with a conviction that overwhelmed her and made her buoyant. Long concerned with the workings of the human mind, the endlessly fascinating but finally predictable reactions of personalities, she now had a new goal: description that would express "the rhythm of the visible world." Her great catalogue of human responses had been filled; for too long she had continued to be the scientist with a notebook, recording mechanically instead of registering the nervous and revealing shocks of imagination and fancy. To weigh the balance toward that side of her personality where the artist was dominant she began a series of improvisations upon nature, then moved on to further improvisations upon domestic objects. Like the cubist painters, and like the psychologists under whom she had been trained, her concern was not with appearances but with relationships. The whole visible world would be her field. Working easily and with speed she completed *Susie Asado, Preciosilla* and *Gypsies in Spain.* It was as if she had suddenly broken new trails through the forest of words in which she continually dwelt, by finding the metaphorical relationship between sight and sound. "This metaphoric process," wrote Donald Sutherland, "or rather this metamorphosis by words is, with differences, a little like the distortions of Matisse in color and line or like the more complete conversions in the cubist paintings of Picasso. That is, as Matisse seeing a fairly rich curve or a pleasant spot of color in the subject matter would exaggerate these into a sumptuous curve or a gorgeous area of color on his canvas, and as Picasso would make any approximately flat or approximately angular surface in the subject matter into a very definite quadrangle on canvas, so Gertrude Stein, intensifying and converting the original qualities of the subject matter by isolation and metaphor, winds up with a result that exists in and for itself, as the paintings do."

But as she followed new trails, misunderstanding and controversy followed her. In ordering his impressions of her work through the period of *Tender Buttons,* Edmund Wilson in his great study *Axel's Castle* finds that typical pieces "would be analogous to a Cubist canvas composed of unidentifiable fragments." But after this exact perception of what she was aiming at, Wilson goes on to identify Gertrude Stein with the heirs of French symbolism and thereby deserts the means that might have urged him to make for her the same significant place in his critical pantheon that he made for Proust, Joyce, Eliot and Valéry. It was Wilson's feeling that "she has out-distanced any of the Symbolists in using words for pure purposes of suggestion — she has gone so far that she no longer even suggests. We see the ripples expanding in her consciousness, but we are no longer supplied with any clew as to what kind of object has sunk there."

Actually, she had not outdistanced the symbolists, but had taken an entirely different road. Like her French contemporaries among poets she was in revolt against the heavily aesthetic character of symbolism and its dependence, finally, upon sentiment, assertion and posture. As far as she was concerned, that movement was a matter of a history only the last echoes of which had ever reached her. Furthermore, symbolism was French and she was American, the heiress of the legacy of Henry James and of all that had gone on under the boundless American sky. "One's great objection to the Symbolist school," wrote André Gide, "is its lack of curiosity about life . . . all were pessimistic, renunciants, resignationists, 'tired of the sad hospital' which the earth seemed to them — our 'monotonous and unmerited fatherland,' as Laforgue called it. Poetry had become for them a refuge, the only escape from the hideous realities; they threw themselves into it with a desperate fervor." On intellectual as well as temperamental terms, it is inconceivable that Gertrude Stein could have had any creative connection with a movement so described. Alfred Jarry, far more than Gertrude Stein, is the writer whose qualifications make him the rightful occupant of the place at the ultra end of the symbolist spectrum. Since Edmund Wilson's book has had an enormous influence on academic minds, his tendency to place her in the symbolist dispensation has very likely contributed more to her neglect by responsible critics than any other factor — always saving, of course, the forbidding length and billboard breadth to which she protracted her illustrations of ideas about language and consciousness.

The symbolists, for all their dislocations of thought and chromatic syntheses of language, still worked in reference to the body of known literature and myth. Their aim was representation — by distortion, in suggestions, from highly individual perspectives — of ideas and feelings whose counterparts are the matrix of the world's literature. When they eventually dared to substitute feelings for ideas, to attempt a conquest of reality by emotion, they were simply exploring, by processes of extension and refinement, a new way of providing creative liberation.

156

The cubists, on the other hand, abjured myth, tradition and all the emotions that were the residual part of their associations. To create unique objects — a painting or a poem that would not confirm a truth, or newly dramatize an old subject — they produced visual and verbal artifacts which were in themselves objects of aesthetic contemplation. Until this absolute separation of aims is made clear; until, in the words of Apollinaire, the cubist enumeration is seen as "so complete and decisive of the various elements which make up the object that these do not take the shape of the object," the critic is tempted to apply to cubist creations rules and expectations that the cubist writer or painter has cast aside. Unlike the symbolists, the cubists — at least in the emergent phase of the synthetic period which most influenced *Tender Buttons* — drew less upon the unfettered imagination or the irrational depths of the psyche than upon the ability of the intellect to make surprising new compositions out of the familiar accoutrements of café and studio life. "I was very much struck at this period," said Gertrude Stein, "with the way Picasso could put objects together and make a photograph of them. . . . To have brought the objects together already changed them to other things, not to another picture but to something else, to things as Picasso saw them."

Concentrating upon the lettering and labels of wine and cognac bottles, pipes, tobacco papers, matches, chair-backs, table tops, playing cards and dice, the cubists had turned from the refinements of traditional painting to scenes composed of vulgar, inconsequential elements which they attempted to fuse poetically and make radiant. In a similar turning, Gertrude Stein took naturally to the homely iconography of household life — to "Objects Food Rooms" — in her exploration of the literary possibilities of cubism. A carafe, a box, a plate; celery, asparagus, sausages and salmon — real things in a real room — were her subjects and she attempted to give them a reality that would be poetically fresh and new and yet as solid as the simple reality that might present itself to a household visitor. She did not allow these objects to keep their natural presences, but used them in conjunctions that made a kind of super-synaesthesia in which colors are suggested by activities, sounds by statements and shapes by attitudes. Beginning psychology classes are familiar with the experiment in which the instructor asks his students to shut their eyes while he scrapes the blackboard to produce an intolerable sound which, at the same time, causes a distinct flash of color in the "blind" vision of those who hear it. Deliberate confusion of the senses was part of Gertrude Stein's attempt to provide a shock of attention that would, literally, recreate the experiences implicit in the congeries of her subjects.

In this attempt to apprehend purely, to break through the devices of literature into untrammeled perception, Gertrude Stein used means she had borrowed from painters with utter strictness. She had become one of those writers of whom Picasso said: "Often while reading a book one feels that the author would have preferred to paint rather than to write; one can sense the pleasure he derives from describing a landscape or a person, as if he were painting what he is saying, because deep in his heart he would have preferred to use brushes and colors. . . ." Other writers at the very same time — notably the American and English poets of the imagist movement — attempted to record a similar purity of apprehension. Yet these writers all remained well within the bounds of literary propriety. While it was apparent that the early poems of a poet like William Carlos Williams had unmistakable affinities with the new painting, and that some of his poems could best be understood in terms of cubist techniques, no one could have accused Williams of having tried to paint with his pen. With her childlike literalness, Gertrude Stein was wide open to such an accusation and, in fact, invited it.

Tender Buttons appeared in 1914, published in New York by Claire Marie, a little firm devoted to "New Books for Exotic Tastes." Of Gertrude, the advance brochure said: "She is a ship that flies no flag and she is outside the law of art, but she descends on every port and leaves a memory of her visits. . . . The last shackle is struck from context and collocation, and each unit of the sentence stands independent and has no commerce with its fellows. The effect produced on the first reading is something like terror. . . ." The book proved to be a *succès de scandale,* yet received little serious critical attention, was of no influence whatsoever upon writers and caused no tremor in the course of literary history. Nevertheless, for what they might eventually be worth, Gertrude had made constructions as revolutionary in terms of literature as were the collages, or *papiers collés* as they were sometimes called, of Picasso and Braque in terms of painting. The release provided by the painters changed everything and everyone and made the character of a generation; that provided by Gertrude Stein changed nothing and no one and made only publicity.

In the portraits, as she explained, her method was concentrated upon "the perfectly determined rhythm" that all individuals exhibit, and in "the sense of sound they produce." In *Tender Buttons*, she had tried "to do the same of bodies; that is to say, to get the same sort of feeling out of things that I have gotten out of people. You see, I happen to have a literal mind that thinks things are always based on a perfectly literal and definite appearance and sound that I perceive. If you have anything as literal as that, I have a perfect conviction that you are bound to have a good many people who will understand it, and as a matter of fact you do."

In attempting to "express things seen not as one knows them but as they are when one sees them without remembering having looked at them," Picasso was forced to do away with the sense of a picture as a window through which objects were seen as maintaining their ordinary relationships. When this step was made, distortion was no longer a degree of departure from a norm but the basis of a method. Gertrude's description of this point of view as it applies to Picasso's work exactly accommodates her own: "A child sees the face of its mother, it sees it in a completely different way than other people see it, I am not speaking of the spirit of the mother but of the features and the whole face, the child sees it from very near, it is a large face for the eyes of a small one, it is certain the child for a little while only sees a part of the face of its mother, it knows one feature and not another, one side and not the other, and in his way Picasso knows faces as a child knows them and the head and the body. He was then commencing to try to express this consciousness. . . ."

In the following paraphrase of Gertrude's description of the basis of Picasso's working method, precisely similar ideas governing her own

159

work show clearly. "Really most of the time one sees only a feature of a person with whom one is, the other features are covered by a hat, by the light, by clothes for sport and everybody is accustomed to complete the whole entirely from their knowledge, but Gertrude Stein when she saw an eye, the other one did not exist for her and only the one she saw did exist for her and as a writer, and particularly an American writer, she was right, one sees what one sees, the rest is a reconstruction from memory and writers have nothing to do with reconstructions, nothing to do with memory, they concern themselves only with visible things and so the writing of Gertrude Stein was an effort to make a composition of these visible things and the result was disconcerting for her and for the others, but what else could she do, a creator can only do one thing, she can only continue, that is all she can do."

True to her intention, *Tender Buttons* was concerned only with visible things. Her interest in people, types, classifications of emotional and mental states had been forgotten; she was now interested only in surfaces, in appearances. She attempted to perceive these without reference to what her memory might make of them, without concern for their time-honored places in the scheme of things and to record them in words regarded as objects rather than as references to objects. This abrogation of the conventional order of relations among things and the mind that perceives them represented a kind of deliberate barbarism. French poets had already made similar gestures, and critics had not only justified their bravado but declared it necessary. "It is only in that moment when words are freed from their literal meaning," said Pierre Reverdy, "that they take on in the mind a poetic value. It is at that moment that they can be freely placed in the poetic reality." In a lecture given in 1911, André Gide had quoted Charles-Louis Phillippe's formula, "The time of sweetness and dilettantism is over. What we need now, are barbarians." Commenting upon this statement, Gide said: "The curious thing is that it is through culture that [Phillippe] becomes aware of the *legitimacy* of this feeling." Other critics interpreted the formula to mean simply that they should renounce bookish art and give an account of their experience. But Gertrude Stein's statement was the clearest of all. "I would not know," she said simply, "what I knew."

The critic Marcel Raymond saw this concept of experience as closely related to that of William James, in which "Experience becomes a sense of certainty that penetrates one's whole being and stirs one like a revelation; a state of euphoria that seems to give the world to man and persuades him that he 'possesses' it. But it is accessible only to those who free themselves from habitual vision, from utilitarian convention. . . . To become a barbarian by means of patient and progressive de-intellectualization is, first of all, to receive sensations and to leave them a certain amount of free play, not to place them in a logical frame-work and not to attribute them to the objects which produced them; it is a method of detaching oneself from an inherited civilized form in order to rediscover a greater plasticity and expose oneself to the imprint of things."

Barbarism of this nature is not primitivism and yet, to the tutored eye, its products often seem highly alike. The experience of the primitive, like that of the child, controls his expression and tends to keep him at its mercy. The experience of the "barbarian," by contrast, is selective and controlled. "By combining the functions of critic and poet," wrote Laura Riding, "and taking everything around her very literally and many things for granted which others have not been naïve enough to take so, she has done what every one else has been ashamed to do. No one but Miss Stein has been willing to be as ordinary as simple . . . as stupid, as barbaric as successful barbarism demands. Does no one but Miss Stein realize that to be abstract, mathematical, thematic, anti-Hellenic, anti-Renaissancist, anti-romantic, we must be barbaric?"

In choosing to practice this sort of barbarism, through no inability to practice forms sanctioned by her culture, but under a compulsion to sweep away the underpinnings of language and rhetoric, Gertrude Stein had inevitably approached the point at which literature is no longer cursive but discrete and abstract. In her own insistent belief, however, the vitality of her free transcription of experience was anything *but* abstract, since she felt that anyone could see that "things as they are" lived on her pages, unadorned and without props.

By 1912, Picasso too had come to a point just short of abstraction and his immediate influence on her progress cannot be discounted. Other painters — Malevitch, Kandinsky and Mondrian in particular — were soon to go beyond the phase of collage with which Picasso and Braque were importantly associated, toward pure abstraction, dispensing with subjects and even their physical attributes. But Picasso kept a slim and playful grip on reality, or representation, by his ingenious manipulations of recognizable, if often highly disparate, materials. Since Gertrude Stein could not move into pure abstraction without first making up a synthetic language, *Tender Buttons* remains within the cubist development of collage and can be best explained by references to it. Her "poems" are compositions, but they have neither idea nor theme; they ask the reader to pay attention, not to a writer with a message but to a literary gymnast attempting to put down thought-in-the-process-of-being-recorded. These compositions represent a private ordering, rhythmic and visual, of materials one can recognize easily enough, but which serve to convey no programmatic meaning. She worked as meticulously as Picasso in this free play of the plastic imagination, but the ambiguity and associative penumbra of any given word as opposed to the plastic definiteness of any object guarantees defeat in her efforts to make the verbal equivalent of collage.

Nevertheless, she did to her own satisfaction make versions of collage —"There can be the message where the print is pasted," she wrote — and if the results of her methods do not invite analysis in any terms except those in which one might explore the findings of a Rorschach test, the sources of her method are easy to apprehend simply because they parallel with complete fidelity the methods of Picasso. According to Frank Elgar, "Picasso used to take a sheet of paper as his ground. Then he would cut up natural substances — wood, etc. — and glue them on the sheet. These he surrounded or covered with lines and light shading. At first he produced some very graphic and airy compositions in this way. Later, as the fragments of alien material became increasingly important, the finished works became more compact and solid, finally acquiring an obvious and convincing harmony. In the *Bottle of Old Marc, with Glass and Newspaper* (1912), for instance, all the objects were drawn except for the newspaper, which is actually a newspaper-cutting, and the piece of wallpaper stuck on the table. In the *Bottle, Glass and Violin,* which dates from the winter of 1912, the news-cutting indicates the shape of the bottle, while the imitation wood suggests the violin. In yet another still-life the extraneous elements are used only for spatial definition: the *Student with the Pipe* (1913-14) shows a face which is mischievously suggested by straight lines and a few curves, topped by a dark beret made of gummed paper." With these works (*Student with the Pipe* for a time was part of Gertrude's collection), Elgar goes on to say, ". . . the hermetic Cubism practiced from 1911 onwards was heading, by 1913, towards a more accommodating and broad-minded conception altogether. The meticulous arrangements of details, the breaking-up of forms and proliferations of minute volumes which are all typical of what has been described as 'analytical Cubism' . . . could not survive after the success of the *collage* technique."

The exact parallel in Gertrude Stein's development away from the analytical cubist phase of *Many Many Women* into the collage phase of *Tender Buttons* is notable (even her titles bear a close similarity to the titles of collages) and her explorations of post-cubist possibilities were soon to be as various and free as Picasso's. She had made a revolution and urged its success into constantly broadening phases of freedom. But it was a private revolution in an empty palace. The freedom it made possible was necessary to no one but herself. Daring to do what other writers had merely contemplated or what other writers had vaguely entertained — as an architect of skyscrapers might, on a day off, think of putting up a cantilevered doghouse — she had been courageous, but she had also made clear how quickly a poet could reach the vasts of lunar silence. Sooner or later somebody was bound to make such experiments, if only to make sure that the landscape of the moon could not support human life. Gertrude Stein brought back proof that, as long as literature involves the responsibilities of the rational mind, the known world is its only planet. She published her findings which, in spite of her hopes, still smacked of laboratory data, and she became famous. Whatever she did after this would be looked upon with either absolute outrage or unquestioning respect. Everything depended upon the feelings of the observer about the value of documents from the moon. It was easy to say that she was foolish, and nearly everybody did. But for people concerned with literature as an infinitely viable art, she had approached with heroic singleness, and perhaps had solved, a crucial problem — whether or not is it possible to have an absolutely personal idiom and still have communicable meaning.

While Picasso silently supported her through *Tender Buttons* (since he did not read English, he had no notion, except through hearsay, that she was his literary counterpart), another source of confidence and one in no way dependent upon the theories of painters was her long-held conviction that words preceded ideas in the development of culture. She believed that in every new period of literary achievement the sense of words as entities to be played with, jumbled, reversed and made into patterns, was abundantly evident. "The English from Chaucer to the Elizabethans," she wrote, "played with words they endlessly played with words because it was such an exciting thing to have them there words that had come to be the words they had just come to use then . . . In the early English writing words did move around they moved by themselves we get that with the period that ended with the end of the Elizabethans, words moved then, they made their own existing they were there and they enjoyed that thing they enjoyed being there the words did and any one having anything to do with them anything to do with the words being there knew that of them knew that the words were enjoying that thing were enjoying being there."

In all of English literature, the high point of the consciousness of words as pliable and tangible entities was, she felt, the Elizabethan era, when Shakespeare "teased words and amused himself." Even Swift, she felt, referring to his tract on the Irish beggars, "had a poignant sense of the quality and weight and native force of words." But gradually, towards the end of the eighteenth century, this sense became grandiose and then moribund. By the nineteenth century, the rich old sense of words had almost been forgotten. The only way to recover this property of words, she believed, was to reconstruct the very sense of words and that was what she and her

American predecessors had done: "In the American writing words began to have inside themselves those same words that in the English were completely quiet or very slowly moving began to have within themselves the consciousness of completely moving, they began to detach themselves from the solidity of anything, they began to excitedly feel themselves as if they were anywhere or anything, think about American writing from Emerson, Hawthorne Walt Whitman Mark Twain Henry James myself . . . and you will see what I mean, as well as in advertising . . . words left alone more and more feel that they are moving and all of it is detached and is detaching anything from anything and in this detaching and in this moving it is being in its way creating its existing."

The influence of William James can be read in every example of her work up to *Tender Buttons*, yet she did not care to admit, or did not fully realize, the extent of his dominance. *The Making of Americans* and works just after it, with their emphasis upon the continuous disengaged present, their insistence on the Jamesian time-sense, read like literary illustrations of a psychologist's theories. And yet, even as late as 1914, Gertrude could say: "It does not follow that the strongest impression is produced by the strongest mind. It just happened by accident or circumstance that I came under the influence of William James, but I have not yet found the expression of that influence or impression."

Alice Toklas suggests that, since Gertrude did not consciously think that her writing methods were related to, or generated by, ideas of James's, this statement is literally true. Gertrude still preferred to think of James as an influence on her personality, rather than as a source of her writing career. However, since she was shy about admitting to the slightest literary influence from any quarter, she seems to have suffered, in this instance, from a temporary case of myopia. This lapse represents an exception among the insights into her own development she continually named and tried to elaborate before any audience that would listen to her. Like a scientist obsessed, she had for the moment taken all measures — all, that is to say, but her own.

CHAPTER 12

A door should be a door must be a door should
and must be open or closed. Close the door and
draw the shades. Close the shutter and open the
window. Open the window and open the door.
Anybody can make that song.
Thank you very much.

— GERTRUDE STEIN

AMONG the friends whom Gertrude's
friends brought to "27" was Mabel Dodge, a wealthy American with a
decided taste for art and artists and an indefatigable flair for entertaining personalities who were indiscriminately famous for their charm,
notoriety or accomplishments. Mrs. Dodge, who seemed to spend
all of her days in the restless center of a portable *salon*, had for a time
settled near Florence with her architect husband Edwin, in a house
they had reconstructed to their own design — the Villa Curonia,
Via delle Piazzole, Arcetri. When Gertrude and Alice returned from
their momentous visit to Spain, they were pleased to accept an invitation to come to the Villa Curonia as house guests.

Gertrude's friendship with her hostess had not previously been
close, but she had warmly responded to the enthusiasm Mabel
Dodge had shown toward *The Making of Americans* which she had
read in manuscript. "It is one of the most remarkable things I have
ever read," she told Gertrude in a letter. "There are things ham-

mered out of consciousness into black & white that have never been expressed before — so far as I know. States of being put into words the 'noumenon' captured — as few have done it. To name a thing is practically to create it & this is what your work is — real creation. It is almost frightening to come up against reality in this way. I always get — as I told you — the shivers when I read your things. And your palette is such a simple one — the primary colors in word painting & you express every shade known & unknown with them. It is as new & strong & big as the post-impressionists in their way &, I am perfectly convinced, it is the forerunner of a whole epoch of new form & expression. It is very morally instructive for I feel it will alter reality as we have known it, & help us to get at Truth instead of away from it as 'literature' so sadly often does."

Gertrude arrived at the Villa Curonia on a hot day wearing, in the description of her hostess, "a sort of kimono made of brown corduroy . . . just sweating, her face parboiled. And when she sat down, fanning herself with her broad-brimmed hat with its wilted, dark-brown ribbon, she exhaled a vivid steam all around her. When she got up she frankly used to pull her clothes off from where they had stuck to her great legs. Yet with all this she was not at all repulsive. On the contrary, she was positively, richly attractive in her grand *ampleur*. She always seemed to like her own fat anyway and that usually helps other people to accept it. She had none of the funny embarrassment Anglo-Saxons have about the flesh. She gloried in hers."

In the study of Edwin Dodge who, at the time, was in America, Gertrude worked by candlelight deep into the night during her stay at the villa. Writing only four or five lines to the page in her prodigal longhand, she would leave a pile of manuscript for Alice to gather up and type in the morning. Her preoccupation, much to Mrs. Dodge's relief, had apparently blinded her to the romantic drama that was being enacted almost in her presence.

In the absence of her husband, Mabel Dodge reported in her memoirs, she had "unwittingly" made a conquest in the person of her young son's tutor, a twenty-two-year-old football player, a "blond white boy" whom she found "sweet like fresh hay and honey and milk." One night, as Gertrude labored late, this paragon made his way past the door of her study and urged his way into Mabel's room. The walls were thick; still, Mrs. Dodge was apprehensive. When she put her ear to the wall, there was no sound; she concluded that Gertrude was deaf to every voice but that of inspiration. Several hours later, when the moon was down, Mabel had successfully repulsed the young man's prolonged advances, but not before he had whispered, "I love you so — and the wonderful thing about you is that you're so *good!*" On this note of controlled ardor he had taken his "last, fresh fire," as Mabel described it, past the room where Gertrude, "like a great Sibyl dim against the red and gold damask," scrawled out her syllables.

Mabel Dodge, whom Gertrude in turn and in kind described as "a stoutish woman with a very sturdy fringe of heavy hair over her forehead, heavy long lashes and very pretty eyes and a very old-fashioned coquetry," professed not to be able to understand the personality of Alice Toklas. While Mrs. Dodge would have been the first to admit that she could not understand herself, either (she was once described as "an enigma in search of enigmas"), she thought Alice's lot in life must have been insupportably dull. The only self-interested thing about Alice, she noticed, was an obsession for the care of her fingernails which, daily, she trimmed and polished by the hour. When Mabel Dodge asked her what it was that kept her seemingly so much at peace with the world, Alice replied simply, "My feeling for Gertrude." They were never to become friends. In Alice's aristocratic view, Mabel Dodge was doomed to remain all her life hopelessly *arriviste*.

Nevertheless, Mrs. Dodge valued Gertrude for reasons that many other people were not alert enough to grasp or not charitable enough to allow. She felt that Gertrude, as Leo's first disciple, had learned the necessity of being absolutely free to react to paintings as well as to people, to count upon one's own subjective taste as a first principle. This, according to Mabel Dodge, "made her daring in a snobbish period of art. I remember she adored those ridiculous miniature alabaster fountains, with two tiny white doves poised on the brink, that tourists bought at the shops on the Lung 'Arno, and she had a penchant for forget-me-not mosaic brooches, and all kinds of odds and ends that she liked much as a child liked things." As for more valuable objects, Gertrude was not concerned whether they were *bon goût* or not, *quattrocento* or pre-Raphaelite. Her pleasure, independent of origins or stylish classifications, was always her own point of judgment.

Many other guests came and went during their sojourn at the Villa Curonia, and one who particularly charmed them was Constance Fletcher, who was included in Gertrude's gallery of early portraits and, many years later, introduced as one of the dramatis personae of her last opera. A native of Newburyport, Massachusetts, Constance Fletcher had come to Italy with her mother and her mother's lover who, in their New England home, had been the household tutor. Sensitive, even as a very young child, to the scandal that shadowed her family life, Constance grew up in the Venetian *palazzo* of her errant mother and stepfather and took secretly to writing romantic novels. One of these, published under the pseudonym of "George Fleming," was *Kismet*. When the book became a bestseller, her secret vocation was exposed and, to her acute distress, the family scandal was revived. But the surprising turn of events had provided temporary emancipation from her cloistered life in Venice. As a free woman and a famous author, she went to England, made the acquaintance of Oscar Wilde and Henry James and became engaged, for an extraordinarily long time, to the grandson of Byron, Lord Lovelace. When Lord Lovelace jilted her and went off to Africa, leaving her with lavish gifts of jewels and letters of Byron that had served Henry James as a basis for his short novel, *The Aspern Papers*, she took on a legendary reputation that lasted for the rest of her days. After a successful career as a playwright in London she was gradually drawn back to Venice and into the shadows left by her deceased mother. There, with elaborate daily rituals, she and her sentimental stepfather maintained the memory of her strong-minded mother, strewing the staircase where she once had walked with rose petals. Living perpetually in her troubled past, Constance Fletcher believed she had developed a private pipe line to ghosts that swarmed *palazzi* along the grand canal. When, as often happened, knockings and

169

strange whooshings occurred during the night at the Villa Curonia, she simply took it for granted that she was being visited by one or the other of her departed friends. Her morning-after stories of these visitations drove other guests out of their wits.

André Gide came to the villa for an evening but, in the bleak testimony of his *Journals*, the occasion was not memorable. He and Gertrude had nothing to say to one another. Their failure to find common ground may be put down to differences in personality since, in terms of their respective work, they had more in common than either suspected. Each in his own way, they had perhaps come closer to realizing cubism in literature than any other two authors living. In his novel, *The Counterfeiters*, as the American critic Wylie Sypher has pointed out, Gide had accomplished on the ideational plane of literature certain realizations of cubist methods that Gertrude had begun to achieve on a strictly plastic plane.

The writing of two new portraits — one of her hostess, the famous *Portrait of Mabel Dodge at the Villa Curonia*, and one of Constance Fletcher — occupied Gertrude daily during the length of her visit. Within a few years, the line with which the Mabel Dodge portrait began was to become one of the particular counters of a select circle of the avant-garde: "The days are wonderful and the nights are wonderful and the life is pleasant." After this mild and fairly insipid beginning, the portrait was continued in little paragraphs:

Bargaining is something and there is not that success. The intention is what if application has that accident results are reappearing. They did not darken. That was not an adulteration.

So much breathing has not the same place when there is that much beginning. So much breathing has not the same place when the ending is lessening. So much breathing has the same place and there must not be so much suggestion. There can be there the habit that there is if there is no need of resting. The absence is not alternative.

Any time is the half of all the noise and there is not that disappointment. There is no distraction. An argument is clear.

Several pages later the *Portrait* is concluded with this paragraph:

There is all there is when there has all there has where there is what there is. That is what is done when there is done what is done and the union is won and the division is the explicit visit. There is not all of any visit.

Unlike most of Gertrude's works, the *Portrait of Mabel Dodge* interested Leo and moved him quickly to write a criticism, by way of emulation, which he sent off to his sister at once.

Size is not circumference unless magnitude extends [Leo wrote]. Purpose defined in limitation projected. It is the darkness whose center is light.
Hardly can the movement arrest. Formality is subservience. Liquidation confluent with purpose by involution elaborates the elemental. Its significance protracts but virtue is dissimulated.
All men are so but not in all ways. It is the thought process but not detached. Relations may be elaborated and hence illumination. Though the mole is blind the earth is one.

Gertrude took his critical parody in good grace, and Leo was confounded. "Gertrude and even Alice have the cheek to pretend that they understand this (which I can do in part sometimes)," he wrote to Mabel Weeks, "but as Gertrude thought it very nice and I had very sarcastical intentions we evidently didn't understand it the same way." But Mabel Dodge was so flattered by her portrait that she had it published at once in an edition of three hundred copies bound in Florentine paper. She suggested to Gertrude that it might be profitable for her to become a sort of wandering bluestocking minstrel, and go from country house to country house doing word portraits of the gentry.

Back in Paris, *salon* life at "27" flourished, but Gertrude was restless and dissatisfied. For nearly ten years she had been a prolific and dedicated writer. In her literary storeroom, manuscript was piled upon manuscript; and in spite of the enthusiasms of influential friends, not one publisher showed interest in the new works or in their author. No longer interested in paying her own printers' bills, Gertrude was convinced that her work would and should find its way onto the list of a publisher of reputation. When a friend suggested that John Lane, a leading English publisher, was not averse to considering unorthodox literature, she decided to make a brief trip to England in January, 1913.

On arriving there, she and Alice stayed at the home of a Colonel and Mrs. Rogers in Riverhill, Surrey. In the rituals of country living in the English manner, they loved the pervasive air of comfort, the perpetually burning open fires, the tall maids who stood about "like angels of the annunciation," the formal gardens and polite children, and the way in which all of these things seemed to exist mysteriously in some preordained harmony. Gertrude settled easily into the pleasures of the grand household, but was irritated by the continual flow of random conversation that was always coursing through it. The unceasing flow of the human voice, particularly when it spoke English and was not her own, ruffled her good nature and made her seclude herself for hours on end.

But comfort and largess were never anathema to Gertrude Stein; the business trip began to take on the character of a holiday. They moved on to the country house of Roger Fry, whom they had known from his many visits to "27." Having served as Director of the Metropolitan Museum in New York from 1905 to 1910 and as adviser to J. P. Morgan's activities as an art collector, "Fry, the aesthete, sensitively on the defensive, jaundicedly anti-American and anti-millionaire," in the description of Aline B. Saarinen, had by this time returned to London and deep involvement in the careers of the rising Bloomsbury group. Gertrude regarded the society of Bloomsbury as "the Young Men's Christian Society — with Christ left out," but she was fond of Fry, whose interests were now centered in the progress of his Omega Workshops in Fitzroy Square, where carefully coached craftsmen were busy making adaptations of primitive forms in an effort, it was naïvely hoped, to counteract the spreading influence of industrialism and mass production. In the excitement of his new associations, Fry had moved away from his brilliant yet largely conservative position as a critic to become the champion and promoter of the postimpressionists, to whom he stood in much the same relation as William Morris had stood in relation to the pre-Raphaelites. The art world, or at least its overwhelmingly conservative numbers, had not yet recovered from the shock of his new declaration of allegiance. When the English public was introduced to the new era in French painting through an exhibition Fry

organized in November, 1910 — "Manet and the Post-Impressionists"— it had responded with enthusiasm but also with many signs
of outrage and dismay. "I do not suppose there were fifty people in
England who had looked at pictures of Matisse or Picasso," wrote
Clive Bell, "but all true lovers of art knew instinctively that they
hated them." The show was a financial and promotional success
and a second, even more radical, postimpressionist exhibition was
hung at the Grafton Galleries in 1912. Primitivism became a rage
in England and artifacts from the far corners of the Empire were
suddenly objects of the closest scrutiny. According to Clive Bell,
"Galleries and museums in which were to be found collections of
the primitive and exotic were frequented; and directors of ethnological
departments were perplexed by an influx of lively and inquisitive
visitors, while the poor guardians in the remoter parts of the British
Museum and Victoria and Albert had their slumbers cruelly disturbed."

Fry's pronounced enthusiasm for Gertrude's work was a natural
outgrowth of his broad new interests. "Why," he wondered, were all
British novelists, "engrossed in childish problems of photographic
representation?" Once he had convinced himself that subject matter in art was not of importance, Fry began to find evidences of
support for his position in the works of new painters who sought,
first of all, "systems of relations," and to find further corroboration
in the poems of Mallarmé. Over a period of twenty years he translated many of these and eventually published a book of them. Fry
felt that painters had opened new avenues by returning to "the ideas
of formal design which had been almost lost sight of in the fervid
pursuit of naturalistic representation." Having taken a first in Natural Science tripos at Cambridge, Fry continued his training in explorations of art. Edith Sitwell, in her contribution to the collection of memoirs, *Coming to London,* recalls one of his experiments:
"Mr. Fry invented an instrument, consisting of a piece of string and
a lump of lead, that would register the exact amount of emotion felt
by the person holding it, when brought, for the first time, into the
presence of a great work of art. The legend goes that Mr. Fry, was
taken, for the first time (string in hand) into the presence of a green

173

apple painted by Cézanne, and that the apparatus went completely berserk, striking him violently, first in the stomach, and then upon the forehead, and knocking him unconscious."

When Fry turned his scientific eyes on literature, some of his friends felt that he aimed at reducing all the beauties of the art to a secondary place and that his overwhelming interest lay in formula and abstraction. On one occasion — using Milton's *Ode on the Nativity* as his model — he made up a gibberish poem which, he believed, maintained the essential force of the original poem without "cluttering" it with images. A man who could believe this would naturally find the work of Gertrude Stein made to his order.

On Sunday afternoons Gertrude and Alice attended the regular weekly *salon* of John Lane in London. Lane's wife, an American, had read *Three Lives* and had been sufficiently impressed by it to recommend to her husband that he think of publishing it. When he began to speak seriously about plans for bringing it out, Gertrude wrote to Mabel Dodge, "We are having a very amusing time here and as yet nothing is decided but John Lane and the English Review are nibbling. John Lane is an awfully funny man. He waits around and asks a question and you think he has got you and then you find he hasn't. Roger Fry is going to try to help him land me. . . ." Her hopes for John Lane would ultimately be realized, but the *English Review* did not consider her quite the catch she considered herself. The editor's note read curtly: "Dear Madam, I really cannot publish these curious studies. Yours very truly, Austin Harrison." With the exception of John Lane, literary London showed a vast and adamantine indifference to Gertrude's offerings. Yet she could take heart in news from New York, where Mabel Dodge was beating drums and heralding Messiah. "You are just on the eve of bursting," she wrote. "Everybody wherever I go — & others who go where I don't say the same thing — is talking of Gertrude Stein!"

CHAPTER 13

Hurrah for *gloire*. — GERTRUDE STEIN
This will be a *scream!* — MABEL DODGE

INDEPENDENT to the point of icono-
clasm, Gertrude Stein pursued her own methods in a career remote
from the general world of letters and marginal to the interests of
nearly everyone but herself. A phenomenon for which no one
could adequately account, a kind of cultural sport, she was unique
because she was the only writer in the English language who transcribed literally the lessons of non-literal painting. As a camp follower
of the intrepid bands of artists who ranged the slopes of Montmartre and the boulevards of Montparnasse, it was only natural that
she be introduced to her native American countrymen just when the
painters were making their sensational overseas debut. The event
serving her and them — the epochal Armory Show — opened in
New York on February 17, 1913, and later moved on to the Art
Institute of Chicago. There it had to be protected from verbal and
physical attack by a large part of the population, enraged art students
and the Law and Order League. Finally it went to Boston, where a

woman, fainting in front of a cubist painting, fell against Raymond Duchamp-Villon's bust of Baudelaire and smashed it. But otherwise the citizens of the Back Bay allowed the Copley Society to house the show in comparative serenity. Cooled by the show's scandalous history in alien parts of the country, Bostonians largely left it alone.

Barely two months before its New York opening, even a pioneer as sensitively attuned to cultural currents as Alfred Stieglitz had no inkling of the revivalist spirit about to infect the American art scene. Taking time out from his duties as director of his Little Galleries of the Photo-Secession, familiarly known as "291," Stieglitz wrote to Gertrude: "Times are terrifically hard over here. Then, too, one must remember that there is no real feeling for art, or love for art, in the United States as yet. It is still considered a great luxury; something which is really not necessary. And all this in spite of the so-called interest in old masters and the millions spent for them by people like Altman and Morgan. Was not Altman the landlord of our little '291'? Did he not double the rent virtually on the day on which he bought the property and incidentally bought a new Rembrandt? Did he ever know that '291' was fighting tooth and nail, single handed, in this vast country of ours, for the very thing he thought he loved?"

Signs and minor wonders had been noted before the onslaught from abroad, but mainly by *cognoscenti* and a few collectors like Chicago's Mrs. Potter Palmer who had come into contact with impressionism while traveling abroad, or at the exhibition arranged by the dealer Durand-Ruel in New York in 1886. Painters like Maurice Prendergast, sensing the significance of impressionism, had already applied its methods to native subject matter. Gertrude's good friend and frequent visitor, Alfred Maurer, one of the first Americans to join the "school of Paris," had subsequently abjured naturalism and thrown over the beginnings of a successful academic career. Other American artists who had seen for themselves in Paris — among them Bernard Karfiol, Max Weber, Abraham Walkowitz, John Marin and Arthur Dove — in one way or another had become members of the new dispensation. Stieglitz had exhibited drawings by Matisse, sculptures by Rodin, Japanese prints by Utamaro, assorted works of Toulouse-Lautrec, and had even been so far in advance of his time as to show children's art. In 1909, he had given a joint show to Alfred Maurer and John Marin, followed by exhibitions of Renoir and Cézanne lithographs, Picasso drawings, as well as paintings by such eminent but still unclassifiable Americans as Marsden Hartley and Arthur Dove. Modern art had been introduced to America. Its force, if not always its meaning, was already clear to the habitués of the *salon* and gallery which Stieglitz had, in 1906, opened on the third floor of 291 Fifth Avenue — the famous address which was "a kind of sheltering fort," wrote Van Wyck Brooks, "to so many who felt at the time like pioneers in the Indian country." But not until the Armory Show did Americans in general reap the whirlwind that had swept over Paris and the Continent since the emergence of Cézanne, but which had barely brushed the shores of the New World.

Free spirits like Mabel Dodge, openly hungry for portents that mankind was about to move onto higher planes of rapport with the infinite, tended to think that the show was "the most important public event that has ever come off since the signing of the Declaration of Independence." Others relished the event as a singular incident in the history of bourgeois-baiting. But to a few, including Leo Stein, whose tastes had already transcended the early and, he seemed to feel, already perverted beginnings of the new art, it was old stuff. A week before the opening, he recorded his feelings and removed himself from any claim of sponsorship his earlier position in Paris may have seemed logically to entail. "You people in New York will soon be in the whirlpool of modern art," he wrote to Mabel Weeks. "I, on the other hand, am out of it. The present enthusiasm is for cubism of one species or another and I think cubism whether in paint or ink is tommyrot. It seems to me to be the intellectual product of the unintellectual and I prefer the intellectual to manifest themselves on a merely intelligent plane . . . As for Picasso's late work, it is for me utter abomination. Somebody asked me whether I didn't think it mad. I said sadly, 'No, it isn't as interesting as that; it's only stupid . . .' Cubism may have some results, but I cannot imagine that it can remain long as an integral thing."

177

Sculptor Jo Davidson, later a good friend of Gertrude's, also had objections. In the special number of *Arts and Decoration* devoted to the Armory Show, he presented them soberly: "These people object to objectivity. They point out that all the art up to that of today is founded on reminiscence. If their theory is true it follows that not only in painting and sculpture is it possible to ignore the past, but also in literature, and to substitute sounds for words to express our thoughts and emotions. Language originated that way, but continuous thought only came when a vocabulary had been developed. Take the case of Gertrude Stein's Portrait of Mabel Dodge. This piece of prose — if prose it is — has a certain fascination. But does it convey any idea whatsoever of Mabel Dodge, to even the most intelligent reader? Indeed, if it were not described as a portrait on the cover, who would suspect what it was all about? Look at Picasso's portrait of Kahnweiler. In each case there is that literary clew supplied by the title, which makes us immediately look for some suggestion of Mrs. Dodge or Kahnweiler. And, after all, does not the very word portrait suggest a certain objectivity of approach? It is all very fine to say that the tag is a concession to existing conventions. But why make concessions to existing conventions if existing conventions are all wrong?" Davidson's questions anticipate similar ones by later critics of Picasso and Stein who felt that any shred of representational or programmatic content in their respective works amounted to a kind of deliberate teasing, if not even a kind of cheating. The discernible eye or nose in a cubist painting, or the recognizable name or quotation in a cubist poem, struck them as clues to things impossible to discover. Since they were not disposed to see the humor in this sort of playfulness, they put themselves in the paradoxical position of seeming to call for a "pure" art and no monkeyshines when, actually, their own loyalties went wholly toward an art of representation.

Within a single month of its opening, more than a hundred thousand people came to view the exhibit. Among them were former President Theodore Roosevelt and Enrico Caruso, who made caricatures of some of the paintings and tossed them to amused spectators. The star attraction — the prime object of contumely — was Marcel Duchamp's *Nu descendant un escalier* (*Nude Descending a Stair-*

Pablo Picasso, Fernande Olivier, Guillaume Apollinaire, Marie
Laurencin; from a painting by Marie Laurencin

Picasso portrait of Mlle. Gertrude Stein

case), which one reporter described as "an explosion in a shingle factory." The second sensation was Brancusi's *Mademoiselle Pogany*, a sculptured head with enormous hyperthyroid eyes. All the new moderns unknown in America — Picasso, Matisse, Van Gogh, Gauguin, Braque, Leger, Kandinsky, Picabia — were given strong representation much to the chagrin of the gutter press, which greeted them with outraged sputterings and guffaws barely different in kind from the frightened fulminations that came from the academies.

An explanatory statement published by the Association of American Painters and Sculptors — the name chosen by the loosely constituted group of individuals who had banded together for this one purpose — was forthright and modest: "This is not an institution but an association. It is composed of persons of varying tastes and predilections, who are agreed on one thing, that the time has arrived for giving the public here an opportunity to see for themselves the results of new influences at work in other countries in the art way.

"In getting together the works of the European masters, the Society has embarked on no propaganda. It proposes to enter on no controversy with an institution. Its sole object is to put the paintings, sculptures and so on, on exhibition so that the intelligent may judge for themselves, by themselves. . . ."

But to a general public for whom painting meant sentimental landscapes from James Whitcomb Riley's good old days, tinted views of the Grand Canal, Oriental slave markets and angel children blowing bubbles; for whom sculpture meant Rogers Groups, or Daniel Chester French, or statues of full-bosomed matrons of Enlightenment or Liberty, the show was inevitably regarded as an affront and an abomination. Humorist Irvin S. Cobb spoke for the armies of the middle class: "I was reared in the Rutherford B. Hayes School of Interior Decoration," he wrote in the *Saturday Evening Post*, "I distinctly recall the time when upon the walls of every wealthy home of America there hung, among other things, two staple oil paintings — a still-life for the dining room, showing a dead fish on a plate, and a pastoral for the parlor showing a collection of cows drinking out of a purling brook."

Royal Cortissoz, the influential critic of the New York *Tribune,* dubbed the show "Ellis Island art," thereby lumping it with the infamous contributions to American life the yellow press had already assigned to the great immigrant movement which had but recently passed its height. "Anarchy" was the most common epithet; one alarmed critic said the exhibition was "a revolution igniting a bomb under the populace." "As to Matisse," wrote the painter Kenyon Cox, "it is not madness that stares at you from his canvases, but leering effrontery." In New York, a group calling themselves the "Academy for Misapplied Art" put on a mock Armory Show; and in Chicago, Bible Belt students from the Art Institute met the outrage by burning an effigy of the Matisse *Blue Nude,* which had for years been one of the prizes of "27." They were dispersed by authorities, but the impulse to violence had at last found outlet. FUTURIST ART INCLUDED IN STATE VICE INQUIRY, read a newspaper headline, followed by the subheading: INVESTIGATOR FINDS NUDE PICTURES AT INSTITUTE ATTRACTING GAZE OF YOUNG GIRLS.

Bewildered by reports of such vehemence, Matisse was moved to say to the American journalist Clara MacChesney, who interviewed him in Paris, "Oh, do tell the American people that I am a normal man; that I am a devoted husband and father, that I have three fine children, that I go to the theater, ride horseback, have a comfortable home, a fine garden, that I love flowers . . . just like any man." As they had in New York, the public in Chicago came in multitudes to see the assembled works — some sixteen hundred paintings and sculptural pieces by three hundred artists. Nearly three hundred of the works were sold; two hundred and fifty went to buyers in New York and about fifty more were divided between collectors in Chicago and Boston.

Not all of the early critics of the show were against it, or regarded its masterpieces as "antique corroding neurasthenias spewed out of European capitals." Henry McBride and Joel Spingarn, to name but two of its supporters, became eminent for their perspicacity. McBride, who was shortly to become a close friend and remain a lifelong champion of Gertrude Stein, recalled his first experience of the show as "Enchanting — as enchanting as black magic and as shocking." Spingarn, an American follower of Benedetto Croce's theory of "creative expressionism," also felt new tremors and glimpsed new horizons. "The opening night," he wrote, "seemed to me one of the most exciting adventures I have ever experienced, and this sense of excitement was shared by almost everyone who was present. It was not merely the stimulus of color, or the riot of sensuous appeal, or the elation that is born of a successful venture, or the feeling that one had shared, however humbly, in an historic occasion . . . What moved me strangely was this: I felt for the first time that art was recapturing its own essential madness at last, and that the modern painter-sculptor had won for himself a title of courage that was lacking in all the other fields of art."

Spingarn hoped that American writers would, in turn, follow the painters in their "divine release from custom and convention." During his lifetime this hope was realized in many literary works from England and the Continent but, with the exception of Gertrude Stein, American writers remained comparatively untouched. Nevertheless, Spingarn's breadth of view led him to shape a significant contribution to the history of American letters. It was he who had, in 1911, introduced the term, the "New Criticism," and who had continued to insist that "The first need of American criticism today is education in esthetic thinking." In the years to follow, this much-abused term would echo in the purlieus of literary scholarship and focus a controversy still far from resolution.

While many artists sponsored the Armory Show, few had particular sympathies with the violence of the new work or convictions about its durability. Some of them, like Arthur B. Davies, whom they chose as their director, were famous conservatives. An unabashed disciple of the French romanticist Puvis de Chavannes, Davies had made his reputation painting modestly attired nymphs distributed among comfortable textbookish versions of Arcadia. But tolerance and liberality were the order of the new day; while some of the artists were, professionally, of a die-hard temperament, they were convinced that the strange and the new at least deserved a showing. Every practicing artist had suffered from the stagnation of American culture in general. As time would tell, the support they gave to their foreign colleagues was a gesture resulting in ultimate advantage to themselves. When the Association had first been set up, its aim was to put on a large show of American art that would have as a point of interest only a few radical pieces from abroad. But when financial arrangements bogged down and Arthur Davies was called in to take charge, he transformed the earlier conception of the show and reversed its emphasis. The Americans would have to be satisfied finally with but a marginal place in an international exhibition.

Things had begun quietly enough when, in the summer of 1912, Walt Kuhn, secretary of the Association, went to Europe. His itinerary included Cologne, Munich, Berlin, Paris and a view of Roger Fry's second show devoted to postimpressionism at the Grafton Gallery in London. Since only great numbers and enormous variety would fulfill the aims of the group, Kuhn borrowed with a lavish hand. Yet the bias of the Association lay heavily in favor of the School of Paris. In the choice of French works, the American painter Walter Pach was particularly influential. Pach had lived in France for several years. Among his friends — Renoir, Monet, Rouault, Braque, Derain, Brancusi and Picasso — were individuals associated with both impressionist and postimpressionist developments. A man highly learned in the history of art, Pach was one of the few Americans who seemed instinctively to understand relationships of the new painting to pre-Renaissance art and to the non-representational art of Egypt, China, Greece and Peru. If the Armory Show was the great demarcation point between tradition and the twentieth century, it was the taste of Walter Pach that had greatly to do with the *risorgimento* of which it was the prime mover. Nevertheless, the show was not wholly representative; in deference to the French, Pach and other mentors of the show tended to slight the Italian futurists and certain of the English avant-garde, notably Wyndham Lewis, who were not given the place which, at least in the historical view, their contributions warranted.

Walt Kuhn was so successful in Europe that the collection he amassed was too large for any conventional gallery to house. After a search, the Association found just what they wanted in the Sixty-

Ninth Regiment Armory, at Lexington Avenue and Twenty-fifth Street. They set about garlanding the walls of the cavernous hall, placing little evergreen trees — the motif of the show — among the sculptural pieces, and reducing the forbidding expanse of the drill hall by corridors and cubicles made from burlap-covered partitions. Solicitous of the sensibilities of the general public, they arranged the exhibition so that the visitor entered into comparatively familiar surroundings where he would view the greater part of the American entries, then proceed by stages to the penultimate shock of Van Gogh and Gauguin, and on to the shattering first sight of the cubist group.

"The New Spirit" was the motto of the show which, historically speaking, brought into close, parallel contact the two main streams of art rebellion shaping the new American scene. "The Eight"— also known as the "Black Gang" — and the "Ash Can Group" were one; the internationalists another. In the works of "The Eight"— Ernest Lawson, Arthur B. Davies, Maurice Prendergast and the Philadelphians, George Luks, Everett Shinn, William Glackens, Robert Henri and John Sloan — grass-roots naturalism, previously concerned with landscape and pastoral subjects, was now concerned with scenes of city life. McSorley's wonderful saloon had replaced Bear Mountain as a subject; working girls drying their hair on midtown rooftops replaced the unawakened milkmaids who graced the verandas of the old homestead. Reflecting the urbanization of American life in one channel, the show pointed to the growing internationalization of American thought in another. The second channel of rebellion was an importation — a wholesale adoption of the aesthetic revolution of Europe — and it quickly found its course on American soil.

The impact of the Armory Show on that part of American consciousness still "accessible to experience" was summed up by Lee Simonson, the set-designer. "Our emancipation has been as swift as it has been complete," he wrote. "Before the Armory Exhibition . . . the existence of painting modern in a different sense than Manet's or Monet's was a rumor. Names such as Cézanne, Gauguin, Picasso and Van Gogh, were shadowy deities of an alien legend. Our critics abroad seemingly had never penetrated . . . Leo Stein's apartment, of a Saturday evening, in the Rue de Fleurus. If any did, they printed no record of their adventure. At Stieglitz' pioneer gallery, '291,' Hartley's and Marin's landscapes, Matisse's drawings and Cézanne's water colors were seen, misunderstood and generally ignored. But no sooner had Arthur B. Davies revealed on a larger scale, at an armory, the development of modern painting from Ingres to Matisse, than the magnitude of what we had ignored overwhelmed us. The insularity of our critics and museums was destroyed at a blow . . . Within a year we disarmed the revolution by domesticating it."

Through the not entirely welcome initiative of Mabel Dodge, Gertrude Stein tagged along with the Armory firebrands and, in a good part of the public mind, correctly came to be identified with them. When satires on the show began to appear, she was the only writer included in the widespread, heavily labored merriment. The following excerpts from *The Cubies' ABC*, a parody on the show in the form of a child's picture book, are typical:

> G is for Gertrude Stein's limpid lucidity,
>   (Eloquent scribe of the Futurist soul.)
> Cubies devour each word with avidity:
> '*Alone* words lack sense,' they affirm with placidity
> 'But *how* wise we'll be when we've swallowed the whole.'
> — G is for Gertrude Stein's limpid lucidity.
>
> S is for Schamberg's fair dame at her 'phone.
>   Conversing with G. Stein, the Futurist scribe.
> The Cubies, eavesdropping, hear Gertrude bemoan:
> 'This one feeling many far seeming alone,
> The bluer the bliss the redder the bribe!'
> — S is for Schamberg's fair dame at her 'phone.*

Undergraduate Edward Estlin Cummings, in an essay entitled, "The New Lot," published in *The Harvard Advocate*, dealt with the graphic products of the new art somewhat hesitantly. But in regard to Gertrude Stein he showed a prescience that set his remarks apart from the tiresome parodies and endlessly similar attacks appearing

* Morton L. Schamberg, a once well-known painter of machine-like forms, who died in 1918 at the age of thirty-seven.

in the popular press. "Gertrude Stein subordinates the meaning of words to the beauty of the words themselves," he wrote. "Her art is the logic of literary sound painting carried to its extremes. While we must admit that it is logic, must we admit that it is art?"

In spite of abuse by wiseacre journalists and angry academicians, it was apparent, at least in a field of art other than painting or sculpture, that Gertrude Stein alone had made a bid for the "title of courage" Joel Spingarn had long looked for. Gertrude's chance to participate directly had come about when Frederick James Gregg, an editorial writer for the *New York Sun* and publicity man for the show, was discussing pertinent matters with Mabel Dodge. Suddenly, Mrs. Dodge reported, he flung up his hands and exclaimed, "Oh! I'm all up in the air about this post-impressionistic literature — now this Gertrude Stein — !" Sighting opportunity, Mrs. Dodge remembers having said, "Well, you believe that there is too much smell of death in most of the painting you know. You want the new spirit. You want fresh life. Why don't you see that you can apply that to words? Words originally in primitive man were pure sound expressing directly an emotion. That is some time since. The life has gone out of them, their meaning is lost, blurred — Gertrude Stein —" On the basis of this unlikely conversation, Mabel Dodge was asked to write an article. Intrigued by an assignment she considered momentous, she restudied her favorite example of Gertrude's work, The *Portrait of Mabel Dodge at the Villa Curonia*, and turned out a piece which was published in the special number of *Arts and Decoration*. Entitled "Speculations, or Post-Impressionism in Prose," the article was prefaced by an Editor's Note: "Post-Impressionism, consciously or unconsciously, is being felt in every phase of expression. This article is about the only woman in the world who has put the spirit of post-impressionism into prose, and written by the only woman in America who fully understands it."

In a somewhat breathless manner, Mabel Dodge identified Gertrude as a disciple of Henri Bergson (which she never was) and of Picasso; and contributed further to the "sibylline" aspect of the Stein legend by reporting that "she always works at night in the silence, and brings all her will power to bear upon the banishing of preconceived images." Aggressive, dogmatic, the article inveighed against apathy — "indifference reeks of death. It is the tomb of life itself"— but still managed to convey something of the real background and intention of Gertrude Stein. "In a large studio in Paris, hung with paintings by Renoir, Matisse and Picasso, Gertrude Stein is impelling language to induce new states of consciousness, and in doing so language becomes with her a creative art rather than a mirror of history." She quoted a passage from her own portrait, and concluded the article with rising, if anticlimactic, eloquence: "Many roads are being broken — what a wonderful word — 'broken'! And out of the shattering and petrifaction of today — up from the cleavage and disintegration — we will see order emerging tomorrow. Is it so difficult to remember that life at birth is always painful and rarely lovely? How strange it is to think that the rough-hewn trail of today will become tomorrow the path of least resistance, over which the average will drift with all the ease and serenity of custom. All the labor of evolution is condensed into this one fact, of the vitality of the individual making way for the many. We can but praise the high courage of the road breakers, admitting as we infallibly must, in Gertrude Stein's own words, and with true Bergsonian faith — 'something is certainly coming out of them!' "

Undismayed by the extravagant impressionism of the outburst, Gertrude congratulated Mabel: "Really it is awfully well done," she wrote, "and I am as proud as punch. Do send me half a dozen copies of it. I want to show it to everybody. *Hurrah for gloire.*"

Quite early in the proceedings, Mabel Dodge had apparently come to regard the Armory Show as a major sortie in her own privately sponsored revolution. Identifying herself with Gertrude, and uninhibited by her presence, she was thrust into a limelight where a good measure of *gloire* would be deflected to Mabel Dodge. Arthur Davies was sufficiently impressed with the article in *Arts and Decoration* to ask her to participate in putting the actual exhibition together, and to send her about to beg pictures from wealthy New York friends and to cajole acquaintances abroad into lending theirs. She had an automobile and a bearskin-muffled chauffeur, and no demands upon her bank account other than for flowers and cig-arettes. Electrified by a sense of mission, she toured Manhattan ring-ing the death knell of tradition in art. Only now and then, she said, was she moved to drop a tear for those who would soon find them-selves displaced and dispossessed. Her errand was grim, but she moved forward in the role, as she chose to see it, "of Fate's chosen instrument." Gertrude, meanwhile, was not one knowingly to ac-cept the notion of Mabel Dodge as the chosen instrument of any-thing — unless it might be the advancement of Gertrude Stein. Mrs. Dodge garnered so much publicity as Gertrude's "faithful and incomprehending Boswell" and so much curiosity by her presentation and defense of the Stein manner that Gertrude herself was relegated to second place. As Mabel Dodge wrote, and as Ger-trude might well have echoed: " 'Well, who is Mabel Dodge?' they exclaimed. And thousands of copies of *Arts and Decoration* were sold, for Gertrude Stein's portrait of her, serving as an example of her style, was in it, and she had signed that article — and there was something new under the sun and everybody's blood ran quicker for it! . . . I found myself in a whirlpool of new, unfamiliar life and if Gertrude Stein was born at the Armory Show, so was 'Mabel Dodge.' "

It did not take Gertrude long to see what was happening, or long for Mabel Dodge to sense that the tone of Gertrude's letters was dropping to the freezing point. Mrs. Dodge later professed to be puzzled by the anger Gertrude eventually directed toward her. "Leo told me it was because it appeared to her that there was some doubt as to which was the more important, the bear or the one leading the bear. . . ." But, remembering Alice Toklas's earlier animosity, she ultimately felt — with perfectly good reason — that Gertrude's earlier affection for her had been studiously and persistently un-dermined. Never for a moment had Miss Alice Toklas of San Fran-cisco accepted Mabel Dodge or her "Buffalo sort of vulgarity."

CHAPTER 14

And everybody came and no one made any difference.

— GERTRUDE STEIN

THE Saturday evenings once reserved by the Steins for the convenient entertainment of particular friends were now occasions open to almost anyone who cared to cross the courtyard and ring the bell. The only necessary credentials were the curiosity to look and to listen and an ability, without a drink in sight, to maintain the proprieties of the drawing room. From the meeting place of the largely local *cognoscenti* that it had once been, the Stein atelier had undergone a transformation that now made it an international forum for the exchange of gossip, addresses and — as long as this was done with more grace than earnestness — ideas.

British visitors began to arrive in numbers, shepherded often by the faithful Roger Fry, who introduced young Wyndham Lewis, "the displaced genius of English letters" and later one of Gertrude's harshest critics, and the assertive, cantankerous painter, Augustus John. Fry had been first interested in Gertrude as a consequence of his admiration of Picasso's portrait of her, about which he had written an account in the *Burlington Review*. But as soon as they had become acquainted he began to show interest in Gertrude herself and to look into her work. Aware of his commanding position in the London Bloomsbury group, she found his attentions gratifying and, no doubt, promising for the furtherance of her publishing career. Through him she was introduced to figures of the English literati, among them Logan Pearsall Smith, whose exceedingly warm praise she could hardly have anticipated. "He went quite off his head about your portrait," she reported to Mabel Dodge, "and is reading it to everybody. Never goes anywhere without it and wants to do an article on it for the English Review. Among other things he read it to Zangwill and Zangwill was moved. He said, 'And I always thought she was such a healthy-minded young woman, what a terrible blow it must be for her poor dear brother." And it seems he meant it. Then when Logan would persist in reading it and re-reading it, Zangwill got angry and said to Logan: 'How can you waste your time reading and re-reading a thing like that and all these years you have refused to read Kipling.' And the wonderful part of it was that Zangwill was not fooling."

Since everybody was free to bring somebody, nobody who was anybody failed to turn up at "27." Individuals who had participated in at least one Saturday evening made up a network of artists, scholars, collectors and *jeunesse dorée*, spreading across Europe and America. A smattering of aristocracy had also begun to make its appearance in the atelier, individuals with decorative yet often purely nominal titles and hyphenated names from the *Almanach de Gotha*. Baronial matrons from Chicago, among them Emily Crane Chadbourne came on one pretext or another, and there was always someone who kept the door open to proper, and sometimes raffish, visitors from Boston. The international pilgrimage came and went, giving honest homage at the shrine of modern art or, in many cases, secretly looking in upon the center of what they felt must surely be a gigantic hoax. All the while, Gertrude continued to sit peacefully in her chair by the iron stove, talking and listening and, above all, being that hostess of whom Bernard Faÿ said, "the greatest and most beautiful of her gifts is her presence."

When Mabel Dodge returned to Europe exhausted from her triumphs during the winter of the Armory Show, she was happy to find that their contretemps had been put aside, if not forgotten, and that she was still on speaking terms with Gertrude. In the wake of her fluttering passage came the young men of talent or special charm of whom it was her tendency to make personal ornaments. One by one, they came to present their letters of introduction to Gertrude: Robert Edmond Jones, the young theatrical designer; John Reed, the young revolutionist from Harvard whose bones would soon be resting in the walls of the Kremlin; and Carl Van Vechten, a young music critic for the *New York Times* who would soon be more famous as a novelist.

Van Vechten had first known of Gertrude when Mabel Dodge gave him one of the three hundred copies of her portrait which, on her return to America in 1912, she had distributed with a free hand. Subsequently he had read *Three Lives*, as well as the portraits of Picasso and Matisse that were published in *Camera Work*, and had become an unquestioning admirer. He came actually into Gertrude's life through a series of scenes that Henry James would have been intrigued to elaborate. Before their first meeting, Gertrude's English friend, Miss Gordon Caine, had come to the Rue de Fleurus with Van Vechten's first wife, Ann. To Gertrude's discomfort, Ann Van Vechten talked at length about "the tragedy of her married life." This visit was all but forgotten a week later when, with a friend, Gertrude and Alice attended the second performance of *Le Sacre du Printemps*. Stravinsky's music was the contentious aspect of this new ballet, which had been commissioned by Serge Diaghilev, and for which Nijinsky was choreographer. The *première* performance had resulted in an uproar — one critic said it would be better named "Le Massacre du Printemps" — and fireworks of one sort or another were expected to accompany the second. Van Vechten, after having presented his letter of introduction to Gertrude by post, had been invited to the Stein household for dinner for the following Saturday. On the evening of the performance, Gertrude and Alice were sitting in their box contemplating the behavior of Guillaume Apollinaire and his lady companions in a box below theirs, when just before the curtain went up, a tall, well-built young man appeared through the dimming light and sat down beside them. His clothes were elegant and he looked Scandinavian, they thought, or perhaps American; he was in any case a striking personality with whom to share a box. Hisses and catcalls greeted the performance; canes and umbrellas were brandished as the audience, pre-heated by reports of the *première*, showed its fiercely divided response. In lieu of the music, which was barely audible, Gertrude enjoyed the melée, and was so delighted by the mysterious stranger in exquisite evening clothes that when she returned to "27" she sat down and wrote a portrait that she entitled simply *One*.

When Van Vechten arrived for dinner a few evenings afterward, he was immediately recognized as the Scandinavian intruder. Their cook had prepared a somewhat whimsical meal — endless courses of hors d'oeuvres followed by a wet omelette — but table talk was seasoned by Gertrude's casual and, to her guest, bewildering references to his married life. Her cat-and-mouse game failed to un-pleat Van Vechten's composure, however, and before the evening was over they had come to the beginnings of a lifelong friendship. "It was on all sides love at first sight," Alice Toklas has said, "and the beginning of a long rare friendship, indescribable loyalty on his side, complete dependence on Gertrude Stein's. . . . It was he who found her first and years later her last publisher."

Like Alice herself years before, Van Vechten on first acquaintance was struck with the beauty of Gertrude's voice. He felt that even the "celebrated *voix d'or* of Sarah Bernhardt . . . before it had lost its metallic resonant glamour" was no match for the richness of hers. But his immediate and deep interest in Gertrude was based on a knowledgeable, if somewhat marginally oriented, appreciation of what she represented as an artist. Independent in his taste both in music and in literature, Van Vechten confessed that his preferences ran toward "the odd, the charming, the glamorous." He admitted that he was quite willing to subscribe to the superior genius of Beethoven and Milton, but that his deeper pleasure lay in listening to Scarlatti and in reading the slighter works of Thomas Love Peacock. His concern for Gertrude became one of the happiest and most durable elements in her life. More than any other individual who has interested himself in her work and in her person, Van Vechten had both the will and the means to keep her name before the public. It was he who made famous her phrase, "Rose is a rose is a rose is a rose"; who wrote introductions for her works, edited them, and made arrangements for their publication; and it was he who was eventually to become her literary executor, only in 1958 relinquishing the role to Donald Gallup of the Yale Library because of "advancing age."

By 1912, estrangement between Gertrude and Leo had come to a critical point. Having lost one another in effect years before, they had learned to exist without irritation as far as the household went, but with an indifference in regard to one another's creative pursuits so deep that separation seemed inevitable. Leo had already begun to withdraw from the Saturday evenings when, in his words, "My interest in Cézanne declined, when Matisse was temporarily in eclipse, when Picasso had turned to foolishness." But there was an even stronger reason: "27" was no longer his private forum. To his own way of thinking, at least, he had won his great debate and was no longer interested in lesser ones that might be argued there. The decline of the atelier as a place of miraculous conversions has been described by the art critic Henry McBride: "After the Armory Show had ended and everybody in America had said something witty about Marcel Duchamp's Nude Descending the Staircase, the crowds of pilgrims became too dense for even Gertrude's energy to cope with, and her 'Saturday nights' gradually became less frequent and certainly less tumultuous. By the time I reached them . . . an evening party with Gertrude Stein and Alice Toklas . . . (Leo Stein had already lost the faith and deserted the ship) was much like a party anywhere else though, of course, livelier. What made it lively was the presence of all the striking new young artists in Paris talking shop, the pleasantest kind of talk there is for those who talk it.

"But there were no altercations. How could there be? Everyone had been vindicated. Cézannes had suddenly increased in price and the Metropolitan, much against its will, had been obligated to buy one."

Only a few years earlier, to many people Leo and Gertrude had seemed to live but for one another; now they showed neither dependence nor affection. Gertrude had developed swiftly as a writer and, even more expansively, as a personality in the art world while her brother remained creatively stagnant and had become, in terms of his old society, uncommunicative and withdrawn. Even his ambitions had become atrophied, while various obsessions confirmed the depth of his still undiagnosed neuroticism. That he was difficult to live with may be taken for granted. His aggressive intellectualism was never relaxed, his convictions of his own dammed-up genius never dissipated. In order to sharpen his perceptions, far from blunt to begin with, he would often fast for days on end. This habit led often to curious states of superconsciousness in which his insights were like those of a drug addict, and his behavior almost as irresponsible. His speculations in such states were usually turned in upon himself — toward rationalizations of his failures and elaborate, tedious analyses of the nature of his brilliance. Just as often, he was morbidly preoccupied with his digestive processes. In 1907 he had taken up the fad of Fletcherism, chewing each mouthful of food exactly thirty-two times and wondering aloud about the results of his new dietary regime, completely self-absorbed.

His good friend Hutchins Hapgood, whose long relationship with Leo had to survive many vicissitudes, had described his temperament as it showed itself at this period with considerably less generosity toward him than Gertrude, publicly at least, ever expressed. "He was almost always mentally irritated," said Hapgood. "The slightest flaw, real or imaginary, in his companion's statements, caused in him intellectual indignation of the most intense kind. And there seemed to be something in him which took it for granted that anything said by anybody except himself needed immediate denial or at least substantial modification. He seemed to need constant reinforcement of his ego, in order to be certain that all was well with the world and that God was in his heaven. I remember in Paris days, he got a letter from one of his oldest and best friends, who had been of great service to him and who was one of the few men whom he wholeheartedly admired. But this letter contained one phrase — which seemed to me insignificant, and which I have now forgotten — which caused Leo the greatest indignation, and caused him to wipe his friend off the tablets of his sympathetic memory; and the friend remained obliterated for many years."

Gertrude had long ago learned to tolerate and live with his autocratic sensitivity. The most difficult thing to deal with now was the irritation arising out of their constant, uncompromised, intellectual differences. These had developed to a point where, as Leo confessed in a letter to his old friend Mabel Weeks, "there is practically nothing under the heavens that we don't either disagree about, or at least regard with different sympathies. The crucial thing is of course our work. In my case this is of comparatively little importance because in the first place I never suspected Gertrude of having any interest in the criticism of ideas, and in the second place I have no desire for glory."

Gertrude's writing had long seemed to Leo an "abomination" and he continued to feel about it, as he wrote, "exactly as I do about Picasso. Picasso was for essentials a feeble, not a powerful artist. He tried to circumvent this by novel inventions of form. Gertrude couldn't make ordinary syntax and words in their ordinary meanings have any punch, and like Picasso she wanted Cézanne's power without Cézanne's gift. So she perverted the syntax."

Differing ideas, competitive careers and irritating personal habits all contributed to discord, but the crucial factor leading toward their breakup was of quite another nature. This was Leo's protracted, torturous relationship with the woman he was, many years hence, to make his wife. The relationship had begun in 1905 and was continued through a series of disruptions, doubts, renewals and leavetakings year after year. Nina Auzias was the woman's name, and at the time of their meeting she was already famous as a model and as the mistress, from time to time, of a number of figures well known in the artists' quarter.

Nina Auzias had come to Paris from the provinces at the age of eighteen, presumably to study singing. But soon after her arrival in the city she had taken up with a socialist laborer who occupied a great deal of her time, causing her to fail in studies that might have insured her admission to the Conservatoire. Her father, a professor of mathematics, refused to supply further funds for her support. When her socialist lover became unemployed, Nina began a career of singing in the streets for whatever money passers-by might toss her way. Through constant exposure to the elements over several years, she lost her voice. When her liaison finally broke up, she took to modeling and soon to accepting the favors of young artists and men-about-Paris, Americans in particular.

According to her memoir of their first encounter, Nina Auzias fell in love with Leo at first sight: "Yes, that was May, 1905, a May filled with sunshine, azure skies, and fresh green. A martial fanfare concluded the *Freishutz* overture. Seated beside my dear friends Miko and Polo I dreamed and gazed at the beauty around me. Magda had loaned me an old dress, too large, but I had altered it to my measurements. . . . We were relaxed and silent beneath the chestnut trees of Luxembourg. Suddenly along the terrace, in the full sunshine, I saw him — like an Egyptian statue of a handsome giant he approached. His hat and golden beard hid from me his features, but I was certain that he was the mate of my desires. His arms swung in rhythmic balance, and his supple, elastic stride added to the grace and beauty of his ecclesiastical appearance. Deeply moved and surprised I cried to my young friends, 'See that man who is passing. He will be my husband. I know it.' 'Mad girl,' they cried, laughing, 'you do not know who he is — he is the great American Maecenas Leo Stein. Do not be angry, but fearful!' "

They did not meet on this occasion, or on a number of later occasions when they passed on the street or sighted one another in a café. They were not even introduced when a friend took Nina to the Rue de Fleurus where, among a crowd of visitors, she sat, "Like a lark fascinated by a shining mirror . . . motionless, silent, unable to take my eyes from Leo." She met Gertrude that evening and thought her "a wonderful strong person," and confessed that "her magnificent voice, like heavy velvet, came to me, but senseless I knew not what she was saying." Years later, after another series of chance encounters, they finally met in a café where, in the midst of writing a letter, Nina turned to Leo to ask the spelling of the word *bacchante*. She began posing for him within the week.

Nina's numerous romantic involvements and Leo's own hesitations about a permanent attachment kept their relationship tenuous and full of contradictions. Gertrude was party to the progress of the affair, but only as a sounding board for Leo's self-questionings, a position she found onerous and tiresome. Writing to a friend in 1910, Leo expressed his feelings toward Nina, for whose favors three other men were at the same time contesting: "I'm perhaps not passionately in love, but at all events I'm very deeply absorbed. She's a woman of twenty seven. She looks a good deal like a feminine version of The James The Less in Correggio's Dome picture in Parma and in her moments of radiance she's extraordinarily like the Angel in his Madonna with St. Jerome." These analogies with painting might have been expected from one of Leo's tastes, but when his romantic feelings were subject to the same kind of analytical treatment, he began to distrust emotions and gestures anyone else might have accepted as normal reactions. Nina's title as "the soul of the Quarter" he accepted easily enough, even though, as he archly said, "her figure is much better," and managed to hide whatever jealousy he was capable of feeling. As time went on and his rivals became fewer, he watched developments with a sense of relief and began to devote himself to formulating various "tests" by which Nina might, by conscious application or by unconscious behavior, "prove" herself adequate to his notions of a proper wife.

Leo and Gertrude parted in 1912, thereby freeing themselves of one another and of the burdens of mutual toleration. Years later, Leo analyzed those differences which, he felt, had doomed their early relationship. Beside the difference of his basic intelligence and her basic stupidity, there was her ability to drive ahead while he was driven only back upon himself, her hunger for glory and his concern only to understand himself. When the crisis came, he saw it as being to his advantage: ". . . this domestic discord," he wrote to a friend, "has had its importance in urging what Alice's coming has facilitated, my freeing myself from about the only thing that was in any serious way a check on my independence."

No single outburst accompanied his leavetaking, another fact which he attributed to Alice's presence which, he said, was "a godsend . . . it enabled the thing to happen without an explosion." His departure for Florence was quiet and sullen, yet at no time did either he or Gertrude express vindictiveness. They divided their paintings along the lines suggested by a letter he wrote to Gertrude, probably in January, 1914: "The Cézanne apples have a unique importance to me that nothing can replace. The Picasso landscape is not important in any such sense. We are, as it seems to me on the whole, both so well off now that we needn't repine. The Cézannes had to be divided. I am willing to leave you the Picasso oeuvre, as you left me the Renoir, and you can have everything except that. I want to keep the few drawings that I have. This leaves no string for me, it is financially equable either way for estimates are only rough and ready methods, and I'm afraid you'll have to look upon the loss of the apples as an act of God. I have been anxious above all things that each should have in reason all that he wanted, and just as I was glad that Renoir was sufficiently indifferent to you so that you were ready to give them up, so I am glad that Pablo is sufficiently indifferent to me that I am willing to let you have all you want of it. I should not have taken the Spanish landscape in the first place if I had not supposed that your interest in the later things had rendered it of minor importance. Since this is evidently not the case, I shall not only propose but shall insist with happy cheerfulness that you make as clean a sweep of the Picassos as I have of the Renoirs, with the exception of the drawings which I want to keep, partly on account of their actual delightfulness and partly on account of the personal note. But then with the exception of the presentations there is among them, I think, nothing of special importance to you. You'll take the little still life, the gouache head, and the little bronze . . . I very much prefer it that way, and I hope that we will all live happily ever after and maintain our respective and due proportions while sucking gleefully our respective oranges."

When Gertrude came to write of the early days of the Rue de

Fleurus, she made emphases which, in fairness to the views of many others who knew her and Leo then, should be qualified and corrected. According to Hutchins Hapgood, commenting upon attitudes later expressed by Gertrude, ". . . one would have thought that Leo was only a family satellite, and that he meant little to her. But if she had written at that time about their life, he would have appeared, not only as the beloved and the important, but as the great spirit of Twenty-seven Rue de Fleurus, where Picasso and Matisse received material and spiritual nourishment, and where she was vouchsafed the daily privilege of his presence. No more remarkable change has probably ever taken place in a human being's personality than that which has happened in the case of Gertrude Stein. In later years, when the critical Leo could not follow the direction of her writing nor the direction of her emotional life, she seemed to feel herself spurned and insulted . . . and to have lost her ordinary sense of justice."

Leo's new home in Florence brought him no promise of happiness. According to Mabel Dodge, the extreme phase of his neuroticism began when he lived alone. "He wasn't very neurotic before that. He was very shut into himself and he had his own queer ways of wearing sandals, eating mostly nuts, and looking down his long ram-ish nose — but after all, he had a human contact with life through his sister — and when Alice supplanted him he was cut off from it completely . . ." Shortly he was back in America for a long visit. To his own way of thinking he had cut himself off from a *ménage à trois* in which, he felt, his life was marginal, sterile, and where his problems were met with little sympathy. Some friends of his and Gertrude's, among them Mabel Dodge, felt that the attachment between Gertrude and Alice had very much to do with his leaving. It was their feeling that by having relieved Gertrude of every onerous activity, by assuming all secretarial duties, and by protecting her from every undesirable and annoying contact with people, Alice had made herself indispensable to Gertrude's comfort. Gertrude, growing helpless, less inclined to do anything for herself, had begun to seem foolish in Leo's eyes. The vine, they felt, was beginning to strangle and vitiate the tree.

Whatever Alice's presence may have had to do with bringing to culmination the differences that would finally separate them, the deeper causes of estrangement were recorded by Gertrude in a work written between 1910 and 1912, yet not published until after her death. If jottings on the flyleaf of one of Gertrude's notebooks may be taken as indicative, this work was apparently at first conceived as being about Leo and his sister-in-law Sarah. But Gertrude also puts down, in her notations, the following: "Complete sound and then a bit of what they did and how. Then do Alice and me and what we did and how, use the introduction for Alice. . . ." Nevertheless, *Two: Gertrude Stein and Her Brother* is finally concerned mainly with its two announced subjects. Written in the style of *Many Many Women*, *Two* belongs with those works demanding inordinate patience and endurance on the part of the reader. And yet it probably constitutes the most meaningful statement of the course of the relationship that has yet been made. While the first hundred pages or so are mesmerizing and without reward, in the last fifty pages occur passages as memorable as any Gertrude Stein ever wrote.

Early in the work she writes: "They are not alike. They are different the one from the other one. The one is hearing himself and making sounds then with that thing. The other one is one hearing some one and being one then making sounds of that thing. They are not alike." In many such childishly simple and interminably iterated passages she dwells upon Leo's self-absorption and the growing self-consciousness and independence of herself and his most intimate and constant auditor who "was thinking about being one and she was knowing that sound was coming out of her and she was thinking about being a very different one in being one than he was in being one."

Her dependence upon Leo and her respect for him is given support and substance in the exercise and, while she begins to define herself by difference from him as a creator — as one who *is* able to break through the trap of self — this evolution is not the result of antagonism or disillusion, as popular report would have it, but of a simple realization of profound differences. "In being one and being working she was expressing that she was completing realising that she was completely changing in coming to be one expressing certain conviction."

When the change is manifest, and separation inevitable, there occurs a break in the monotony of the narrative, a kind of onomatopoeic lift and enlargement of spirit: "She being one, sound coming, she was aspiring in beginning, she was aspiring in needing changing, she was exalting in sound coming, she was escaping in attacking, she was emphasizing in expressing, she was asking in coming, she was coming in changing, she was protected in resting, she was keeping in needing, she was accomplishing having had something."

In the period of her tutelage, Leo's probings were instinctive and his resolutions illuminating. But now that she had developed convictions of her own, not only as a theorist but as a practitioner of a new and unprecedented kind of literature, she found Leo's self-absorbed pursuit of aesthetic certainty intolerable. "He was one who was the one who was certain that in arranging that thing arranging completely listening to himself inside him he was completing something and having been completing something he was beginning the deciding of everything. . . . She was one and being that one she could be telling herself what she was not hearing."

Her new sense of freedom and conviction, supported by the release or escape that her work provided, show in the following passage with its continuous rhythmical overtones of a refrain Gertrude was much attached to: "Right, left, I had a good job and I left": "In working when she did what she did she worked all she worked and she did all she did when she did what she did. She did what she did and she worked. She felt what she felt and she did what she did and she worked. She did what she did and she felt what she felt when she was doing what she did and she worked when she did what she did and she did what she did when she worked. She felt what she felt when she did what she did when she worked. She worked when she did what she did. She felt what she felt when she did what she did. She worked when she did what she did and she felt what she felt when she worked, when she did what she did."

The climax of her release and a demonstration of her ability to achieve power by accumulation comes in a passage of an entirely different tenor. Here she celebrates her freedom and grandly announces her significance. With themes as engaging, to her at least, she rises to the epiphanous: ". . . She is the anticipation of conviction of remembering being existing. She is the anticipating of a new one having been an old one. She is the anticipation of expression having immaculate conception. She is the anticipation of crossing. She is the anticipation of regeneration. She is the anticipation. She is the actualisation. She is the rising having been arisen. She is the convocation of anticipation and acceptation. She is the lamb and the lion. She is the leaven of reverberation. She is the complication of receiving, she is the articulation of forgetting, she is the expression of indication, she is the augmentations of condensing, she is the inroad of releasing." The rhythm and substance of this passage give it the quality of a litany — not an imitation or a parody, but an abstract litany. While the basic repetitions of the litany form are respected, and the liturgical variation of address, there is of course no focus, no propositional center. There are tensions, elevations, and these are engendered almost wholly by rhythm and by the illusion that she is creating something as solemn as prayer. The ability to create and sustain this illusion is one of Gertrude Stein's indisputable talents and may be her most notable. Her accomplishment in this regard, at so early a point in her career, anticipates its elaboration in her plays and its final success, especially in *Four Saints in Three Acts*.

Another aspect of the passage is notable — the sudden introduction of images. Their appearance here in a climactic passage is strategic in quite the same sense that Henry James, after endless disquisitions full of nuance and cerebration, suddenly reports an overt action — an illicit kiss, the smashing of a bowl. Reality is what has been held in reserve, and when the crack is opened and, for a split second, the reader stands in one-to-one relation with its images or gestures, he is shocked, not because reality has been introduced, but because its relevance to what he has been following is suddenly made positive and electrifying.

After this climaxing passage, *Two* moves quietly and repetitively to an ending with less and less consideration of Leo's dilemma and more and more conviction of Gertrude's emancipation. Finally, in the last of some one hundred and fifty pages, occurs the passage: ". . . All she won was that victory. She had that conviction. It was turning and resetting, it was not adaptation, it was the time of day. All the day was that way. And that which was penetration and reversal was the same good-bye. She did turn to die. She was not in that eye. She was the pleasing reunion that was not being in being where there was no seeing. She came to stay that way."

In his own terms, Leo also believed that he had found himself and, as he wrote to Mabel Weeks, "what more strange and wonderful world can any one hope to find than himself." He was glad to be rid of the Saturday evenings and all they stood for. He "would rather harbor three devils" in his insides, he said, than go on talking about art. Besides, he had come to feel, the aesthetic and philosophical attitudes with which he was identified were "too much the attitudes of the intellectual superman to be available as yet for the general profit."

If his messianic impulses had now given way to a guarded sense of insularity, Leo's quest of self-discovery was not finished, as he thought, but barely begun. Rejected by the world of art he had rejected, his interest and influence faded with the years, to be replaced by a sterile, truculent self-assertion and self-justification. In 1915, he wrote to Mabel Dodge, "I believe that at last the insoluble is solved, the mystery explored, the endless ended and the infinite begun. I have found the light in the darkness, the path in the desert, the trail in the ocean, the way in the air where no way is." A pilgrim in search of himself, forever believing that he was about to discover the "map" of his life, the "goal of the quest psychoanalytic," he was to continue decade by decade to believe he had finally come to the shrine of ultimate self-revelation, only to learn that, for him at least, there was no final place.

During a long sojourn in America during the war years, when he lived first in a New York apartment, then in a little stone cottage at Mabel Dodge's "Finney Farm" in Croton-on-Hudson, and later on Cape Cod, he continued to write to Nina Auzias and to contribute to her support. Their love affair was many years along by now, and

Leo had broached the subject of marriage hesitantly. When he made up his mind that the time was appropriate, he tried to arrange for Nina's passage to New York. When he failed in this, old doubts returned. In 1916, he wrote to her, "I love you for always, more than any other woman. But I do not know how, the love which at a certain moment was more than budding, really flowering, has vanished. And now I do not know when it will re-awaken, or how. In any case, time passes. I do not see a rosy-colored future. And I want you to adapt yourself to the conditions which present themselves. . . ." Finally, in 1921, they were married, and for a time Leo seemed to become settled in his role of devoted husband. A year later his constant self-probings had brought him to a new assessment of himself: "I have carried the analysis to a conclusion after two and a half years of constant work," he wrote to his cousin Fred Stein. "The result is interesting, but rather disastrous. My life had been such an utter failure because the foundations had been entirely bad. I have finally cleared away the debris, but there was so much of it bad that when it is all cleared away, it left nothing but the bare ground. This would be quite perfect if I were twenty years younger, or even ten years younger. At fifty, and with rotten health and very little energy, it is quite too big an order to commence building from the ground up."

It is not without a very great sense of pathos that one reads statements, nearly ten years later, that show him harping on the same old raddled string: "I have finally resolved the problems of my neurosis, and in consequence have begun the only work which is natural, and so to speak inevitable for me, painting. All my life has been a spiritual and visual training for painting and only my interior troubles have prevented me from devoting myself to it. Now and henceforth, as long as I shall have physical health, I shall work at painting and I hope, even with (that is to say, in spite of) my advanced age, etc., to succeed with it." He had come to believe that "the lie of lies is the lie we tell ourselves, and the sin of sins is to hide from self-knowledge." And in spite of many fresh, new but doomed starts, he knew the nature of his failure, which he once illustrated by the following anecdote: "When Sir William Rowan Hamilton suddenly had his flash of discovery of the science of quaternians just as he was about to cross a bridge over the river in Dublin he said to himself, 'There I've fifteen years of work before me.' He did the work. I . . . recount a similar story only I never did the work."

Except for a brief note now and then, he made no attempt to come close to Gertrude, and yet confessed that their old antagonism had disappeared and that he felt more amiable about her than before difficulties between them had developed. Living mostly in Florence, at his villa in Settignano, during the twenties, he had no personal contact with his sister, and very little interest in anyone else, preferring to spend his energies on the writing of a book to which he planned to give the title *Others — Do They Exist*. But when Gertrude suddenly became famous as a best-selling author, his curiosity, in spite of his repeated statements of indifference, was piqued. He disapproved of her work almost totally, yet he was fascinated by the public response to her career. He did not read her lectures, but he read clippings about them, and was at moments won over to the point where he could admit that they showed a certain amount of "wit and a good deal of ordinary sense." But his feelings remained ambivalent. "What she says about punctuation is amusingly put and perfectly stupid . . ." he said. "If all the fools were drowned in Noah's flood, the seed was saved."

In 1936 he felt that both he and Gertrude had achieved what they had sought from their earliest years together: "She wanted to be a lion, and she finished by being one. I wanted to reach the point where things to me seemed intelligible — not metaphysically, for I was always anti-metaphysical — but in a pragmatist sense. I've gotten to that now."

In spite of his claims of release, the weight of his past continued to drag him down. On July 28, 1946, less than forty-eight hours after Gertrude had died without his knowledge, he wrote to his friend Howard Gans, "Berenson said to me a little while ago, 'You're damned cocky, aren't you?' and I said, 'Sure, who's got a better right, after all these years of preparation?' My real tragedy, I might rather say, the tragedy in the matter is that it comes so late. I have something now that is four-square and as big as all outdoors, and instead of having before me ten, twenty, thirty years to do something with it worthy of what it is, I am an old man with a ruined stomach and doubtful kidneys and everything practically uncertain."

Leo and Gertrude had grown so far apart that their only contact with one another was through the public press. Nina Stein had heard a rumor of Gertrude's death, but when no one among their Florentine friends could confirm the report, they decided to take it only as hearsay. Finally Leo learned the truth in a news magazine. In a postscript to another letter to Howard Gans, written early in August, he says: "I just saw in *Newsweek* that Gertrude was dead of cancer. It surprised me, for she seemed of late to be exceedingly alive. I can't say it touched me. I had lost not only all regard, but all respect for her."

The best report of Leo Stein in the last days of his life occurs in the Italian Journal of the American critic Alfred Kazin, part of which was published in the *Partisan Review* in May, 1948. Kazin had driven out to Settignano to see Bernard Berenson's villa:

. . . the butler seemed uncertain whether to admit us, Berenson being away, but Leo Stein . . . came out of the library and offered to show us around. Stein is a tall, gentle, gangling old man . . . now seventy-five, who looks like a Jewish Uncle Sam — very rustic, nervous, deaf, but full of talk and little wisecracks, all of them delivered in such a flat, uncompromised Middle Western twang after his 30 or 40 years of Italy, that it was strange in that braided garden to take in his mussed, blue serge suit and hearing aid, the knapsack over one shoulder. . . . I noticed how jumpy Stein became when we stopped too long before some pictures. Of course, showing his friend Berenson's house must have been a bore; he had been in and out of the place for years, and comes almost daily now to work in the library. Yet I was a little surprised, knowing of his life-long concern with painting, to hear him confess that it was not the work of art that mattered to him so much as the mind of the painter. He is very much preoccupied with all sorts of psychological questions and told us that he had just (at seventy-five) finished psychoanalyzing himself. The devouring interest of his life was to discover why men lie. This is something that evidently touches him very deeply. While he had been showing us pictures and rooms with a certain irritation, and made affectionate little digs at Berenson's expense . . . he suddenly, in Berenson's study, went off into a long discourse about psychology and the need for scientific exactitude in determining character. He spoke with a kind of uneasy intensity, as if he had been held in on this topic for a very long time, and wanted our understanding with or without our "approval." It was of the greatest importance to him, this practice of lying; it would be a key to all sorts of crucial questions, if only he could get his hands on the solution; it was, you might say, at the center of the human ambiguity. As he went on he would look up at us every so often, pull irritably at his hearing aid, and grumble: "What? What? You think what? I can't hear you!" riding impatiently over us and his deafness for standing in his way, and rearing up against our passing comments with a loud cry, very moving in an old man, which seemed to come straight from the heart: "It's important! It's the big thing! No one looks these facts in the face! Animals can't lie and human beings lie all the time!"

He was, however, very happy these days; had got over a bad illness and was just publishing a new book (Appreciation) in the States; there was a lot of work ahead of him. He talked about his writing with a mingled anxiety and enthusiasm, as if he were just starting out on his career; though very frail, he gave the appearance of a young writer speculating dreamily on all the books he is going to write. I should have caught on sooner, but didn't until we went into Fiesole to have a drink; he had always suffered from a bad case of being Gertrude's half-noticed elder brother, and now that she was dead probably felt liberated to go on with his own career. His resentment of her shone through everything he said. Talking about their childhood in Europe, when they had been trundled around by a father "who didn't think we could get any kind of decent education in America," he remembered most how Gertrude had always lorded it over him. "But you know," he said simply, "she was the kind who always took herself for granted. I never could." And one saw that she had dominated the situation when they had decided to make their lives in Europe. "She always took what she wanted! She could always talk her way into anything! Why," — discussing her pioneer collection of modern paintings — "she never even *liked* Picasso at first! Couldn't see him at all, *I* had to convince her. And then she caught on and got 'em for practically nothing." After all those years, the bitterness rankled, keeping him young. How often, I wonder, has he been approached only as a lead to his famous sister, and this by people who haven't the slightest knowledge of his interests? It must be this, added to his long uncertainty about himself, which lends that strangely overemphatic quality to his interest in "facts." Facts — the masculine domain of elder brothers humbly and grimly toiling away at *real* things, like aesthetics and psychology, where Gertrude, the mother of them all, took the young geniuses under her wing and, always the last of the feminists, did as she pleased — even to putting the English language in her lap like a doll, and making it babble out of her inscrutable naturalness and humor. . . . Strange to see him now, at his age, going back and back to the old childhood struggle. They had transferred the cultural rivalry in that prosperous Jewish family to Europe and worked it in and out of the expatriate life, making of Paris and Florence new outposts for an old ambition.

A few days before he himself died of cancer, almost a year to the day after Gertrude, Leo wrote to his cousin Fred Stein:

There is in the reviews of my book on *Appreciation* so much said about the relations between Gertrude and myself that it seems to me something should be said to put this matter straight.

The differences between Gertrude's character and mine were profound. My interest was a critical interest in science and art. Gertrude had no interest whatever in science or philosophy and no critical interest in art or literature 'til the Paris period and, apart from college texts, never, in my time at least, read a book on these subjects. Her critical interest was entirely in character, in people's personalities. She was practically inaccessible to ideas and I was accessible to nothing else. She was much influenced by people and I was not influenced by them at all but only by ideas.

From childhood on our private lives were entirely independent. At a very early time before our teens we had come to an explicit understanding not to interfere with each other, and this developed in many implicit ways.

In Paris her critical interest in art and literature was awakened by her personal problems in writing. The Cézanne, Matisse, Picasso pictures that I bought were of great importance to her in respect to her work and then became an interest independent of that and in time this interest in pictures came to be only second to her writing.

Some reviewers speak of a feud or quarrel between us. We never quarrelled except for a momentary spat. We simply differed and went our own ways. Later I would sometimes criticize her work or comment on her character in reference to it as I would do in the case of any other writer, not thinking that the hearers would interpret this as a consequence of personal relations. There is no more quarrel or feud in my relations to Gertrude than in my relations to Picasso. In both cases I have impressions and opinions which are not necessarily in agreement with certain opinions widely prevalent. That is all.

CHAPTER 15

If you want to clamber and sing with delight
you want to have grey hair turning white and
then lose a watch and then find a memorandum
and then have multitudes of red curtains and
then in an agreeable moment go to London.
What is it darling. Nothing dearie.

— GERTRUDE STEIN

WHEN their mutual disagreement had become as deep as the devotion that was once the most impressive thing about them, Gertrude and Leo Stein had found and set out upon roads which, in each case, would make all the difference. Leo was out of sight by 1913, but his presence remained a part of the atelier and the echo of his voice would never entirely be gone from its walls. In a burst of energy that seemed to be directed at exorcising Leo's troubled and daily more insubstantial ghost, Gertrude and Alice set about making plans to renovate their living quarters and started to look for new furniture to fill the gaps left by his removal of his own things. While they had at first resolved to put an end to an era of "27" by removing themselves to an apartment that overlooked the Palais Royal gardens, the landlord there would not agree to changes they had in mind. Using part of the four thousand dollars received for three Picasso paintings she sold to the dealer Kahnweiler, Gertrude concentrated upon long-desired improvements and addi-ions to their Rue de Fleurus apartment. She had a covered passage-way built between the studio part of the establishment, the atelier, and their living quarters, the *pavillon,* had electricity installed to replace the elaborate and bothersome gas lamps (they had no central heating until 1927, no telephone until the early '30's), and was having the whole apartment repapered when she received an unannounced visit from John Lane, the English publisher. He said he had just about decided to bring out an English edition of *Three Lives* and indicated that he was open to discussion of plans for other volumes to follow. Because of its length, he felt that *The Making of Americans* was out of the question. Then Gertrude suggested he do a collection of all of the portraits she had by this time completed. Lane said he would think about this, and left the Rue de Fleurus with Gertrude's promise to come to London for final discussions.

An ill wind heavy with rumors of war blew through the streets when Gertrude and Alice descended at Victoria Station on July 5, 1914, but whatever uneasiness they may have felt was allayed when, on the following Sunday, they went to John Lane's regular afternoon *salon.* War, they were relieved to find, was but one of a score of subjects about which the faithful Sunday afternoon guests were concerned. Before the tea party was over, Lane asked Gertrude to come to his office for the signing of contracts for *Three Lives.* But when they could not agree on a date, they decided to put the business meeting off until some time within the ensuing weeks when they would both be free. With two weeks or so of holiday ahead of them and no other business to attend to, Gertrude and Alice spent their days pleasantly, shopping and theater-going and renewing English friendships they had made at "27." Gertrude had confessed in a letter to Mabel Dodge that she would, during her London visit, do her best to "look like a genius." With the essential collaboration of Alice, she had apparently struck just the right note. Muriel Draper, who lived then in London, remembered her "stalking through crowds, adorned in a short corduroy skirt, a white silk shirt, sandals, and a tiny hat perched up on her monumental head. She was usually shadowed by a friend who was always draped in some semi-Oriental gauze of sorts, with clinking bracelets, tinkling chains and ear-rings as big and oval as her gaunt eyes. A strange pair. They came to Edith Grove, where Gertrude would sit in Buddhistic calm until some topic of conversation arose which stimulated her interests. And then she would talk for hours, a steady flow of ideas in an almost boring logical sequence, some of them profound and others merely a form of brilliant dialectic. Her point once gained or, in any case, her opponent once retired, she would sink back into calm and absorb intuitively what no longer aroused her intellectuality. She was fascinated by my turbans and could give an accurate description of one, seen from as far away as an upper theatre-balcony, that would be complete in every detail, even to the setting of a stone that would dangle from it between my eyes . . . She was sensitive about attacks upon her own peculiar form of literary expression, at least sensitive to any expressed or felt doubt of her sincerity. The technical aspect of it she would debate for hours, but her motive for developing it she would protect to the last drop of her mind's blood. She would say abruptly: 'I don't know anything about it. I take things in and they come out that way, independent of conscious processes. I don't know anything about it.' "

Muriel Draper's husband Paul was fond of Gertrude but could not accept her literary pretensions as anything but fakery. To pull her leg, he wrote a parody of her portrait style and, through a friend, had it forwarded to Gertrude anonymously. The parody, according to his wife, came back with a note from Gertrude saying that "if his friend had any literary gift at all, which she was in no position to judge from the one article submitted, it was most certainly temperamentally unsuited to the style he had so flatteringly chosen; he had best follow his natural writing direction, which was doubtless of a scholarly and conservative trend."

Alvin Langdon Coburn, the photographer, arranged with his friend, Henry James, a meeting with Gertrude and Alice. But when the appointed day arrived, James was ill and sent a wire canceling the engagement. As time would tell, this was their last and only chance to meet the great writer to whom Alice was devoted and whom Gertrude was gradually coming to regard as her most immediate literary ancestor. From both the pleasures and disappointments of London they were soon glad for respite. When they accepted a friend's invitation to come to Cambridge, Gertrude was taken to lunch to meet Jane Harrison, the classical scholar. This encounter was a fiasco. The celebrated Miss Harrison shared nothing of Gertrude's zeal for the twentieth century and, in fact, had said for the record that she was interested in nothing that could not be traced "back to its first known beginnings." Attuned to centuries thousands of years apart, she and Gertrude had nothing to say to one another and made no effort at more than party conversation.

But the occasion at least provided material for one of Gertrude's short pieces, "Crete," written during the English visit. In the first lines of this work, which follow here, "Miss Clapp" is of course Miss Harrison, and the text is a matter of the tags and rhythms of small talk: "Is Miss Clapp at Newnham now. She has been about ten days in bed. Oh I am so sorry. I relieve that mention of a yes, I relieve that mention of a yes. Oh I am not so sorry. Not so sorry. Official time table. Official time table art dyers. French dry cleaning. Official time to table. I wonder if they mean to be begged. I wonder if they mean to be begged. Oh I am so sorry. It might yes. It might be possible that something delayed the train especially as the wind went Westward. Shall it be an appeal. Yes. What a pity. What a pity."

The failure of their interview is not surprising. Gertrude either disliked or was indifferent to most eminent members of her own sex, and could not easily abide having anyone presented to her as a peer; the few warm friendships among women she cherished were made, so to speak, on home ground, when reputations and worldly eminence stood in the far distance, and where amenities of daily life gave color and spice to casual conversation.

The sortie into the university town was not altogether without rewards. Alice's silent, inner bells, which acted like radar, had been muffled now for seven long years — ever since the evening when Picasso arrived trying to look like Abraham Lincoln. But they were about to ring out clarion-clear. This happened, once again at a dinner party. Although Alfred Edward Housman was one of the guests, it was not for the poet-don that the bells sounded, but for

Alfred North Whitehead. Gertrude, too, was taken at once with Whitehead and with his wife, and the attraction was apparently mutual. Alice talked about fish and literary personalities with Housman throughout the meal, but most of the time her attention was directed toward the philosopher, already famous around the world for his collaboration with Bertrand Russell on *Principia Mathematica*. When the company wandered into the garden after dinner, Whitehead took an arbor seat next to Alice and they talked about the sky; not its metaphysical aspects, to be sure, but how it looked that evening. Before the party broke up, Gertrude and Alice were invited to come for the weekend at the Whitehead home, Sarsen Land, Lockridge, near Salisbury Plain.

They returned to London for a few days, mainly to shop for furniture. When they could find nothing readymade that seemed suitable, they had themselves measured into chairs and a couch, and signed an order for delivery to Paris. When Gertrude was finally able to keep her deferred appointment with John Lane, she came away from his office with the first bona fide contract of her career. She was, at last, no longer a self-sponsored author, but a name on the list of a famous publisher. Relieved to feel that their long-drawn-out trip to England was handsomely justified, they took the train to Lockridge for what they expected would be their final weekend away from Paris. But the weekend stretched into more than forty anxiety-ridden days.

The Whitehead home was crowded with young people, guests of the Whiteheads' son and daughter, Eric and Jessie. But the pastoral weekend had hardly begun when declarations of war, like separate explosions all across the face of Europe, blighted the holiday and dispersed the guests. Return to Paris was, for the moment at least, impossible. They decided to go to London to hold themselves in readiness for a possible early passage, but Mrs. Whitehead persuaded them to stay on at Lockridge until guarantees of safe-conduct were clarified. "Do you remember it was the fifth of September we heard of asphyxiating gases," Gertrude wrote. "Do you remember that on the same day we heard that permission had been withheld. Do you remember that we couldn't know how many h's there are in with-held."

They made a brief visit to London to get their trunks and arrange for money, and there Gertrude was interviewed by an Irish journalist, J. P. Collins, of the *Pall Mall Gazette,* who had been intrigued by the first American reviews of *Tender Buttons* published in New York only a few weeks before. Like many others of Gertrude's readers, he felt the book was a great "stunt" and suggested that "after a time she might come forward and say she had done all this in order to test the credulity of the public." Gertrude answered him straight-forwardly. "If you mean that this is what we call a stunt, then let me tell you that stunts are not created in this way. They are in-variably the product of one mind reacting on the work of another or the caricature of a thing somebody else has created. . . . A stunt is always founded on something that somebody else has done; and another point of difference between the counterfeit and the reality is that the original is always done slowly and imitation, unless it is very elaborate, may be hit off at once. Nothing that can hold the attention a certain number of years can fail to have reality."

They returned to Lockridge to wait out the apprehensive days and weeks. As the Germans moved toward Paris over the smoking ruins of the Belgian plain, Gertrude and Alfred North Whitehead occupied themselves with long walks about the countryside. She found him generous, humble and retiring, and expressed the be-lief that, in his collaboration with Bertrand Russell, it was he who had contributed most of the ideas that had made their book a philo-sophical landmark. Since, before his meeting with Whitehead, Russell had already published a number of these ideas, her conclusions were affectionate but inaccurate.

Overriding everything in their path, the Germans came within striking distance of Paris; at Lockridge the peripatetic conversa-tions came to an end. Gertrude was too mournful even to leave her room; and she was further upset by her observation that all of the Whiteheads seemed much more concerned with the destruction of libraries and historical buildings in Belgium than they were with the

213

war itself. Not until the Spanish Civil War, when landmarks in places she herself had known and loved were destroyed, did she come to understand their attitude. Thinking about this eventually led to the bit of dialogue in *Four Saints in Three Acts* where St. Teresa, asked what she would do if she could kill three thousand Chinamen by pushing a button, replies through the chorus, "St. Teresa not interested." Like her favorite saint, Gertrude was but remotely interested in what happened beyond her ken. She was her own best continuous present and, while she could be moved personally by the threat of the destruction of Paris, to the destruction of so much else in her violent century she continued to be "not interested."

When Paris seemed doomed, she sat in solitude, unable to read or to write. Like millions of others around the world, she suffered out the Battle of the Marne terrified and disbelieving. When, finally, it became apparent that the Allies had stemmed the tide, Alice was the first to hear the report. She rushed to Gertrude's room calling out the news, but Gertrude refused to believe her. Convinced, finally, she wept, and Alice wept.

Life at Lockridge brightened. Recovering bravado and intransigence, Gertrude met all comers with airy confidence. When Lytton Strachey came she thought him fairly dull but was entertained by the sound of his high faint voice and the sight of his silky beard. With Bertrand Russell she quarreled about American education, defending with a maximum of zeal her minimum of information about what she considered "progressive" methods against his classical preferences. Most of the Englishmen who came to the Whiteheads made her impatient, especially when, as so many of them did, they spoke fearfully of "the German genius for organization." It was her belief that the Germans had no organization at all, that they had merely formulated and imposed a plan of action, and that was not organization, that was *method*. Only the Americans had genuine organization, she felt, because they conceived organization in terms of naturally assumed cooperation, without imposition. Because it was so mechanical, the German idea was not modern and could not therefore ultimately prevail.

They got money from America — Alice from her father, and Gertrude from her Baltimore cousin, Julian — and after weeks of inquiry at Thomas Cook's in London were told that they could return to Paris on October 15th. With imperturbable single-mindedness, Mrs. Whitehead decided she would go with them: her eldest son, North, had left for the front without a proper overcoat and, to give unwitting support to the widespread notion that this was a "schoolboys' war," she worried mainly that he might catch cold. To make sure that he was warmly clothed for the battlefield, she used her influence to get papers of transit from the War Office and from Field Marshal Kitchener personally. These documents worked like charms, and the three ladies were shuttled across the Channel and into Paris like persons of state.

"Your King and country need you," said the ubiquitous posters from which the steely eyes and pointing index finger of Lord Kitchener reiterated their one point. "When I came back to Paris," said Gertrude, "I was surprised not to see these notices up." Blackouts, food shortages, relentless apprehension had deadened the spirit of the capital. The city seemed half empty, its life shuffling and mean. It was the beginning of the years Gertrude described as "a period of fashion without style, of systems with disorder, of reforming everybody which is persecution, and of violence without hope." A few visitors came to the Rue de Fleurus, but the old *esprit* had vanished in the hard shadow of the war. "Montmartre and Montparnasse were under dictatorial rule," according to Jean Cocteau. "Cubism was going through its austere period. Objects that could be placed on a cafe table and Spanish guitars were the only distractions permitted." Old friends and acquaintances were going to war or preparing to go. Georges Braque was already in the frontline trenches. Apollinaire, "learning to ride and getting fat," was in training to be "a conductor of cannon." Matisse, called up three times, was rejected because of his poor eyes. A touch of the old excitement had come to Gertrude in her acquisition of two new paintings by Juan Gris. But since the painter himself was living in the country, at Collioure, she had to be content with long-distance rapport. Juan Gris, who had begun to paint in a manner somewhat

215

similar to Picasso and Braque as early as 1910, had long been an outstanding but notably unsuccessful figure among the cubists, most of whose works by this time commanded a steady market. Gertrude was among the first to buy Gris' work and had recently joined with Matisse in helping the painter survive by agreeing to send him money in monthly payments. But conflicting loyalties on Gris' part involving his dealer friend Kahnweiler, who was forced into exile in Switzerland, and the expectations of his new patrons resulted in misunderstandings which caused a break between the painter and Gertrude that was not made up until after the war. Matisse said later that he stopped seeing Gertrude because of her mistreatment of Gris, but Kahnweiler seems to possess the truth of the matter. In 1914, Gris wote to him: "Gertrude Stein, hearing of my difficulties, has been so kind as to send me two hundred francs. Matisse, who has gone to Paris for a few days, has succeeded in arranging with Gertrude and Brenner that, between them, I shall receive one hundred and twenty francs a month." Michael Brenner, an American sculptor and art broker, had indeed promised to join with Gertrude in financial support of Gris. But when Gris decided that the option that went with the agreement conflicted with Kahnweiler's long-standing first claim on his work, he withdrew from the proposed arrangement. Matisse remained under the impression that it was Gertrude who had reneged. After the war Gertrude and Juan Gris became intimate friends until his early death in 1927. Then she paid him the tribute of one of her finest short pieces, *The Life and Death of Juan Gris*. "I remember he said Kahnweiler goes on," she wrote, "but no one buys anything and I said it to him and he smiled so gently and said I was everything." According to her, Gris was the only painter whom Picasso "wished away." In her last years, it was customary for Gertrude to speak of Gris as "the great one."

The days were long, monotonously alike; Paris, fearful and subdued, seemed hushed and desolate. Except for brief visits to their old friend Mildred Aldrich, who had found herself trapped on a battlefield at the outbreak of hostilities (her book, *Hilltop on the Marne*, became a best-seller), they passed a sullen winter cut off from old friends and old interests. Carl Van Vechten, who had recently married Fania Marinoff, a Russian actress who became a familiar figure in early American movies, was trying to place some of Gertrude's things, among them *Aux Galeries Lafayette*, with editors of magazines in New York. But the dealings were long-drawn-out, muddied by conflicting advice from other friends, and unpromising. Gertrude was losing her monumental patience. "I know I am doing more important things than any of my contemporaries," she wrote to a friend, "and waiting for publication gets on my nerves." To make matters worse, money was short and wartime living expenses came high. To meet financial emergencies, Gertrude sold to her brother Mike, for four thousand dollars, the last Matisse still hanging on her walls, *La Femme au Chapeau*.

In March, bombing alerts and, finally, a zeppelin raid over Paris at night terrified her and Alice. With the first signs of spring they decided they would leave the city, at least for a little while. Seeking haven in neutral territory, they chose Palma de Mallorca which they already knew and liked. Life in Palma was such a relief from the austerities of Paris that they decided to stay. They found a house, 45 Calle de Dos de Mayo, in a little community, Terreno, just beyond the town limits and with a Breton servant, Jeanne Poule, and a dog, Polybe, settled down for a summer interrupted only by a five-day visit to Valencia to see bullfights with the great Gallo Gallito and Belmonte. Even though Gertrude felt the Majorcans were "a very foolish lot of decayed pirates with an awful language," the geographical change proved to be a spiritual refreshment. Once more Gertrude felt the creative impulses generated by Mediterranean landscapes and seascapes. These propelled her toward writing a series of the literary oddities she was satisfied to call plays.

The conviction that there was a distinct relationship between a landscape and a play, things which "anybody can see by looking," was already a part of Gertrude's thinking. One of her most successful and famous works, *Four Saints in Three Acts*, written many years later, was based on this notion; but the conception of this opera, produced in 1934, was already firmly established in the plays she wrote as early as 1913. These compositions are attempts to transcribe scenes, landscapes and events, without premeditation and without using the means by which a conventional playwright calculates his maneuvers and controls his effects. Her approach has little in common with that of the writer who establishes situations and, by one means or another, explores and resolves conflicts within them. Gertrude Stein's plays are conceived within the cubist dispensation, which is to say that the materials of a landscape, or the actions and gestures accompanying an event, are motifs with which she does quite what she pleases. Since she is not going anywhere, she begins and ends where she likes. Since she has nothing to resolve, she maintains her snatches of conversation, her random observations and her often kittenish stage directions on the level of fanciful exposition, continually surprising herself and, possibly, her audience. The typical result is a kind of word-ballet in space in which the simplest verbal movements are elaborated in chants and rituals. Many of these plays read like verbal counterparts of certain paintings of Joan Miro where distorted and fragmented figures and objects tumble about one another like a circus in full swing.

Such works are naturally hermetic, and open to all the limitations of literary cubism. If she did not solve these problems in terms of communication, in terms of theater as a ceremony of the imagination, she had made a valid point. In making this point she contributed to the restoration of a quality largely missing from the English and American drama of her time. She had always disliked the stories of plays and, from her earliest childhood, was fascinated by the ritual movement of plays. It was only natural that her own plays would omit stories in favor of something like continuous ritual in which movement to entertain the ear and eye would replace dramatic action. While she knew that experiments in a dramatic form so remote from the existing theater would find no wide sanction, she also knew that the visual power of any play, like the undeniable attraction of any cubist construction, was magnetic. If she put aside story and action in favor of emotion and time, and thereby robbed her audience of their normal expectations, she nevertheless felt that any play forced its attention upon the spectator who could only give in to its demand. This conviction led her to a relaxation of all conventional dramatic standards and she went along merrily entertaining herself with the writing of such *divertissements*. During her stay in Terreno she completed most of the pieces eventually included in the volume *Geography and Plays*.

It was easy for Gertrude to beguile the days of war with the leisurely contemplation of landscapes and local customs, but she could not escape the war itself. Whenever there was news of a German victory, the governess in a neighboring household would hang out a flag. Piqued by this arrant display of nationalism in a neutral country, Gertrude and Alice responded by hoisting the tricolor over their house whenever there was news of an Allied victory. But most of the time they had to look on sadly while the German imperial standard floated in the breeze. Their life of exile in Terreno was uneventful, and they were well cared for by Jeanne, the servant girl of whom Gertrude wrote, "In recounting the glories of France she never forgets the father of her child." Turnips, tangerines and almonds grew in their garden; the weather was mild; there were gentle hills and semitropical byways for walking and, not far away, curio shops to visit. They spent the evenings reading aloud from volumes of memoirs, the letters of Queen Victoria, miscellaneous diaries; and Alice put her needlewoman's talent to use in producing a formidable series of garments for the soldiers. Summer came, but reports from Paris were like echoes from a tomb. Picasso was in anguish watching over the lingering death of Eva (Marcelle Humbert) who since 1912 had replaced Fernande Olivier in his affections. Braque had been wounded, Leger was a stretcher-bearer, Apollinaire brigadier of an artillery company; and Juan Gris was living in the Bateau Lavoir, which everyone else had long ago deserted, supporting himself in the humble capacity of *professeur de dessin*. Such dispiriting information made them decide to stay where they were. But finally in the summer of 1916, heartened by the outcome of the Battle of Verdun, they wanted to go home. They returned to Paris, observed a new lift in spirits everywhere, and were themselves at last ready to stop being mere bystanders and get into the war if, of course, they could do so on their own terms.

Strolling down the Rue des Pyramides one morning, they saw a

Ford car being driven by a uniformed American girl. On one side of the car was painted "American Fund for French Wounded." Gertrude nudged Alice. "There, that is what we are going to do," she announced, then sought out the headquarters of the organization and guided Alice to it. They were quickly accepted as being fit for relief duty, but were told that they would have to secure their own means of transportation. Gertrude wrote to her cousins in New York who raised enough money to have a Ford shipped over.

While they waited for their car, Gertrude wrote war poems, two of which were published in *Life*, the comic predecessor of the present Luce publication. This unusual sponsorship for authentic Stein came about as a consequence of Gertrude's staunch and reasonable defense of what she was doing. Not long before, *Life* had run a series of satirical imitations of *Tender Buttons*. When Gertrude read them she wrote to the editor telling him that since the original Stein was so much funnier and more interesting than the pallid imitations, why should he not publish samples of the real thing? She was astonished when he agreed, and immediately sent him a poem on Woodrow Wilson and another on war work.

When the Ford arrived, it was fitted out like a truck and, with a bottle of white wine, christened "Auntie" in honor of Gertrude's Aunt Pauline "who always behaved admirably in emergencies and behaved fairly well most times if she was properly flattered." Gertrude had been taught to drive by her friend from Majorca, William Cook, who had given her lessons in a two-cylinder Renault taxicab which had seen service in the Battle of the Marne. But Cook had never succeeded in teaching her how to drive in reverse. Driving her new car home from the garage for the first time, she went into a dead stall between two tramcars and had to enlist the aid of passers-by to push her off the tracks. This was but the first of a plague of troubles attendant upon her learning to handle the Ford, but soon she was busy delivering supplies to hospitals in and around Paris. Then the ambitious volunteers got their first big assignment: to open a distribution depot in Perpignan serving several *départements*. Things were always going wrong with "Auntie," but Gertrude had a genius for getting help in the most unlikely circumstances. This useful faculty was something that other relief workers could not comprehend; whenever *they* got stuck they had to get out by themselves. Gertrude had a simple explanation for their failures: they looked too efficient. She, on the other hand, with a genius for being as helpless as she was charming, convinced potential Samaritans that she was democratic, good-humored and, in spite of her inability to deal with the mechanics of a situation, knew exactly what needed to be done. Above all, she felt as a personal first principle that if you had an obvious sense of equality people would do anything for you.

From the banquet hall of a hotel which they had succeeded in requisitioning as depot and regional office, they distributed relief supplies to military hospitals around Perpignan, making personal visits to each soldier for whom they had packages. Gertrude's easy and infectious sociability was put to the highest test on these visits, many of which were fairly grim. Since Alice was put in charge of accounts, Gertrude was free to dispense cheer and maternal warmth and to be the entertainer. As a team, they were not only efficient but, at the very first glance, good for a laugh. They both wore helmet-shaped hats and belted, big-pocketed coats approximating uniforms; and Gertrude continued to wear sandals and the knitted vest and shirtwaist with gathered sleeves that had already become her trade-mark. Dedicating themselves wholly to their work, they were often deeply touched by the plight of the men they came to know, and they did not fail to realize what anomalies they must have been to many of those whom they visited. As Gertrude wrote:

> We meet a great many without suits.
> We help them into them.
> They need them to read them to feed
> them to lead them.
> And in their ignorance.
> No one is ignorant.
> And in their ignorance.
> We please them.

When their work in Perpignan was finished, and they had been photographed with their Ford truck in front of the birthplace of

Marshal Joffre, at Rivesaltes nearby, they closed up their depot and returned to Paris. The United States had entered the war by this time and, at the suggestion of the American Fund for French Wounded, they opened up a new depot meant to serve a territory including the Gard, the Bouches-du-Rhône and the Vaucluse. Nîmes became their new headquarters and there they took residence in the Hôtel du Luxembourg.

Their activities in Nîmes were the subject of a short poem by Gertrude entitled "The Work," and published in the A. F. F. W. Bulletin. Perhaps in deference to the essentially non-literary character of her audience, Gertrude for once put aside the hermetic manner of most of the other pieces written at this time and easily communicated what she saw and felt, as the following excerpts show:

THE WORK

Not fierce and tender but sweet.
This is our impression of the soldiers.
We call our machine Aunt Pauline.
Fasten it fat, that is us, we say Aunt Pauline.
When we left Paris we had rain.
Not snow now nor that in between.
We did have snow then.
Now we are bold.
We are accustomed to it.
All the weights are measures.
By this we mean we know how much oil we use for the machine.

. . .

Hurrah for America.
Here we met a Captain and take him part way.
A day's sun.
Is this Miss.
Yes indeed our mat.
We meant by this that we were always meeting people and that it was
     pleasant.
We can thank you.
We thank you.
Soldiers of course spoke to us.
Come together.
Come to me there now.
They read on our van American Committee in aid of French wounded.

All of it is bit.

Bitter.

This is the way they say we do help.

In the meaning of bright.

Bright not light.

This comforts them when they speak to me. I often discuss America with
them and what we hope to do. They listen well and say we hope so
too.

We all do.

.   .   .

This is apropros of the birthplace of Maréchal Joffre. We visited it and
we have sent postal cards of it. The committee will be pleased.

It is not a bother to be a soldier.

I think kindly of that bother.

Can you say lapse.

Then think about it.

Indeed it is yet.

We are so pleased.

With the flag.

With the flag of sets.

Sets of color.

Do you like flags.

Blue flags smell sweetly.

Blue flags in a whirl.

We did this we had ribbon of the American flag and we cut it up and we
gave each soldier one with a pin and they pinned it on and we
were pleased and we received a charming letter from a telephonist
at the front who heard from a friend in Perpignan that we were
giving this bit of ribbon and he asked for some and we sent them
and we hope that they are all living.

The wind blows.

And the automobile goes.

Can you guess boards.

Wood.

Naturally we think about wind because this country of Rousillon is the
windiest corner in France. Also it is a great wine country.

.   .   .

This is apropos of the fact that I always ask where they come from and
then I am ashamed to say I don't know all the Departments but I
am learning them.

In the meantime.

In the meantime we are useful.

223

That is what I mean to say.

In the meantime can you have beds. This means that knowing the number of beds you begin to know the hospital.

Kindly call a brother.

What is a cure.

I speak french.

What one means.

I can call it in time.

By the way where are fish.

They all love fishing.

In that case are there any wonders.

Many wonders are women.

I could almost say that that was apropos of my cranking my machine.

And men too.

We smile.

In the way sentences.

He does not feel as we do.

But he did have the coat.

He blushed a little.

This is sometimes when they can't quite help themselves and they want to help us.

We do not understand the weather. That astonishes me.

Camellias in Perpignan.

Camellias finish when roses begin.

Thank you in smiles.

In this way we go on. So far we have had no troubles yet and yet we do need material.

It is astonishing that those who have fought so hard and so well should pick yellow irises and fish in a stream.

And then a pansy.

I did not ask for it.

It smells.

A sweet smell.

With acacia.

Call it locusts.

Call it me.

I finish by saying that the french soldier is the person we should all help.

Much to the delight of the ministering angels, American soldiers in great numbers began turning up at Nîmes. Gertrude sought out the doughboys, and soon they sought her, eager to tell her their life stories, to explain the latest slang from Kansas and Wisconsin, and to exist for a few hours in the resonance of the earth-mother warmth she generated. One of these acquaintances, W. G. Rogers, eventually became Gertrude's first biographer when, shortly after her death, he published *When This You See Remember Me*. Rogers came to know her and Alice while he was with the Amherst College ambulance unit and had come on furlough to Nîmes to see Roman ruins. "They pumped me," he wrote, "for all they were worth. Where was I born, who were my parents, what did my father do, where did I go to college, who were my professors, how did I happen to be in the Army, was this my first visit to France, what would I do when the war ended? One spelled the other, like police grilling a prisoner for hours on end, until they dragged my whole history out of me." Instead of finding this sort of interview an irritation, Rogers found it enormously comforting. Their curiosity, he felt, was more solicitous than prying. When, later, he came to study Gertrude's writings, he realized that he was then being subject to her insatiable need to be, at the same time, "talking and listening," and to her scientific investigator's talent for adducing information the uses of which were sometimes contributory to her work, sometimes wholly gratuitous.

Such encounters were invigorating to Gertrude; she had forgotten how American she was and loved being reminded. After having not written for many months, she began to do a series of short works, the most famous of which, *Have They Attacked Mary He Giggled*, found its way into the pages of *Vanity Fair*.

Just after the signing of the armistice, the relief workers were called back to Paris where they immediately got orders assigning them to liberated Alsace. Equipped with a big basket of bread and butter and roast chicken, wearing fur-lined aviators' gloves and jackets, they set out for Strasbourg. There they were assigned to Mulhouse from which they distributed supplies to the shelled cities and burned-out villages through the length of a long cold winter. When, finally, it was the season "of orange blossoms and storks," they were able to close their depot (refugee relief had by this time been taken over by the government) and start back to Paris "by way of Verdun and Mildred Aldrich."

At first the city seemed more proud and beautiful than it had ever been, and they spent the days in a happy fever of gadding about to renew old acquaintance, to lunch and dine with friends from abroad who had turned up in the service of the Allies, or the American Army, or the Peace Commission, and to re-establish "27" as the meeting place of everyone worth anything. They had no servant, and domestic difficulties were increased by the fact that, having spent large sums of money on the soldiers in their care, and on the soldiers' families, they were both seriously overdrawn at their bank. Undaunted, Alice decided they "would live like gypsies, go everywhere in left-over finery, with a *pot-au-feu* for the many friends we should be seeing." But soon they discovered the great emptiness the war had made in the only way of life they had known. Everyone seemed restless, everything unsettled; the old ways were dead and gone. Cousins from Baltimore turned up to see Gertrude, but she was bored with them. She had not seen them for eighteen years and, as she said, "Certainly there is no use in seeing anybody you have not seen for eighteen years, and I hoped it would not happen again." Picasso was about and, under the influence of American movies, had taken to addressing Gertrude as "Pard." This annoyed her and they quarreled "over nothing at all." People came and went, talked pictures and gossiped, but the old sense of "27" as the still center of a whirling movement had been dissipated. No act of will could renew the excitement that had once been spontaneous and self-sustaining. The old faces were absent; the new ones had nothing to offer.

As if to seal the doom of the Paris they had once known, the shocking news of the death of Guillaume Apollinaire saddened them and put a pall on the city's haunts of writers and painters. Suffering from head wounds caused by a shell fragment in 1916, Apollinaire had apparently recovered sufficiently to return to Paris and embark on a new marriage and a new life in his famous quarters on the Boulevard St. Germain. Two days before the armistice, his condition weakened by Spanish grippe and a long series of operations on his wound, he died suddenly in a city decked with flags of triumph. Gertrude had lost an old professional ally who was the beloved mentor of many of her first Parisian friends. Except for the decisive barriers of language, he would have been her rival both as a theorist and as a writer whose roots lay in cubism. Yet from their first meeting in her neophyte days in Montmartre, when Apollinaire was already the roaring boy and unpredictable leader of the Bateau Lavoir set, she looked upon him fondly and with respect. His influence as organizer and promoter of the emergent art of the century far surpassed hers in its real effects and he had become by general fiat the patron saint of literary men. Yet Gertrude seems never to have envied his position if, indeed, she recognized his significance or suspected that he would take a larger place in literary history than the one she was slowly and hopefully defining for herself. She even forgave Apollinaire his championing of the movements succeeding cubism — futurism, the Italianate version of cubism, and Dadaism, the cul-de-sac of nihilist aesthetics — both of which she abhorred. While his work had tonic effect upon a generation of writers, Gertrude always maintained that she had little interest in it; his lively, ingratiating personality was the thing that impressed her.

After Apollinaire's death, those who knew him came to realize with sorrow how much he had meant to the world of art. Not since Baudelaire had there been a French aesthetician more deeply attuned to new artists and new currents or more intimately concerned to push forward the frontiers of the estate of letters. Painters and writers who, under Apollinaire's easy yet commanding auspices, had enjoyed without thinking about it an exhilarating sense of communication among themselves felt suddenly cut off. He was but one of the victims of a war that had dispersed a brotherhood and ended a society nothing could reconstitute. "When mobilisation was decreed in August 1914," said Picasso, "I accompanied Braque and Derain to the railway station at Avignon. We have never found each other again." The undefined but pulsating center of the old Paris was gone; and it was into this widespread sense of vacancy that Gertrude and Alice had returned.

On the outs with Picasso; far away from Matisse, who had gone to Nice to settle down permanently; fondly worried about Juan Gris who was ill, discouraged and uncommunicative, Gertrude felt alone and rootless in a city full of transient strangers. Only Mildred Aldrich, now puttering away among the flowers in her battlefield garden in the afterglow of her best-selling success, seemed to be a link with the happier past.

From Leo, back from America and now at home in Settignano Gertrude received an unusually mellow and characteristically self-obsessed letter:

DEAR GERTRUDE:

I sent you a note from N.Y. before I left as I found that the antagonism that had grown up some years ago had gotten dissipated and that I felt quite amiable, rather more so even than I used to feel before the strain developed. It's rather curious, the change that has come over me in the last month or so. You know all those digestive troubles & most of the others that I had, I eventually found to be merely neurotic symptoms & all the time in America or at least intermittently during all that time I was trying to cure the neurosis. But they're damned hard things to cure & it was as it was with the digestive cures always up and down, till recently I was in almost utter despair. Then . . . I got on a tack that has led to better states. This has finally led to an easing up & simplifying of most of my contacts with things and people and bro't about a condition where it was possible to write to you. . . . "The family romance" as it is called is almost always central in the case of a neurosis just as you used to get indigestion when we had a dispute. So I could tell pretty well how I was getting on by the degree of possibility I felt of writing as I am doing now.

It's a curious thing to look back upon one's life as I do now as something with which I have nothing to do except to stand for the consequences because it was really a prolonged disease, a kind of mild insanity. . . . Unfortunately my first attempts at psychoanalysis did not work satisfactorily, every little advance was countered by as great a relapse. If it hadn't been for that I might have had a successful time over there. . . .

The Dadaists, led by Tristan Tzara, appeared noisily in Paris in 1920, but Gertrude would have nothing to do with them. In the 1930's, Clifton Fadiman dubbed her "the mama of Dada," but the mildly clever epithet is notable mainly for its total inaccuracy. She was in every way opposed to the Dadaists, as a writer, as a thinker, and as a person. Their insistence upon nihilistic extravagance in art and personal behavior was polar to her insistence upon a new order of apprehension and expression, not to mention her taste for the old-fashioned amenities of daily existence. She became friendly with Tzara for a brief period, but never felt the stimulation others professed to find in his fiery career.

It was a time of transition, protracted by the war and its after-effects, a time in which the Americanization of France, according to Gertrude, was evident in "hygienes, bath-tubs, and sport," a time in which her most important personal associations would tend to be with Americans who wrote rather than with Europeans who painted. The great invasion and temporary settlement of the American expatriates had begun and if art was in the air, so was talk of jazz, skyscrapers, the newest tango from Argentina, machinery and advertising slogans. Gertrude was there to welcome all the disillusioned, idealistic and talented young men and all their hangers-on just as, a few years later, with no less enthusiasm, she was there to bid them good-by.

A key event in the new constitution of things was the establishment by Sylvia Beach of Shakespeare & Company, in the Rue de l'Odéon. This bookshop, catering to English readers of a high degree of literacy, offered not only a handsome display of new publications and a gallery of literary celebrities photographed by Man Ray, but a comfortable back parlor with a fireplace. There tea was served among manuscripts of Walt Whitman on perpetual display. Gertrude became friends with the shop and its proprietress at once, signaling her support by becoming the first annual subscriber to the rental library. Sylvia Beach, who came from Princeton, New Jersey, where her father was a clergyman, had been an ambulance driver during the war. A clean-cut, small woman with a masculine air, she impressed her customers with the intelligent enthusiasms she showed for the creative milieu into which she had ventured. Sylvia Beach had been introduced to the bookman's world by Adrienne Monnier who ran another famous shop, La Maison des Amis des Livres, also in the Rue de l'Odéon. Like Shakespeare & Company, La Maison paid little attention to the bulk of publishers' listings and determinedly featured the unconventional and experimental. Among its many famous customers were André Gide, Paul Claudel, André Breton and the leaders of Dada, as well as the composers who became famous as *Les Six:* Darius Milhaud, Georges Auric, Francis Poulenc, Germaine Taillefer, Arthur Honegger and Louis Durey.

One of the earliest projects of Shakespeare & Company was the publication of James Joyce's *Ulysses,* and it was from the shop's premises that the enormous and, to many Americans, deliciously illicit business of selling a proscribed book was carried on. Sylvia Beach had little notion that so rarefied a venture, as it seemed then, would turn into a very profitable and illustrious business. Her close friendship with Joyce himself, which led eventually to her handling his correspondence and much of his typing, did not at first aversely affect her good relations with Gertrude. It was Sylvia Beach, in fact, who introduced the two writers to one another. Gertrude and Joyce had previously shown interest in knowing one another, but things had gone awry with plans made by mutual friends and the event never took place. Once they had even been in the same room together at an Edith Sitwell reading, but their actual meeting did not occur until they were both guests at a party Jo Davidson gave to celebrate the completion of his statue of Walt Whitman. On this occasion, Miss Beach approached Gertrude to tell her that Joyce was present and would like to meet her, but that because of his eyes he could not move around. Gertrude allowed herself to be led to Joyce's side and, according to a letter she wrote to W. G. Rogers, said "we have never met and he said no although our names are always together, and then we talked of Paris and where we lived and why we lived where we lived and that was all. . . ." At other times, Gertrude was often touchy about the coupling of her name with that of the Irish master mainly because, by suggesting affinities of outlook and method that did not exist, such mention did disservice to both writers. Her wish to dissociate herself from all connection with Joyce was based not only upon her profoundly different practice but upon her conviction that it was a writer's business to stick to English. Joyce, she felt, had not resisted temptations she well understood but had indulged in the fabrication of a language of his own. Of modern masters, she preferred to be mentioned in the same breath with Proust. But as far as her own reading tastes were concerned, she enjoyed detective stories more than the works of either.

CHAPTER 16

> It was the time of a kind of renaissance in the
> arts, in literature, a Robin's Egg Renaissance.
> . . . It had perhaps a pale blue tinge. It fell out
> of the nest. It may be that we should all have
> stayed in Chicago.
>
> — SHERWOOD ANDERSON

"SO it was to be the Lost Generation . . .
Gertrude Stein made a famous remark to Hemingway, and Hemingway used it as the inscription for a novel (*The Sun Also Rises*), and
the novel was good and became a craze —" So wrote the American critic Malcolm Cowley who grew up with the generation, then
away from it and became with the publication of *Exile's Return* its
most authentic and perhaps most sympathetic historian. "Young
men tried to get as imperturbably drunk as the hero, young women
of fairly good family cultivated the heroine's nymphomania, and
the name was fixed. It was a boast at first, like telling what a hangover one had after a party to which someone else wasn't invited.
Afterwards it was used apologetically, it even became ridiculous;
and yet in the beginning, as applied to writers born at the turn of
the century, it was as accurate as any tag could be.

"They were, in the first place, a generation, and probably the
first real one in the history of American letters. They came to matu-

232

city during a period of violent change, when the influence of the time seemed temporarily more important than that of class or locality. Everywhere after the war people were fumbling for a word to express their feeling that youth had a different outlook. The word couldn't be found for years; but long before Gertrude Stein made her famous remark, the young men to whom she referred had already undergone the similar experiences and developed the similar attitude that made it possible to describe them as a literary generation."

Hemingway soon regretted the apologetic connotations that came to fasten and cling like barnacles to the epigraph he had chosen for his book, and tried consistently to disabuse readers of its over-publicized meaning. It was true that the young men of his generation had been dumped out of their porch swings by the tremors of militarism, and it was a matter of record that they had been sent or cajoled into battlefields by the ripples of patriotism and the rhetoric of high-minded slogans. In the cross fire of other men's wars, they had watched their Christian democratic idealism become the first victim of its own pretensions, while the generation itself was dispossessed, disillusioned, and fed to the teeth with a bitterness they would taste, retaste and spit out for years. Yet, said Hemingway, "damned if we were lost except for deads, *gueules cassées*, and certified crazies. Lost, no. And Criqui, who was a real *gueule cassée*, won the featherweight championship of the world. We were a very solid generation. . . ."

Gertrude claimed no personal part in the coining of the immensely durable epithet and, in fact, doubted that she had uttered it. If, as people said, the phrase was her invention, the idea must have been the result of a talk she once had with M. Pernollet, the hotelkeeper in Belley, where she was later to take up summer residence. It was M. Pernollet's conviction that every man becomes civilized between the ages of eighteen and twenty-five. If the civilizing experience does not occur within that period, the individual has lost his chance. And that is what had happened to those who went to the war. Missing their opportunity, they had become "*une génération perdue*."

233

Homesick just beneath the skin, the young and the lost came to the Rue de Fleurus where they might take refuge in "the mature Gertrudian bosom," as Van Wyck Brooks put it, "much like that of their far-away prairie mothers, but of a most gratifying sophistication. Miss Stein gave them back their nursery rhymes and they had fine babbling times together." Worse than that, Brooks felt, she provided "a diet of nightingales' tongues for boys who knew nothing of beef and potatoes." They came in multitudes — valedictorians fresh from the colleges of the Eastern seaboard, misunderstood children from small festering towns in the Deep South, cynics in corduroy from the wastelands of the great Middle West where culture was Caruso on the gramophone and Millais' *Hope* twanging her harp over the imitation fireplace. Greenwich Village was but a stopping place on their inevitable trek to the "City of Light" and the crooked streets of its Left Bank. After the French Line had ferried them across and they had established a beachhead at American Express, they were like children let loose in a grand bazaar. "Everyone was in Paris," wrote Margaret Anderson in *My Thirty Years' War*, one of many accounts of hairsbreadth escape from the middle class and the Middle West which in their time were as familiar as stories of escape from Hitler's Germany or Stalin's Russia in the following decades:

The Swedish Ballet gave nightly galas in the Théâtre des Champs Elysées. Jean Cocteau's Les Mariés de la Tour Eiffel was given for the first time, with costumes by Jean Victor Hugo. Groups of insurgent artists prayed for scandal, hissing, booing, blowing on keys. Cocteau came in with his high hair, his unique hands and his woolen mittens. After a ballet Satie and Picabia appeared on the stage in a motor car to acknowledge applause. . . . Stravinsky gave his Noces with the Ballets Russes, Milhaud, Auric, Poulenc and Marcelle Meyer played the four pianos. . . . The Ballets Russes had a new curtain by Picasso — two running women a hundred times larger than life. Picasso sat in Diagleff's loge, determined to be seen without evening clothes. Braque threatened to hold up a performance — one of his greens had been tampered with. . . . Satie was discovered in tears because his ballet was applauded less than others. James Joyce was discovered at all the symphony concerts — no matter how bad. Juan Gris was making beautiful dolls. Gertrude Stein was buying André Masson. Man Ray was photographing pins and combs, sieves and shoe-trees. Fernand Leger was beginning his cubist cinema, Ballet Mécanique, with music by George Antheil. The Boeuf-sur-le-Toit . . . had a negro saxophonist, and Milhaud and Jean Wiéner were beginning their worship of American jazz. The Comte de Beaumont presented his Soirées de Paris, including Cocteau's Roméo et Juliette with Yvonne George. The Dadaists gave performances at the Théâtre Michel where the rioting was so successful that André Breton broke Tzara's arm. Ezra Pound made an opera of Villon's poetry and had it sung in the old Salle Pleyel. . . .

With an inordinate amount of musical accompaniment, the twenties had begun to roar. The dedicated expatriates and the sensation-shopping transients who would communicate the excitements of Paris to Main Street had found at 27 Rue de Fleurus a figure who, in stature, temperament and wisdom, transcended both Paris and Peoria. "It is very pleasant," wrote Professor Carlos Baker in *Hemingway: The Writer as Artist*, "to think of the Pallas Athene, sitting among the statuary in one of her temples like Gertrude Stein among the Picassos . . . and murmuring to the Achaeans, homeward bound from the battle of Troy: 'You are all a lost generation.'" Before Gertrude Stein had become the mother of all the sad young men, a momentous event in her life was the first visit of Sherwood Anderson. While history associates him with the Lost Generation, Anderson by reason of his advanced age and artistic maturity was never really one of their number. He may have shared the indeterminate sense of loss that was part of the emotional equipment of most of them, but feelings of separation and dislocation had, in his case, already been transformed into a positive sense of freedom and a profound intuition that his own life, at least, was dedicated. He had long since got clear of Ohio, as a fact and as a state of mind, and had observed the nature of home-grown Bohemia in Cleveland, Chicago and New Orleans. In the long-delayed realization of his talent he had achieved a personal security that allowed him to be a sponsor of the expatriate movement, rather than a participant. Like almost everyone else who came to Paris, he went to Sylvia Beach's shop, expressed his desire to meet Gertrude, and was shortly escorted to "27."

On his first visit when, along with Miss Beach, he was accompanied by his wife and the American critic Paul Rosenfeld, he showed

"a winning brusquerie, a mordant wit and an all-inclusive heart"
— a combination of virtues which Alice Toklas found irresistible
Anderson's first impression of Gertrude was no less delighted. "Im
agine a strong woman with legs like stone pillars sitting in a room
hung with Picassos," he wrote in his notebook. "The woman is the
very symbol of health and strength. She laughs. She smokes cigar
ettes. She tells stories with an American shrewdness in getting the
tang and the kick into the telling." While the geniality of her *salon*
accommodated everyone, as far as Gertrude and Anderson
were concerned the occasion was theirs alone. After years of neg
lect, while her manuscripts went not to a publisher but to the
shelves of the heavy *armoire* in the vestibule, while even now she
had scant hopes of publication or wide recognition, Gertrude
had become pessimistic and not a little bitter. When Anderson told
her simply what he thought of her work and what, in his own
development, it had meant, she took it as a declaration of love and
was quick to answer him in kind. "I don't think you quite realize
what it meant," she wrote to him, "to have some one and you have
been the only one quite simply to understand what it is all about
simply understand as any one would suppose everyone would un
derstand and to so charmingly and directly tell it to me." From the
first exchange, their correspondence reads like a series of love letters.
"Gee I love you," Sherwood would write. Gertrude would answer, "I
can't tell you how much you always mean to me"; and the current
of mutual praise flowed back and forth for years. "You know some
day Sherwood you must write a novel that is just one portrait.
You are a peach of a portraitist do sometime do a novel that is
just one portrait and nobody else's feelings coming in." In comment
ing on an article praising some piece of hers, she wrote, "I like
your article a lot, I like the fact that you can and do see them where
they are, and where you are, my dear, there is only you doing that."
Meeting but infrequently during the course of their lives after
ward, they nevertheless kept up an intimacy the basis of which can
be most clearly read in their happy recognition of their own
peculiarly American temperaments and personalities and in their
embattled sense of having broken with tradition and confounded it.

Like Gertrude, Anderson was most alive when he was actively struggling to break through into new reaches of expression, even when the effort came to something far short of his hopes. They both had an incorrigible tendency to make a romance of the nature of creative wrestling, and this attitude often led them to neglect to appraise results in their eagerness to praise intentions. In differing ways, they strained to force the language of common speech to express areas of feeling or visual perception that may finally be intractable to the demands of verbal communication. Anderson's straining showed in his passion to give himself wholly to experiences which he was at the same time attempting to delineate. Gertrude Stein's straining was apparent in her remorseless tendency to drain passion from experience and to present the residuum of experience in the shape of a verbal artifact. While their most representative works are not remotely alike, they are products of a shared striving to bring into literature something beyond the means of literature — in Anderson's case, the attempt to make words do the messianic offices of something as vague as the religion of humanity and, in Gertrude Stein's case, the determination to make words do what only painting or the cinema can do. In each case, their achievements bear witness to a kind of genius that will not settle for the satisfactions of mere talent.

Anderson most clearly stated the nature and extent of his professional debt to Gertrude in 1934. In that year, Professor B. F. Skinner, in an article, "Has Gertrude Stein a Secret?" published in the *Atlantic Monthly*, brought forth the notion that the methods of Gertrude Stein were not only influenced by her early laboratory experiments at Harvard, but that much of her writing was indistinguishable from the automatic writing which those experiments were set up to investigate. She had stumbled upon a good thing, Professor Skinner implied, and had subsequently parlayed it into an international reputation. In defense against these charges, Anderson wrote an article for *The American Spectator* in which he analyzed the relationship between the conscious and unconscious aspects of writing in terms that made automatic writing an aesthetic impossibility. He went on to praise Gertrude Stein because she was a "path-finder" and because she had "dared, in the face of ridicule and misunderstanding, to try to waken in all of us who write a new feeling for words." In a letter to his daughter-in-law, Mary Chryst Anderson, he expressed himself further:

I have always thought it quite possible to make the habit of writing words with the hand, the arm, so automatic that something within is released. This is surely not automatic writing, and yet I think that all of the more beautiful and clear, the more plangent and radiant writing I have done, has all been done by a kind of secondary personality that at such times takes possession of me.

In this article the writer speaks of the fact that Miss Stein does not know what she is writing, nor do I, whereas while she denies any secondary self, I attribute all to the secondary self.

You can see the advantage of this. The poet thus escaped the nuisance of parading before the world as poet.

And there is something else; the poet lives only as writer. He has no other life, and I can truly say that the person my friends, my own family, etc., know, has nothing to do at all, or at least very little to do, with the second person, the writer as person.

This, I think, might bring me to what Stein did for me. I am always amused by the talk about her. The point is always missed. Suppose she taught me to recognize the second person in myself, the poet-writing person, so that I could occasionally release that one.

And not to blame it for the anxious person, myself as known by others.

You can see the great gain in that to me and why I think that Stein is a genius.

I think that the man in this article also misses it.

After Anderson had returned to America, among the first of the young men to come to the Rue de Fleurus was big, red-haired Robert Coates, a novelist who later became art critic for the New Yorker. Gertrude and Alice liked him as a person and as a writer and their affection was returned in Coates's praise of Gertrude's work during a long friendship. Constant in expressing his feelings to her personally, Coates also published his appreciation in places strategically important for the growth of her reputation. He was followed to "27" by Ezra Pound, whom Gertrude and Alice liked neither as a person nor as a poet. Pound's special interests at this time ran to Japanese prints, political economy and Oriental music. Gertrude shared none of these, and there was little else about his thinking, his person or his manner that attracted her. A nervous, self-conscious young man with a high voice, a laugh described as being like the triumphant bray of a jackass, and a robust, red-blond bearing, Pound struck many people as being in perpetual motion. "His beard, his open collar, his earring, the lopsided table he had made for himself, the coats he wore, his aggressive mannerisms," said critic Herbert Gorman, "proclaimed to the world in the most militant way that he was continuously either lashing or thumbing his nose at the Philistines." One of Gertrude's objections to the man was his avuncular attitude toward women; with no warrant or warning, he might kiss them on the forehead or draw them upon his knees with no concern for their wishes in the matter or their taste for such displays. Gertrude was nevertheless taken with Ezra "in a sort of way" at first, but soon found him "not amusing." She felt he was a "village explainer" (a term she had once used in describing her brother) which meant that his talk was "excellent if you were a village, but if you were not, not." In particular she took exception to his attempts to "explain" to her the significance of the paintings hanging on her walls. Since they both had widely celebrated reputations as discoverers and sponsors of new talent, it was perhaps fortunate for the peace of letters that they never found themselves in contest over the same prodigy. Gaudier-Brzeska, Pound's brilliant young sculptor friend, had been killed in the war, and George Antheil, the young composer who became his later enthusiasm, had not yet arrived in Paris. The competitive air that emanated from Ezra Pound was certain to keep Gertrude at a distance, even had she been able to overlook his lack of personal charm. Any sort of competition was anathema to her, and she was continually on the alert for signs that circumstance might force her into it. Pound took exception to the pointedly cool treatment she gave him, but she was adamant in refusing him welcome to her atelier. In retaliation, Ezra advertised Gertrude as a mere parasite on the body of literature and delighted in opportunities to refer to her as "old tub of guts."

For the young in the full flush of the Jazz Age, Gertrude's name had become inextricably associated with rebellious stances and attitudes. The fact that these same young men would not or could not read her work was unimportant; since the era of revolt needed figures and symbols, Gertrude Stein became one of its eponymous heroes. As the blue notes of Gershwin's *Rhapsody* "seeped through the gothic twilight of Oxford," so did the spirit and the melody, if not the letter, of *Tender Buttons*. Gershwin's "total rhapsody," wrote the English novelist and self-proclaimed aesthete, Harold Acton "never so slickly performed as in the days of its pristine freshness, with each instrument enjoying its separate tinted spotlight, cast a twentieth-century spell which dove-tailed into the divagations of Picasso, Mr. Prufrock and Gertrude Stein."

Inevitably, the writer most closely identified with the Jazz Age, F. Scott Fitzgerald, came to join the charmed circle about her feet. From their first meeting, he had her deepest confidence and affection. In Gertrude's estimation, Fitzgerald was "the first of the lost generation . . . the only one at that time of their descent on Paris to have already given proof of a gift." She felt he "really created for the public the new generation," first by being the generation's representative and then by becoming its symbol. Fitzgerald was impressed with Gertrude, but also amused by her. He described her as looking like "the Great Stone Face" and once remarked to a friend, "What an old covered-wagon she is!" According to Alice Toklas, he was then "distinguished, highly intelligent and completely attaching." On a later visit with them on his thirtieth birthday, he said it was unbearable to have to face the fact that his golden youth was over. When Gertrude insisted that, after all, he had been writing like a man of thirty for many years, he thanked her for telling him what he wanted to believe. She had warmly praised *This Side of Paradise*, and when *The Great Gatsby* arrived, she told him that she believed he was creating a contemporary world with the same degree of success that Thackeray had achieved in *Pendennis* and *Vanity Fair*. Fitzgerald responded to these praises with a tribute as profound as any ever expressed by the writers of her "lost generation": "I am so anxious to get The Making of Americans & learn something from it and imitate things

out of it which I shall doubtless do. . . . You see, I am content to
let you, and the one or two like you who are acutely sensitive, think
or fail to think for me and my kind artistically (their name is not
legend but the word like it), much as the man of 1901, say, would
let Nietche (sp.) think for him intellectually. I am a very second
rate person compared to first rate people — I have indignation as
well as most of the other major faults — and it honestly makes
me shiver to know that such a writer as you attributes such a significance to my factitious, meritricious (metricious?) This Side of Paradise. It puts me in a false position, I feel. Like Gatsby I have only
hope." This hope was to remain with Fitzgerald all through his
short life. In his notes for *The Last Tycoon*, the novel interrupted
by his death, he recorded: "I want to write scenes that are frightening and inimitable. I don't want to be as intelligible to my contemporaries as Ernest who as Gertrude said, is bound for the
Museums. I am sure I am far enough ahead to have some small
immortality if I can keep well."

Alfred Kreymborg, the American poet, en route to Rome to establish *Broom*, a magazine he was planning to edit with his ex-Prince-
ton friend, Harold A. Loeb, came to "27" and talked of his new
venture which, presumably, would make a clean sweep of everything. Gertrude made the most of the opportunity his visit presented. "Pulling open a row of ponderous drawers in a cabinet,"
Kreymborg recalled, "she disclosed a pile of huge manuscripts she
had been working on for years, none of which had ever been published in book form and only slight portions of which had been
accepted by magazines." This information, and the sight of the un-
wanted manuscripts, stunned Kreymborg and he took two of the
bound volumes containing *A Long Gay Book* for his co-editor to
examine. Loeb could not be talked into enthusiasm for this work,
but was finally agreeable to publishing one small narrative of Gertrude's, *If You Had Three Husbands*, to be issued "in short, serial
doses."

A lady refugee from a house full of aged invalids and the gloom
of New England winters, journalist Kate Buss of Medford, Massachusetts, led a Boston contingent to the Rue de Fleurus and be-

came herself one of its regulars. In spite of her hazy understanding of Gertrude's work and her unsettling suspicions about its validity for years Miss Buss kept the readers of the staid pages of the *Boston Evening Transcript* au courant with the name of Stein. While her personal devotion to Gertrude never resulted in comprehension of her work, she was one of the few people who could, directly, question Gertrude on this or that intention without being suspected of a breach of loyalty. With Kate Buss came the severely handsome Djuna Barnes, who would eventually write the remarkable novel *Nightwood*. Gertrude did not read this book. Had she done so, she would have found that it illustrated certain theories of hers on a scale and in a depth she might well have envied. As a theorist, she had many ideas that remained subject to more positive proof in creative acts than she was herself able to produce. But the insularity she cultivated in regard to nearly all but the very youngest of her contemporaries kept her from seeing further than her own nose. Myopia in relation to some of the most significant literature of an era she considered her own was but one of the consequences of her engulfing egotism.

Another figure who received from the sometimes imperious hostesses of "27" less attention than his distinction would seem to warrant was Glenway Wescott, the celebrated young novelist who came trailing behind him the rich dust of Wisconsin and the Byronic cloak for which he was famous at the University of Chicago. Gertrude decided that, while Wescott had "a certain syrup" in his personality, "it just doesn't pour." (Years later, these words were turned against her when, in the same culinary spirit, Malcolm Cowley offered the notion that Gertrude had "a certain pepper, but it clogs in the shaker.")

While T. S. Eliot had attained in these years a solid but somewhat austere and limited reputation, his stature was already outlined clearly enough to indicate the great range of his ultimate influence. Within the walls of "27," his name had first been mentioned by Ezra Pound. Through a mutual friend of Gertrude's and Eliot's, Lady Rothermere, who was financing the publication of *The Criterion* which was edited by the poet, an evening was arranged at which

Miss Stein and Mr. Eliot were to become acquainted. Gertrude professed to be but halfhearted in the prospect, but Alice and others told her that this was one young man she should not miss knowing. Alice was putting finishing touches on a new evening dress Gertrude was going to wear for the occasion when, unexpectedly, Lady Rothermere and Eliot, along with Jane Heap, the editor of *The Little Review*, arrived at the Rue de Fleurus. Alice remembered Eliot as "a sober, almost solemn, not so young man who, refusing to give up his umbrella, sat clasping its handle while his eyes burned brightly in a non-committal face." With Gertrude he had a sober conversation about split infinitives and other grammatical solecisms, and her knack of bringing them into her work. Eliot suggested that he would be pleased to have her give him something for publication in an early issue of the *Criterion*. But, he insisted, what he wanted was her very latest thing. As soon as he and his companions had departed, she sat down and wrote a portrait of Eliot which, since his visit had been made on November 15, she entitled *The Fifteenth of November*. Eliot accepted this piece but, in spite of his insistence on the freshness of what he might publish, its appearance was repeatedly delayed for nearly two years.

The Eliot portrait was merely one in a series of such works in a now familiar method. However, since it was published in an organ as highly regarded as *The Criterion* and since the renown of its subject was great, the portrait served to buttress Gertrude's rapidly solidifying reputation as underminer of traditions and menace to the academies. The seismographic pen of Henry Seidel Canby registered tremors that were beginning to shake the world of established literature, in the center of which, like an ivy-covered Kremlin, stood Harvard University. "If this is literature," wrote Canby, "or anything other than stupidity worse than madness, then has all criticism since the beginning of letters been mere idle theorizing. If it is literature, then alas! for literature. Thank Heaven, that there are still Professor Lowes and Harvards to conserve tradition and guide taste, and to make the world unsafe for eccentricity. To raise the grotesque and the absurd to the plane of the serious is to render a disservice to literature. More, it is to render an insult to intelligence and evoke a curse on criticism."

Gertrude professed to be pleased when, some time later, she heard that Eliot had said in a lecture at Cambridge that her work was "very fine but not for us." What Eliot actually said was "it is not improving, it is not amusing, it is not interesting, it is not good for one's mind. But its rhythms have a peculiar hypnotic power not met with before. It has a kinship with the saxophone. If this is the future, then the future is, as it very likely is, of the barbarians. But this is the future in which we ought not to be interested." While deploring her influence, Eliot nevertheless granted the effectiveness of some of her methods, and admitted in a letter to her that he was "immensely interested" in everything she wrote.

In this era of great personalities, as a renewed Paris became the crucible for experimentation in every art form and the symbol of freedom for artists of every degree of talent and restlessness, Gertrude continued to write in serenity and deep self-conviction. She wrote every day, and under any circumstance imposed by the domestic routine which she and Alice were at meticulous pains to observe. Instead of the long unbroken nighttime sessions of the earlier years, she had now learned to work in concentrated short periods — sometimes for minutes, sometimes for hours, through the course of every day. She had even learned to write while posing and, through a series of sittings for the sculptor Lipschitz, sat pencil in hand. But most of her writing was done in the high front seat of "Godiva," the Ford that had recently replaced the war-worn "Auntie," as she waited for Alice to complete the daily round of errands to grocers and tradespeople. Street sounds, she discovered, and the movements of traffic, provided counterpoint and impetus to creation. She developed a method of setting a sentence for herself as a sort of tuning fork or metronone and then writing to that tempo and tune. Among the works put together in this way were *Mildred's Thoughts*, which Gertrude felt best represented her work of the immediate postwar period, and the *Birthplace of Bonnes* and *Moral Tales 1920-1921*.

With another completed manuscript in hand, and no prospects

for its acceptance by a commercial publisher, she once more had to resort to subsidizing her own wares. On the advice of a friend she made arrangements for the publication of *Geography and Plays* with the Four Seas Company, of Boston. This obscure house, only a few years earlier, had been devoted wholly to such publications as *School Ethics* by Eleanor Marchbanks, *Running and Training*, by the coach of the Harvard track team, and *Manna for the Months*, by Helen Elizabeth Jeffers, "a series of original thoughts for mental, physical and spiritual progress." But after a period of undiluted wholesomeness, the Four Seas Company had suddenly gone in for Literature. Books by forceful new writers like Conrad Aiken, John Gould Fletcher and William Carlos Williams were now on its list, and Gertrude's friend, Kate Buss, had arranged with them to publish her *Studies in the Chinese Drama*.

In the hope of gaining attention in America, Gertrude asked Sherwood Anderson if he would be interested in writing an introduction to the book, telling him again that his response to her work was unique, and that she had never ceased to cherish it. Anderson replied that he would rather do an introduction for her work than any other literary task he could think of, and shortly produced an essay which included the following passages:

One evening in the winter, some years ago, my brother came to my rooms in the city of Chicago bringing with him a book by Gertrude Stein. This book was called *Tender Buttons* and, just at that time, there was a good deal of fuss and fun being made over it in American newspapers. I had already read a book of Miss Stein's called *Three Lives* and had thought it contained some of the best writing ever done by an American. I was curious about this new book.

My brother had been at some sort of a gathering of literary people on the evening before and someone had read aloud from Miss Stein's new book. The party had been a success. After a few lines the reader stopped and was greeted by loud shouts of laughter. It was generally agreed that the author had done a thing we Americans call "putting something across" — the meaning being that she had, by a strange freakish performance, managed to attract attention to herself, get herself discussed in the newspapers, become for a time a figure in our hurried, harried lives.

My brother, as it turned out, had not been satisfied with the explanation of Miss Stein's work then current in America, and so he bought *Tender*

Buttons and brought it to me, and we sat for a time reading the strange sentences. "It gives words an oddly new intimate flavor and at the same time makes familiar words seem almost like strangers, doesn't it," he said. What my brother did, you see, was to set my mind going on the book, and then, leaving it on the table, he went away. . . .

Since Miss Stein's work was first brought to my attention I have been thinking of it as the most important pioneer work done in the field of letters in my time. The loud guffaws of the general that must inevitably follow the bringing forward of more of her work do not irritate me but I would like it if writers, and particularly young writers, would come to understand a little what she is trying to do and what she is in my opinion doing.

My thought in the matter is something like this — that every artist working with words as his medium, must at times be profoundly irritated by what seems the limitation of his medium. What things he does not wish to create with words! There is the mind of the reader before him and he would like to create in that reader's mind a whole new world of sensations, or rather one might better say he would like to call back into life all of the dead and sleeping senses.

There is a thing one might call "the extension of the province of his art" one wants to achieve. One works with words and one would like words that have a taste on the lips, that have a perfume in the nostrils, rattling words one can throw into a box and shake, making a sharp, jingling sound, words that, when seen on the printed page, have a distinct arresting effect upon the eye, words that when they jump out from under the pen one may feel with the fingers as one might caress the cheeks of his beloved.

And what I think is that these books of Gertrude Stein's do in a very real sense recreate life in such words. . . .

For me the work of Gertrude Stein consists in a rebuilding, an entire new recasting of life, in the city of words. Here is one artist who has been able to accept ridicule, who has even forgone the privilege of writing the great American novel, uplifting our English speaking stage, and wearing the bays of the great poets, to go live among the little house-keeping words, the swaggering bullying street-corner words, the honest working, money saving words, and all the other forgotten and neglected citizens of the sacred and half forgotten city.

Would it not be a lovely and charmingly ironic gesture of the gods if, in the end, the work of this artist were to prove the most lasting and important of all the word slingers of our generation!

When *Geography and Plays* was finally dispatched to its publisher in Boston, Gertrude and Alice packed their luggage into their Ford runabout and made a midsummer trip to Saint Rémy to explore again the countryside they had come to love during their wartime errands of mercy. Seduced once more by the charms of the valley of the Rhône, they lingered contentedly into the autumn. Their hotel was not a particularly comfortable one, but when they agreed that the country about had a poignant beauty that would compensate for any material shortcomings, they settled down for the winter. Relieved to be out of the whirl of their usual Parisian society of earnest pilgrims and dilettante transients, they spent their days wholly with country people except on occasions when they had visits from their friends, the sculptress Janet Scudder, and Camille Sigard, the opera singer, who had taken a house nearby. So began Gertrude's "Saint Rémy period," and during the ensuing months she produced some of the loveliest, most lyrical writings of her career. Landscape was again the thing that set the tune and sustained the melody. She visited the remains of Roman monuments that studded the area; she watched huge flocks of sheep pouring through mountain passes and spreading themselves out upon the fields; and interminably she wandered the little Alpine hills meditating upon the uses of grammar and the nature of poetical forms. These were months when, she said later, "I concentrated the internal melody of existence that I had learned in relation to things seen into the feeling I then had . . . of light and air and air moving and being still. I worked at these things then with a great deal of concentration and as it was to me an entirely new way of doing it I had as a result a very greatly increased melody." Music had suddenly begun to shape everything that she wrote. Her visual subjects were still disrelated, juxtaposed and atomized without any concern for representation except in cubist terms, but there was a new lift and buoyancy in the measures she made of them. *Saints in Seven* and *Talks to Saints in Saint Rémy* were among the happiest results of the sojourn, and with these pieces came the beginning of the long preoccupation with her other-worldly yet curiously non-celestial view of the nature and temperament of sainthood. She wrote her famous *A Valentine for Sherwood Anderson,* and a series of other love poems of an airy delicacy and playfulness, and she wrote

Capital Capitals, a "conversation" among the four capitals of Provence — Aix, Arles, Avignon and Les Baux — which, within a few years, would provide her with her first important text for music. It was a winter of great creativity and intense happiness, far from the restlessness of the postwar generation and the distractions of forceful and often importunate friends and visitors. But even the concentrated "melody of existence" was something she could not endure for long. "I was rather drunk with what I had done," she said. "And I am always one to prefer being sober. I must be sober. It is so much more exciting to be sober, to be exact and concentrated and sober. So then as I say I began again." When March came and the relentless mistral blew for days on end and spring was barely in sight, they were glad to return to "27" and its solid familiar comforts.

CHAPTER 17

I very recently met a man who said, how do you
do. A splendid story.

— GERTRUDE STEIN

THE young man with the "passionately in-
terested rather than interesting eyes" who came to dinner one winter
evening in 1922 with his pretty wife, Hadley, was Ernest Hemingway. His hostess, Gertrude Stein, knew nothing about him except
brief information conveyed in a letter from Sherwood Anderson,
which she had received a few days before, saying that his friend
Hemingway was an American writer "instinctively in touch with
everything worth while" and that she would find him delightful to
know.

Miss Stein did find him delightful. She was struck with his extraordinary good looks, and was above all completely charmed to
find that he was "a born listener." From their very first encounter
he seemed to want only to sit before her, an immense audience of
one, and listen to the slow deliberations of her entrancing voice.
When, now and then, *he* talked, she liked what he said, but had to
admit that she preferred his long absorbent silences. She knew they

would become friends and, as a first gesture, offered to teach him how to cut his wife's hair.

In the Hemingways' apartment in the Rue Notre Dame des Champs near the Place du Tertre a few days afterward they conferred, piece by piece, about most of the work he had written — a part of a novel, some very short stories and a number of poems. The poems interested her for what she felt was their forthright Kiplingesque manner, but the novel struck her only as inept, the stories as often too frank. She felt that Hemingway should stick to "poetry and intelligence" and eschew the hotter emotions and more turgid vision that informed his prose. However, since he would be a novelist, her advice was simple: begin all over again, and concentrate.

They met often after that, taking long conversational walks about the Left Bank, mulling over Hemingway's writing problems and the practical living problems which curbed his freedom to write. In March, he wrote to Sherwood Anderson, "Gertrude Stein and me are just like brothers, and we see a lot of her." As correspondent for the Toronto *Daily Star* and feature writer for the *Star Weekly*, he had to face every day the dilemma of professional necessity and creative ambition. Now, to complicate everything, his wife was pregnant. He said he was too young to be a father. Gertrude helped him to face the inevitable. She advised him to save up enough money through journalism to enable him to turn to literature exclusively for a long solid period, because if he did not somehow get out of journalism and write, she was afraid that one would use up the juice needed for the other. Accepting her counsel, he returned to Toronto. There he was continuously homesick for Paris and sorely burdened by financial difficulties. He wrote to Gertrude saying that he could finally understand why businessmen committed suicide. But Gertrude's words of advice had made a deep impression and helped to sustain him through a bad time. "She has a wonderful head," he told Edmund Wilson, "she is where Mencken and Mary Colum fall down and skin their noses."

When his first child, a boy, was born in October, 1923, Hemingway was eager to take his leave of Toronto for good. Within a few months he was back in Paris, still forced to take on journalistic assignments, but determined to put first things first and concentrate on his writing. His apprehensions about the baby had been dispersed on its arrival; now he was concerned about the circumstances under which it should be baptized. With no previous church ties to direct his choice, he finally decided on the Episcopal, and Gertrude Stein and Alice B. Toklas became the godmothers of John Hadley Hemingway.

Like everyone else who knew him well, Gertrude was aware of the multiple personality of the young Hemingway and was fearful that his need for protective disguises would eventually lead to his losing himself. The individual she knew on her own terms was obviously not the one in the legend he had begun to generate in the personality-conscious environs of the Dôme and the Sélect. "Hemingway is so soft-hearted that it must be as much as he can bear to beat a punching-bag," said Margaret Anderson. "If I had to choose a single adjective to describe Hemingway I should choose simple." Jane Heap, Miss Anderson's co-editor on *The Little Review*, thought that his animal prototype would be a rabbit, "pink and white face, soft brown eyes that look at you without blinking. As for his love for boxing and bull-fighting — all that is thrashing up the ground with his hind legs." His way of changing poses bewildered many others and tended, often, to keep potential friends at arm's length. He was the hard-boiled American reporter with a hard self-confident smile, coming at you with a chip on his shoulder; he was also the wide-eyed "*Sensitif*," still trying to assimilate the experiences that had swiftly transported him from Oak Park, Illinois, to the Boulevard Montparnasse. "Hemingway was a type not easy to size up," according to the American novelist and publisher Robert McAlmon. "At times he was deliberately hard-boiled and case-hardened; again he appeared deliberately innocent, sentimental, the hurt, soft, but fairly sensitive boy trying to conceal hurt, wanting to be brave, not bitter or cynical but being somewhat both, and somehow on the defensive, suspicions lurking in his peering analytic glances at a person with whom he was talking. He approached a café with a small-boy, tough-guy, swagger, and before strangers of whom he was doubtful a potential snarl of scorn played on his large-lipped, rather loose mouth."

But he was also "Beery-poppa," the family man who addressed his wife as "Feather-kitty." With the infant, "Bumby," they lived in a squalid apartment without a toilet or running water, with a mattress spread on the floor for their bed. The only note of comparative affluence in the ménage was a baby carriage luxurious enough to cause a stir in the Luxembourg Gardens when, in the afternoons, it was trundled through the buzz-saw whine and floating sawdust in the carpenter's yard that served as the "court" on which their apartment faced.

Though she did not particularly encourage him, Hemingway sought out Gertrude time and again. He hungered for her private and special regard and, while she was never distant to his advances, she accepted him with a preference that was no more or less than that she granted to many other engaging and talented young men who came into her preserve. When on occasion she left Paris for the country, he said the city was empty without her, sent nostalgic postcards begging her to come back because he had just discovered sleep and what a fine way it was to spend the winter and needed her to cheer up the town, and otherwise counted the days until her return. Like a child showing off before an only half-attentive parent, he was, on the one hand, continually calling her attention to his exploits in boxing, bullfighting, skiing and fishing and, on the other, telling her how mightily he was struggling with creative problems and how much, under her guidance, he was learning. A little more than a year after their first meeting, he wrote to her saying, "It was a vital day for me when I stumbled upon you." While Ezra Pound and other eminent figures were his sometime mentors, Hemingway later made no secret about who it was had helped him most. Speaking with the American poet John Peale Bishop, he said, "Ezra was right half the time, and when he was wrong, he was so wrong you were never in any doubt about it. Gertrude was always right."

He moved about restlessly — Spain, Italy, the Tyrol — sometimes on minor newspaper assignments, but more often in pursuit of another inexpensive place in which to live and write, where the fishing or the skiing was good or, best of all, where there was someone willing to put on boxing gloves with him. But he was never out of touch with Gertrude, and never lost his hunger for her advice and approval. He sent her word-counts of his progress, reported in detail the all-night writing hours he kept, and analyzed for her every shift in his creative impulse, including those bad times when his head was "like a frozen cabbage."

When they were both in Paris at the same time they followed current gossip like bloodhounds and were in at the death of many a reputation. But their central concern was always for tokens or premonitions of their own success. Every new acceptance, however minor or from whatever fiercely obscure little magazine, was occasion for extravagant congratulations. They both had a clearly defined feeling, if only a vague picture, of coming glory, and shared their confidence like an illicit secret. Believing that it was "the best stuff I have ever read," Hemingway tried to get Gertrude's magnum opus, *The Making of Americans*, written nearly fifteen years before, into the possibly sympathetic hands of the American publisher Horace Liveright. This led to a series of dealings that seemed hopeful, but finally a flat rejection from Liveright came through. He took the rejection personally ("I feel sick about it but don't you feel bad, because you have written it and that is all that matters a damn"), and tried to hearten Gertrude by saying that it was only a matter of time before it would all come about and that she should believe him because his optimism was "not Christian Science."

His prophecy was not without immediate support. Ford Madox Ford was preparing to bring out a new magazine, *The Transatlantic Review*. Under the urgings of Hemingway, who served as an associate editor and literary scout, Ford decided to begin serialization of a portion of *The Making of Americans*. To make this possible, excerpts had to be copied from the original sewn and bound manuscript which had long been stashed away among other reams of unpublished Stein. Since there was but one copy of the manuscript in existence, Hemingway was entrusted with the job. His labors as copyist for Gertrude Stein's favorite writing touched her deeply; from then on her attitude toward him was always one of "indulgent weakness," quite in contrast to that of people who, unaware of his strict and sober attentions to his work, came to regard him as one of the bogus Bronco Bills of Montparnasse who from the Dôme and the Rotonde would set off on nightly *bistro* binges flourishing verbal lassos and do their daily writing stints in the mists of the inevitable hangover.

Hemingway's taste in literature tended to be rather indifferently catholic, especially where the work of his contemporaries was concerned. But he disagreed sharply with Gertrude on the virtues of a book she heralded — E. E. Cummings's *The Enormous Room.* Hemingway felt sure that it had been copied from somewhere. He had no idea where or from what, but still he was sure that the book was not the original work it seemed to be. Gertrude insisted that its originality was authentic and, in view of Cummings's ingrained New England outlook, that its individuality could be logically presupposed. Hemingway was unmoved by her explanation, and didn't care; he still thought it was all cribbed from somewhere. Not two years later, however, he was saying that *The Enormous Room* was the greatest book he had ever read.

Hemingway's regard for Sherwood Anderson apparently lessened to a degree commensurate with the advancement of his own career and gradually led to his complete renunciation of the older writer. It was a familiar story as, once more, temperament and circumstance drove a brash tyro to the point of baiting and satirizing the old master from whom he had received only kindness. In a creative burst during seven days in November, 1925, Hemingway wrote *The Torrents of Spring.* This book, wrote Professor Carlos Baker, "a satirical *jeu d'esprit* with a serious core, got its title from Turgenev, its locale from the State of Michigan, and its *raison d'être* from the writings of Anderson and (to a lesser degree) Gertrude Stein." In writing it, Hemingway made an attempt, partly, to ridicule Anderson's style and to discredit his worth as the "present ace and best-seller" among his contemporaries; and, though he made no particular point of it, to take a satiric swipe at Anderson's trick of imitating Gertrude, as in the following passage:

254

Going somewhere now. En route. Huysmans wrote that. It would be interesting to read French. There was a street corner in Paris named after Huysmans. Right around the corner from where Gertrude Stein lived. Ah, there was a woman! Where were her experiments in words leading her? What was at the bottom of it? All that in Paris. Ah, Paris! How far it was to Paris now. Paris in the morning. Paris in the evening, Paris at night. Paris in the morning again. Paris at noon, perhaps. Why not? Yogi Johnson striding on. His mind never still.

And when he entitled Part Three of his book "The Making and Marring of Americans," the message he had for Gertrude was clear. When the book was finished, he sent Anderson a letter which the latter regarded as "the most self-conscious and probably the most patronizing letter ever written. . . . There was something in the letter that was gigantic. It was a kind of funeral oration over my grave." As for *The Torrents of Spring* itself, Anderson felt that it was a parasitic book that might have been funny if someone like Max Beerbohm had cut it down to about twelve pages.

Still, he was puzzled about Hemingway's having turned upon him and took seriously the one possible clue that Gertrude supplied. She had reason to believe that Hemingway had resented Anderson's stories *I'm a Fool* and *I Want to Know Why* because they frustrated Hemingway's determination to stake out the whole field of sports for himself. In any case, Anderson eventually came to share much of Gertrude's feeling about their erstwhile protégé: "I think that, in the case of Hemmy, there is too much talk of style. In the end the style is the man. I keep wondering why the man feels life as he does. It is as though he saw it always as rather ugly. 'People have it in for me. All right. I'll go for them.' There is the desire always to kill . . . he cannot bear the thought of any other men as Artists . . . wants to occupy the entire field.

"There is this sharp difference between the man and, say, Wolfe or Faulkner. They may write of terrible happenings, but you feel always an inner sympathy with the fact of life itself."

When Anderson visited Paris later in the twenties, Hemingway, in spite of urgings from mutual friends, made no effort to see him. On his last day in Paris as he sat in his hotel room among his packed

255

bags, Anderson later recalled, "there was a sudden knock on the door, and there Hemingway was.

"He stood in the doorway.

" 'How about a drink,' he said, and I followed him down a stairway and across a street.

"We went into a small bar.

" 'What will you have?'

" 'Beer.'

" 'And you?'

" 'A beer.'

" 'Well, here's how.'

" 'Here's how.'

"He turned and walked rapidly away."

When Gertrude admonished Hemingway for having taken an attitude so ungrateful, he said that it had to be made clear that he and Anderson were and had always been poles apart in the matter of taste. Gertrude was not interested. She loved Anderson and was convinced that he had a genius for using the sentence to convey a direct emotion which made him permanently important. There was no one else in America, she said, who could write so clear and passionate a sentence. Hemingway thought this was false and, even if it were true, was still sure that Anderson was deficient in taste. Gertrude's answer was that taste had nothing to do with sentences. What's more, she added, with a shift of attention he perhaps found slightly chilling, among the younger writers it was only Scott Fitzgerald who wrote naturally in the kind of sentences that distinguished a good novel from a bad one.

Alice Toklas was one of several people, among them Pablo Picasso, who claimed they had first "sent Hemingway to Pamplona," where he was introduced to bullfighting. Whether or not she was directly responsible, she and Gertrude had whetted his interest by many accounts of bullfighting, stemming especially from their stay in Majorca during the early days of the war. From the first time that he witnessed a bullfight Hemingway looked upon boxing as "paler and paler," as he wrote on a postcard from Spain, and was obviously well on his way toward becoming the *aficionado* author of *Death in the Afternoon*. Some of his friends suspected that his response was less love at first sight for the sport than it was a need to love the art of the bullfight because Gertrude had praised it to him. At any rate, between brief stays in Paris and excursions about the Continent, there was always a trip to Spain to catch the performance of some sensational new torero. Bullfighting had become an obsession. It was too late for him to do anything about it, he said with a straight face, but there was "Bumby," the kid, and when eventually they would have to move back to Canada, Ernest was going to buy him a bull calf to practice veronicas with.

But writing was always the main thing and to write happily meant having the approval of his new master, in spite of his association with such worthy literary friends as Malcolm Cowley, John Dos Passos, Archibald MacLeish, Donald Ogden Stewart and Ezra Pound. He quoted Gertrude to herself in letters, began to emulate something of her manner in his own letters to others, and even for a time attempted, as she had years before, to find the literary equivalence of the methods of Cézanne. From Spain, where he was experimenting with the Cézanne approach, he wrote, "Isn't writing a hard job, though? It used to be easy before I met you. I certainly was bad, gosh, I'm awfully bad now but it's a different kind of bad."

Just what Hemingway meant by "a different kind of bad" can only be surmised. From Gertrude, as his early works began to show, he had learned the value of skillfully maneuvered repetitions, the simple power of the declarative sentence, and the necessity for saturation in an attitude within which the writer can write as a possessed and still self-possessed being, rather than as mere reporter or analyst. Her passion for charts and diagrams and the bones of a thing, the scientific exactitude she had retained through many years when she had nothing to do with science, was obviously of great value to him in assessing his own work. As he wrote to Edmund Wilson, "Her method is invaluable for analyzing anything or making notes on a person or place." While this reference to her "method" undoubtedly takes in the whole of Gertrude Stein's approach to literature, in specific terms it likely applies to her determination to isolate experience as well as words, and to study it

257

in terms of its feeling content, its visual content and, by all means, to keep it alive by keeping it away from a creatively debilitating dependency on memory. But advice can do no more than make a writer aware of himself and perhaps lead him to excision — which can be a creative act in itself — of what he recognizes as bad. Gertrude apparently helped to channel and refine Hemingway's talent by helping him to brush aside the dead hands of many influences that had kept his work either too conventional or too clever, abrupt and highly colored. He was a good pupil, and it was inevitable that for a time he should have taken over some of the characteristics of Stein that belong particularly to the pre-cubist phase of her career. While nobody, not even Hemingway, was ever to follow her into literary cubism, the following paragraph from his story, *Up In Michigan*, cannot be read without immediate echoes from Gertrude Stein's *Three Lives:*

Liz liked Jim very much. She liked it the way he walked over from the shop and often went to the kitchen door to watch for him to start down the road. She liked it about his mustache. She liked it about how white his teeth were when he smiled. She liked it very much that he didn't look like a blacksmith. She liked it how much D. J. Smith and Mrs. Smith liked Jim. One day she found that she liked it the way the hair was black on his arms and how white they were above the tanned line when he washed up in the washbasin outside the house. Liking that made her feel funny.

No single event marked their estrangement and no isolated reason can account for it, but Hemingway and Gertrude drifted apart through the middle years of the twenties and no act of will or momentary relapse into affection would ever bring them together again. Gertrude bore no animosity, but as she watched his progress she came to some unhappy conclusions. She felt that bit by bit Hemingway was throwing away the talent with which he was endowed, and which was so brilliantly evident in some of the stories he wrote during the early days of their acquaintance. She had tried to save what was finest in him, she felt, but was unable to prevail against Hemingway's growing obsession with sex and violent death. It was here, she felt, that his talent had been arrested by his false solution of a personal problem: he had compensated for his incredibly acute shyness and sensitivity by adopting a shield of brutality. When this happened he lost touch with his true genius, she believed, and could only go on endlessly repeating a role for which he was not inherently fitted, and for which he had no basic conviction. His rise to fame following the publication of *The Sun Also Rises* and *A Farewell to Arms* lifted him beyond the category of those who were "struggling" and to whom she was exclusively attracted. The breadth of his public success, and the measure of Hemingway's new status as an expatriate symbol, was deftly registered in a cartoon which appeared in *Life*: several tipsy Americans are sitting in a Parisian bar rather like the Dôme. Piled beside them are copies of *The Sun Also Rises*. One of the group asks, "Garçon, what's that the orchestra's playing?" And the waiter answers, "Why, Sir, that's the Star-Spangled Banner."

As Hemingway's career was being pursued in far-flung corners of the globe in the quest of big game and big fish, she continued to regard him with a sort of maternal amusement. His attitude toward her seemed gradually to stiffen into indifference — until she published her memoirs in which, as Sherwood Anderson said with relish, she took "such big patches of skin off Hemingway" with her "delicately held knife." In *The Autobiography of Alice B. Toklas*, she reports a conversation with Anderson, just after Hemingway had sent Sherwood the offensive funeral-oration letter. "Hemingway had at one moment, when he had repudiated Sherwood Anderson and all his works, written him a letter in the name of American literature which he, Hemingway, in company with his contemporaries was about to save, telling Sherwood just what he, Hemingway, thought about Sherwood's work, and, that thinking, was in no sense complimentary. When Sherwood came to Paris Hemingway naturally was afraid. Sherwood as naturally was not. As I say he and Gertrude Stein were endlessly amusing on the subject. They admitted that Hemingway was yellow, he is, Gertrude Stein insisted, just like the flat-boat men on the Mississippi as described by Mark Twain."

When *The Green Hills of Africa* was published shortly after the

Autobiography, a newspaper reviewer, spotting passages pertinent to the feud, commented that Hemingway "went all the way to Africa to hunt, and then when he thought he had found a rhinoceros, it turned out to be Gertrude Stein. . . ." Recording a conversation with his wife, Hemingway in *The Green Hills* makes his riposte to the passage from the *Autobiography*:

"Yes, and he doesn't have to read books written by some female he's tried to help get published saying how he's yellow."

"She's just jealous and malicious. You never should have helped her. Some people never forgive that."

"It's a damned shame, though, with all that talent gone to malice and nonsense and self-praise. It's a god-damned shame, really. It's a shame you never knew her before she went to pot. You know a funny thing; she never could write dialogue. It was terrible. She learned how to do it from my stuff and used it in that book. She had never written like that before. She never could forgive learning that and she was afraid people would notice it, where she'd learned it, so she had to attack me. It's a funny racket, really. But I swear she was damned nice before she got ambitious. You would have liked her then, really."

"Maybe, but I don't think so."

There is obvious bitterness in both of these passages, yet Gertrude for her part continued to feel for "Hem" an "indulgent weakness," in spite of their failure ever again to achieve rapport. When she ran into him by accident some years later on the Faubourg St. Honoré, he said he was "old, and rich and tired; let's be friends." Gertrude answered that she was neither old nor rich nor tired and that she would prefer to let the relationship stand. The relationship did stand, but in the years to come neither of them could resist expressions of feeling that showed how time had all but obliterated the intimate warmth that was once the whole of their Parisian idyll.

In *For Whom the Bell Tolls*, Hemingway's hero, Robert Jordan, is discussing onions with the character named Augustin:

"What hast thou against the onion?"

"The odour. Nothing more. Otherwise it is like the rose."

"Like the rose," he said. "Mighty like the rose. A rose is a rose is an onion."

"Thy onions are affecting thy brain," Augustin said. "Take care."

"An onion is an onion is an onion," Robert Jordan said cheerily and, he thought, a stone is a stein is a rock is a boulder is a pebble.

Gertrude made no public comment, but sometimes at home she would seize a handkerchief and, maneuvering in front of her poodle, Basket, would play-act the toreador while the dog was supposed to play the enraged bull. "Play Hemingway," she would say to the pampered white dog, "be fierce."

Some years later, in an interview with the novelist John Hyde Preston, Gertrude elaborated upon her opinion of Hemingway's development. When Preston expressed the view that Hemingway "was good until after A Farewell to Arms," she disputed him, saying, "No, he was not really good after 1925. In his early short stories he had what I have been trying to describe to you. Then — Hemingway did not lose it; he threw it away. I told him then: 'Hemingway, you have a small income; you will not starve; you can work without worry and you can grow that way'; he wished to grow violently. Now, Preston, here is a curious thing. Hemingway is not an American novelist. He has not sold himself and he has not settled into any literary mould. Maybe his own mould, but that's not only literary. When I first met Hemingway he had a truly sensitive capacity for emotion, and that was the stuff of the first stories; but he was shy of himself and he began to develop, as a shield, a big Kansas City-boy brutality about it, and so he was 'touchy' because he was really sensitive and ashamed that he was. Then it happened. I saw it happening and tried to save what was fine there, but it was too late. He went the way so many other Americans have gone before, the way they are still going. He became obsessed with sex and violent death. . . .

"Now you will mistake me. Sex and death are the springs of the most valid of human emotions. But they are not all; they are not even all emotion. But for Hemingway everything became multiplied by and subtracted from sex and death. But I knew at the start and I know better now that it wasn't just to find out what these things were; it was the disguise for the thing that was really gentle and fine in him, and then his agonizing shyness escaped into brutality.

No, now wait — not real brutality, because the truly brutal man wants something more than bull fighting and deep-sea fishing and elephant killing or whatever it is now, and perhaps if Hemingway were truly brutal he could make a real literature out of those things; but he is not, and I doubt if he will ever again write truly about anything. He is skillful, yes, but that is the writer; the other half is the man."

When Preston asked, "Do you really think American writers are obsessed by sex? And if they are, isn't it legitimate?" Gertrude answered, "It is legitimate, of course. Literature — creative literature — unconcerned with sex is inconceivable. But not literary sex, because sex is part of something of which the other parts are not sex at all. No, Preston, it is really a matter of tone. You can tell, if you can tell anything, by the way a man talks about sex whether he is impotent or not, and if he talks about nothing else you can be quite sure that he is impotent — physically and as an artist too.

"One thing which I have tried to tell Americans," she went on, "is that there can be no truly great creation without passion, but I'm not sure that I have been able to tell them at all. If they have not understood it is because they have had to think of sex first, and they can think of sex as passion more easily than they can think of passion as the whole force of man. Always they try to label it, and that is a mistake. What do I mean? I will tell you. I think of Byron. Now Byron had a passion. It had nothing to do with his women. It was a quality of Byron's mind and everything he wrote came out of it, and perhaps that is why his work is so uneven, because a man's passion is uneven if it is real; and sometimes, if he can write it, it is only passion and has no meaning outside of himself. Swinburne wrote all of his life about passion, but you can read all of him and you will not know what passions he had. I am not sure that it is necessary to know or that Swinburne would have been better if he had known. A man's passion can be wonderful when it has an object which may be a woman or an idea or wrath at an injustice, but after it happens, as it usually does, that the object is lost or worn after a time, the passion does not survive it. It survives only if it was there before, only if the woman or the idea or the wrath was an incident in the passion and not the cause of it — and that is what makes the writer.

"Often the men who really have it are not able to recognize it in themselves because they do not know what it is to feel differently or not to feel at all. And it won't answer to its name. Probably Goethe thought that *Young Werther* was a more passionate book than *Wilhelm Meister*, but in *Werther* he was only describing passion and in *Wilhelm Meister* he was transferring it. And I don't think he knew what he had done. He did not have to. Emerson might have been surprised if he had been told that he was passionate. But Emerson really had passion; he wrote it; but he could not have written *about* it because he did not know about it. Now Hemingway knows all about it and can sometimes write very surely about it, but he hasn't any at all. Not really any. He merely has passions. And Faulkner and Caldwell. . . . They are good craftsmen and they are honest men, but they do not have it."

CHAPTER 18

It would be quite wise to have followers.
— GERTRUDE STEIN

THE great disparity between the fame of Gertrude Stein as one of the giants of modern literature and the inconsequential number of her published works made up a paradox that outraged her sense of justice and subdued her hopes for lasting consideration through all of the early and middle years of her professional life. Popular reviewers kept her name prominent in the columns of American newspapers, and sometimes even spoke of her with respect instead of quoting her sentences for easy laughs. In a discussion of the newly arrived Hemingway, the book reviewer Burton Rascoe wrote: "He must be counted as the only American but one — Mr. Sherwood Anderson — who has felt the genius of Gertrude Stein's *Three Lives* and has evidently been influenced by it. Indeed, Miss Stein, Mr. Anderson and Mr. Hemingway may now be said to form a school by themselves. The characteristic of this school is a naïveté of language, often passing into the colloquialism of the character dealt with, which serves actually to convey profound emotions and complex states of mind. It is a distinctively American development in prose. . . ."

She was talked about, listened to, made into a legend. But for many reasons she was not read, and the most important of these was simply that she was not published. Her despair at this neglect brought her at times to a poignancy of expression which, normally, would be the last thing one might expect from her. "Sometimes I think it would be nice," she said, "to sell typewritten copies of me in a store but I don't know of a store. . . ." While her manuscripts were always readily available, the "adventurous publisher" for whom she had long waited failed to show. Carefully bound, the completed works of more than twenty creative years stood in proud isolation upon the shelves of a Spanish *armoire*. Meantime, Gertrude and her friends made plans, cooked up schemes and tried "angles," enlisting aid from any quarter that might lead to the ransom and rescue of the well-dusted but long neglected manuscripts.

In 1920, John Lane had reprinted *Three Lives* in England, and its modest second-round success had whetted Gertrude's appetite for more. From New York a friend sent advice that echoed the feelings of a hard core of devotees and a few critics: "Last spring I dined with Walter Arensberg & Duchamp and we talked of a new book of your things and the best way to put it over etc. My opinion was that you ought to print it privately at your own expense and once a thousand volumes were printed they could be sold somehow. I think in the end it would pay for itself. You see you are handicapped by writing in a language that is behind in the arts. *There is a public for you but no publisher.* . . ."

When Robert McAlmon, the young director of the Contact Press and husband of the wealthy English writer Bryher, came within striking distance, Gertrude issued an invitation to tea. She and McAlmon found common ground in their passion for "documentary, autobiographic and biographic things" and for the novels of Trollope. But the occasion was only partly social; Gertrude had business in mind. During the course of talk she suggested that McAlmon publish *The Making of Americans* in a series of four to six volumes over a period of two years. He responded to the notion that her book

265

might be suitable on the list of his Contact Editions, but felt that since the work was "all of a piece" and offered no obvious divisions for serial presentation, it had better be published as a single volume. Gertrude quickly sanctioned this improvement on her own scheme, and promised McAlmon that she would see to it that at least fifty friends bought advance copies. The manuscript was shortly on its way to the press of Maurice Darantière in Dijon, a firm which had already served the cause of modernism by printing James Joyce's *Ulysses*.

The printing job, as might be expected, was a nightmare for the French compositors. Countless repetitions, minute inversions, infinitesimal variations, all the characteristic tricks and turns of the early Stein were quite beyond them. And yet the circumstance of working in a language foreign to them was perhaps in its way an advantage, since they were not influenced by notions of their own about customary syntax or sentence balance. But Stein in any language would pose its special problems, and the possible advantage of ignorance was not enough to prevent them from committing hundreds of errors that were not only serious but barely discernible. When proofs came back, Gertrude and Alice were faced with a job that brought them to the edge of desperation and blindness. The worst trial from the compositors was their tendency to drop out whole sentences, making long arduous checkings necessary before corrections were possible. Rereading the book for the first time since she had written it, Gertrude found the experience a mixed pleasure. She was greatly worried that people might think some of the book's unorthodox uses of tenses, persons, adjectives and divisions were not to be taken as written, but that they would be ascribed to the whimsies of typesetters. "Though it does seem a bit profound to my twenty year older eyes," she admitted, she was on the whole eminently satisfied with the literary merit of the manuscript as it stood. She toyed with the idea of making certain minor revisions, but always found herself reverting to the original way of putting things. In her personal judgment, the long-buried work had assumed the solidity of a classic. "There are some pretty wonderful sentences in it," she wrote to Sherwood Anderson, "and we know how fond we both are of sentences."

The Making of Americans, more than nine hundred literally transparent and almost unreadable pages, paper-bound, was published finally in September, 1925, but not before Gertrude's forwardness had cost her the friendship of the man who published it. In McAlmon's absence from France she had taken it upon herself, against his instructions, to order delivery of the printed volumes from the press of M. Darantière in Dijon for immediate shipment to New York. When McAlmon discovered this unwarranted intervention, he was angry — not without reason, Gertrude conceded — and wrote to her detailing other matters he regarded as breaches of their understanding. He felt that Gertrude had done nothing herself to promote distribution of the book, noting that "no evidence of any order [has] come in through your offices except from your immediate family." He concluded his letter with accusations and a threat: "Incidentally, you have never been financially incapable of putting your book before the public if *your* art is of prime importance for you. If you wish the books retained, you may bid for them. Otherwise, by September — one year after publication — I shall simply rid myself of them en-masse, by the pulping proposition. . . ." McAlmon's threat was never carried out, but his personal relations with her had come to an end. Friendship or no, *The Making of Americans,* the cornerstone in a career dedicated to unorthodoxy on the largest scale ever entertained by a serious writer, was at last available to anyone who cared to buy.

In the wide net of literary, romantic or bar-stool relationships that self-exiled Americans and Englishmen had cast over artist-quarter Paris and its Spanish, Italian and Riviera suburbs, Robert McAlmon was an ubiquitous figure. His own work as a writer came to nothing much, but his services as the publisher of Contact Editions and the Three Mountains Press were of enormous value. Besides Gertrude Stein, authors whose work he brought out in editions which for the most part are rare items today included Ernest Hemingway, Ezra Pound, William Carlos Williams, H.D., Djuna Barnes and the painter Marsden Hartley, whose *Twenty-five Poems* appeared in 1923. If the expatriate period tends, today, to be notable mainly for the great fame of a very few writers and painters, it was also a period that beautifully accommodated scores of marginal artists like McAl mon, and hundreds of brilliant failures. Participation in the restless excitements of the milieu was a compensation for many individuals whose work would come to nothing but whose hopeless ambitions could be kept alive in endless talk and, now and then, in vicarious enjoyment of the success of those who had "come through." As an observer of a life to which he was intimately bound, McAlmon took issue with the already overpublicized version of expatriate existence. The legend of the "roaring twenties" had not then congealed into its present form, but the flighty character of the period was already a journalistic cliché. In his book of memoirs, *Being Geniuses Together*, he commented:

. . . there were appearing in American magazines and newspapers a number of articles about the life of the deracinated, exiled and expatriate, who lived mainly in Paris leading, the articles implied, non-working and dissolute lives. An American journalist, long a resident of Paris, was riled and asked me to collect a list of the foreign artists who had been in the Quarter throughout the last year or so. He suggested that I note also what work they had accomplished, and jot down a note about their dissipations, if any. One night, with several others who had been in Paris for some time we noted down a list of two hundred and fifty names, English and American, and some were the names of persons responsible for the American articles against so-called exiles in Paris. The report indicated that said righteous article-writers had been known by several to have indulged in Montparnassian dissipations as extensively as any. In that list were the names of none but working writers or painters, one of the writers has since gained the Nobel prize; several others have been . . . acclaimed great writers. The same is true amongst the painters and sculptors, and I now, looking over the list which we compiled and which was never used, remember that a quantity of these people started and completed books which brought them fame, in Paris and during those days. One wonders what fixed idea American newspapers had, and what obsession persisted in the writers who returned to America, which caused them to find it necessary to throw off on Paris, a city which gave them material and stimulus, and which helped them to grow up mentally, if they did.

It has been said that Paris is the parasite's haven because it is easier to go to hell there comfortably than anywhere else. On the other hand, if somebody stands its racket for a long period and emerges purposeful and a producing person it means talent and strength, and it means that he has dissipated a quantity of soppy ideas and has a sounder chance of being an rtist in a respectable sense, intellectually. For the rest, any art quarter is olerant of weaknesses, and the hangers-on might as well go to hell in 'aris as become equally spineless, futile, and distressing specimens in their ome villages. A Parisian drunk is not nearly so sad to watch as the small town down-and-outer. He isn't alone or lonely.

If Gertrude's literary success was still but thinly substantiated by published works, and if dissidents like McAlmon considered her "a stammering, repetitive and somehow inarticulate person," her social success as a leading figure in the expatriate world was radiant and beyond question. "On sunny mornings," recalled the social historian Lloyd Morris, "when the streets of the Right Bank were full of people, a hallucination would sometimes overtake you. From around a corner there appeared the vision of a great Buddha on wheels, erratically charging down the thoroughfare, divinely indifferent to the fate of mortal traffic, heedless of laughter or imprecations. The sudden vision was all too real; it was merely Miss Gertrude Stein single-mindedly bound upon some practical errand in her model-T Ford. . . . Miss Stein was massive, monumental, majestic; she had the grandeur of a major scenic phenomenon. . . . A summons to her home was an invitation to present oneself to Mont Blanc. . . ."

Through the early and mid-twenties, "27" had assumed the aspect of something between a court and a shrine. Proximity to the throne, where Gertrude sat with legs crossed, one sandal dangling from her big toe, was much to be desired by the young men who curried royal favor. There was, in the course of time, always one among them who, unofficially yet with authority, served as major-domo to the royal establishment while all about him jockeyings for position went on. In the background, over the noise of the teacups, one could hear the sound of rolling heads, the rumble of dead reputations being carted away.

Not the least noticeable thing about the *salon* was the way its dramatis personae changed from month to month, week to week. Both Gertrude and Alice preferred variety in their relationships; and Alice often blithely quoted the jingle, "Give me new faces, new faces, new faces. I have seen the old ones." Gertrude had said for years that she liked to see people come but, just as much, she liked to see them go. As a shrine, the atelier was already historical and impressively decked with propitiatory gifts. A patina of fame had settled on the paintings, and the brushings of thousands of pilgrims had mellowed and polished the heavy furniture. It was only natural that Gertrude, to whom Bernard Faÿ often referred as "our lady," should have become its aureate and heavyset madonna. American composer Virgil Thomson, who was probably amused by both the royal and sacred aspects of the place, recalled his first impression: "I saw two old ladies sitting by the fire; they were waiting, and I couldn't help thinking of the line: 'Will you come into the parlor said the spider to the fly?' "

Others who did not know and perhaps would not have cared about the nice hierarchical divisions in Gertrude's retinue came to her door as sober and interested as they would come to Sainte Chapelle or Les Invalides. In search of "all that Paris had to offer," they regarded a visit to "27" as a visit to an academy where examples of almost every phase of modern painting could be studied at leisure and discussed with one who had been among its earliest champions. Whatever the social climate, the paintings remained the focal point of interest around which the deeper life of the *salon* revolved. Gertrude was continually rearranging the works, featuring new ones or attempting to revive interest in an old one by placing it in a position of prominence. She also had her own *Salon des Refusés*, a small room into which were dispatched paintings she had acquired as white-elephant gifts, or had bought by mistake, or in which she had finally lost interest. "I never know when or why a picture suddenly becomes beautiful and loses its quality of irritation," she said. "There was a time when I had to cover that Cézanne portrait with a glass for no one would believe that it was finished; it irritated everyone and even angered some. Without liking it, I had recognized its quality, and then one day — as one turns over in sleep — it became beautiful and I could not see it in the way I had seen it before." Because of this lively changing attitude, there was always some new point of interest in the *salon* which so easily might have taken on the dead air of a museum.

While her great collection of paintings gave Gertrude's *salon* a pecific luster, a number of people, painters among them, felt that she actually knew little about painting and tended to feel that her taste was, at best, whimsical. Even an intimate like the painter Harry Phelan Gibb, her closest English friend, was disturbed on one occasion by a most unexpected reaction from Gertrude. Gibb had sent her one of his works, on the back of which was a sketch of the sort he turned out for calendars and greeting cards as a way of making a living. To his astonishment, Gertrude altogether dismissed the gift painting, but said she thought the sketch was very fine. Gibb wrote: "I don't know what to make of it. The sketch you give praise to was one of my worst pot-boilers too bad to sell at any price. I therefore used the back and painted the other one. I thought it had something in it though I knew it did not hold together yet I thought I had got just that something out of the commonplace. Then I thought it might amuse you. It never occurred to me you would look at the one on the back. However you have looked at it. You have said what you think and I am left perplexed."

Since both she and her brother had "made" so much of their pictures — he in his *salon* lectures and later in his writings, she in her literary transcriptions of cubism — many observers came to regard them mainly as theorists, lacking in any real feeling for visual art, whose pictures were merely pegs on which they could hang hypotheses. In support of this view, their critics — granting they had taken up Picasso and Matisse in the very earliest days of their collection — pointed to their later divergent interests which led Leo away from nearly all contact with modern art and led Gertrude to give support to artists whom many knowledgeable people regarded as being without distinction. In this view, their connection with Picasso and Matisse seemed wholly a matter of chance; except for the useful notoriety it brought, almost any other association might have served them as well.

Many people felt that, even as she sat as proprietor in the midst of her collection, Gertrude could not wholly disguise the fact that she was really more interested in the individuals who had contributed works to it than she was in the paintings themselves. Her concern, they felt, was with personalities and public success rather than with actual achievement. They noticed often that she tended to rate a new painter's promise in terms of the strength of his resistance to her. An indifferent newcomer was met with indifference, and when he was shown to the door his work was banished with him. Her inveterate gallery-going was interpreted as a search for new personalities, new faces that might brighten and adorn "27," if only for a prescribed time. "Yesterday evening Bravig and John were here," she wrote in *A Diary*. "They will be here again. Several times other people have been here. There is a difference of opinion as to the desirability of their being here." Few people felt that she was searching for new art experience or that she was even accessible to it. This feeling, though undoubtedly springing in many cases from jealousy and malice, can nevertheless be supported by evidence from her earlier life. The switch of interest she had shown in the course of her work under William James, from the experiments to the subjects, from the reactions to the reactors, had already been repeated in far different circumstances. Throughout her life Gertrude showed very little interest in the work of artists she did not know, unless they were dead and comfortably separated from her by at least a generation. There was no distant idol in her life at any time, no one beyond her immediate circle toward whom she looked with respect and admiration, unless it were someone as remote from the world of art and as thoroughly dead as Ulysses S. Grant. She had come to be satisfied with self-adulation, knowing, as she said, that in her time she was the only one. Her affection for others was reserved for those whom she could appropriate. Whether or not the world agreed, Picasso was the only painter, Sherwood Anderson was *the* great American writer, and Virgil Thomson, as soon as he showed interest in putting her works to music, was the greatest living master of prosody.

In spite of such reservations as to the true depth of her interests, Gertrude's prestige as an arbiter of painting was not to be dismissed. According to the English novelist Ford Madox Ford, she was "both Pope and Pharaoh of the picture-buying world." Her early identification with the career of Picasso had given her the aura of a prophetess which, in a business way, some dealers were eager to exploit. Her appearance at the opening of a new exhibition was considered the first augury of its success. Her entrance was awaited always, and was unfailingly dramatic; she kept up a running stream of chatter as she moved at will through the gallery and was never without an audience. Holding forth in the center of a hundred paintings, she blessed this work with her popish hands and damned that with a glance of indifference. Unlike her brother, she never lectured on paintings which attracted her. She was not even particularly informative. When the editors of a magazine sent her a questionnaire among which was the question, "What is your attitude toward art today?" Gertrude dismissed all pretension. "I like to look at it," was her whole answer. In place of Leo's exhaustive, groping interpretations, she offered only immediate acceptance or rejection. She had to like a painting in order to think about it. Leo's approach was quite the opposite; he had to think about a painting before he could allow himself to like it.

In her own preserve, perpetually attended by her dark guardian angel with the long earrings, her apparent remoteness caused many people to feel they might at any moment "catch fire from the sacred flame." Something timeless about her — Max Jacob once said, "I must have known the admirable Gertrude Stein in the prehistoric age"— was alternately repellent and attractive. Most of the visitors succumbed to her charm, and many who remained inarticulate about her work easily found words to describe her fascination.

When William Carlos Williams, the American poet and physician, came with Robert McAlmon to see her, she gave him tea, then one by one showed him her great collection of unpublished works, and asked him what he would do if he were in a similar position. "It must have been that I was in one of my more candid moods," Dr. Williams wrote in his *Autobiography*, "or that the cynical opinion of Pound and others of my friends about Miss Stein's work was uppermost in my mind, for my reply was, 'If they were mine, having so many, I would probably select what I thought were the best and throw the rest into the fire.'" There was a shocked silence. Then, as McAlmon recalled, Gertrude became vehement. "No, oh no, no, no," she said, "that isn't possible. You would not find a painter destroying any of his sketches. A writer's writing is too much of the writer's being; his flesh child. You may, but of course, writing is not your métier, Doctor." "But Doctor Stein," said Williams, "are you sure that writing is your métier? I solve the economies of life through the profession of doctoring, but from the first my will was toward writing. I hope it pleases you, but things that children write have seemed to me so Gertrude Steinish in their repetitions. Your quality is that of being slowly and innocently first recognizing sensations and experience." This was too much; the door of the atelier had already closed silently on William Carlos Williams. "I could not see him after that," Gertrude said. "I told the maid I was not in if he came again. There is too much bombast in him."

But the contretemps did not change Dr. Williams's deep appreciation of what Gertrude Stein was doing in the way of pioneering American paths into the overgrown forests of a literature moldy with imitative leaves from the pages of Spenser and Wordsworth and Tennyson. "Having taken the words to her choice," he wrote, "to emphasize further what she has in mind she has completely unlinked them from their former relationships to the sentence. This was absolutely essential and inescapable. Each under the new arrangement has a quality of its own, but not conjoined to carry the burden of science, philosophy, and every higgledy-piggledy figment law and order have been laying upon them in the past. They are like a crowd at Coney Island, let us say, seen from an airplane. . . . She has placed writing on a plane where it may deal unhampered with its own affairs, unburdened with scientific and philosophic lumber."

George Biddle, the American painter, came and left independent of her spell. George Antheil had taken Biddle to "27," and the latter recalled their evening in his autobiography, *An American Artist's Story*:

Nothing seemed very comfortable and there were some Picassos and a good many Juan Gris' hanging around. Gertrude was a dominating personality, massive, powerful, and always, I suppose, by way of indirection. I felt that she might have been a Bethlehem Steel Magnate — she had the same thin lips and breadth between the temples; better still a labor politician or a Catholic cardinal. For there was that about her that sized up people and situations — perhaps even better than pictures. She said

27 rue de Fleurus: part of Gertrude and Leo Stein's collection
of paintings

Gertrude Stein sitting for Jo Davidson

something about Juan Gris being one of the great unrecognized creative spirits of his epoch. I have forgotten her exact words, but they were, with a certain calculating, inscrutable inflection, in the superlative.

I said nothing. She and George kept up the conversation. She asked us if we would like to see some of her very early Picasso drawings. They were quite unknown to the outside world, she said, looking even more sapient and impenetrable. We said: Yes, indeed; we would love to see the early Picasso drawings. We sat around a table and from an album Miss Stein selected and presented for our delectation one after another of the master's earliest moods. They had real charm and gaiety and life . . . We knew that we were in the presence, in this unostentatious and somewhat uncomfortable house, of the early, unpublished masterpieces of a very great creator.

"May I see that one just another moment, Miss Stein? Amazing formality of line. What delicacy and what packed design! Interesting the way he echoes his diagonals — don't you think so, George? — in reference to his masses."

Something inside me kept getting tighter and tighter, more and more belligerent. Toward the end of the seance Miss Stein asked me, politely, if somewhat unconventionally, what at the moment I was painting. I was ungracious enough to say that I did not think my work would interest her. Miss Stein, who in her own massive and rarefied manner had also perhaps been inwardly smoldering, broke out in an Old Testament prophetic indictment of my attitude toward art and my own limitations. I would never "understand" or "realize," because of my birthplace, my background, my family, my morals, the Quaker, the Puritan in me. I have forgotten just what. We shouted at each other. I argued with her coldly. I think she called me a lawyer. We parted not entirely on unfriendly terms.

Generally, at home, her ways were easy and genial; yet this did not mean that she might allow just anyone who happened to come to assume that he was on intimate terms with her. Alice saw to that, in her unobtrusive way, by serving as a screening agent; the bores, the incompetents, the overly talkative, the untalented nobodies and the opportunists seldom eluded her subtle delaying tactics. When one of the untouchables did manage to get through to Gertrude, likely as not he would find himself shunted away in the middle of a sentence without knowing quite what had happened. This imperious behavior on Gertrude's part resulted in much ill-will. The price she paid for refusing ever to be bored was the echo of retribution in the biographies and memoirs of a generation of the rejected. Those who bored her, of course, eventually found her and her circle boring. As Robert McAlmon wrote, "She accepts too readily the adulation of people that a person of healthy self-confidence would dismiss at once as parasites, bores, or gigolos and pimps." But others felt that, having lived conspicuously in Paris for more than twenty years, Gertrude "had become part of it, like Picasso and the Eiffel Tower; too individual to be merged in any clique. . . . She seemed timeless. . . . As she scratched her head and fixed you with her eagle eye, you felt you were taking tea with a monument." In her own mind, she was both the Parisian figure and the four-square American that she wanted to be. "For one thing, for all of the time I've been in France," she said, "I have never been called an expatriate and that is the thing I am proud of. I proved you could be a good American anywhere in the world."

Subterranean currents might be coursing through an evening's assemblage of personalities, but the over-all tone of the *salon* was one of a strict and formal politeness. Yet on some occasions, Gertrude and Alice, who actually lived in a singular and complementary harmony, might drop guards and come to the brink of a quarrel. One of these rare incidents occurred after Alice, who had always been notably thin, had gone on a diet out of sympathy with Gertrude's determination to reduce. Alice became accustomed to the short rations, and soon found she had altogether lost her normal appetite. Gertrude thought this hilariously funny and could not control her laughter when she told of it. Unsmiling, Alice quietly announced to the company that Gertrude was having one of her "stupid" days. Gertrude would seldom tolerate eccentric behavior in anyone but herself, and was quick to cut those whose manner was odd, or presumptuous, or snide. But boorishness was never the only reason for a snub. Dullness and conventionality were just as vulnerable. She preferred the interesting fake to the distinguished good character. Normal people bored her to distraction and as a result the regulars at "27" came to include "Young men who did not know precisely what they were, and distinguished elderly gentlemen who knew only too well, and assorted ladies in pairs," along with a complement of figures of every conceivable artistic type and temperamental persuasion.

When Bernard Faÿ, who was to be a faithful friend of Gertrude's for many years, first entered her circle in the mid-twenties, he took a dim view of what he encountered. "Around her I could see a great many writers young and old," he said, "who were cultivating their literary talents just as Ripley's freaks cultivate their oddities. . . . These men are amusing; they often do original work; they sometimes write good books; and they happen now and then to make a great piece of writing — but they are responsible for most of the unpleasant atmosphere and bad reputation that surrounds contemporary literature."

Katherine Anne Porter, then living in Paris, was no less harsh in assessing the pretensions of the *salon* and its fledglings. "Miss Stein herself sat there in full possession of herself," wrote Miss Porter in *The Days Before*, "the scene, the spectators, wearing thick no-colored shapeless woolen clothes and honest woolen stockings knitted for her by Miss Toklas, looking extremely like a handsome old Jewish patriarch who had backslid and shaved off his beard." Among the late-comers trying to elbow their way into the "lost generation" were some who, according to Miss Porter, "announced that they wished their writings to be as free from literature as if they had never read a book, as indeed too many of them had not up to the time. . . . A few of them were really lost, and disappeared, but others had just painted themselves into a very crowded corner."

Those who were already enjoying Gertrude's favor were apt to view her coterie attachments in quite a different light. "She was supposed to exert a deleterious influence on the young," said Harold Acton, "but as far as I could see she solved their problems with rare sympathy and common sense. I considered her an excellent critic. To me she gave sound advice, though I was neither a disciple or an imitator. I showed her my latest poems and . . . a fable in prose which I had just finished, and she saw in them what she was looking for: the rhythmical connection between my writings and my personality."

The regulars cherished their sense of coterie, yet the group was continually riddled with dissension. To have paid respects to Gertrude and to have sat with Alice was to have been admitted into the charmed circle of those whose pretenses, at least, were interesting and fashionable, and to have received the benediction which, a short time past, had been famously granted to Picasso and Matisse, to Anderson and Hemingway. Virgil Thomson, whom Gertrude first met in the fall of 1926 when he came to visit her with composer George Antheil, was perhaps the most genuinely distinguished among them. He did not always get along very well with Alice, but he soon found himself in Gertrude's good grace simply for having chosen to compose musical settings for her *Susie Asado* and *Preciosilla*. Thomson had for years been one of her admirers, and his understanding of what she was up to was based on firsthand knowledge of her writing ever since his Harvard days when he inconclusively experimented with putting some of *Tender Buttons* to music. But he was no sycophant and his objective sense of Gertrude's personality was as clear as the affection in which he would hold her for many years. "She expected to be granted the freedom of a man," he observed, "without allowing anyone to sacrifice the respect due her as a woman." Whereas there was nearly always some elusive note of patronizing in Gertrude's clucking attendance upon her mixed brood, this did not extend to Virgil Thomson. She seemed to have recognized his brilliance as a critic and his self-assurance as a composer from the very beginning of their relationship and to have accepted him as an equal.

The painter, Pavel Tchelitchew, who for a time served in the unofficial and uneasy capacity of major-domo, witnessed the rise and decline of his personal influence, and went on to become the leader of a group of painters Gertrude flirted with, favored, and finally consigned to the enormous oblivion of those who she felt had not fulfilled their promise. More easily than any of the others, novelist Elliot Paul came and went impervious either to favor or the lack of it. George Antheil, quickly rising to a short-lived prominence as the *enfant terrible* of American music, blazed about for a while with his *Ballet Mécanique*, a violent composition meant to make listeners aware "of the simultaneous beauty and danger" of their era's "unconscious mechanistic philosophy, aesthetic." This work was scored for eight pianos, a player piano, xylophones, bass drums, rattles, electric bells and an airplane propeller. (Antheil would soon retreat to America, to re-emerge in the public eye much later as the author of a syndicated column dispensing advice to the lovelorn.) And then, suddenly, a young Dutch painter, Kristians Tonny, was the new thing. . . . In Gertrude's words, "One does like to know young men even though as soon as that they are not any longer young. As soon as one really knows them they are not any longer young."

According to Bravig Imbs, a young novelist fresh from Dartmouth College, who served a short term as major-domo, "we were a coterie and most of us young enough to think it very important. We were all going to be great artists and we had all sat with Alice and we had all given our homage to Gertrude. . . . So it was perfectly normal to attach importance to the fact that Virgil mulled over his melodies whilst walking in his favorite park, the Parc de Saint Cloud, that René Crevel was acting like a madman in the night clubs of Berlin (though it inevitably meant his return to some dismal sanitarium in Switzerland), that Poupet had acquired an adorable crystal canary in a crystal cage to decorate his dining room, that Elliot Paul had bought a new accordion, a magnificent Italian one, that Pavlik [Tchelitchew] had been threatened with mumps and as a result had become interested in Christian Science, that Gertrude was going to take elocution lessons from a professor at the Sorbonne as it was almost certain she would be invited to speak at Oxford, that Alice was having trials at her dentist — Gertrude who was never ill always treated Alice's infirmities with such quietly Olympian detachment that Alice was forced to seek consolation elsewhere — that Allen was looking wretched since he had started to work in a deluxe travel agency, that Sherwood Anderson was coming that very afternoon to meet Picasso and that Sherwood had a new wife who was a charming creature and that no one had taken him seriously at Mrs. Jolas' dinner when he announced that if he were wealthy he would have fresh pyjamas every night and a new wife every three years, that the luncheon of Sherwood with Joyce had been a fiasco because Sherwood had started out beautifully by asking Joyce what he thought of Ireland, that Janet Scudder had persuaded the French government to change the name of the street she lived on, that Juan Gris was better after having been very ill and had had success in Berlin, that George and Boske Antheil looked like Babes-in-the-Wood after their unsuccessful venture in New York, that Robert Coates had a lovely address: the City Hotel. . . ."

With so many personalities to deal with, Gertrude's favorite sport, according to Bravig Imbs, was the deliberate framing of contretemps which were apt to result in emotional fireworks. This Machiavellian game took place while she sat "majestically like a Roman emperor, taking a deep malicious pleasure in the all but mortal combat she had encouraged among her guests. She was not only extremely versed in the French art of 'brouille' but had this extra accomplishment of stirring up quarrels between people without ever once stepping into the shadow of blame herself. She had observed Guillaume Apollinaire who was past master of this highly civilized art, and had learned from him. Alice would always reprove Gertrude for letting herself fall into such temptations, and Gertrude would answer with Juan Gris' favorite proverb: One must always yield to temptation."

The friendship of Gertrude Stein and Edith Sitwell which, in time, became a firm one, began inauspiciously. In 1923, Miss Sitwell had published in the *Nation and Athenaeum* a review of *Geography and Plays*, in which she said: "To sum up the book as far as possible, I find in it an almost insuperable amount of silliness, an irritating ceaseless rattle like that of American sightseers talking in a boarding-house (this being, I imagine, a deliberate effect), great bravery, a certain real originality, and a few flashes of exquisite beauty. . . . She is, however, doing valuable pioneer work." Gertrude felt that the review was condescending and dismissed it as but another report from the alien world. A year later, the London *Vogue* published an article by Miss Sitwell in which she stated that she had spent the year reading almost nothing but *Geography and Plays*, and that she considered it an important and beautiful book. Gertrude forgave and forgot. When Edith Sitwell next came to Paris, a meeting was arranged. Gertrude was deeply impressed with her, thought that she looked like Queen Elizabeth as she might have been painted by Modigliani, and soon one of her few friendships with anyone she might have considered one of her peers was affectionately joined.

In later years, Edith Sitwell and her brother Osbert remembered Gertrude mainly for her incorrigible tendency to misinterpret every human relationship with which she came into contact. When Gertrude said that so-and-so was in love with so-and-so but that the emotion was unrequited, or that Mme. X. was about to sue M. Y. for slander in a matter involving Mlle. Z., the Sitwells came to the conclusion that they would approach the truth only by assuming just the opposite of Gertrude's assertions. But their fondness for her as a person and respect for her as a writer was constant and long-standing. "She is the last writer in the world whom any other writer should take as a model," Dame Edith wrote, "but her work, for the most part, is very valuable because of its revivifying qualities, and it contains, to my mind, considerable beauty." Reporting one of their early conversations, she recalled that Gertrude had said, "The difference between Picasso and inferior painters is that inferior painters put in all the leaves on a tree, with the result that you see neither tree nor leaves. Picasso paints one leaf upon a tree, and you see the life of the tree." In a similar sense, commented Dame Edith, "She throws a word into the air, and when it returns to the ground it bears within it the original meaning it bore before custom and misuse had blurred it."

Gertrude and Alice saw Edith Sitwell often in Paris, and introduced her to Pavel Tchelitchew who painted several widely reproduced portraits of her and who became her close friend. When Miss Sitwell returned to England, it was upon her urgings and assurances that Gertrude consented to lecture at Cambridge. When the president of the literary society there had written to Gertrude to speak in the early spring of 1926, the idea terrified her. She wrote a quick and definite refusal. Hearing of this rejection, Edith Sitwell wrote immediately to say that it was of the first importance that she change her mind, that Gertrude's "actual presence in England would help the cause" since "it is quite undoubted that a personality does

281

help to convince half-intelligent people." Contingent upon Gertrude's acceptance of the Cambridge invitation, she prodded, Oxford was also about to ask her to lecture. Gertrude did change her mind, but the prospect of a public appearance sent her into an extended period of depression and anxiety.

She brooded for days, decided to take elocution lessons from a professor at the Sorbonne, then decided not to. She could make no beginning on what she was going to say until one afternoon in Montrouge when, waiting for a mechanic to finish repairs on her car, she sat on the fender of another car in the garage and began to write. By the time her Ford was repaired, she had completed all of *Composition as Explanation*. To make sure that she would be stylishly caparisoned, her friend Yvonne Davidson provided her with a stately robe of blue Chinese brocade. The next step was to get the reaction of anyone who might be willing to listen to a preview performance of her lecture. Everyone had ideas, not so much on the content of the lecture, since no one ever argued with Gertrude about the validity of her thoughts, but on the manner of delivery. After much confusing advice, and with no belief that she had learned anything, she arrived in London in the grip of a fearful case of stage fright. Osbert Sitwell who, she felt, looked like "the uncle of a king," came to her hotel, extended his sympathy and tried to help. "He so thoroughly understood every possible way in which one could be nervous," said Gertrude, that she was "quite soothed."

The evening at Cambridge was a resonant success and when, at Oxford a few days later, Gertrude again took the platform in her robe of Chinese blue, she had begun to feel like a prima donna. Harold Acton, who had invited her to address the members and friends of the "Ordinary," a literary society, recalls the event in his *Memoirs of an Aesthete:*

Edith, Osbert and Sacheverell Sitwell accompanied Gertrude as well as Miss Alice Toklas, her inseparable companion, who looked like a Spanish gipsy and talked like a Bostonian. Gertrude had left all her nervousness at Cambridge; it was a fine summer day and she was ready to enjoy herself. Her audience was even larger than I had anticipated and many had to stand. Owing to the critics, the popular conception of Gertrude Stein was of an eccentric visionary, a literary Madame Blavatsky in fabulous clothes, the triumph of the dream and escape from life personified, with bells on her fingers as well as on her toes, or a mermaid swathed in tinsel, smoking drugged cigarettes through an exaggerated cigarette holder, or a Gioconda who had had her face lifted so often that it was fixed in a smile beyond the nightmares of Leonardo da Vinci. One was aware of the rapid deflation of these conceptions, as Gertrude surpassed them by her appearance, a squat Aztec figure in obsidian, growing more monumental as soon as she sat down. With her tall bodyguard of Sitwells and the gipsy acolyte, she made a memorable entry.

Nobody was prepared for what followed, a placid reading of *Composition as Explanation* and several word portraits, including one of Edith Sitwell, who sat so near that the portrait could be compared with the original. The litany of an Aztec priestess, I thought, uttered in a friendly American voice that made everybody feel at home until they pondered the subject matter. What a contrast between manner and matter, between voice and written page! . . . Though we had heard dozens of lectures, nobody had heard anything like this before. There was no nonsense about her manner, which was in deep American earnest, as natural as could be . . . While she read Edith Sitwell's portrait I glanced at the model. No, I could not see the likeness, nor, apparently, could Edith, for she was trying not to look as embarrassed as she felt. Sachie looked as if he were swallowing a plum and Osbert shifted on his insufficient chair with a vague nervousness in his eyes. The audience sat attentively; some were taking notes. Gertrude Stein was casting a spell with her litany which might go on for ever and ever amen. The illusion that we were living in a continuous present was certainly there, a little too continuous for my taste.

Discussion after her talk lasted for an hour. When someone asked her why she thought she was on the right track with her unique sort of work, she replied that it was not a question of what she thought, or of what anyone thought. She had been going her own way for twenty years and now both at Oxford and Cambridge they wanted to hear her lecture. The climax of the evening came with a touch of Gertrude's wit that left nothing more to be said. In his memoirs, Osbert Sitwell recalls the moment: "I remember . . . a certain commotion arising and some accompanying laughter when . . . she remarked 'Everything is the same and everything is different.'

"Many undergraduates had come to the hall to amuse themselves after the lecture at the expense of a writer widely and angrily derided, her work dismissed as the 'stutterings of a lunatic.' But in the presence of this obviously distinguished woman, the wiser of them recognized that there was not much to be done in this line. At the end, two young gentlemen [David Cecil & Robbie Calburn], not so easily discouraged, shot up to heckle her from different parts of the audience: but they asked an identical question: 'Miss Stein, if everything is the same, how can everything be different?' In a most genial, comforting manner, Miss Stein replied: 'Well, just look at you two dear boys!' "

CHAPTER 19

What we buy is this and with it we satisfy the
longing for a solitude *à deux*.
— GERTRUDE STEIN

WITH her English lecture, *Composition
as Explanation*, happily placed for publication in England with
Leonard and Virginia Woolf's Hogarth Press, and in America with
the *Dial*, of which Marianne Moore was then managing editor, Gertrude with Alice went in the late spring of 1926 to Belley, to stay
once more at Pernollet's hotel. From there they meant to explore
the countryside in the hope of turning up a house they would find
suitable to buy or lease. Their previous visits had convinced them
that this particular corner of the Rhône valley, perpetually fresh-
ened by air from the snowfields of the Alps, was more to their taste
than any other part of France they knew. An old garrison town of
some five thousand inhabitants, Belley is situated in the Bugey,
part of the department of the Ain, in the east of France equidistant
from Chambéry, Lyon, Grenoble and Bourg-en-Bresse. The little
town is the metropolis of a rich farming country, with a hospital, a

seminary, country court, a *souspréfecture*, a garrison including a battalion of Moroccan troups, and a number of schools.

Though they took long drives for many days on end, they found nothing in the way of a house to please them and finally put off further explorations until the following summer. Then, as they were driving along one afternoon, they sighted a house in Bilignin, an outlying part of Belley. Perched comfortably on an elevation across a gentle valley, this house was nothing less than "the summer house of our dreams." They learned upon inquiry that it was occupied by a lieutenant in the French regiment stationed in Belley, and soon learned further that the lieutenant had no intention of moving elsewhere. Undaunted, they were determined to get his house for themselves. One of their friends suggested that they might pull some strings and have the lieutenant made a captain; since there was no room for another captain in Belley, he would have to go elsewhere. Setting to work on this suggestion, they prevailed upon influential friends in Paris to try to arrange a promotion for the officer. They were told that this was impossible, but the man was in any case soon transferred to Africa. Their behind-the-scenes maneuvering took many months to bring to conclusion, but they finally succeeded in dislodging the lieutenant's family and in signing a lease on a residence they had still not seen from a distance of less than two kilometers.

Back in Paris they resumed their "court" season. Paul Robeson, a friend of Van Vechten who had gained by this time the reputation of having singlehandedly "discovered" the American Negro for art, came to Paris with the hit show *Revue Nègre*, and Gertrude gave a large party for him and members of the cast. She was attracted to Robeson immediately because she felt he knew American values and American life as only one in it but not of it could know them, and perhaps because he could easily understand her contention that the Negro in America suffered not so much from persecution as from "nothingness." But Robeson's having made a specialty of singing spirituals was rancorous to her; spirituals, she felt, belonged no more to him than did anything else American. In basing his career on the singing of spirituals, he had made a false emphasis.

The expatriate movement had largely spent itself by the late twenties, but Gertrude, monumentally in Paris as she had been years before the famous migration of the artists had begun, was still the outstanding figure to meet and still the widely acknowledged "Mother Goose of Montparnasse" and "queen-bee of the expatriate hive." In the minds of many young literary pilgrims, James Joyce was by all odds a greater writer, but his ill-health and natural reclusiveness made him unavailable to all but a few. Gertrude, by contrast, kept perpetual open house; one new arrival after another made for a continuity of fresh interest and kept up a chain of introductions that seemed without end. The American poet Hart Crane turned up in France where before long his demoniac behavior had got him bounced out of Le Sélect and into La Santé, the local jail, for a period of ten days, and he had to be rescued by Gertrude's friend Bernard Faÿ and others. But before his troubles with the gendarmerie had begun he came to the Rue de Fleurus. "I went to see Gertrude Stein despite my indifference to her work," he wrote to a friend. "One is supposed to inevitably change one's mind about her work after meeting her. I haven't, but must say that I've seldom met so delightful a personality. *And* the woman is beautiful!"

Sherwood Anderson came to Paris in December with his two children, and a Christmas Eve party was given for them at "27." He and Gertrude spent a good deal of time exchanging stories about Hemingway in the days before fame had taken him away from them, and in spinning fantasies about books upon which they might themselves someday collaborate. Of all American figures, they were both most fond of Ulysses S. Grant. To write a book about the Civil War, especially one that would put the "stuffed shirt," Robert E. Lee, "in his place," was a fantasy Anderson had indulged for years. Together, they felt, they could really rejuvenate Grant as a proper American hero and give him a shining new place in national history. The project was never to come about as a collaboration but, in *Four in America*, Gertrude, at least, finally had her say about Grant.

Following the example of one of the stylish Rue de Fleurus regulars, the Duchesse de Clermont-Tonnerre, Gertrude decided to have her hair cut very short. One rainy Sunday Alice set to work, and as her scissors snipped and sheared, Gertrude read from a book and, incidentally, made a discovery which impressed her enough to report it later in attempting to clarify an aspect of her work. "I found that any kind of a book if you read with glasses and somebody is cutting your hair and so you cannot keep the glasses on and you use your glasses as a magnifying glass and so read word by word reading word by word makes the writing that is not anything be something.

"Very regrettable but very true.

"So that shows to you that a whole thing is not interesting because as a whole well as a whole there has to be remembering and forgetting, but one at a time, oh one at a time is something oh yes definitely something." In very careful stages, the shearing process lasted all one day and well into the evening of another. When Sherwood Anderson came to call, only a cap of hair was left on the imperial head. Alice and Gertrude watched his reaction apprehensively. It made Gertrude look like a monk, he said. They both thought this was a charming thing to say, and breathed with relief.

Picasso, at first sight of the new tonsure, was openly dismayed. "My portrait," he said, staring at Gertrude with wounded eyes. But when he had carefully studied the living version of the head he had painted with such protracted care, he became genial. "After all," he said confidently, "it is all there."

As the long procession of talented, fashionable, rich and possibly interesting young men continued to pass over the threshold of the atelier, Gertrude was almost daily confronted by letters from friends in America and England, of which the following are typical:

DEAR GERTRUDE,

This will introduce you to —— twenty something, and a year out of Harvard — a charming acquaintance of mine who is just starting for Europe and asked me for a letter to you whom he admires in the way young men would who know about you as much as read you. I told him you were away just now but that I would send him word when you returned. He writes. Is very well bred and entertaining. Is perhaps a little la de dah but most likeable. I never suggest this kind of thing to you unless I think it will be a benefit to your ultimate book sales over here. And unless I also think it is a person who will not bore you.

288

Dear Gertrude,

A young friend of mine —— asked me for a letter of introduction to you, and so I had to give it to him. Doubtless he'll present it soon as he is eager to enrol himself among your disciples. . . . He is what you call a "fils de famille" — he has ancient lineage and, I believe, some money. He buys modern paintings occasionally from artists who sell but seldom. Be as nice to him as you can, though of course I know you are over-run with these petitioners for friendship.

Bravig Imbs had for a long time been regarded as one of the brightest and most winning of these young men and, like many of the others, lived in fear that circumstances would soon force him to go home just when Paris was most enthralling. But, like most of the others, he managed to stay on for years; it was he who first brought Elliot Paul to "27." "I have never seen two persons become friends more quickly than Gertrude and Elliot," said Imbs. "The very first contact was electric. Elliot, generally reserved and shy, was talking as if he had had things to say to Gertrude for years, and Gertrude interrupted him with peals of laughter and told him how much she had enjoyed his books. . . . Elliot was, of course, of a courtesy which charmed men and women alike, and Alice was quite swept off her feet by his manner. Gertrude was sensitive to his flattering remarks of attention as well, but she liked him because of his mellow ironic talk, the fact that he was an important writer, interested in her own work, and contributing literary articles to the Chicago *Tribune*, and because he had the quality of evanescence."

Not long after their meeting, Paul, whom Gertrude liked to refer to as "a New England Saracen," wrote the first serious estimation of her work to reach a wide audience, an account published in the Paris edition of the Chicago *Tribune*. His warm open manner made him unusually privileged at "27" and he began coming frequently. On one of these occasions, Imbs reported: "To talk about Joyce in Gertrude's salon was rushing in where angels feared to tread, but that was exactly what Elliot was doing, and I realized then what great affection both Gertrude and Alice must have for him, for if anyone else had dared praise Joyce to their faces they would have read the Riot Act forthwith. Elliot was blissfully unconscious of the fact that he was being more than impertinent, and went on and on talking about this wonderful 'Work in Progress.' . . ." Gertrude allowed him to express himself for a while but, finally, with one limply generous concession, brought the discussion to a close. "Joyce and I are at opposite poles," she said, "but our work comes to the same thing, the creation of something new."

The happiest consequence of her friendship with Elliot Paul was the opportunity to become identified with the early days of the greatest of all the expatriate magazines, *transition*. The announced ambition of this review was nothing less than "to forge a chain that would link together Europe and America." In its pages the work of Gertrude Stein was warmly welcomed — to such an extent that in the list of contributors for one issue was the legend: "And Gertrude Stein sends what she wishes and when she wishes and she is pleased and we are pleased." Before he had assumed the role of assistant to Eugene Jolas, editor of *transition*, Elliot Paul had come to Gertrude with news of the job that had been offered. He was not sure that he should accept; but Gertrude sent his doubts flying. "After all," she said, "we do want to be printed. One writes for oneself and strangers but with no adventurous publishers how can one come in contact with these same strangers?" Paul accepted the job, but in the course of selecting the contents of the first issue became fearful that the magazine might become too popular. The absolute limit in the number of subscribers, he felt, would be two thousand. More than that would mean that it was not fulfilling its special and rarefied purposes. As it turned out, he need not have worried. At its highest point of influence, *transition* never had more than one thousand subscribers.

Among the pieces Elliot Paul chose for Volume 1, Number 1, and paid for at the rate of thirty francs (about three dollars) per page, was an excerpt from Joyce's *Work in Progress* and the short text of *An Elucidation* by Gertrude Stein, her first effort to "explain" herself. But the typesetters failed her. "Through an inadvertence in the printing establishment," Paul explained, "the text of *An Elucidation* was printed in toto but in the wrong order." Gertrude was profoundly upset at having this, of all pieces, subject to a mangled presentation in public, and was not placated until *transition* offered to print the work in a separate pamphlet and to guarantee the proper succession of every syllable.

"Everyone knows the difference between explain and make it plain," Gertrude insisted, and in *An Elucidation* she attempted to "make it plain" simply by presenting for the reader's dalliance a garland of playfully designed sentences. In spite of the promise of the title, this work is no more an elucidation of her methods than a series of problems in calculus would be an elucidation of algebraic notation. Gertrude had a contempt for critics and criticism, except in a few instances when some critic would compare her work to that of Bach or jeopardize his reputation by leaping over critical hurdles in order simply to shake her hand. Because of this feeling on her part, one senses that *An Elucidation* was motivated by a determination not to use the paraphernalia of a critic in stating the problems of an artist, and to avoid altogether the terms and references that might allow her readers to take bearings in relation to the analyses of other artists and critics. Because she did not believe that analysis analyzed anything, she refused to divide herself into critic and creator. She wanted to *be* the thing she was talking about. In order to accomplish this she produced a teasing intellectual exercise in which she played around with a few puns such as "Halve Rivers and Harbours. Have rivers and harbours"; showed a number of the cinematic tricks that words can do; declared that "Action and reaction are equal and opposite"; and took time to congratulate her reader on having followed the very strict terms of her letter and spirit: "I can see and you can see, you can see and so can I see that I have not made more of it than needs to be made of it. In every way you are satisfied and we have given satisfaction and we have not meant to be swamped by other considerations."

On the whole, the piece fails to accomplish what it was meant to do, not because it stands outside the range of logic a reader might grasp and follow, but because it conspicuously lacks charm in rhythm, diction or design, and because her habit of coyly inviting the reader to solve for himself problems she has been at no pains to present amounts finally to a kind of patronizing. In most instances, particularly in her critical writings, Gertrude Stein's manifest confidence in what she is doing goes a long way toward winning sympathetic attention. She firmly believed that "Anything once it is made has its own existence and it is because of that that anything holds somebody's attention," and she felt that clarity was much less to be desired than force. But when she fails to communicate her own self-confidence, she immediately appears naked and not a little absurd. The reader suspects that her true difficulty lies in the fact that, even when she is addressing herself, she sometimes loses consciousness of her audience. Losing that consciousness, and momentarily unnerved, she throws in irrelevant matters in an attempt to restore the illusion of control. But the false lead remains false and sets up the further suspicion that while she may be on her way she has little notion of where she is going. As Edmund Wilson remarked on typical works of her middle period, "We see the ripples expanding in her consciousness, but we are no longer supplied with any clew as to what kind of object has sunk there."

Gertrude was pleased when Elliot Paul told her that he thought the essay was a more effective statement than *Composition as Explanation*. The latter work, he felt, was one in which she had not succeeded in doing without a number of the conventions of critical explanation. In *An Elucidation*, on the other hand, she had withheld the last iota of information, and had provided instead a series of examples which made her "point" less obvious and consequently, at least to those readers who could bring themselves to go the route, more striking.

Under Paul's editorial and personal favor, Gertrude's name was always prominent in the early issues of *transition*. But within two years the editorship passed exclusively to Eugene Jolas, whose wife Maria was footing the bills, and under whose regime the work of Stein appeared less frequently. When her name was no longer in the contributors' column, the magazine collapsed. Gertrude drew the obvious conclusion.

But according to Maria Jolas, her highhanded dismissal of *transition*-without-Stein was a pose. When, late in 1930, there were rumors that the magazine was about to reappear, the coolness that had set in between her and the Jolases was suddenly a thing of the past.

Under a barrage of notes, telephone calls and other forms of invitation, the Jolases allowed themselves to be persuaded to publish Gertrude in the next issue of the revived magazine. Later, when Maria Jolas felt that Gertrude chose "to play the queen in public," striking off the heads of the innocent or the indifferent, she considered it imperative "to inform Miss Stein that *Transition* was not conceived by Eugene Jolas as a vehicle for the rehabilitation of her own reputation, although it undoubtedly did do this. Nor was her role in its development different from that of many other well-wishing contributors. *Transition* was conceived, and the personal and financial sacrifice gladly accepted, in order to create a meeting place for all those artists on both sides of the Atlantic who were working towards a complete renovation, both spiritual and technical, of the various art forms. Miss Stein seemed to be experimenting courageously, and while my husband was never enthusiastic about her solution of the language, still it was a very personal one, and language being one of his chief preoccupations, she obviously belonged with us. Her final capitulation to a Barnumesque publicity none of us could foresee. What we should have foreseen however, was that she would eventually tolerate no relationship that did not bring with it adulation."

Above the little storms for which she was sometimes responsible but in which she was seldom deeply involved, Gertrude as usual had work to do and, as usual, she was doing it. An event of particular import to a new phase of her work had been the first exhibition at the Galerie Druet in 1926 of a group of painters who began to be referred to as the "neo-romantics." The most prominent members of this group were Pavel Tchelitchew, Eugene Berman and his brother Léonid, Christian Bérard and Kristians Tonny. Most of their works showed a determined reaction against cubism in particular, as well as against the various kinds of abstraction that had for many years superseded the purer forms of cubism. Neo-romantic paintings bore a distant but definite relationship to Picasso's early Blue and Rose Periods and, like the paintings of those periods, showed easily recognizable human figures in dramatic settings suffused with soft, exotic and sentimental color.

Gertrude called these painters "the Russian School" — probably as a gesture toward her particular friends, Tchelitchew and Berman — and they made the first reasonably coherent movement in painting to which she gave favorable attention since the early days of cubism. For a few years, she maintained a mild enthusiasm for the neo-romantics and bought a good number of their pictures; but eventually she quarreled with some of the painters and finally chucked all of their works out of her collection. But in the years when she was looking at neo-romantic paintings and thinking about them, she became acquainted with the works of her last great love in painting, Francis Rose. From him she eventually acquired sixty paintings, and through him she became reacquainted with his professional master, Francis Picabia, an old cubist hand who had recently begun to interest her by developing in the romantic vein a method based technically on a strong linear bias.

Under the general influence of these men, she began to concentrate upon ways to get more emotional content into her work. "There are all these emotions lying around," she said, "no reason why we shouldn't use them." In this spirit she undertook the composition of a long poem, *Patriarchal Poetry*, trying to analyze and illustrate the structure of emotion as it might show itself in a kind of spooling verbal movement, and went on to write the most lyrical and melodic work of this period, *Lucy Church Amiably*. With the latter she returned to the novel — her own definition and brand of novel, to be sure — but one in which a heroine, Lucy Church — a name derived from the little church with a pagoda-like steeple at Lucey in the region of Belley — and the heroine's neighbors figure as recognizable characters, and in which the relation of characters to their setting is often fairly clear.

An increased melodiousness in the line-to-line composition provided a change from the brisk syncopations that had marked most of her earlier work. In her own words, *Lucy Church Amiably* "altogether makes a return to romantic nature that is it makes a landscape look like an engraving in which there are some people." For the "advertisement" with which the book is prefaced, she devised a paradigm sentence that represents the note of a pitch organ, a sort of rhythmical key, to set the tone and method of the novel as a whole: "Select your song she said and it was done and then she said and it was done with a nod and then she bent her head in the direction of the falling water. Amiably." As in most of her plays, landscape dominates *Lucy Church Amiably* and is its main subject. The beauties of Gertrude's particular corner of the Ain are directly named and the words for everything are lovingly caressed. But her intention was not merely to record the pleasures of landscape or to gather bouquets of its images, but to catch the effect of a landscape self-contained and perpetually alive in the movements of weather, clouds, birds, beasts and butterflies as they play about her person and entertain her meditations. Her heroine, Lucy Church, is often unmistakably Gertrude Stein herself, so that the ultimate effect of the work is a sense of her mind continually thinking and recording its thoughts in the midst of a pastoral that is itself perpetually in motion. She was determined to dwell in sentiment, to make a sort of old-fashioned valentine of "climate and the affections," yet she remained playfully aware of her own wry toughness in regard to conventional expressions of sentiment. She had not gone "soft," and in the text of the book itself she pointedly reminds her reader of the fact. "To put into a book what is to be read in a book, bits of information and tender feeling," she says. "How do you like your two percent bits of information and tender feeling."

In the spring of 1928, she bought a white poodle at a department store and a new Ford car. She named the poodle "Basket" and, for once, left her car unnamed. Then she and Alice set out for their new summer home, hopeful that the lieutenant whom they had displaced would be assigned to Morocco forever. When, finally, they could inspect close up and at leisure the home they had chosen at a distance, they could see that it was a typical manor house with white plaster walls, two vegetable gardens, and a terrace commanding a long view in the direction of the upper Rhône and the French Alps. Here, for seventeen consecutive years, they would spend six months out of every year.

Their new house was even finer than their dreams of it, according to Alice Toklas, but their dreams of finding publishing outlets for the great accumulations of Gertrude's work remained unanswered. However, in the aftermath of Gertrude's widely praised lecture appearances in England, Oxford and Cambridge men had begun to come to the Rue de Fleurus in great numbers, and with them came Joseph Brewer, a sympathetic young publisher associated with the firm of Payson and Clarke. With gratifying speed and efficiency he arranged for the publication of a book-length selection of Gertrude's pieces, "put together from every little that helps to be an American," and brought them out under the title of *Useful Knowledge*. This volume was handsomely produced and Gertrude was hopeful that she had finally laid the foundations for a continuing series of works to be published in England and America. But the book was a heavy financial loss and, once more, she found herself without a publisher and without prospects.

It was Alice Toklas, of all people, who redeemed the sad situation and fulfilled the long hope by herself becoming the "adventurous publisher" of the works of Gertrude Stein. To provide her with capital, Gertrude sold Picasso's *Girl with a Fan* to Marie Harriman, wife of the future governor of New York, and soon the new publishing house which, on Gertrude's suggestion, was named Plain Edition, was ready to go into business. Maurice Darantière, who had already printed *The Making of Americans* at his press in Dijon, was helpful with plans, and *Lucy Church Amiably* duly appeared as the first book on the list.

Distribution was the knottiest problem for the new publisher. But with advice from professional friends and amateur promoters, Alice got the volume into the windows of many Paris bookstores. Gertrude spent days walking about the city to look at their modest displays of her wares. Collectors in America, of whom there was a small, far-flung, but faithful number, responded at once, and soon the publisher of Plain Edition had an active little overseas business to attend to. Besides the novel, four other works were eventually brought out under the imprint: *Before the Flowers of Friendship Faded Friendship Faded; How to Write; Operas and Plays;* and *Matisse Picasso and Gertrude Stein.*

With the shape of each year now happily established, Gertrude and Alice were as completely delighted to set off for Bilignin each spring as they were to return to the Rue de Fleurus every autumn. Scores of visitors came to see them in the country, and they were continually preoccupied with their gardens and the succession of little dogs that were given to them as companions to the sovereign Basket. But none of these caused Gertrude to neglect the demands of her genius and she was as deeply involved in her work and as prolific as ever. Once she had exhausted the romantic seam, and turned away from the calligraphic attenuations of that period, she began to revert to a more closed and cerebral kind of composition and in this mode produced a series of compositions published under the title *How to Write*. This work, concerned with "equilibration" and the technical aspects of grammar, narrative, vocabulary, is perhaps the most opaque of all of her books.

She had become interested, almost to the point of obsession, in the relations of paragraphs and sentences. "Paragraphs are emotional," she said, "sentences are not," and she wrote long abstract treatises-by-example in an attempt to clarify the conviction for herself and for her readers. The pieces in *How to Write* are as strict and uncompromising in their denial of "content" or melodiousness, and as deliberate in their innocence, as some of the musical compositions of Erik Satie or of his American follower John Cage. Gertrude Stein was no longer "painting" as she had been for a good part of her writing career and while she would not as a rule tolerate comparisons to music, music as it had developed in her lifetime offers the best reference. The experience of listening to twenty or thirty of John Cage's "sonatas" in succession is much like reading *How to Write*. In both cases the listener or reader, if he is going to accept anything at all, must accept random fragments and oddly matched pieces that are remarkable for what they scrupulously do not do in terms of literature or music rather than for what they do. In Gertrude Stein's case, the reader follows a process that is essentially an examination of the contents of the author's consciousness. What she delineates may finally be brought into some shape, but this demands a more intimate knowledge of her personality and her cerebrations than is humanly possible. To read *How to Write* is finally to learn what language sounds like when it is consciously divorced from sense, in the ordinary sense of sense, and when the impulses and ideas it means to express have been vaporized with the absolute efficiency of a nuclear explosion.

The appearance of this most hermetic of all of her works caused the kind of consternation that was now commonplace yet, compared with the reception of *Tender Buttons,* the breadth of interest in the book was narrow and the expression of outrage reduced to scrannel pipings. If the book is to be accounted for in sober terms, it may best be regarded as a logical part of the body of her work, nearly all of which ignores objections put clearly by Leo Stein when Gertrude first began to write. With accuracy and candor, Gertrude reported Leo's early reaction: "He said that it was not it it was I. If I was not there to be there with what I did then what I did would not be what it was. In other words if no one knew me actually then the things I did would not be what they were." Since Leo's statement introduces a consideration that obtained through all but the last phase of her career, and because this consideration is of paramount importance in relating Gertrude Stein to other writers with whom she is constantly and erroneously grouped, it provides an introduction to a matter that overarches and circumscribes any account of her creative career.

This matter is simply the relationship of the artist to the world from which his compositions come and the audience for whom they are intended. When William Butler Yeats said of William Blake, "He was a man crying out for a mythology . . . trying to make one because he could not find one to his hand," he spoke not only for Blake but for a host of modern writers who wanted the prerogative of composing epics in a world lacking the cultural coherence on which epics are based. As the myths of Western religion waned, and political systems showed themselves inadequate to provide the secular counterparts of religious mythology, many modern writers came to feel that their central challenge was to find some substitute for the myth-structures that had made possible the epics of the past. They looked back with nostalgia on the comparatively ordered bodies of belief that had served the Greek dramatists, and upon the comparative religious and philosophical unities that had allowed great poets like Virgil and Lucretius and Dante and Milton to write in the intellectual security their respective eras made available. Searching for this substitute, modern poets and novelists began to entertain various possibilities — history as interpreted from the points of view of Freud, Jung or Marx, or from the point of view of those men who have elaborated upon the cyclical theories of Vico; a single culture viewed as an entity in which the present and the past are equally alive and reciprocally related; or even a total account of man viewed as both the agent and creature of his science. Like Joyce, some writers would hit upon the notion of borrowing piecemeal the mythological unity of some period of the past and use it to contain and carry the chaos of the present.

When portions of *Ulysses* began to be published, T. S. Eliot made a famous statement that called attention to the particular nature of Joyce's achievement: "In using the myth, in manipulating a continuous parallel between contemporaneity and antiquity, Mr. Joyce is pursuing a method which others must pursue after him. They will not be imitators, any more than the scientist who uses the discoveries of an Einstein in pursuing his own, independent, further investigations. It is simply a way of controlling, of ordering, of giving a shape and a significance to the immense panorama of futility and anarchy which is contemporary history. It is a method already adumbrated by Mr. Yeats, and of the need for which I believe Mr. Yeats to have been the first contemporary to be conscious. It is, I seriously believe, a step toward making the modern world possible in art."

In their separate quests to find something to substitute for a mythology, other writers who at first glance seem as difficult to comprehend as Gertrude Stein had assumed dependencies that would ultimately make their work explicable. By the time she had accepted painting and laboratory psychology as the sources of her method, these writers had begun to make use of suggestions from the still new sciences of psychology and anthropology and, in some cases, were groping vaguely for expression of new conceptions attendant upon the formulations of space-time physics. These extraliterary sources were logical and justifiable points of departure from nineteenth-century conventions of fiction and poetry, and they provided systems of thought and bodies of knowledge within which the experiments of many of the new writers might be reasonably accommodated.

Among these writers were some to whom the sciences were meaningless and far too remote to provide any sort of literary background or framework. Yet, like many of the others, they tended to see the modern world as a chaos filled with the ruined arches of religion and the roofless porches of philosophy. When they could take shelter in neither, they looked for any structure stable enough to provide even temporary residence. When they could not find these in fact, they began to devise them in imagination. The search for accommodating structures would lead some of them to single out certain objects and then to endow them with an enormous freight of symbolic meaning — the method of Franz Kafka in *The Castle*, for instance, or that of Hart Crane in *The Bridge*. The same search would lead others to the greater bravado of making mythological structures of their own, even to the point of devising completely arbitrary systems of philosophy and versions of history. This was the case of Yeats with *A Vision* and the poems dependent upon it, and that of Ezra Pound with the *Cantos*.

However, not all writers would make their own new versions of myth. Others would base their work upon an idea, a method, or perhaps on a perspective related to the findings of scientists and the meditations of philosophers. But in nearly all cases, their final literary manifestations of their excursions into the world of ideas would stand in open relation to the particular sources which suggested them. So Virginia Woolf's "interior time" and the works exemplifying the belief that intuition is deeper than intellect stood clearly in relation to Bergson. So T. S. Eliot's *The Waste Land*, with its "historical culture, intellectual tradition and legacy of ideas and forms," stood in relation to the published researches of Sir James Frazer and Miss Jessie Weston.

Any writer is distinguished by his selective eye, tone of voice, and the rhythms in which his imagination registers its play. Yet the particular identity of a writer is not clearly established until he is seen in

300

relation to his times. Historically speaking, Gertrude Stein's place is likely to remain tentative and to be peculiarly dependent upon notions of what literature can properly achieve. Even her admirers despair when they must account for the discrepancy between the canny, wise and deeply erudite cast of her mind and spoken words, and the vast wastes of utter "thoughtlessness" which are the most of her written words. She may come to be regarded as one who stopped short of the common goal to which other major writers addressed themselves, and she may be regarded as one who, refusing to acknowledge the common goal, set her own challenges and met them with resounding success. If the common goal continues to be the solution of the problem of myth or, at least, the setting of a clear and adequate "frame of reference" by which a work of literary art is made generally accessible, Gertrude Stein cannot be fairly judged in relation to either. Her only "usable knowledge" was and continued to be the day-by-day reality of her existence as she lived it and recorded it. Her writing was loosely based in what she had learned from William James, and its sources can be traced back to certain of his experiments and pronouncements on the nature of consciousness. But the connection with James is neither strong enough nor consistent enough to base a theory upon. Except for those affinities that might be explained as merely coincidental, she herself quite naturally denied the relationship between the "vision" of her works and the laboratory documentations of her old master. Her deeper and more immediate sources lay in painting; and by the time she had transcribed the lessons of painting into her own practice, connections that might possibly have indicated her dependence on any but her own existential "frame of reference" were severed. Instead of solving the problem of myth in terms of literature, she turned to painting and ignored the problem. When she had made this step, she largely confounded literary criticism of her work and forced those who would evaluate her work to accept her on her own terms or to leave her alone. Since her own new terms were based in painting, it is essential to discover just what these amounted to.

By and large, the twentieth-century painters with whom she joined company have not had to deal with challenges confronting the poet or novelist — at least those poets and novelists like Proust and Mann, Yeats and Eliot, whose scope has tended toward the epical. Whether the painter's work is conceived as a window looking out upon the world, or as a window reflecting, like a mirror, only what is in his own mind, he works in reference to a given, comparatively settled and existing thing. The world is his reference and his "mythology," and if he finds problems in recording his world these problems are largely technical rather than ideational. His art is spatial, which means that it is governed by what can "happen" in space or be expressed in space, and his materials have specific properties which he uses to produce the lines and planes that define space. (Open to many kinds of assessment, the painter's space in recent years has become a commodity in a spectacular market. "Inch by inch," Janet Flanner has written, "a Cézanne landscape is the highest priced newly discovered land known in the Western World.") The painter's fundamental effort is concerned with the plastic potentialities of his medium, and his success lies in the ingenuity and power with which he can employ his available means. When, in the course of history, he is led to incorporate a new sense of time, a fourth dimension, into his work, he makes this step by recording angles of vision or by devising the graphic representation of a process. He is not urged, as the writer is, to account for an object, a figure, an idea, through all of its permutations or to relate any of these subjects to their total background. By the definiteness of his materials, the painter is released to pursue his art to its abstract limits without having to lug with him an impending baggage of associations. The writer, on the other hand, is called upon to assume the function of creator, lawgiver and philosopher before he can begin to exercise his pure gift as lyric singer, and before he dares to examine the sound, gravity, color and texture of words as things having their own discrete existences.

Like that of her painter contemporaries, Gertrude Stein's world became less a world of ideas than one of new perspectives, new forms, and plastic possibilities that seemed to develop out of the medium of language as easily as new colors might be mixed on a palette. Assuming the freedom of a painter, she proceeded as if the visible world were the only world and attempted to bring bits and pieces of her observaton into compositions by which her mosaic sense of experience would, as in the case of paintings, be apprehended as a whole. Like the painters who influenced her, she was determined to maintain the logic of nature, even though her methods led her to deny the appearance of nature. She succeeded in maintaining the logic of nature, but only insofar as the logic of the free-playing mind as it flits and swims around any subject can be considered to be natural. The appearance of nature which, in writing, is the illusion of a thing to which the human mind can respond in the same terms as the mind responds in life was, in her case, obscured or replaced by intellectual constructions almost exclusively related to the mind that produced them.

The eye, more tolerant than the mind, allows a painter the license of denying appearance in favor of a beguiling illusion. But when a writer persists in denying appearance as completely as did Gertrude Stein, the mind of the reader is left with no object upon which to fix, no point at which to rest. Adrift in the interstices of her free-playing world of suggestion, and taunted by fragments of "reality" that loom and disappear before they can be grasped, he is apt first to become weary and, soon after, rebellious. Her audience tends finally to consist only of the few individuals who can tolerate literature reduced to a series of tensions generated by the impact of participles, verbs and pronouns, to the formula predicted by Valéry —"de l'algèbre et des sensations"— or to the anarchic data of objects waiting to be sorted.

For myth, legend and symbol, Gertrude Stein substituted pure intellectual experience, "an apprehension of process composed of perspectives and integers in a continuum." She thereby broke sharply with the whole development of literature in America or in Europe and advanced — or retreated — toward that primitivism which is possible only when a whole tradition has been absorbed and dismissed. Intellect had revised the interpretation of phenomena in her lifetime; the solid world of Western man had been atomized; new methods of measurement and analysis had arrived in the development of science and the life of art. Yet to all appearances Gertrude Stein reverted to that kind of poetry which Vico regarded as the first form of living history, "the metaphysic of man whilst he is still living in a direct sensuous relation to his environment . . . before he has learned to form universals and to reflect." By the play of intellect she had tried to cancel out intellect in order to bring literature to the purity of something like birdsong or a game of chess.

No other writer had been so daring or, perhaps, so foolish. In *Finnegans Wake*, James Joyce brought acrostic methods of mythological reference to their ultimate complication. Yet Joyce is bound by references; his technical puzzles can be solved with erudition, patience and ingenuity. As Picasso supposedly said of him when he turned down an offer to illustrate an edition of *Ulysses*, "He is an obscure writer all the world can understand." Because she offers no references by which bearings can be taken, Gertrude Stein cannot be "solved," she can only be accepted. In relation to the cabalistic arabesques and top-heavy historicism of Joyce, her methods are as simple and flat as those used in rock-painting. Joyce met the early challenge he set for himself by working through knowledge to achieve that state in which the artist is "like God, indifferent, paring his nails." Gertrude Stein had assumed this divine indifference to begin with. Joyce's gargantuan work, *Finnegans Wake*, may be the final encrustation of Byzantine technique after which Gertrude Stein, her pages swept clean of propositional content, represents the ABC's of a new literature. In any case, among writers in English she was alone in her attempts completely to forego the support of history and knowledge, and has remained alone.

The subject of much of her work, like that of many of the painters, was composition itself. Like the painters who make variant versions of the same composition, keeping the original relationships but changing the objects and colors, she made compositions in pure sound and offered them in several versions. Maurice Grosser, in his book *The Painter's Eye*, comments upon this aspect of her practice: "For example, a poem entitled 'Suzy Asado,' after a Spanish dancer whom she knew, whose name rhymes with *'leche helada'* . . . becomes (since *asado* in Spanish means 'roasted'): 'Toasted Suzy is my ice

:ream.' But even if all such references could be tracked down and understood, they would explain very little. Because Gertrude Stein's subject matter — at any rate in the poems which form the greater part of her work — is purely composition in sound. There is, for example, a 'Portrait of F.B.' which has the same cadences and the same shape as the . . . poem 'Rooms.' But the actual words used in the two poems are completely different."

In the "explanation" she reports, Leo believed that one had to know her personally in order to understand what she was writing; to be possessed of all the little domestic facts of her existence; to know what she ate, how she was dressed, where she went and whom she saw, along with the whole range of her literary background and interests, if one were to recognize the proper clues by which her work might be interpreted. He was correct in this analysis, but if Gertrude knew that he had hit upon the fundamental thing that would limit her audience and keep her work from the scrutiny of critics and, with few exceptions, from scholars, she made no sign then or later. Her confidence was as weighty as her presence and she simply proceeded to write what seemed to her real and self-justifying.

Her single-mindedness may, with some qualifications, be put down as self-assurance, and the drive of an artist who had sighted her own way through a general cultural dilemma. Any single life, fully documented in an expressive medium, may suggest that individual experience has applications wholly as valid as any system of thought or body of belief to which readers might be directed for guidance since, after all, no life is wholly unique or without relevance to the human condition. Gertrude Stein did use the data of her private existence, but since she seldom bothered to present the time, place and particularity of her sources or the background against which her works should be read, she seems guilty of a flagrant irresponsibility. If she is defensible, we must look to the explanations of the painters and poets to whose methods she was committed. She had, in practice, anticipated and then followed a deliberate theory of irresponsibility put forward by the French cubists: "We will even willingly confess that it is impossible to write without employing readymade phrases, or to paint if we totally neglect the familiar symbols. It is for each to decide whether he should scatter them all through his work, mix them intimately with personal symbols, or boldly exhibit them, magical discords, shreds of the great collective lie, at a single point of the plane of the higher reality which he appropriates to his art." With indifference to such difficulties as almost any reader would encounter, she proceeded with the large expectation that intuition objectified in abstract word-patterns would sustain her, and she had confidence that the initial resistance of her readers would give way before the force of "the created thing." This unyielding attitude necessarily limited sympathetic response to her work, caused her to be neglected while exhaustive critical inquiry was given to figures of far less importance, and proved an insurmountable barrier in bringing her work to any group of readers larger than bands of devotees.

After the ultimate hermeticism of *How to Write* and other works of its period, Gertrude was exhausted and disposed to relax. She knew that she had gone as far as she could go in her laboratory investigations of the bones and integuments of expressive language, and if she had not found answers to all of her questions she had at least sorted out the integers of which questions are made. Language was still her own button box, and she had sorted and arranged its contents in every conceivable way. She was ready now to put it aside, and to tell the world in the language of the world just who she was and why the world should take her into account.

Leo Stein late in life

Alice B. Toklas in
America

Gertrude Stein at the height of her fame

CHAPTER 20

She will be me when this you see.
— GERTRUDE STEIN
But God what a liar she is!
— LEO STEIN

"ONE does not in one's heart believe in mute inglorious Miltons," Gertrude confessed, and in the summer of 1932, when the weather at Bilignin was dry and beautiful, she made a gesture to prove her point. Choosing a style meant to register on every page the speaking voice of Alice Toklas and written from a point of view assumed to be Alice's, she put down the anecdotal history of their long life together. "This is her autobiography one of two," said Gertrude. "But which it is no one which it is can know," and then, revising a phrase — "When this you see remember me" — that had punctuated passages in her work for many years, she prophesied, "She will be me when this you see." She wrote to be understood unequivocally, and what she wanted to be understood was, first and last, herself. The result was a spectacular bestseller, *The Autobiography of Alice B. Toklas*, which inevitably brought her into the lecture halls of the United States and imposed upon her name celebrity of such proportions that her eminence on the American scene was for a time shared only by gangsters, base-ball players and movie stars.

She had long had premonitions of being a celebrity of greater reputation than the precincts of the art world would ever allow. In her search for literary subjects she had never really gone any further than herself. But now "the important thing was that for the first time in writing," she said, "I felt something outside me while I was writing, hitherto I had always had nothing but what was inside me while I was writing." She felt that if she told her own story as simply as Defoe had told the story of Robinson Crusoe, her adventures on the storm-swept island of avant-garde Paris would strike readers as equally irresistible. "Think of Defoe," she said, "he tried to write Robinson Crusoe as if it were exactly what did happen and yet after all he is Robinson Crusoe and Robinson Crusoe is Defoe and therefore after all it is not what is happening it is what is happening to him to Robinson Crusoe that makes what is exciting every one." The actual writing of this momentous book took only six weeks. When she returned to Paris with the manuscript in hand, the first thing she did was to phone Picasso to tell him about it.

He came to "27" with his wife Olga, to whom he had been mar-ried since the end of the war. Mme. Picasso, under the name of Olga Koklova, had been a ballet dancer when Picasso met her while he was doing sets for the famous Satie-Cocteau-Diaghilev ballet, *Parade*, and she was now the mother of his first child, Paulo. When Ger-trude translated parts of the manuscript for the two of them, Picasso, according to Gertrude, found it all "very exciting." However, in the course of the reading of the translation, the name of Picasso's first Parisian mistress, Fernande Olivier, came importantly into the story. Offended, Mme. Picasso picked up her things and walked out in a huff. Picasso was perplexed and hesitant but Gertrude urged him to follow his wife. When he did, he disappeared from Gertrude's life for a period of nearly two years.

The literary agent for the *Autobiography* was William Aspinwall Bradley, who handled most of the well-known Parisian writers who were published in America. Gertrude instructed Bradley to try to place the book with the *Atlantic Monthly* for serialization. Of all

American magazines, this was the one in which she had always hoped her work might sometime appear. Her own efforts had always ended in rejection, and even a sponsor as influential as Mildred Aldrich could not prevail upon the editors to let Gertrude Stein in. Only a year before, the *Atlantic* had returned one of Gertrude's frequent submissions with the following letter:

DEAR MISS STEIN:

We live in different worlds. Yours may hold the good, the beautiful, and the true, but if it does their guise is not for us to recognize. Those vedettes who lead the vanguard of picture arts are understood, or partly understood, over here by a reasonably compact following, but that following cannot translate their loyalties into a corresponding literature, and it would really be hopeless for us to set up this new standard.

I am sorry.

Yours sincerely,
ELLERY SEDGWICK

Simon-pure Stein was one thing, but Stein as raconteur was another. Her next letter from Sedgwick showed a change of heart, if not a change of tune:

DEAR MISS STEIN:

There has been a lot of pother about this book of yours, but what a delightful book it is, and how glad I am to publish four installments of it! During our long correspondence, I think you felt my constant hope that the time would come when the real Miss Stein would pierce the smoke-screen with which she has always so mischievously surrounded herself. The autobiography has just enough of the oblique to give it individuality and character, and readers who care for the things you do will love it. . . .

Hail Gertrude Stein about to arrive!

Believe me,

Yours sincerely,
ELLERY SEDGWICK

As soon as the first installments of the *Autobiography* appeared, fan letters by the score began to come across the ocean. With them also came big checks representing more "earned" money than Gertrude had ever known. "I love being rich," she said, "not as yet so awful rich but with prospects, it makes me all cheery inside. . . ." But this feeling soon gave way to new worries and a period of soul-searching: her relations to her work had become confused by a new idea of the potential rewards of work. Slowly, she began to feel, everything was somehow changing inside her. The sense of public success was the thing she had once regarded as the cause of a crucial change in the "bottom nature" of Matisse, and now the same thing was beginning to trouble her. "Suddenly it was all different," she said, "what I did had a value that made people ready to pay, up to that time everything I did had a value because nobody was ready to pay. It is funny about money." Even her daily life in Paris began to show changes she could never have anticipated. Somehow "it was less Paris than it had been. . . . The thing is like this, it is all the question of identity. It is all a question of the outside being outside and the inside being inside. As long as the outside does not put a value on you it remains outside but when it does put a value on you then it gets inside or rather if the outside puts a value on you then all your inside gets to be outside. I used to tell all the men who were being successful young how bad this was for them and then I who was no longer young was having it happen."

She had phrased her personal version of the problem awaiting any serious writer whose work might or does find a commercial outlet. She had always worked without a thought of a market in the broad sense, and her judgment was urged only by considerations proper to her task; her bravado, in spite of many disappointments, had remained uncurbed; her vision unimpaired. But once the notion of a market entered her calculations, once she was forced to listen to the voice of Mammon, she had found herself in jeopardy. To follow this voice would be to go further and further from the sound of the one voice in the world that could ever answer her search for approval — her own. In the works of her late years she did to a degree become a victim of several alluring voices — songs from the "outside." But for the present, at least, "inside" reservations about success and its dangers were not sufficiently compelling to halt her progress. In conference with Bradley, she decided that Harcourt Brace should have the book in America and that, for sentimental reasons associated with John Lane, his successors, the Bodley Head, should be its English publisher.

The Autobiography of Alice B. Toklas was published in August, 1933. The book charmed reviewers and a large new public, but its reception received no swelling of trumpets from Leo Stein. In spite of his belief that "The historian investigates his facts, the autobiographer just remembers them" — and in spite of his sympathy for General Grant who, having been reproached for misinformation in his autobiography, had said, "That's the way I remember these things. Let those who remember them otherwise write what they remember . . ." — Leo refused to make similar concessions to his sister. Writing from his home in Florence to Mabel Weeks, he said, "I read Gertrude's autobiography the other day and thought it maintained very well the tone of sprightly gossip rising at times to a rather nice comedy level. But God what a liar she is! . . . Practically everything that she says of our activities before 1911 is false both in fact and implication, but one of her radical complexes . . . made it necessary practically to eliminate me." Shortly after, in another letter to Mabel Weeks, he said: "Her autobiography did seriously annoy me for a while. I had long since ceased to say anything at all about my relations to the art movement of the early 1900's, and always declined to write or say anything about it in public. Therefore I had no desire to be "recognized" in the matter, but it was a still different matter to have a sort of official lie given to such relations as were generally supposed to have existed." Rancor came through more clearly in letters to art collector Albert Barnes in which he referred to the book as "that farrago of rather clever anecdote, stupid brag and general bosh," and as "a rather clever superstructure on a basis of impenetrable stupidity. Gertrude and I are just the contrary. She's basically stupid and I'm basically intelligent."

Long before the book was in print, an American lecture agent had turned up to bid for Gertrude's services. With only vague notions of going to America, she nevertheless entertained his propositions for what they might be worth. When she told him that Alice and the two dogs would of course have to go along on any lecture tour she might conceivably undertake, the agent cooled, and she put aside the idea of America. Promise of vast amounts of money apart, she was deeply bothered by something she had known all along: the

American public was more interested in her person than in her work. "After all," she said, "there is no sense in it because if it were not for my work they would not be interested in me so why should they not be more interested in my work than in me. That is one of the things one has to worry about in America."

A scintillating public success, the *Autobiography* was also a relentless personal trial. Nothing was natural after its appearance, not even the charms of a summer in Bilignin. Worried about identity because she was not writing and had no urge to write — "Was I I when I had no written word inside me?" — Gertrude found herself in a continual fuss about servants and householding, misgivings attendant upon her success, and melodramatic happenings in the neighborhood. Before September came, the arrival and departure of four different servant couples had disastrously disturbed her summertime quiet; Mme. Pernollet, the hotelkeeper's wife, for whom she had great affection, had mysteriously fallen from a high window to her death in the cement courtyard of the hotel; and an Englishwoman visiting a neighbor had shot herself in a nearby ravine. Visitors arrived inconveniently, or stayed too long; nothing was right.

Picabia came with his Swiss wife and talked against Cézanne with such force and authority that Gertrude found herself dismayed, not because of the attack itself, but because of the "truth" of Picabia's insights. Other visitors — Janet Scudder and William Aspinwall Bradley and Francis Rose and William Seabrook and Mme. de Clermont Tonnerre — came and went, but nearly all occasions seemed more irritating than pleasurable. Gertrude never liked anyone to stay for long, "not because they are in the way but because after a time they are part of the way we live every day or they are not and I prefer them to be not." Without writing or feeling the urge to write, there was no anchor by which she felt moored to her "island of daily living." Finally, she made the beginnings of a sort of tour de force of a detective story based on the unsettling events of the summer. This *divertissement* was published, years after her death, under the title *Blood on the Dining-Room Floor*. This short "novel" has the quality of a literary pastiche in its genre and is full of numbers and suspicions and an indiscriminate air of portentousness. A little *roman à clef*, in which Gertrude's visitors and neighbors are transparently present, the story begins with the time-honored convention of a dead body, but then, unlike most detective stories, makes no headway whatsoever toward unmasking the criminal. Conditions for criminal activity are suggested in a score of ways, many motives are hinted at, and every event is touched with presage, but nothing is solved, resolved, or brought to any conclusion other than mystification.

Back in Paris in the late autumn, with acclaim becoming more intense and intrusions more frequent, she continued in a troubled spirit to work on her contribution to the detective story genre. She wrote daily, but could take little satisfaction in what she turned out. "Although I did it," she said, "I did not really do it." She was literally beside herself. Now everyone wanted her to meet someone. She began going out to one engagement after another. "It was pleasant being a lion," she confessed, but still there was the inner worry because "everybody was writing to me and I did not do any writing." In the evenings, with Basket, she would wander alone about her corner of Paris, increasingly aware of the political tensions radiating in waves from Berlin and from Moscow and from Rome.

She had lost even the old satisfaction of looking at paintings. The only painter whose work pleased her was that of the Cuban, Francis Picabia. "I thought I understood all about what we had done," she wrote, "and now understanding Picabia made me start all over again." She had known this painter for many years, but he had never before arrested her attention. His new work, coming at a time when Picasso was, as she said, "writing" in the same sense that in her middle period she had been "painting" — and when she had lost interest in her "Russian group" — struck her freshly and she became interested in his beginnings. She was fascinated by his stories of his early years and eventually wrote about them in a catalogue for an exhibition in which Picabia showed paintings composed of several pictures placed one over the other in a transparent manner, so that boats and classical heads and birds of paradise and shrubbery were mixed, giving the effect of several photographs on the same plate.

"His grandfather who brought him up and with whom he lived," she wrote in the printed introduction, "was one of the inventors of photography. He was a friend and companion of Daguerre, who invented the daguerreotype. Picabia, when he was a young boy was always with his grandfather. They used to travel a great deal and always visited museums and his grandfather, who was doing experiments in coloured photography at the time, being a well-known savant, was always given permission to photograph. So they photographed all day and they developed all night, and this his early experience, so Picabia believes, and I am not sure he is not right, has had a good deal to do with the development of modern painting. Picabia got from the constant contact with photography, which gradually bored him very much in spite of his admiration and affection for his grandfather, got something which did give him the idea of transparence and four dimensional painting, and this through him certainly had a great deal to do with everything. Even now in his later painting and certainly in his drawing he has achieved a transparence which is peculiarly a thing that has nothing to do with the surface." Such considerations made her feel for a time that she would have to revise her whole sense of the advance of painting through the years of which she had just written so eloquently. "Painting," she had already said, "now after its great moment must come back to be a minor art." And yet, she seemed not really sure, and not to be sure was unsettling.

When her agent Bradley went to America, she authorized him to arrange for the publication of everything still unpublished in her own country: *The Making of Americans* first and, after that, "everything." Bradley succeeded in getting Harcourt Brace to accept a revised and shortened version of her magnum opus. Just after she had signed the contract, Gertrude was dismayed by a cable from Bennett Cerf of Random House. He offered to bring out the whole book, just as it stood, in the Giant Series of the Modern Library. But it was too late to accept his offer. She kept on wandering about the Left Bank, reading political posters that proliferated on billboards, thinking about Roosevelt (who she said was like Louis Napoleon because he had "no personality but a persistence of insistence in a narrow range of ideas" and whom she regarded as a minor dictator in a succession begun by Theodore Roosevelt), about events in the wake of her success, about everyone suddenly wanting to meet her when, of course, she had been available to everyone these many years. With a good part of her thoughts concerned with America and its destiny, she began to write *Four in America*, a work which occupied her through most of the winter. She hoped that it might divert her from the self-probings that were beginning to discolor her whole existence, but she could not avoid carrying her problems into the book itself and, in fact, made her ingenious composition serve as a way out of dilemma. "I am not I when I see," she said, and began to think of American personalities who had achieved great fame, and to write about them in relation not only to the work they did but to the work they *might* have done. In this undertaking she wrote long remarkably uninformative portraits of Ulysses S. Grant, Wilbur Wright, Henry James and George Washington, trying to see each of them "do other things than they did so as to try to find out what it is that what happens has to do with what is." She made Grant a religious leader, Wright a painter, Washington a novelist, because he "began a novel the novel the great American novel," and James a general.

She had tried to get away from painting in the old cubist sense, and had succeeded in shifting the emphasis from spatial to linear effects from the time of *Lucy Church Amiably*. But when she came to analytical work she reverted to her older method. Like *The Geographical History of America*, *Four in America* is "spatialized" in that she took a few ideas about each of her figures, endlessly dissected them, displayed the component parts resulting from her operation, and made them integers in a process. She had definite things to say in each case, but instead of using discrete, logical, discursive language to make her points, she forced the reader — by many hints, beginnings, repetitions — to formulate, to think, to say: she must mean this . . . or that.

Four in America is a fantasy made even more remote than the fantasies one is accustomed to in literature or psychological case-books by the fenestrations of her thinking as she records it. The subject of the book, according to Thornton Wilder, was her answer to the question: "What are the various ways in which creativity works in everyone?" In praising her effort, Wilder in a moment of detachment

L* 315

makes a point which the greater part of Gertrude Stein's career confirms: "I think it can be said that the fundamental preoccupation of Miss Stein's life was not the work of art but the shaping of a theory of knowledge, a theory of time, and a theory of the passions."

The seriousness of her quest was deep enough to allow her relief from the intrusions of the great world and to conserve herself in terms that success and publicity could only serve to exploit. "I am and have been very full of meditation," she wrote to Sherwood Anderson, "about direct and indirect vision, and the relation between the writer and an audience either actual or not actual. I have just been writing about four Americans and one of them Henry James has cleared up a lot of things for me that is in trying to put him down. There are so many things to say and there is nothing to do but say them. . . ."

But others had decided it was time to say things, too, and these were not complimentary to Gertrude. Angered by the *Autobiography*, the editor of *transition*, Eugene Jolas, had opened the pages of the magazine "to several of those she mentions who, like ourselves, find that the book often lacks accuracy. This fact and the regrettable possibility that many less informed readers might accept Miss Stein's testimony about her contemporaries, make it seem wiser to straighten out those points with which we are familiar before the book has had time to assume the character of historic authenticity . . . There is a unanimity of opinion that she had no understanding of what really was happening around her, that the mutation of ideas beneath the surface of the more obvious contacts and clashes of personalities during that period escaped her entirely. Her participation in the genesis and development of such movements as Fauvism, Cubism, Dada, Surrealism, Transition etc. was never ideologically intimate and, as M. Matisse states, she has presented the epoch 'without taste and without relation to reality.' *The Autobiography of Alice B. Toklas*, in its hollow, tinsel bohemianism and egocentric deformations, may very well become one day the symbol of the decadence that hovers over contemporary literature."

In *Testimony Against Gertrude Stein*, published as a supplement to *transition* 1934-1935, Georges Braque, the Jolases, Matisse, André

Salmon, Tristan Tzara each in turn took issue with Gertrude's account of her relationships with them. Matisse, by and large, corrected small details about the prices of paintings and his domestic situation; stated that, according to his recollection, Braque had made the first cubist painting; and expressed the view that Sarah Stein, whom Gertrude did not mention, "was the really intelligently sensitive member of the family." Maria Jolas documented Gertrude's misunderstanding of Elliot Paul's function in the early days of *transition* and, as a consequence, her lack of clarity about the role of the Jolases as her long-time befrienders. Tristan Tzara felt that her book had exposed "a clinical case of megalomania," and asked by what right his name had become part of it. "Far be it from me to throw any doubt upon the fact that Miss Stein is a genius," he wrote. "We have seen plenty of those. Nor that Miss Toklas is convinced of it. To tell the truth, all this would have no importance if it took place in the family circle between two maiden ladies greedy for fame and publicity. But the immense apparatus which has been put in motion in order to arrive at this affirmation finds an obviously noisy echo in the well-known process by which the aforementioned maiden ladies thought they had the right to quote names and tales indiscriminately, thus accounting for the fact that, among others, my name is associated with what they so candidly call their memoirs. . . . They tell us the infinite pains they took to lure to their house, where their collection of canvases constituted an irresistible bait, people who might be useful to them in publishing an article in this or that review. I have no objection to their revealing the secrets of their literary kitchen, if they feel inclined to do so. It can all be used, even the left-overs . . ."

Braque stated categorically, "Miss Stein understood nothing of what went on around her," and felt that her "tourist" sense of cubism was simply a distorted view of the personalities associated with the movement. André Salmon took issue with her version of the banquet for Rousseau and expressed astonishment at Gertrude's flightiness. ". . . I had thought, along with all our friends, that she had really understood things. It is evident that she understood nothing, except in a superficial way."

317

Gertrude showed no sign of having been perturbed by the widely circulated riposte. Except for pockets of resistance, choruses of praise drowned out the demurrers of those who felt themselves wronged. Her attitude about such matters had already been put down succinctly: "An error is easily made between 1924 and 1925.

"I said 1925 and I should have said 1924. This is because I made a mistake and beside that I was not able to remember and we all of us said 1925 and it was 1924.

"Also they were able to be very happy about how much better it was to be different in detail if it was to that that they listened."

She had her own work to do, and, with lecture-tour possibilities continually in the air, a decision to make. While her agent was looking into arrangements, she had from Ford Madox Ford just the sort of letter she found most persuasive. "Come with me," he wrote, "they feel hurt that you do not come, and you would not want to hurt their feelings, come with me, come this January." America was getting closer, certainly; yet it was still a long way from the nightly gatherings of soapbox orators at the corner of the Boulevard Raspail and the Boulevard Saint Germain.

CHAPTER 21

I will be well welcome when I come.
Because I am coming.
— GERTRUDE STEIN

        EVER since 1913 Gertrude had written plays that were not really plays in any known theatrical convention but unique attempts to "verbalize" landscapes. One of these, *Four Saints in Three Acts*, was published in *transition* in 1929 and thereby started on a career as the most successful of all of her theater pieces. Its eminence among her works was not assured, however, until Virgil Thomson had come into her orbit. Thomson was already a mature artist who quietly guarded his independence and who at first maintained none but sardonic attitudes toward the whole Stein circle. Yet he had soon demonstrated that he could work with Gertrude without compromise of his own standards and without making her feel that she was giving up artistic autonomy. He had finished his operatic score for *Four Saints* as early as 1928 and had played it to friends in New York, among them Mabel Dodge (Luhan) who felt that "it would do to opera in America what Picasso did to Kenyon Cox" and Carl Van Vechten who thought that it could have "a regular boob success." But plans for an American production were not put into effect until the *Autobiography* was causing its great stir.

It was Gertrude's opinion that general recognition of Picasso's work had not come until 1917, when his *décor* and costumes for the history-making *Parade*, were put on the stage. "When a work is put on the stage," she said, "of course every one has to look at it and in a sense if it is put on the stage every one is forced to look and since they are forced to look at it, of course, they must accept it, there is nothing else to do." She naturally had hopes that her own work on the stage would result in a similar capitulation. However, there was still the matter of a quarrel with Thomson to be overcome. "In the meantime," she wrote, "it is not to be not remembered that I had quarrelled with Virgil Thomson and I had heard nothing from him, he had gone to America and the opera with him." This quarrel had mainly to do with Gertrude's disinclination to abide by the usual contractual arrangement by which the composer of an opera receives the greater part of the royalties from its performances. But Thomson's firm and tactful handling of the matter soon led to the dissolution of differences and, as well, to an equitable assignment of royalty rights.

The painter Maurice Grosser had meanwhile begun to shape the scenario of *Four Saints* to the practical demands of the stage, and had approached the designer Florine Stettheimer with the idea of mounting the opera as an elaborate take-off on entertainments in which petrified Sunday School children play out scenes from the Bible. On Thomson's suggestion, young John Houseman was chosen as director. It was also Thomson's idea that the cast be composed entirely of Negro performers — a notion that had come to him during a visit to a Negro night club. Gertrude was at first resistant to this plan because, as she wrote to him, "Your Negroes may sing and enunciate ever so much better than white artists, but I still do not like the idea of showing the Negro bodies. It is too much what modernistic writers refer to as 'futuristic.' I cannot see its relevance to my treatment of my theme." But, she wisely admitted, "it is for you to make a success of the production."

On December 6, 1933, Thomson reported the progress of plans in a letter to her: "The cast . . . is hired and rehearsals begun. I have a chorus of 32 & six soloists, very, very fine ones indeed. Miss Stettheimer's sets are of a beauty incredible, with trees made out of feathers and a sea-wall at Barcelona made out of shells and for the procession a baldachino of black chiffon & bunches of black ostrich plumes just like a Spanish funeral. St. Teresa comes to the picnic in the 2nd Act in a cart drawn by a real white donkey & brings her tent with her and sets it up & sits in the doorway of it. It is made of white gauze with gold fringe and has a most elegant shape. . . . Frederick Ashton is arriving from London this week to make choreography for us. Not only for the dance-numbers, but for the whole show, so that all the movements will be regulated to the music, measure by measure, and all our complicated stage-action made into a controllable spectacle. Everything . . . is shaping up so beautifully, even the raising of money (it's going to cost $11,000), that the press is champing at the bit and the New York ladies already ordering dresses & engaging hotel rooms."

It was a practical report and should have been a heartening one. In her disturbed state, Gertrude could not really believe that the show would come off. Her trouble, as she diagnosed it, was that she was "not there to believe." Yet the production did beautifully come off, and when cables began arriving from Van Vechten and people from whom she had not heard in years, she decided that she would have "to believe." At the same time she asked herself: "What is it that makes anybody certain that nothing is really going to happen. It is all that about time and identity and not existing undoubtedly it is."

After a preview performance, Van Vechten was unequivocal about the importance of *Four Saints*. He wrote to Gertrude, saying that the opera was "a knockout and a wow. . . . I haven't seen a crowd more excited since *Sacre du Printemps*. The difference was that they were pleasurably excited. The Negroes are divine, like El Grecos, more Spanish, more Saints, more opera singers in their dignity and *simplicity* and extraordinary plastic line than *any* white singers could ever be. . . . Frederick Ashton's rhythmic staging was inspired and so were Florine's costumes and sets. Imagine a crinkled sky-blue cellophane background, set in white lace borders, like a valentine against which were placed the rich and royal costumes of saints in red velvets, etc. and the dark Spanish skins. . . ."

On the next night, February 8, 1934, *Four Saints in Three Acts* was given its first public performance in the Avery Memorial Auditorium of the Wadsworth Athanaeum in Hartford, a museum which, under the direction of A. Everett Austin, Jr., had already made a name for itself in the annals of modern art when, in 1931, it served to house the first exclusively surrealist exhibition in America. Austin had raised money through The Friends and Enemies of Modern Music, an organization he had founded, and advance publicity had made most of the fact that "a circus is guaranteed to pack a house while a serious experiment in music and drama is not." News releases were carefully calculated to play up the circus idea, and conservative Hartford allowed itself to be spieled into the tent where Gertrude and her saints were ready to go into their act. According to the report of W. G. Rogers, "A perfumed air of chi-chi pervaded the opening, which had been preceded by the arrival of carloads of the fashionable from New York and festive doings in the best houses in the Connecticut Valley. A ticket to the opera was, as well, a ticket to the event of the season." Consequently, the audience assembled before the first curtain was naturally one delighted to be able to tell that they had been there and only too ready to spread talk of a *raffiné* occasion, rather than one notably capable of assessing the merits of the opera as a revolutionary piece of theater.

Nonetheless, it was an immediate hit on all scores, including the ingenious one supplied by Virgil Thomson. Plans for its New York *première* were accelerated. She was still regarded as elusive and teasing, but Gertrude Stein had at last made a forceful communication to an American audience on her own terms. Anger and dissent fanned argument about the work, and perhaps contributed as much to its popular success as did conspicuous praise. For the most part, people who came with open minds found themselves enchanted by the brilliant ingenuity of the production which dramatized in a hundred ways the curiously integrated simplicities and sophistications of the text. Many spectators, happily admitting they had no notion of what was going on either in dramatic or operatic terms, said they were nonetheless carried into fantasy so beguiling that they simply put aside any urge to analyze. It was true spellbinding for many susceptible souls, and hundreds who had seen it once came back again and again.

Unlike the *Autobiography*, *Four Saints* does not lend itself to classification as one of the happier accidents or byproducts of Gertrude's career, but stands as a work rooted in her long-standing theory and practice. It was uncompromised Stein, made palatable to a large general public by Virgil Thomson, by the ingenuity of Frederick Ashton who in his choreography called upon memories of Peru where as a child he had absorbed a sense of Indian ritual, and by others who exploited with great imagination the remarkably short text she had provided. In his earliest experiments with Stein, Thomson had sought no wide public hearing. But when the little preludes to their ultimate collaboration had been performed before private gatherings in New York, he had learned how effectively his music and her words could be joined. Of one of these evenings, Henry McBride had reported to Gertrude: "We've had lots of fun and one of the pleasantest things was the hearing of your poems to the music of Virgil Thomson. We roared with enjoyment but Carl Van Vechten who sat opposite me, pulled a serious face and shook it at me reprovingly as though to say we were not taking it the right way. But young Virgil Thomson really is a wonder. I never saw such self-possession in an American before."

Thomson had once confessed to Gertrude that her writings troubled his dreams. For all that, she felt he was one who really understood her. When he had broached the idea of her writing an opera, she had begun to think about saints. Her mind did not run toward saints as agents of divinity or even as manifestations of the largess of divine grace, but as human beings who had a beatific attitude toward the natural and human wonders of existence. Of the three saintly figures for which she had always kept a special affection — Teresa of Ávila, Ignatius Loyola, and Francis of Assisi — two were Spanish. She felt it was essential that the saints she would write about be Spanish because there had to be "really weather in which

323

to wander in in order to be a saint. . . . A saint a real saint never does anything, a martyr does something but a really good saint does nothing, and so I wanted to have Four Saints who did nothing and I wrote the Four Saints in Three Acts and they did nothing and that was everything."

Implicitly, she was comparing sainthood with genius — her kind of genius. Like saints, geniuses had to spend an awful lot of time intensely doing nothing. If they became busy and responsible they became commonplace and dull. Sainthood was a condition, not an achievement.

The landscape, then, would naturally be Spain, especially the landscape around and about Ávila where, as a current guidebook points out, "We must not forget that in walking about the city and surrounding countryside Santa Teresa acquired her deepest fervor." And here, of course, one would expect pigeons everywhere. Picasso already had *his* pigeons — the beginning of a succession that would eventually include his Communist version of "the dove that goes boom" — and now Gertrude would have hers, al fresco and "on the grass Alas."

Her explanation of the meaning of the opera was straightforward; it was, she said, "a perfectly simple description of the Spanish landscape." Again she was describing and attempting to express the disrelated images and visual rhythms that had always been the memorable facts and, for her, the creative materials of any landscape. Discrete meanings a reader might take from piecing together words in such works as *Four Saints* would only reflect his enslavement to connotation; such meanings were but incidental to her intention. As she said, "it made a landscape and the movement in it was like a movement in and out with which anybody looking on can keep in time. I also wanted it to have the movement of nuns very busy and in continuous movement but placid as a landscape has to be because after all the life in a convent is the life of landscape, it may look excited a landscape does sometimes look excited but its quality is that a landscape if it ever did go away would have to go away to stay." This explanation is a literal rendering of her conception of a play as static. All of her plays — with the debatable exception of *Yes*

Is for a Very Young Man — are static simply because they are conceived as paintings, paintings that can be apprehended "all at once," and yet which are full of internal movement. They are not plotted narratives, but meditations; instead of directing the attention and guiding it through stages of mounting interest, they arrest the attention and invite it to dalliance. *Four Saints* in particular not only exemplifies these personal conceptions of Gertrude's but relates them characteristically to the Spanish theater where verbal excitement continually sustained is far more important than the development of plot and more basically dramatic than any possible action.

Virgil Thomson's attitude toward the work was as uncomplicated as Gertrude's. He later asked a radio audience about to listen to *Four Saints* to disabuse themselves of the weird preconceptions that had come to surround it. "Please do not try to construe the words of this opera literally," he said, "or to seek in it any abstruse symbolism. If, by means of the poet's liberties with logic and the composer's constant use of the simplest elements in our musical vernacular, something is here evoked of the child-like gaiety and mystical strength of lives devoted in common to a non-materialistic end, the authors will consider their message to have been communicated."

After a week's run in Hartford, *Four Saints* went on to New York, opening there on February 20, 1934. In photographs sent to Paris by Van Vechten, Gertrude could see her name in electric lights on the marquee of the Forty-fourth Street Theatre and a display window at Gimbel's advertising "Four Suits in Two Acts." Still, everything seemed distant and unbelievable. Success thousands of miles away had little meaning for her; she could never in all her life participate in any excitement without being on the spot. "I rarely believe in anything," she said, "because at the time of believing I am not really there to believe." This self-indulgent and illogical response led her to offend Thomson and others by not sending well-wishing cables on either of the opera's openings. Her sense of remoteness had led to her seeming to be indifferent. As she was eventually to learn, this did little to strengthen bonds with friends who had worked hard for a success which redounded almost wholly to her and but incidentally to them.

The New York critics were at sixes and sevens. *Four Saints* was called the most important dramatic event of the season, and it was called tommyrot. "Pigeons on the grass, alas," they said, "was pigeon English," and they called it "cheap vaudeville humor." Writing in the *Nation*, Kenneth Burke professed to be stumped. "I should like to discourse easily and familiarly on the plot of Stein's piece," he wrote, "but must admit that I cannot. The words show evidence of a private playfulness which makes them more difficult to fathom than if they were written under gas." An article in a medical journal put forth the notion that Gertrude Stein was perhaps a victim of palilalia — "a form of speech disorder in which a patient repeats many times a word, a phrase, or a sentence which he has just spoken." Music critic Lawrence Gilman remarked that a Ph.D. thesis or a wine list would have made as good a libretto; and in *The Conning Tower*, the popular columnist Franklin P. Adams expressed an "unyielding . . . opinion of the libretto. I say it is spinach."

Division of opinion marked discussions carried on by high-, middle- and low-brow alike. "The smart thing among the younger artists," novelist and composer Paul Bowles wrote to Gertrude, "is to be violently against it. Stieglitz decides also to side with them. Most of the defense must be taken for Virgil, against whom they allow them-selves to rage for having had the audacity to give Gertrude Stein in modern dress. That is all I make of their fun, anyway. People walking on Broadway and sitting in Automats talk of 'the Saints play' and usually sound doubtful as to whether it would be worth while to try to get tickets for it. . . ." Publisher Alfred Harcourt re-ported to Gertrude that on the evening he saw *Four Saints*, "Tos-canini was in the orchestra chair behind me . . . he seemed com-pletely absorbed in the performance and applauded vigorously."

For many people, notions of Gertrude's that had previously seemed cerebral, or vague, or absurd, had suddenly been realized and bril-liantly justified. You did not have to discuss what she was getting at because you could see it and feel it. Of the many people who were moved to write to her, few said they "understood" her, and few wanted to enter into discussion of her meaning or her possible mes-sage. They simply said, according to Gertrude, "that they are having a good time while the opera is going on a thing which they say does not very often happen to them at the theatre." Henry McBride, who regretted having seen *Four Saints* only four times during its New York run, and who felt that "it now ranks with the two or three exalted experiences that I have had, with Mei Lang Fang and the Mme. Sadda Yacco of years ago," wrote to Gertrude that he found the opera "indeed, indescribable. With all this, the regular music critics (who know nothing of painting) did not 'get' it; and quite a few people who were bowled over by the performance tried to repudiate their emotional collapse afterward, and keep ringing my telephone to 'explain' it to them. 'What is the real meaning underneath, for clearly it must mean something?' they ask. All this is tiresome. After twenty years of cubism and abstract art, it seems that these unfortunate people have not yet heard of it. . . . What I really feel is, that people who do not feel greatness in the best things of Picasso and Braque . . . do not know what painting is; and those who do not see poetry in your Four Saints do not know what poetry is."

Above the furor, it was apparent that Gertrude Stein had given the American theater a plotless work in which all the conventions of time, exposition, crisis, denouement were dismissed, and yet a work which remained compelling because, like the visions of the saints with whom it dealt, it was of an intensity and calm that finally defied analysis. She had taken an instant of comprehension and, so to speak, elaborated it in space — the space of an evening. The audacity of what she had done was something for endless parody and laughable publicity, but it was also something that brought the American stage a new dimension a full generation before the emergence of Samuel Beckett and Eugene Ionesco. Stark Young, perhaps the one great theatrical critic of the period, had a word that was, as time would prove, resonant if not final. In the *New Republic* he wrote: "I wish I knew some way to make sure of being taken seriously when I say that 'Four Saints in Three Acts' is as essential theatre the most important event of our season. Bullying cliches and fad talk would help out temporarily, but such an approach is not needed at all. This piece of theatre art is the most important for one reason because it is the most delightful and joyous — and delight is the fundamental in all art great or small — what a joke on the hard-working, hard-punching, expensive and self-evident aspect of the average musical show this whole event is! It is important because it is theatre and flies off the ground. . . . It creates instead of talking about. After all, we can imagine writing a play about a professor's home, a boy's troubles, capitalists, et cetera, good matter enough, just as our legs, our blood, our hats and problems are good. But only now and then in the theatre can we hope for something of the quality of a thing in nature (a tree, a melon, a sheet of water, a flight of birds). The point in such a case is not that it is beautiful or not beautiful, but that it lives in itself, and is in essence a constant surprise; and that from it we make our conclusions and applications, deep or trivial, to art and to delight."

William Aspinwall Bradley had meanwhile gone ahead with new preparations for a lecture tour. When Gertrude huffily rejected all his plans, he gave up and walked out of any further involvement with her. But an American tour now seemed next to inevitable. As early as 1914, Van Vechten had tempted her: "You are as famous in America as any historical character, and if you came over I think you might have as great a reception as say Jenny Lind." But as late as 1929, Robert McBride had warned her against any such idea: "Our reporters will simply kill you." Perhaps more dismaying than any other advice was that of her old friend Janet Scudder, who wrote just when Gertrude was feeling most unsettled: "I think that you should follow your usual severe habits and allow America to come to you. In other words the oracle on the mountain top should *stay* on the mountain top. Anyhow you have been away too long. You and Alice will be like two Rip Van Winkles over there." Sherwood Anderson's entreaty, on the other hand, promised just what Gertrude wanted: "I am in the country, on my farm in the hills of Virginia," he wrote. "Why don't you and Alice come to America as a great adventure next summer, Ford around, come see us and others? . . . You ought now to have one big taste, square meal of America again, don't you think?"

Warnings and entreaties only increased Gertrude's new but relentless personal turmoil. Success, publicity, *la gloire* — she had attained them all. But their frightening cost was creative atrophy. "All this time I did no writing. I had written and was writing nothing. Nothing inside me needed to be written. Nothing needed any word and there was no word inside me that could not be spoken and so there was no word inside me. And I was not writing. I began to worry about identity. I had always been I because I had words that had to be written inside me and now any word I had inside could be spoken it did not need to be written. I am I because my little dog knows me. But was I I when I had no written word inside me. It was very bothersome. I sometimes thought I would try but to try is to die and so I did not really try. I was not doing any writing."

Just before their breakup, Bradley had told her that she was throwing away a chance to get rich. She had answered, "I do want to get rich but I never want to do what there is to do to get rich." She knew that he was upsetting carefully laid plans, but she definitely did not intend to assume the large commitments prepared for her signature. With tempers growing short and inner confusion mounting, she decided not to go to America. For a brief period she was relieved. Instead of making money, she began to spend it. Royalties from America made it possible for her to indulge old daydreams: "When I was wishing and sitting I wished for a clock. I meant to pick out an expensive one. I did so and now dear one is economising. That isn't right. I meant it is right. I meant it is right for bathing in one. It is right to be economising. It is right for dear one to be economising. And some day we will be rich. You'll see. It won't be a legacy, it won't be selling anything, it won't be purchasing, it will just be irresistible and then we will spend money and buy everything a dog a Ford letter paper, furs, a hat, kinds of purses, and nearly something new that we have not yet been careful about." She did now buy a new Ford V-8, had a new coat made by the designer Hermes, and ordered two studded collars for Basket. For the first time, a telephone was installed in the Rue de Fleurus, and instead of the usual single servant, a couple was engaged.

Yet America remained in the air as well-wishing friends, convinced

329

in their own minds that the time was ripe, gradually persuaded her to overlook all possible difficulties. During the summer in Bilignin Carl Van Vechten came for a twenty-four-hour visit during which he took nearly one hundred photographs of her and Alice. He wanted Gertrude to come to America and his zeal in photographing her for publicity purposes made the trip seem all but definite. Alice attempted to get assurances from him. "Carl," she asked, "will there be anyone over there who will say, 'There goes Gertrude Stein'? as I have heard of their doing that and I would love it to happen."

"Oh, yes," said Van Vechten, "I think it will happen."

"You mean," said Alice, "you will hire some small boys to do it so as to give me the pleasure of it."

"Perhaps," said Van Vechten, "we will not have to hire them."

The turning point about America was the visit of W. G. Rogers, the doughboy from Nîmes who came to see them in Paris and a few weeks later joined them in Bilignin. Now a successful newspaperman as well as an old and trusted friend, Rogers had Gertrude's deepest confidence. She questioned him on all phases of what she might expect in America. He wanted her to make the tour, but he also had extreme doubts, which he could not bring himself to express to her, about the wisdom of the venture. The thing he feared most was a barrage of ridicule which, at this uneasy point in her life, might prove shattering. But he, at least, was willing for her to take the chance. Spurred by his assurances, Gertrude set to work composing lectures. There was to be a series of six, and she wanted to be certain that every word was put down before she left France.

Bernard Faÿ and nineteen-year-old James Laughlin, later the publisher of New Directions, had encountered one another in Salzburg that summer and had come on to Bilignin together. Gertrude decided that Laughlin could be "extremely useful." She asked him to make short versions of the lectures featuring excerpts that could be used for publicity purposes. Laughlin found it difficult to make synopses that would satisfy her, but she refused to be discouraged by his troubles. Like everyone else who came to visit, Laughlin was ordered to take a hot bath every day and, like everyone else, he was terrified of the gas-heating apparatus which seemed always on the verge of exploding. But Gertrude would have no shilly-shallying. His terror of the gas, she said, was only a childish evasion, he just didn't want to take a bath.

Between conferences, Gertrude was often at the piano. Her improvisations, since she had no training, were somewhere between Bach and boogie-woogie, according to Laughlin, but owed nothing to either. She called her improvisations "sonatinas," but this cut little ice with Virgil Thomson, who simply said that she was no pianist. When he later visited her, he wrote his Piano Sonata No. 3 for the white keys — "for Gertrude Stein to improvise at the pianoforte," as he put it. But since Gertrude could barely read music, he considered his directions as "purely dedicatory." "I like to improvise on a piano," Gertrude said, "I like to play sonatinas followed by another always on the white keys I do not like black keys and never two notes struck by the same hand at the same time because I do not like chords. . . ." Her performance was always a pleasure, to herself at least, because she felt "no musical estrangement." Emerging from the recitals her visitors were helpless to avoid, she was always refreshed and beaming.

When, at last, America was inevitable, Gertrude expressed her random doubts and her expectations in a piece, the complete text of which follows:

MEDITATIONS ON BEING ABOUT TO VISIT
MY NATIVE LAND

I am being so very busy in being about to visit my native land that I have not been meditating not meditating very much but if I were not so busy and were to meditate I would meditate a great deal and I would and in a way do meditate upon what they are to say to me and what I am to say to them, those who make my native land my native land.

What will they say to me and what will I say to them. I cannot believe that America has changed, many things have come and gone but not really come and not really gone but they are there and that perhaps does make the America that I left and the America I am to find different but not really different, it would be impossible for it to be really different or for me to find that it was really different.

I wonder and I ask everybody who has been in America or who comes from America what everything is like, what hotels are like what homes are

331

like, what they eat and the answers sound a little different but not really very different. It will be nice so very nice if it is not really different.

What was the America that I left. It was an America where as Mark Twain said in the first diary he ever kept he got up and washed and went to bed. He was proud that every day nothing happened but that but that he did get up every day and that he did wash. And they are still doing it, and the hotels and what they eat do not seem to have changed much and the homes do not seem to have changed much, nor what they do when they go to school. Twenty-five years roll around so quickly even when they do not seem to be rolling around at all.

And now I am going back to visit my native land. It may not mean so much to anybody but it does mean a lot to me and I feel gradually a pleasant pleasure both near and far away.

Will they ask me questions and will I ask them questions and which will ask the questions most and first, and will they listen to me and will I listen to them. I am not really meditating about these things because I am being kept so very busy but if I were not so very busy I would certainly meditate about these things.

I love to ask questions and I do not dislike answering them, but I like to listen and I like to have others listen, and there is something that I can not remember not really remember did they listen in that America that I remember did they listen to the answer after they had asked the question. I always listen to the answer after I have asked the question and I hope that in that as in other things I am a good American and that they did and still do listen to the answer after they have asked the question. That would make America more than pleasant, it would make it interesting, it would make it more than interesting it would make it exciting.

What America looks like puzzles me more as I meditate as I would meditate if I had more time just now in which to meditate about being about to visit my native land. I do not quite feel that I know what it looks like, a young Harvard man has been here with me and as we talk about Concord and the country in Massachusetts I do know quite that it looks as I remember it, but the cities do seem to have much less to do with my memories, they seem to be different, but I hope not. I hope they are not really different. One does not like to feel different and if one does not like to feel different then one hopes that things will not look different. It is alright for them to seem different but not to be different.

I have no more serious meditations now that I am about to visit my native land because and that is very important to me I always see and talk to and listen to Americans as they come and go and so I have had many meditations about Americans all along. Naturally one of the things that all Europeans tell about when they come home from America is what

Americans eat. What Americans eat does not seem to conform itself in any way to what Europeans that is the French eat, and they are all puzzled and they tell us about it and as we are Americans we say yes but French eating in hotels and restaurants is bad too. Yes they say but not like that. American eating is so moist, so they say, and I really did not know what they were talking about. I did not remember American food as moist. But now a friend has just sent me a great many menus from hotels, breakfast lunch and dinner and I must confess that the food does sound wet very wet indeed compared to French food. Will I like wet food when I eat it when I visit my native land or will I not.

To be sure I have always rather had a tendency to find French food dry as I do not drink wine with my food and so I have a Chinese servant who cooks well the way I remember American food, but is it the way American food is cooked now.

In the interval of being very busy I meditate a great deal about that.

If you are busy very busy you have not time to meditate very much but no matter how busy you may be there is always a moment in which one can meditate on what one is going to eat and whether one is going to like what one is going to eat. Meditation on eating and what is going to be eaten can be done at any odd moment or at meal time when one does not meditate much, and so I do meditate upon what I am to eat now as I am about to visit my native land.

And these are some of my meditations on being about to visit my native land.

CHAPTER 22

You are a dear — and at last all America's forever.

— SHERWOOD ANDERSON

SHE would not go back to America, she had
always said, until she was a lion, a real lion. Now — on October 24,
1934 — as the S.S. *Champlain* slid through morning mist and, port-
side, Staten Island dimly floated past, and the Statue of Liberty beckoned, she was about to see the proof writ larger than she had ever
dreamed.

With America point-blank before her, the hundreds of needling
uncertainties that had plagued her from the earliest thought of coming suddenly vanished all at once. When the press launch drew alongside and a horde of reporters climbed aboard, she met them with a
large show of confidence. Anticipating their questions — they were,
after all, the very same questions she had been asked for twenty
years — she took them off guard. "Suppose no one asked a question,"
she led off, "what would the answer be?" And when they asked,
"Why don't you write the way you talk?" she replied, "Why don't
you read the way I write?"

On the voyage from France her most distinguished shipmate was the best-selling philosopher, Abbé Ernest Dimnet, who was also a target for reporters. When they asked him about conditions in Europe, he said that a recent bicycle trip he had taken through Germany and the Saar had convinced him that Hitler, because of his personal attractiveness, would remain in power indefinitely. "Hitler has a charm that appeals to the emotions," he said, "whereas Premier Mussolini's charm is the charm of force and intellect." City editors who wanted something equally unintelligible from Gertrude Stein found only that she persisted in being logical.

"I do talk as I write," she said, "but you can hear better than you can see. You are accustomed to see with your eyes differently to the way you hear with your ears, and perhaps that is what makes it hard to read my works." When one of the reporters asked if she had been upset by comparisons of her writings to the babblings of the insane, she said no, not one bit, because there was an important difference. "You can continue to read me, but not the babblings of the insane. Besides," she added with a softening glance, "the insane are frequently normal in everything except their own phase of insanity."

Those who had come to challenge her were themselves challenged. Taking the initiative, she answered them with a confounding simplicity, and won them with easy good humor. When they asked if she believed she had introduced anything new into writing, she answered, "I have not invented any device, any style, but write in the style that is me. You have material in yourself and in humanity and you apply it, that's all. I describe what I feel and think. I am essentially a realist." About influences her work may have had on American writers she was succinct. "If you can influence yourself," she said, "it is enough." And when, finally, they asked about "all those repetitions," she answered, "No, no, no, no, it is not all repetition. I always change the words a little." In their notebooks they detailed her costume, her thick woolly stockings, round-toed, flat-heeled oxfords, her cerise vest and mannish shirt of cream and black stripes, her coarse tweed suit and the baffling hat she wore — a sort of deerstalker's cap modeled after a thirteenth-century one Alice had seen in the Cluny Museum — and hurried back to their desks. The afternoon

335

papers blossomed with references to the "Sibyl of Montparnasse," "the high-priestess of the Left Bank," and every story about her bore the inevitable Steinese caption. Typical among them was:

GERTY GERTY STEIN STEIN
IS BACK HOME HOME BACK

More than six months later, "wedded to America," as she told the Paris newspapermen who covered her return to France, she could look back upon every evidence of being the lion she had hoped to become, and upon the renewal of a love affair with her native land that remained passionate to the day of her death.

She had seen the news of her arrival announced in lights crawling around the New York Times Building, had found herself so famous in the big city that she was addressed on the street more often than if she were in Bilignin. She took New York traffic in stride, never hesitating as she stepped from any curb into the midst of it. When an anxious friend asked her why she acted with such bravado, she answered, "All these people, including the nice taxi drivers, recognize and are careful of me." She had crisscrossed the nation by air from Massachusetts to California in a series of some forty-odd appearances, each of them surrounded by fanfare and adulation. At the Hotel Algonquin in New York where literary and theatrical celebrities had long been the rule, she had aroused more comment and interest, according to Manager Frank Case, than anyone who had ever stopped there. Nothing could have pleased her more. "I was very surprised to see how gentle people are today. Everyone is so courteous and polite, so friendly. I am not speaking of the people I know, I have not seen anyone yet. I mean the people in the streets — they seem to recognize me. And they come up to me and say, 'Miss Stein?' And I say, 'Yes,' and then we talk in the most friendly fashion, not at all as if they were seeking out some one who had attained some notoriety. I find it perfectly charming. I went into a stationer's to buy a note pad, and a young man greeted me. He had a baby three months old he told me and we talked about where was the best place to bring up a baby, in the town or in the country. He was so gentle, not a bit intrusive. Before we parted he asked me if I would write my name

336

for his baby, who he said would treasure it for the next generation. He was just an ordinary man, not well dressed or anything, and I found him perfectly charming."

She had enjoyed reunions with many old friends, among them Scott and Zelda Fitzgerald, with whom she had spent part of Christmas Eve in Baltimore. A few days later Fitzgerald had written to her: "I was somewhat stupid got with the Christmas spirit but I enjoyed the one idea that you *did* develop and, like everything else you say, it will sing in my ears long after everything else about that afternoon is dust and ashes. You were the same fine fire to everyone who sat upon your hearth — for it was your hearth, because you carry home with you wherever you are — a home before which we have always warmed ourselves." She had seen Sherwood Anderson, first at his brother-in-law's home in Fall River, Minnesota, and later in New Orleans, where they spent a long evening eating oranges and reviewing the marvelous turns of events that had brought them once more together. A happy meeting, it was their last.

Of new friends, the first in her affection was Thornton Wilder, who was then teaching at the University of Chicago. After the great success of her first lecture there, the University's young president, Robert Maynard Hutchins, asked her to return to conduct ten sessions of a seminar made up of thirty selected students. In one of these sessions she made the most forceful answer to an essential question she had ever spoken. When, according to Thornton Wilder, one of her students asked her for an "explanation" of her most famous line, "Rose is a rose is a rose is a rose," Gertrude fixed her attention on the young man and launched into eloquence. "Now listen!" she said, "Can't you see that when the language was new — as it was with Chaucer and Homer — the poet could use the name of a thing and the thing was really there? He could say 'O moon,' 'O sea,' 'O love' and the moon and the sea and love were really there. And can't you see that after hundreds of years had gone by and thousands of poems had been written, he could call on those words and find that they were just wornout literary words? The excitingness of pure being had withdrawn from them; they were just rather stale literary words. Now the poet has to work in the excitingness of pure being;

337

he has to get back that intensity into the language. We all know
that it's hard to write poetry in a late age; and we know that you
have to put some strangeness, something unexpected, into the structure of the sentence in order to bring back vitality to the noun. Now
it's not enough to be bizarre; the strangeness in the sentence structure has to come from the poetic gift, too. That's why it's doubly
hard to be a poet in a late age. Now you all have seen hundreds of
poems about roses and you know in your bones that the rose is not
there. All those songs that sopranos sing as encores about 'I have a
garden; oh, what a garden!' Now I don't want to put too much emphasis on that line, because it's just one line in a longer poem.
But I notice that you all know it; you make fun of it, but you
know it. Now listen! I'm no fool. I know that in daily life we don't
go around saying 'is a . . . is . . . is . . .' Yes, I'm no fool; but I
think that in that line the rose is red for the first time in English
poetry for a hundred years."

In Thornton Wilder Gertrude had found not only a close personal friend, but a man of letters more receptive to her work and
more acute and articulate about its meanings than anyone she had
ever met. For his part, Gertrude Stein had already become one of the
devotions of a life divided almost equally between teaching and
writing. Wilder's own work was not even remotely akin to hers, yet
when he recorded his insights into the meaning and methods of Stein
he spoke as a disciple. But he was a disciple who could influence as
well as be influenced, and Gertrude freely admitted that many of the
solutions to her later writing problems were the result of conversations with him. She was fascinated by his energy, his manifold interests and his wide-ranging activities; it seemed to her that instead of
dispersing his sterling qualities, these activities somehow managed to
concentrate them. She hoped he would write more fiction. In her estimation, *Heaven's My Destination* was *the* American novel, thereby
differing with Sigmund Freud who told Wilder, "I could not read
your latest book — threw it away. Why should you treat of an
American fanatic; that cannot be treated poetically." During Gertrude's lifetime and afterwards, no one wrote more knowledgeably
of her methods than Thornton Wilder; and no one has had more

338

uccess, quite free from coterie bias, in conveying a sense of her
work in relation to the broad developments in twentieth-century art
and science with which it must be accommodated.

During the course of her trip, Gertrude began to feel that a good
part of her decision to return was a desire to see for herself whether
suspicions that she had finally lost her American roots were justified.
"I think I must have had a feeling that it had happened or I should
not have come back," she told John Hyde Preston. "I went to California. I saw it and felt it and it had a tenderness and a horror
too. Roots are so small and dry when you have them and they are
exposed to you. You have seen them on a plant and sometimes they
seem to deny the plant if it is vigorous . . . Well, we're not like
that really. Our roots can be anywhere and we can survive, because
if you think about it, we take our roots with us. I always knew that
a little and now I know it wholly. I know because you can go back
to where they are and they can be less real to you than they were
three thousand, six thousand miles away. Don't worry about your
roots so long as you worry about them. The essential thing is to have
the feeling that they exist, that they are somewhere. They will take
care of themselves, and they will take care of you, too, though you
may never know how it has happened. To think only of going back
for them is to confess that the plant is dying."

In spite of momentary wonderings at why so little of her past
seemed to return as she crossed and recrossed the continent, she decided that America had become, as she said, "*my* business," and she
wanted to be involved in all of it. She had been entertained at the
White House. "Mrs. Roosevelt was there and gave us tea," she wrote
with vastly mitigated enthusiasm, "she talked about something and
we sat next to some one." With George Gershwin she had sat on a
piano bench while he ran through the score of his new opera,
Porgy and Bess. She had been guest of honor at an epicurean dinner
at Miss Ellen Glasgow's in Richmond, Virginia. After she had
watched the last lap of one of the "marathon dances" which had become a national craze, she wrote to Carl Van Vechten: "A most extraordinary thing, they are like shades modern shades out of Dante
and they move so strangely and they lead each other about one

asleep completely and the other almost, it is the most unearthly and most beautiful movement I have ever seen it makes the dance nothing at all." She had ridden in a police car of the homicide squad on official duty on Chicago's South Side. She had discussed theories of education with Robert Maynard Hutchins and Mortimer Adler, theories of drama with Charlie Chaplin. Chaplin reminded her of her favorite matador, Gallo, "who could not kill a bull but he could make him move better than any one ever could and he himself not having any grace in person could move as no one else ever did."

Bird's-eye views of American terrain (they traveled almost entirely by air) had been a surprise and an affirmation. She felt for the first time that she knew what the ground really looked like, and related what she saw to cubism. "When I looked at the earth I saw all the lines of cubism made at a time when not any painter had ever gone up in an airplane. I saw there on the earth the mingling lines of Picasso, coming and going, developing and destroying themselves. I saw the simple solutions of Braque, I saw the wandering lines of Masson." Thinking about this, she was moved to make one of the few assertions of her lifetime in which she directly related her own career to the world of the painters. "Straight lines and quarter sections, and the mountain lines in Pennsylvania very straight lines," she said, "it made it right that I had always been with cubism and everything that followed after . . . once more I knew that a creator is a contemporary, he understands what is contemporary when the contemporaries do not know it yet, but he is contemporary and as the twentieth century is a century which sees the earth as no one has ever seen it, the earth has a splendor that it never has had."

Just before boarding the *Champlain* for the return crossing, she asked Bennett Cerf, president of Random House, about her publishing future. He told her simply to decide each year what she wanted printed and he would see that it was done.

Paradoxes trailed in the wake of her passage across the United States, and not the least of these was the fact that the most obscure writer of the century had, for a time, become the most famous. Her name had studded the conversation of the more literate segment of the population for years but now, suddenly, it had also become a household word on every level of society. "It is very nice being a celebrity a real celebrity," she said, "who can decide who they want to meet and say so and they come or do not come as you want them." But the new, official aura of celebrity distressed some of her old friends who were used to the informalities of "27." When parties were given in her honor, Gertrude took very seriously the place of honor and "each aspirant was led to the footstool like a mule to a well." A party for Gertrude, they felt, had become too much like an audience with the pope. But others were delighted with the team of Gertrude and Alice — "a large lady firmly dressed in a shirt-waist and skirt and jacket, and a smaller lady in something dark with a gray astrakhan toque . . . slightly suggestive of a battle-ship and a cruiser." Gertrude's appearance was almost as much cause for comment as were her utterances. Americans had known famous bluestockings, but never one who had quite so completely ignored the dictators of feminine fashion. When Louis Bromfield brought his mother and father to meet Gertrude, there was a lull in conversation after introductions had been made, during which the senior Bromfield was heard to say, "I didn't quite catch the gentleman's name, Mama."

References to her cropped up interminably in movies, musical revues, comic strips and random newspaper stories; a high school newspaper in Utica, New York, put out a special Gertrude Stein number; on the Pathé newsreel, movie audiences could see and hear her reading "Pigeons on the grass"; she was quoted as often in barrooms and in courts of law as she was in classrooms. It was an eccentric sort of celebrity, yet it was attended by far more good humor than malice. The public was able to tolerate and accept her as a person while, among the occupational literati, she was widely regarded with envy, suspicion and a curiously puritanical impatience. Young writers, without vested reputations to guard or critical positions to defend, were apt to be her champions. One of them, William Saroyan, wrote to her in the hope of an interview when she would come to San Francisco: "Some critics say I have to be careful and not notice the writing of Gertrude Stein but I think they are fooling themselves when they pretend any American writing that is American and is

341

writing is not partly the consequence of the writing of Gertrude Stein and as the saying is they don't seem to know the war is over." In the opinion of Sinclair Lewis, on the other hand, she was promoting a racket.

Bernard Faÿ, who was in New Orleans during the early part of her visit, looked at the phenomenon of her amazing reception through the eyes of an historian. "I feel that what is going on now in America," he wrote, "what this trip of yours is doing is tremendously important in the mental life of America. What you bring them, nobody had brought them since Walt Whitman . . . and they know it, they feel it. You know I have watched them very closely since 1919 — and seen them get excited over all kinds of things: the new Ford cars, Mr. Hoover, Al Smith, air-travel, the Queen of Rumania, speak-easies, etc.; but I have never seen them act as they do now with you. — It is something deeper and more personal. What your work and yourself stir up in them had not been stirred up for decades."

Whatever the true nature of its interest, the public went on reading of her comings and goings with good-humored indulgence. Even so famous a die-hard as Henry Seidel Canby — who had said earlier that, like the work of E. E. Cummings, hers was without content — was moved to qualify his distaste: "I never chanced to meet her until she came home, and then found her a sensible, intelligent woman, in appearance one of the executive type of highly civilized Jewish women so familiar in philanthropic and art-management circles in New York. . . . Yet," he had to admit, "I still cannot read her without losing my temper." Nevertheless, Canby was newly aware of her power even as a writer, and went so far as to suggest that the young editors of *Time*, in their efforts to differentiate their new magazine from the declining *Literary Digest*, were "subtly and unconsciously influenced by the experimenting going on in the early 1920's, and perhaps directly by Gertrude Stein's twists of sentence order."

Not the least of paradoxes was the fact that the sale of her books continued — with the exception of *Three Lives* which for a time was the best seller in the Modern Library — to be vastly out of proportion to her fame. Random House brought out handsome editions of

Portraits and Prayers, Four Saints in Three Acts and *Lectures in America*, but sales were sparse and all of the titles could shortly be found on bookstore tables reserved for publishers' overstock and remainders. If neglect on such an essential level puzzled observers who could not reconcile it with her astonishing notoriety, this did not puzzle Gertrude. She knew that her publicity came from the fact that perhaps one person in a thousand could say that she was doing something of value, and that the voices of all of the others were not strong enough to drown out the one that spoke with conviction. It had become a cliché to accuse her of writing nonsense, and a very tiresome one. The stubborn point on which her reputation rested and from which her publicity issued was simply the point of conviction that made itself heard beyond and above the reams of good-humored ragging and the choruses of mockery.

No one had ever made better copy for a depression-ridden population than this earthy, articulate mother-image from Paris. She had an undeniable way with reporters of every stripe and could beguile them into putting aside all the prejudices with which they had approached her. At the sight of her comfortable and comforting presence, at the first sound of the inflections of her soft American voice, they were quite put off. Since many of them still came expecting to meet "a languid woman . . . smoking cigarettes, sipping absinthes perhaps and looking out upon the world with tired, disdainful eyes," they were at first surprised, then altogether disarmed. In this aura of good feeling they wrote more copy than they had planned, and turned in engaging accounts of the woman they had expected only to jeer.

In New York, twelve full columns of largely front-page space had been devoted to her within twenty-four hours of her arrival. A number of these stories were carried throughout the country on news-service wires. Local papers took the cue and when she turned up in one city after another she was nearly always front-page news. An account of her visit to Boston began: "Put away any notion that Gertrude Stein is either slightly cracked, or a literary sideshow faker of the kind Barnum liked to handle. This pleasing, thick woman with the close-cropped iron-gray hair, the masculine face and the marvelously pleasant smile, voice and manner, is doing something she thinks is good and no abracadabra, simon-pure, could come from her wittingly."

Once, when she was being interviewed by several reporters at one time, she noticed that a photographer sitting in on the conference followed what she was saying with particularly close attention. "It's funny," she said to the reporters, "but the photographer is the one of the lot of you who looks as if he were intelligent and was listening. Now why is that?" Turning to the photographer, she asked, "You do, you do understand what I am talking about, don't you?" With words she might have put into his mouth and which, in *Everybody's Autobiography*, she *did* put into his mouth, he answered, "Of course I do. You see, I can listen to what you say because I don't have to remember what you are saying. They can't listen because they have got to remember."

In St. Paul she came across the account of an interview written as if it were the report of a wrestling match, in which the reporter quoted from her works sentences which were among her favorites. The story was well written, she thought, and the cribbed sentences were aptly and amusingly related to what she had said in the course of the interview. At a luncheon party that same day she told her hostess she considered the article just about the best writing about her that she had read. The hostess was appalled. She explained that the local literati were in an uproar about the piece because it was vulgar and could only reflect badly upon the taste of St. Paul. Complaints had reached the ears of the paper's editor, and the young reporter was expected to lose his job. Gertrude was unable to talk to the young man herself, but the hostess sought him out and reported Gertrude's feelings. With tears in his eyes, she reported back, he said that Gertrude had saved his life.

America could not take her seriously, but since it could not ignore her, America made her into a popular darling. Her style — or at least, journalistic versions of her style — became a nationally recognized trade-mark. But among intellectuals she still carried less weight as an artist than as a symbol. She was, after all, the intimate of Picasso and Matisse and the school of Paris. Individuals who

344

had never read a line of her work beyond the *Autobiography* defended her with a vehemence that often merely disguised ignorance. She represented the questing American spirit in Paris, that exportable product which, at a distance, constituted a bulwark against native Babbittry. For the middle-brow to deny Gertrude Stein meant denying the new era of all things marvelously irresponsible and inscrutable, meant lining up with George Babbitt as he scratched his balding head in front of a cubist canvas. To deny *Tender Buttons* and *Four Saints* was somehow to sanction the "booboisie" morality whose zealots had threatened to put the publishers of James Joyce behind bars, banned *The Captive* from Broadway, and elevated Bruce Barton to the status of the thirteenth apostle. For the highbrow, to deny Gertrude Stein was to support critics such as Van Wyck Brooks, whose worried appraisals of the dominant literature of the century had already made him déclassé. "Most of our critical writing," wrote Brooks, "deals with technical questions, and technical novelty, as it seems to me, is almost the only virtue it demands or praises. Not whether a writer contributes to life, but whether he excels in some new trick, is the question that is usually asked. It is their formal originality that has given prestige to writers like Joyce, Eliot and Gertrude Stein; and perhaps this is natural in an age of technics. But how can we ignore the larger questions involved in this drift of the modern mind? It seems to me it represents the 'death-drive,' as certain psychologists call it, the will to die that is said to exist side by side in our minds with the will to live. Defeat and unhappiness can reach a point where we accept them and embrace them and rejoice in our enervation and disintegration. And whether we rejoice in it or not, this literature is disintegrating." Gertrude Stein, he felt, had reduced the position of writers "to the last absurdity. In her theory of aesthetics, neither thought nor feeling matters. Nothing counts but the word-pattern, and the greatest thing in life is a nursery-jingle."

Gertrude never wrote answers to attacks upon her, but, face to face with an adversary, was quick to her own defense. Once at the question period after a lecture, a woman in the audience accused her, and certain of her contemporaries, of sensationalism. Gertrude's answer was blunt: "People today like contemporary comforts, but they take their literature and art from the past. They are not interested in what the present generation is thinking or painting or doing if it doesn't fit the enclosure of their personal apprehension. Present day geniuses can no more help doing what they are doing than you can help not understanding it, but if you think we do it for effect, and to make a sensation, you're crazy."

Attacks, from sanctuaried critics or from the scribes of the tabloid columns, merely swelled her progress. As people fought to get tickets to her lectures and jostled for positions in her vicinity at the many luncheons held in her honor, Gertrude Stein was becoming an American institution. She had, at the outset of her tour, decided to limit her audiences to five hundred because she felt she could not, at one time, interest more people than that. This decision in itself resulted in an increased interest no trick of publicity could have matched. At Princeton, the scene of her first college lecture, the police had to check crowds trying to fight their way into the lecture hall. After that there was never any question that audiences *less* than five hundred would ever assemble to hear her.

In Chicago, at the Auditorium Theatre, she saw *Four Saints in Three Acts* for the first time: "I think it was perfectly extraordinary how they carried out what I wanted," she said. "It was absolutely a conversation between saints. . . . It looked very lovely and the movement was everything they moved and did nothing and that is what a saint or a doughboy should do they should do nothing, they should move some and they did move some and they did nothing and it was very satisfying."

For months on end her joy was unclouded; all America, it seemed, was all hers. "I found that Americans really want to make you happy," she told a reporter. "This does not mean that they lack sophistication, but the fact that their gentleness has persisted while they have been becoming sophisticated shows that it is genuine. In Europe, on the other hand, a person's neighbor doesn't really count for much." When she was asked if she thought the country had changed during the many years she had been away, she said "no neither America nor Americans after all when you say changed how could they change what after all could they change to, and when you ask that of course there is no answer." And to Sherwood Anderson she wrote, ". . . it was beautiful that American country it was it is there is nothing to be said about it but that that it was and it is beautiful. . . ."

But toward the end of her visit a question asked on the editorial pages of the Hearst press must have struck Gertrude as the very darkest echo of her own secret thoughts. "Is Gertrude Stein not Gertrude Stein," the editorial queried, "but somebody else living and talking in the same body?" The writer's implication tended to make Gertrude the victim of a psychosis, and might have been dismissed as part of the general campaign of ridicule. But in a sense the writer never could have guessed, the question was oracular, touching on the quick an issue Gertrude could not resolve.

The name and nature of identity had been part of her meditations ever since the days of her adolescent *Weltschmerz*. All her life she had wondered who she was. Her work was an objective register of personality, and should have been a solid answer, but she could not accept even the great bulk of it as sufficiently conclusive. "I am I because my little dog knows me," she said, and then deliberately checked herself. "That does not prove anything about you it only proves something about the dog." Since she believed that "the essence of being civilized is to possess yourself as you are," she was worried now about what happens to people who, like herself, had become the objects of the media of mass publicity in the twentieth century. Since publicity was one of the measures of success, she would of course have to bear with it. But the problems it brought were real. Henry James had said that the theme of an artist remained interesting only so long as the artist was a failure — that so long as he was a failure he was a person. But when he succeeded, he disappeared into his work, and there was no person left. Picasso had said a similar thing to her when he was reviewing his own transition from poverty to fame. Gertrude echoed both him and James in *Lucy Church Amiably* when she said: "A genius says that when he is not successful he is treated with consideration like a genius but when he is successful and has been as rich as successful he is treated like anybody by his family." She herself could not finally stand the effacement of her unique personality in the mills of notoriety, and came to the conclusion that, like war, publicity "prevents the process of civilization."

She had always hoped there would be paintings that would live outside of their frames. But a personality that refused to be framed, especially if that personality were her own, troubled her to the point of obsession. She turned to investigations of time and of all the possible ways in which the human psyche can perceive it. Only by an act of memory, she concluded, are we conscious of time. Without memory, without a specific taking of bearings in relation to past events, the psyche is timeless. Much of her life's work had been directed toward an appreciation or comprehension of this timelessness. Brooding anew, she assayed works which, she hoped, would prove clarifying and, perhaps, comforting. For the next years of her fame she would be devoted to meditations that might save her for herself, and for the writing that the vulgar hands of publicity or the attentions of an admiring public would almost totally neglect.

CHAPTER 23

I am I because my little dog knows me. The
figure wanders on alone.
— GERTRUDE STEIN

OUT of the swing of her crowded new pub-
lic world, Gertrude coveted the privacy of another summer in the
Rhône valley when she might devote the long days to meditation —
when she might "fill up" to the point where writing would be the
simple consequence of "brimming over." But there were inter-
ruptions, as always, and the most unsettling one was the French
army. A regiment of twenty-five hundred men was assigned to little
Bilignin where each of the village's twenty-eight families was expected to assume its share of the billeting. Twenty-five of the reserv-
ists moved into Gertrude's barn. Alarmed by the invasion, Basket and
Pepé, the little Mexican dog given to her by Picabia, could not get
used to the day and night commotion, but Gertrude and Alice accepted their military burden with resignation. As threats of hostilities
crackled along the length of the Maginot Line, the young men of the
village began to be called up at an accelerated rate. Gertrude felt
their household was in "full panoply of war." Yet, in spite of all the

dressings for war, she did not really believe war would come because "after all anybody had done a really big war it is not so easy to do it again." There had *been* a war, and she had made it hers. Another one was just too tiresome to think about.

She would rather move through the pastoral days and weeks comparatively at peace with everything except the elusive problem of identity. Her own identity was now something recognized around the world; yet fame was as much a worry as it was a pleasure. Identity had become a matter of mirrors and metaphysics. Mother Goose, with her "I am I because my little dog knows me," was no comfort at all. To reduce her confusion Gertrude followed a practice she had maintained since childhood: to see a problem clearly she set it down on paper — not as a set of propositions, but as a sequence of meditations and ruminations that welled from her mind as twisted, tumbled, smoothed and as fascinating as flotsam. She began to write *The Geographical History of America or the Relation of Human Nature to the Human Mind*, a work primarily of ideas or, more precisely, of one idea.

Identity, in particular the identity of genius, was the main subject of this book and, in several other books succeeding it, became the last large topic Gertrude Stein would exhaustively examine. Her point of departure, which is also her point of a thousand returns, can perhaps best be stated in the form of a question: What is the difference between that part of consciousness which is absorbed by the affections, events and interests of every sort, and that part of consciousness that dwells wholly unto itself, above the battle, unmoved by the surprises of existence? The first, she decided, was what human nature was all about; the second had only to do with the human mind. A genius is a representative of the human mind, partly because he understands, without submitting to, the force of human nature. Unlike artists who, slaves to human nature, are bound by resemblances, subject to sorrow, disappointment and tears and all the conditions of man's fate, "the human mind writes what it is. . . . And the writing that is the human mind does not consist in messages or in events it consists only in writing down what is written and therefore it has no relation to human nature."

The sense of audience is inevitably involved in these considerations because an audience should be the ideal witness to identity. Yet Gertrude had found that neither an audience of millions nor the audience of just her little dog was able to confirm the identity of her genius. Audiences were too much involved in human nature, she decided, and were thereby prevented from knowing the human mind which, finally, is a law and an identity only to itself. "To know what the human mind is," she wrote, "there is no knowing what the human mind is because as it is it is." In the notably lighthearted course of these meditations, which Thornton Wilder has called "metaphysics by an artist in a mood of gaiety," she circles, attacks, shakes, shreds and finally abandons the remains of the problem with which she began. Since the thesis, or the quest, of the book is comparatively simple, the hundreds of pages which expound it tend to seem like a vast reservoir of inconclusive footnotes.

Perception of one's human mind naturally involved one's sense of time. "I meditated as I had not done for a very long time," she wrote, "not since I was a little one about the contradiction of being on this earth with the space limited and knowing about the stars in an unlimited space that is nobody could find out if it was limiting or limited, and now these meditations did not frighten me as they did when I was young, so that much was done.

"I meditated a good deal about how to yourself you were yourself at any moment that you were there to you inside you but that any moment back you could only remember yourself you could not feel yourself and I therefore began to think that insofar as you were yourself to yourself there was no feeling of time inside you you only had the sense of time when you remembered yourself. . . . And so I began to be more and more absorbed in the question of the feeling of past and present and future inside one and naturally that led me to meditate even more than I had in the lectures I had written for Chicago on the subject of history and newspaper and politics."

In dead earnest about a matter which she seemed to feel would clarify much about herself and her work, she nevertheless remained playful as she kept her subject going with the balance of a juggler.

The following excerpt from *The Geographical History* is a typical one:

The relation of superstition to identity and the human mind.
Please remember the cuckoo.

CHAPTER IV
There are so many things to say about the cuckoo.
I think I will say them all.
I have always wanted to talk about the cuckoo.

CHAPTER III and IV
About the cuckoo.
Long before the cuckoo sang to me I wrote a song and said the cuckoo bird is singing in a cuckoo tree singing to me, oh singing to me.

But long before that very long before that I had heard a cuckoo clock.

And in between I had heard a great many cuckoos that were not cuckoo clocks.

Indeed since then I have never seen a cuckoo in a cuckoo clock.

So then I did hear that a cuckoo not in a clock but a cuckoo that is a bird that sings cuckoo if you hear it sing for the first time in the spring and you have money in your pocket you will have it all the year. I mean money.

I always like to believe what I hear.

That has something to do with superstition and something to do with identity. To like to believe what you hear.

Has that something to do with the human mind that is with writing.

No not exactly.

Has it something to do with human nature. Well a dog likes to believe what he can hear.

You tell him what a good dog he is and he does like to believe it.

The cuckoo when he says cuckoo and you have money in your pocket and it is the first cuckoo you have heard that year you will have money all of that year.

It did happen to me so you see it has nothing to do with the human mind to believe what you see to like to believe what you hear.

But it did happen to me there was a cuckoo and he came and sat not in a cuckoo tree but in a tree right near to me and he said cuckoo at me and I had a lot of money in my pocket and I had a lot of money all that year.

Now you see what a cuckoo has to do with superstition and identity.

When the soldiers she had been quartering finally departed, her English friends, Sir Robert Abdy and his wife Diana, came for a visit and they were followed soon after by Thornton Wilder. No visitor could have pleased her more. For one who talked incessantly, in public and in private, and nearly always about herself, Gertrude had curiously few confidants in her lifetime. Her conversation, as a rule, was neither confessional nor self-analytical, but a mixture of small talk and *pronunciamento*. In Thornton Wilder with "his serious beliefs and precision," she had found a spirit with whom she was not concerned to buttress her importance, or on whom she did not try to impress her point of view, or even to register her opinions. To him, as to no one else, she was ready to expose her most profound doubts. Faith in his faith in her lay at the bottom of this unique confidence, and she could speak openly of her most intimately secret misgivings. "I am not leading him, I am confiding in him," she said, and they walked up and down the hills of Bilignin, talking about the passage of time and the psyches of dogs and the relation of human nature to the human mind.

She felt she would like to have commentaries, like Caesar's *Commentaries*, appended to her new book, and importuned Wilder to supply them. He began to write them for friendship's sake, but finally disappointed her by refusing to print them. Instead, he wrote an introduction to the book. Ruefully, Gertrude accepted his second-best gesture. His refusal to do what she most wanted was one of the few denials of Gertrude's wishes that did not result in a breaking of personal relations or in some blunt or subtle form of retribution.

Wilder visited them again when they had returned to Paris, as he was about to sail for New York early in November. In a long farewell evening, they strolled about the Left Bank and Gertrude reviewed her career. She felt she had written poetry, plays, philosophy, but that she had not "simply told anything." *The Autobiography of Alice B. Toklas*, she felt, "was a description and creation of something that having happened was in a way happening not again but as it had been which is history which is newspaper which is illustration but is not a simple narrative of what is happening not as if it had happened not as if it is happening but as if it is existing simply that thing." With the particular goal in mind of achieving "a simple narrative of what is happening," she wrote *Everybody's Autobiogra-*

phy, by almost any measure the least "stylish" of all of her works, the most journalistic and fact-bound.

Ten eventful years after the triumphs and trepidations of her first visit, Gertrude was again invited to lecture at Oxford and Cambridge, in January, 1936. On a brief visit to England, she and Alice stayed with Lord Berners at Faringdon House, Berkshire, and later with the Abdys in Cornwall. Of all of Gertrude's new friends, none was more eccentric in his own quiet way than Gerald Berners, for whom composing was but one of many aesthetic pursuits. Beverley Nichols, in *The Sweet and Twenties*, gives this account of him: "He was remarkably ugly — short, swarthy, bald, dumpy and simian. . . . He had a tiny piano built into his Rolls-Royce. In this vehicle he used to travel abroad, usually on his way to Rome, where he had an exquisite house in the shadow of the Forum . . . idly strumming snatches of Scarlatti while the chauffeur coped with the traffic." In the car, according to Nichols, he kept a papier-mâché mask — a "white, hideous mask, the mask of an idiot"— and "sometimes, when the light was fading, and the Rolls-Royce was purring through a tiny Italian village, he would put it on, and lean his head out of the window, to the terror of the local inhabitants — a terror that was enhanced by the fact that as the car vanished into the dusk there came, from inside it, the echoes of ghostly music."

Seasoned by her trouping in America, Gertrude was not this time plagued by the stage fright that had once made an ordeal of each of her public appearances. The whole trip, as she reported in a letter, was a pleasure: ". . . I came over to lecture in Oxford and Cambridge and it has gone off very well, it is very sweet the way the American boys in these colleges look upon me as the American flag. . . . We have been staying in some beautiful houses . . . one of the pleasantest was Lord Berners the musician who is a charming person and there was hardly a moment when we were not all lords and ladies but we liked it, there was so much beautiful needlework and so many orchids that Alice was all pleased and so was I, glory is pleasant, it may not be lucrative but it is pleasant, and perhaps it will be lucrative, who shall say?"

Back in Paris she went on with the recollections that made up

Everybody's Autobiography, until it was time again to transfer activities to Bilignin. Spain was torn apart that summer, but their little village remained peaceful, if not sequestered, and they spent the time with many visitors, among them Bennett Cerf and Jo Davidson. Later came Lord Berners, bringing the music for A *Wedding Bouquet*, the ballet version of *They Must. Be Wedded. To Their Wife.* Gertrude had written this piece in 1931, and the Sadler's Wells Company was now about to include the work in its repertoire. As she came to the concluding pages of *Everybody's Autobiography*, she had grave doubts about her style, which she confesses in the course of the book itself. "I had always wanted it all to be commonplace and simple that I am writing," she said, "and then I get worried lest I have succeeded and it is too commonplace and too simple so much so that it is nothing." Bennett Cerf, mindful of the success of the earlier *Autobiography* in the hands of another publisher, and already contracted to the publication of the sequel, expressed nothing but enthusiasm for the chapters Gertrude showed him. Reassured, Gertrude went on being commonplace, filling in the pages with all the people, places and random thoughts that had arrived with fame and fortune in America.

When the directors of the *Exposition Mondiale*, to be held in Paris in 1937, were choosing a committee of jurors for the Petit Palais show, Gertrude was asked to serve as one of the judges. In spite of her old reputation as "pope and pharaoh of the picture-buying world," this was actually her first experience as an official critic. In this capacity, she succeeded, against the wishes of certain other jurors, in gaining space in the show for two paintings of Francis Picabia, the old acquaintance who had just recently come into the fold. The time was ripe for something really new in painting, she felt, and Picabia was the one most likely to meet her expectation. She had seen the rise of the cubists, the Dadaists, the surrealists and "the Russian school" and now, when there was no obvious group or school to represent the tendencies of Paris, she looked to Picabia and then to Sir Francis Rose.

In April, 1937, they again went to London for a week, to attend the *première* of A *Wedding Bouquet* in which leading parts

355

were danced by Margot Fonteyn, Ninette de Valois and Robert Helpmann. Choreography for the ballet had been worked out by Frederick Ashton. Having previously worked with *Four Saints*, Ashton had come to feel for Gertrude something close to adoration. Sensing his deep feelings, Gertrude decided he was a genius. For corroboration, she turned to Alice and her bells, but there was only silence. Lacking Alice's imprimatur, Ashton was but provisionally admitted to the company of geniuses.

Watching a rehearsal conducted by Constant Lambert, Gertrude was, as usual, delighted — "the music and all went together and really there is no use in going to see a thing if you have not written it no use at all." Once more, music and theatrical staging had given a communicable vitality to words of Gertrude's which, on the page, remain comparatively inchoate. At a socially brilliant opening night she took curtain calls, and afterwards commented: "each time a musician does something with the words it makes it do what they never did do, this time it made them do as if the last word had heard the next word and the next word had heard not the last word but the next word." Again, her words in the theater had pleased her more than they did anywhere else. "I like anything a word can do," she said. "And words do do all they do and then they can do what they never do do." Happy in another success, they returned home, wondering if London and Paris had not changed characters. "It is London that is gay and Paris that is somber," she wrote to W. G. Rogers, "too much work and no play can make Jack a dull boy but too much play makes Jack a dismal boy."

She had not seen Picasso for nearly two years, not since the day when he had followed his offended wife Olga from the first reading of the *Autobiography of Alice B. Toklas* on the Rue de Fleurus. Now, to sharpen the vague differences that had kept them distant, Gertrude learned that he had not only taken to writing poetry but to publishing it. Picasso had separated from Olga in 1935, the year in which she bore his daughter Maya. Unhappy in this circumstance and preoccupied with tedious divorce proceedings, Picasso had altogether abandoned any attempt to paint. Instead, he turned to poetry, composing shapeless surrealist poems and plays in French and

Spanish. While Gertrude had little reason to suspect that he was deliberately following her lead, Picasso was also doing poetic portraits. Among these, typical was one written for his friend, Sabartés:

Live coal of friendship
clock which always gives the hour
joyfully waving banner
stirred by the breath of a kiss on the hand
caress from the wings of the heart
which flies from the topmost height
of the tree of the fruit-laden bower
when the gaze turns its velvet toward the window
armchair stuffed with the vest torn from the shrieking goose
shaped with all the patience of the worm
and dyed by the ribbon of Mediterranean hue
table so gracefully set
upon the hand of the beggar
dressed only in flowers
alms garnered from all those worlds he drags
trench of rose-colored bows
so braided
as to spell the words which alone
must sing their names

Had he merely regarded his writing as an avocation, it would probably have caused no disturbance on Gertrude's part. But when Picasso began to publish his effusions, she felt she had to look into the matter.

On Picasso's special invitation, Gertrude went one evening, with Thornton Wilder and Alice, to hear him read examples of the new work. After Picasso had read for a while, he looked to Gertrude for a reaction. "It is very interesting," she told him. He read on, then looked toward Wilder. "Did you follow?" asked Picasso. "Yes," said Wilder, "it is very interesting." By the time they were ready to say good night, Gertrude had "a funny feeling," she said, "the miracle had not come the poetry was not poetry it was — well . . ." "Like the school of Jean Cocteau," said Wilder. "For heaven's sake do not tell him," said Gertrude.

Some months later, after Gertrude had made the acquaintance of

357

Salvador Dali, who was also writing poems, she told the surrealist painter that she "was bored with the hopelessness of painters and poetry." This report soon came back to Picasso. When, in a matter of days, Gertrude encountered him by chance while he was visiting a gallery with Braque, he was quick to remind her of her faithless opinion. According to Gertrude, the following drama served to bring his poetic dalliance to a close:

PICASSO: You said that painters can't write poetry.

GERTRUDE: Well, they can't. Look at you.

PICASSO: My poetry is good. Breton says so.

GERTRUDE: Breton! Breton admires anything to which he can sign his name, and you know as well as I do that a hundred years hence nobody will remember his name. You know that perfectly well.

PICASSO: Oh well, they say he can write.

GERTRUDE: You do not take their word for whether somebody can paint. Don't be an ass.

BRAQUE: A painter *can* write. I have written all my life.

GERTRUDE (striking back at Braque's statement published in *transition's* "Testimony Against Gertrude Stein"):

Well I only saw one thing of yours that was written and that in a language you cannot understand. And I did not think much of it, that is all I can say.

BRAQUE: But I did not write that.

GERTRUDE: Oh, didn't you? Well, anyway, you signed it, and I have never seen any other writing of yours so you do not count. And, anyway, we are talking about Pablo's poetry, and even Michael Angelo did not make much of a success of it. (Turning to Picasso.) You can't stand looking at Jean Cocteau's drawings. It does something to you; they are more offensive than drawings that are just bad drawings. Now that's the way it is with your poetry. It is more offensive than just bad poetry. I do not know why but it just is. Somebody who can really do something well, very well, when he does something else which he cannot do, and in which he cannot live, it is particularly repellent. You never read a book in your life that was not written by a friend, and then not then. You never had any feelings about words. Words annoy you more than they do

358

anything else. So how can you write? You know better, you yourself know better.

PICASSO: You yourself always said I was an extraordinary person. Well, then, an extraordinary person can do anything.

GERTRUDE (Catching him by the lapels of his coat and shaking him): Ah, you are extraordinary within limits, but your limits are extraordinarily there. You know it, you know it as well as I know it. It is all right you are doing this to get rid of everything that has been too much for you. All right, all right! Go on doing it but don't go on trying to make me tell you it is poetry.

PICASSO: Well, supposing I do know it. What will I do?

GERTRUDE (Kissing him): What will you *do?* You will go on until you are more cheerful and less dismal, and then you will —

PICASSO: Yes — ?

GERTRUDE: And then you will paint a very beautiful picture and then more of them. (Kisses him again.)

PICASSO: Yes.

In the summer of 1937, after a long visit by Thornton Wilder, who worked on his manuscripts on their terrace at Bilignin and in the Belley café, Gertrude and Alice made "a sentimental journey" with their old doughboy friend W. G. Rogers and his wife. The project was "sentimental" in Gertrude's terms, since they planned to cover territory they had visited when she and Alice first knew him while they were doing war work twenty years before. They started out from Bilignin, Gertrude at the wheel, on an itinerary that took them to such places as St. Marcellin, Viviers, Avignon, St. Rémy, Arles and Nîmes. Traveling as sightseers and as gourmets, they were rewarded on both accounts. During the trip, Gertrude confided to Rogers her immediate writing plans. "I want to write a novel about publicity," she said, "a novel where a person is so publicized that there isn't any personality left. I want to write about the effect on people of the Hollywood cinema kind of publicity that takes away all identity. It's very curious, you know, very curious the way it does just that." The problem, of course, was her own, and the novel, with which she was to struggle intermittently for years, was *Ida.*

In the same period, Gertrude produced a book for children,

359

The World Is Round, a little allegory about a girl named Rose who climbs by adventuresome stages to the top of a mountain and, having brought her blue chair with her, just beautifully sits there. Ida is the grownup version of Rose, or perhaps Rose after she has reached the summit. Both girls have a dog named Love, and both are wonderfully disconnected from the world in spite of the little fears and bothers and pleasures which preoccupy them. Unlike Ida who moves like tumbleweed across a good part of America, Rose is assertive and, on her way up the mountain, stops to carve her name on a tree: "And Rose forgot the dawn forgot the rosy dawn forgot the sun forgot she was only one and all alone there she had to carve and carve with care the corners of the Os and the Rs and Ss and Es in a Rose is a Rose is a Rose is a Rose."

One of her most lighthearted books, *Ida* is the story of a woman whose mere being is more important than anything she does or might think of doing, simply because she is Ida, the dream girl made flesh. Existing not only in the dreams of others but in a dream of herself, she moves around a lot, marries blithely every now and then, but for the most part simply remains and is Ida to whom it is not necessary for anything to happen. Gertrude conceived of Ida as a "publicity saint" and, like the saints in her opera, it was not necessary for her to do anything but stand around and let the aureole of her beatitude be visible. Ida lives in the realm of the "human mind" and is consequently unaffected by events that occur on the level of "human nature." She is, of course, Gertrude Stein, the short, squat loadstone of a woman who had drawn generations to her doorstep and who, lately, through the offices of mass publicity had moved into the company of Garbo, the Duchess of Windsor and all the somnambulistic heroines of legend whose power lay less in what they did than in who they were. This had happened not because she was a writer, or anything else that she was or might have been, but because she was, after all, Gertrude Stein.

CHAPTER 24

Climate and the affections. I have often been
quoted as quoting that.
— GERTRUDE STEIN

SUCCESS, in all the superficial and ordinary
ways she had coveted its name and 36-point bold-type nature, had
come late to Gertrude Stein. Its glow would last no longer than the
antique light of Indian summer, but for the time it was nevertheless
ample and warm. She moved in its ambience immensely enjoying
the secure knowledge that she was one of the great public figures of
her time. Fame dictated no change in the tempo or conduct of her
intimately comfortable life with Alice, no variation in the casual yet
consistent daily working habits into which she had settled some
thirty-odd years before. But with fame came the temptation to
channel her creative energies into new outlets. She did not resist
these, and while the works they called forth added considerably to
her fame and moderately to her fortune, they also led to a dimming
of her distinction as an artist and brought her to a point where,
with no little pathos, she could ask, "Why have they thought I
sold what I bought?" Her reputation, once a very special and exotic

thing, was now a widely public legend. Most of the old forbidding connotations of her name had disappeared; she was now considered to be charming, amusing, harmless — a clever woman whose Yankee wit and good horse sense had overcome all adversaries. Responding to opportunities that came with general recognition, she moved into the comparatively brief and least distinguished phase of her career during which she quickly wrote and quickly published books palatable to the popular appetite. Frustrated for many long years in attempts to market her genius, she could not resist easy chances to sell her talent. She wrote an intimately rambling account of Picasso which found a large audience; and she wrote *Paris France*, a memoir and act of homage in which she capitalized on the desire of readers to gain a further sense of personal contact with the particularly ingratiating Gertrude Stein whom *The Autobiography of Alice B. Toklas* had made familiar.

As Hitler's black shadow brought Europe to brink-of-war tension in the late 1930's, she remained calm and tried to stay remote from its portents. Preoccupied with herself, the pleasures of celebrity, and the happy new role she played as a writer with a ready and waiting audience, she moved with the seasons from Paris to Bilignin. During winters in the city, she went about socially more than ever before. For the first time in her life, she began to visit the *salons* of *other* figures in art and literary circles. "You will go anywhere once," she said, "Anyway, I will." But her new interest in seeing and being seen outside of her own atelier was short-lived. Even a lion, she found, can get bored.

The epochal history of 27 Rue de Fleurus came to an uneventful ending in 1937. Their landlord, who wanted to take over the residence for his son's family, decided to terminate their lease. Gertrude at first thought of legally opposing his demand. But finally, without tears, she gave in. "I guess 27 got so historical," she wrote to Sherwood Anderson, "it just could not hold us any longer." Presently they moved to a new apartment in the Faubourg St. Germain, just around the corner from the studio Picasso kept on the Rue des Grands Augustins. The apartment was unimpressively situated over a bookbinding establishment on the second floor of V Rue Christine, a little street off the Rue Dauphine which goes down to the Seine near the Pont Neuf, and which takes its name from the Swedish queen who had once kept a flat there. Limited in size yet comfortable, their new quarters soon took on the old aspect of household-cum-museum.

Visitors would arrive by an outdoor staircase looking onto the bookbinder's yard, and come into the apartment by a tiny entrance hall leading to a foyer of perfectly square dimensions. On its walls they might first note a few Japanese prints, then serried ranks of unframed paintings, mostly of Picasso's early cubist phase — especially the nearly monotone works he had composed on summer vacations in Spain — but also of the periods immediately preceding and following. From the foyer, one doorway led into a hall toward the bedroom, and another into a drawing room crowded with furniture onto which northern light fell through tall curtained windows. On every flat surface one might see *bibelots* of wood or glass or stone, and a selection of the "breakable objects" Gertrude particularly cherished. But the paintings would be the overwhelming thing — for their number, their variety and, to the knowledgeable eye, their value. And yet most of them were already mementos, documents of an era written and talked into history. Most of the newer paintings were by Francis Rose; their prominence on her walls confined her loyalty to works that had never received the acclaim or fashionable attention given to almost all of her other acquisitions. Incongruous among them all was a small, ineffably lovely painting of a yellow-green apple, solidly framed and somehow all by itself. Years before, Gertrude had given in to Leo's request that he take one of Cézanne's paintings of apples as his part of the just division of their possessions. Unhappy about this, she had bemoaned the fact to Picasso. Soon afterwards, he had redeemed the loss of all of the Cézanne apples with the gift of his perfect single one.

The deep, down-pillows of the horsehair furniture she had bought in London in 1914 were still in good repair; and Alice's petit point, stitched from designs Picasso had made especially for her, delicately colored the seats and backs of antique chairs. Nothing was arranged for display, nothing catered to the decorator styles that had become widely popular. They were simply home again in the sort of tolerable

363

confusion that characterizes a residence dedicated wholly to comfort.

In the fall of their first year on the Rue Christine, Gertrude was grieved by the loss of her famous pet, Basket. Friends advised her to get another white poodle just like him right away. But Picasso told her he felt this advice was mistaken. He had tried it once, he said, "and it was awful, the new one reminded me of the old one and the more I looked at him the worse it was . . . supposing I were to die, you would go out on the street and sooner or later you would meet a Pablo, but it would not be I and it would be the same. No, never get the same kind of a dog, get an Afghan hound. . . ." Gertrude put his attitude down as the Spanish refusal "to recognize resemblances and continuation." *"Le roi est mort, vive le roi,"* she said, went to a dog show at the Porte de Versailles, acquired another white poodle, and named him Basket II.

As omens of war loomed, raged and disappeared, Gertrude took scant notice as she went on writing a new opera, *Doctor Faustus Lights the Lights,* for which she hoped Lord Berners would supply a musical score. While she could see many signs of anxiety in the lives of her immediate neighbors, she could not herself participate in their common apprehension. Nevertheless, forever the Radcliffe girl with a notebook, she was interested in all the different ways in which people might manifest their alarm. One crisis after another, false threats and true, mobilizations and defense preparations, she could see, had made Paris tense and then weary. Even in the Belley countryside, currents of uneasiness charged everything and made every day subtly different. While she was deeply interested in her objective way, she was also plainly annoyed. She continued to feel that, really, there could be no serious war, and stuck to her conviction against the opinion of one as knowledgeable as Clare Boothe Luce who, with her publisher husband, visited Bilignin in the summer of 1939. "I'm sick afraid that you're wrong about the war," Mrs. Luce wrote to her, "Everywhere, in Poland and in the Balkans they've got too many guns, and now nobody can think what to do with them but shoot them off. That's 'raisonable' too, isn't it? We were in Warsaw and the Ukraine. The average Pole is a square short blond fellow with a head that looks bullet-proof. He hasn't a pocket-book, so he has both hands up under his chin. He has nothing but his life to lose. When men are reduced to such ignominious poverty they generally fight. We think they'll fight, and we think we won't. Ours is still an audience psychology." Gertrude saw things differently, and from a less traveled point of view, but she was nevertheless impelled to take the precaution of sending her unpublished manuscripts to Carl Van Vechten in New York. Her brother Mike wanted her to send her paintings, too. But Gertrude did not show the same concern about them and they remained in Paris.

Since she thought only in terms of individuals and had little concept of the forces that propelled men to power, she analyzed personalities with little regard for the movements of which they were executives. Hitler, she rationalized, wanted to destroy Germany. Like Napoleon, who was to France an Italian foreigner, Hitler was to Germany an Austrian foreigner who subconsciously hated the country of his adoption and would bring it to ruin with the same indifference with which Napoleon had squandered French lives to conquer Europe. Just how he was otherwise going to destroy Germany she did not say, but a general European war was not the answer. "Hitler will never really go to war," she told an interviewer. "He is not the dangerous one. You see, he is the German romanticist. He wants the illusion of victory and power, the glory and glamour of it, but he could not stand the blood and fighting involved in getting it. No, Mussolini — there's the dangerous man, for he is an Italian realist. He won't stop at anything." Through one portent after another, she continued to believe that open conflict was unlikely, and refused to be shaken even by the Munich crisis.

When war did come (the news arrived in the middle of a pastoral afternoon she and Alice were spending with their friends, Mme. Pierlot and Baron and Baroness d'Aiguy in Belley) she was appalled. "They shouldn't! They shouldn't!" was all she could say, and her French friends had to comfort her. The shock was soon over. Within a few days she wrote to W. G. Rogers: "Well here we are, I never did think there would be another war for me to see and here we are, well if there is one I would of course rather be in it than out of it, there is that something about a war."

Gertrude secured a military pass, valid for only thirty-six hours, to enable her and Alice to make a swift automobile trip to Paris. They needed their winter clothing and their passports, but mainly they wanted to see what they could do about protecting their paintings from concussion damage in the event that Paris was bombed. To advise them, they called upon their friend and dealer, Daniel-Henry Kahnweiler, and he hurried to the Rue Christine. As he entered the apartment, Kahnweiler later recalled, "I saw Alice with one foot on the frame of the portrait of Madame Cézanne, trying to remove the picture. I stopped her, and set myself to unframing this magnificent work in a less violent manner." They had thought of spreading the pictures flat on the floor, but had to abandon the idea when they realized that their wall space was naturally four times greater than their floor space. Kahnweiler begged them to take at least some of the small Picassos which could be easily wrapped and which would take up little room, but they decided to take only the Cézanne and Picasso's portrait of Gertrude. Leaving most of the pictures in their accustomed places, they returned to the country "to await developments." They did not again leave the Rhône valley until the end of 1944.

"In the beginning, like camels, we lived on our past," wrote Alice Toklas in the cookbook she published after Gertrude's death; yet they lacked nothing but the largess of their customary *haute cuisine*. Someone sent them an American Mixmaster; they had salmon trout from the Rhône and salmon carp from the Lac de Bourget; all kinds of vegetables from their garden. There was plenty of coal and wood to keep fires burning in the grate; plenty of meat and potatoes and bread and honey; and, once their car had been equipped for a change of fuel, enough wood alcohol to allow them to drive about to places as far as Chambéry and Aix-les-Bains. Gertrude had her detective and adventure stories to read, and a book of astrological predictions, *The Last Year of War*, by one Leonardo Blake, to consult. The prophecies in this volume showed marked relevance to what was happening not only in Europe but before her eyes and, in an atmosphere continually dark with presage, she allowed her old belief in superstition to come into full play. With Basket II she took long walks in the daytime and through the blacked-out evenings, chatting with neighbors on her rounds, and sharing their apprehensions. She had once said, "I wish I could be rich in ways to say how do you do/And I am," and now she had many opportunities to confirm it. The gift of her small talk and good humor was extended to everyone, including a little man who led her to pronounce: "I always do shake hands with a dwarf." Her days were rich in terms of human contact, but as for writing, once she had completed *Paris France* in December, 1939, she came to a period when she felt she was "like the fields, lying fallow."

In the early spring of 1940, when *"la guerre des nerfs"* showed signs of turning into a shooting war, her peace of mind was irretrievably shaken. Belley had been chosen as a training ground by the French army; on its rugged terrain, companies of the 13th Chasseurs and the Foreign Legion were being prepared for an invasion of Norway. Gertrude tried to work on her novel, *Ida,* examining and, she hoped, resolving the problem of identity which had obsessed her ever since she had become famous. But in days riddled with rumor and gunshot, meditation was no longer possible. To forget the military maneuvers she could not help seeing from her windows, and to distract herself from the frightening communiqués that came over the radio three times every day, she made up dozens of stories for children. She planned to publish these in two companion volumes under the title, *To Do, A Book of Alphabets and Birthdays* — one a conventional alphabet with stories for each letter; the other a series of narratives with a birthday figuring in each one. She completed this work in May. Alice thought the book was very funny, but felt it was too adult for children and too childish for adults. As it turned out, prospective publishers agreed with Alice's judgment and the book never found a commercial market.

When Italy entered the war in June, and Paris was occupied on the 14th of that month, Gertrude was "scared, completely scared." Since they would be "in everybody's path," she convinced Alice there was nothing to be done but to flee their dangerous corner. The American consul in Lyon confirmed their sense of jeopardy and validated their passports for swift passage into neutral Spain. But at the very point of departure they hesitated. When they asked their friend, Dr. Chaboux, whether they should leave or stay, he answered, "Well, I can't guarantee you anything, but my advice is to stay. I had friends who in the last war stayed in their homes all through the German occupation, and they saved their homes and those who left lost theirs. No, I think unless your house is actually destroyed by a bombardment, I always think the best thing to do is stay. Everybody knows you here; everybody likes you; we all would help you in every way. Why risk yourself among strangers?" All at once they knew they could not carry out their decision. Resolved to accept troubles they knew rather than brave those they could only fearfully imagine, they dug in for the duration. If they were to die, their end would come in the country they loved and in a house they had made their own. In the play she wrote sometime later, *Yes Is for a Very Young Man,* Gertrude echoes the advice of her physician friend in the words of Constance: "Yes I too was about to go, to go not somewhere but anywhere and one of my neighbors, a farmer said to me, mademoiselle, go where, I am an old man and I tell you in time of danger stay where you are, there if you are killed, you know where you are. . . ."

Within a matter of days the sound of cannon fire told them that the advancing Germans were within close range. Over roads crowded with refugees, they drove into Belley to secure provisions ample enough to see them through any eventuality. They were loading the car with sides of ham, hundreds of cigarettes and bundles of groceries when they heard a thunderous rumble that made them stop and stare: two machine-gun tanks painted with black crosses roared through the main street. They hurried home to Bilignin by a side road and, electricity and postal service having been meanwhile cut off, waited there in isolation for what might come next.

In the days following, Gertrude learned to imitate her French neighbors in the policy of regarding *eux* as "invisible." But Nazi soldiers were soon omnipresent. She even came to feel a little sorry for them. They "did not look like conquerors. . . . They went up and down, but they were gentle, slightly sad, polite. . . . They admired Basket II and said to each other in German, 'A beautiful dog.' They were polite and considerate; they were, as the French said, correct. It was all very sad; they were sad, the French were sad, it was all sad, but not at all the way we thought it would be, not at all."

When the armistice was signed by Marshal Pétain, lights came back on in the evenings, and soon came back the young men who had been but recently conscripted. "Everybody forgot about being defeated, it was such a relief that their men were not dead," Gertrude wrote. "But anyway our light is lit and the shutters are open, and perhaps everybody will find out, as the French know so well, that the winner loses, and everybody will be, too, like the French, that is, tremendously occupied with the business of daily living, and that that will be enough." She did not agree with those who felt that Pétain's capitulation was ignominious. Her reasons, and the order of importance which she assigned to them, were simple and characteristic: "in the first place it was more comfortable for us who were here and in the second place it was an important element in the ultimate defeat of the Germans."

How serious the plight of the two American ladies actually was cannot be certainly known. But the experience of others similarly placed indicates that their being allowed to remain anonymous very likely saved them from a concentration camp and possible death. As Jews, and later as citizens of an enemy nation, they would have been subject to any indignity. They knew this well. Yet, in spite of repeated requests by the consul at Lyon that they seek safety in America, they remained adamant. Lecture agencies had been trying with rich offers to persuade Gertrude to make another tour ever since she had left America. While she was disposed to undertake another visit, she changed her mind when she found no assurance that she would be allowed to return to France. When she had convinced the consul in Lyon that going to America was out of the question, their only protection was the affection of their French neighbors. The Germans demanded that all inhabitants of the area be listed, but their names were deliberately overlooked. As the bald, dignified little mayor told Gertrude: "You are obviously too old for life in a concentration camp. You would not survive it, so why should I tell them?"

Their only crises were domestic ones. They found themselves without money. One of their neighbors, Paul Genin, a silk manufacturer of Lyon who was interested in literature, provided them with a substantial sum in six monthly installments. To pay him back, they sold to a Parisian friend the Cézanne portrait under which Gertrude had written *Three Lives* nearly forty years before. Once more, Gertrude's early acumen had paid off in the most practical way — by providing the means for taking care of an acute necessity. As a rule, she was curiously uninterested in knowing what prices her paintings might bring. Since she had paid so little for them, she felt she had no right to sell them for the astronomical prices many of them could later command. Interpreted in terms of the cost of a particular want, however, she felt that a sale at a well augmented price was justified. During World War I, a Manet went for subsistence needs and, at various other times, when money was needed for the printing of her books, or for an electric heating system, or for some other major revision in their household, she sold Picasso's *Girl with a Fan* and, to Walter P. Chrysler, Jr., the same artist's *Women at a Bar*, or some other work that time and her changing taste had made dispensable.

In January, 1941, she received a letter from Sherwood Anderson: "Eleanor and I are now planning to go off to South America late in February. We have a passage engaged on a boat and plan to take a long sea voyage and land far down somewhere on the west coast, probably in Chile. We may stay down there several months.

"I dare say you have heard of Hemingway's huge success with his new book and of the sudden death of Scott Fitzgerald. His wife went insane and he himself rather went to pieces, over drinking badly. He has for some time been making his living as a movie writer out in Los Angeles."

Within a matter of weeks, they learned of Anderson's own death, suddenly, on March 8 in the military hospital at Colón in Panama where he had been removed from the S.S. *Santa Lucia* with peritonitis. In their isolation, such news seemed to come from another time, another world. They went on meeting the little challenges of every day, the greatest of which was the securing of food. By her efficient management through a long period which seemed to Alice a "protracted, indeed a perpetual, Lent," and Gertrude's willingness to walk many miles for a loaf of bread, they survived in meager comfort. "As Alice does know how to make everything be something," Gertrude said, "we get along fine." Whatever they had was shared with their neighbors, and they supplemented their own fare with fish they caught themselves and with nuts, mushrooms and salad greens gathered in the nearby woods and fields. Yet Gertrude was continually homesick "for the quays of Paris and for a roast chicken, a roast chicken and the quays of Paris," and continually waiting for the American army, "waiting for them, to bring us shoes and stockings and dental floss."

Through a good part of the years 1941 and 1942, Gertrude was busy on a novel, *Mrs. Reynolds,* to which she appended an epilogue stating: "This book is an effort to show the way anybody could feel these years. It is a perfectly ordinary couple living an ordinary life and having ordinary conversations and really not suffering personally from everything that is happening but over them, all over them is the shadow of two men, and then the shadow of one of the two men gets bigger and then blows away and then there is no other. There is nothing historical about this book except the state of mind." The two men are, of course, Hitler and Stalin, to which she gives the names Angel Harper and Joseph Lane, respectively. Throughout the novel they figure as imminent presences, half real, half imagined, that qualify the pleasant idiocy of the domestic life in which worried Mrs. Reynolds and her placid consort, Mr. Reynolds, are exclusively preoccupied. The substance of the book is the same as that of the account of these years Gertrude eventually published as *Wars I Have Seen.* But in the case of the novel, events have been subtracted from their historical continuum and only feelings remain. Above all other feelings, a vague but constant imminence dominates a time when "there was so much going on that it was just as if nothing at all was happening." The style of the novel is clear, but its interminable small talk is apt to give most readers the feeling that they are listening for days and weeks on end to one side of a telephone conversation. Gertrude Stein had again succeeded in making real the relation between time and events, but she had not succeeded in making "reading time" anything more interesting than subjection to a laboratory experiment.

Their lease on the Bilignin house ran out early in 1943, and they were asked to vacate. Since the landlord and his wife did not plan to live in the house, Gertrude was angered by his request and instituted a lawsuit. She lost her case in court but was subsequently granted a period of time in which to look for another domicile. When finally the landlord returned to civilian life, they had to go. In good time, a modern house in Culoz was offered to them. It was named Le Colombier or the Dovecote and it was "a nice big modern house alone against a mountain with a lovely park full of bushes and big trees, and firs," situated only twelve miles from Bilignin. They were heartbroken to have to leave their beloved summer home, but two servants came with their new lease and life promised to be supportable. They packed up their water heater, their bathtub, electric kitchen stove and refrigerator and made the short journey to their new home. "Our final, definite leaving of the gardens," wrote Alice Toklas, "came one cold winter day, all too appropriate to our feelings and the state of the world. A sudden moment of sunshine peopled the gardens with the friends and others who had passed through them. Ah, there would be another garden, the same friends, possibly, or no, probably new ones, and there would be other stories to tell and hear. And so we left Bilignin, never to return."

Once more they were warned, upon specific threat of being interned in a concentration camp, to leave the district and go into Switzerland. Since the warning came directly from Vichy, Gertrude was alarmed. But after consultation with Alice she only confirmed her earlier decision. "No, I am not going, we are not going," she said, "it is better to go regularly wherever we are sent than to go irregularly where nobody can help us if we are in trouble . . . they are always trying to get us to leave France but here we are and here we stay."

Increasing hardships of daily life brought them into close contact with their neighbors and taught them the real and hidden cost of war in the sad records of broken families and the terror of casualty lists. But most of all they learned the meaning of a simple lack of freedom. "There is one thing that is certain," Gertrude wrote, "and nobody really realized it in the 1914-1919 war, they talked about it but they did not realize it but now everybody knows it everybody that the one thing that everybody wants is to be free, to talk to eat to drink to walk to think, to please, to wish, and to do it now if now is what they want, and everybody knows it they know it anybody knows it . . . even if they are not free they want to feel free, and they want to feel free now, let the future take care of itself all they want is to be free, not to be managed, threatened, directed, restrained, obliged, fearful, administered . . . they do not want to be afraid not more than is necessary in the ordinary business of living where one has to earn one's living and has to fear want, disease and death. . . . In 1914-1918, it was still the nineteenth century, and one might still think that something would happen might lead one to higher and other things but now, the only thing that any one wants now is to be free, to be let alone, to live their life as they can, but not to be watched, controlled, and scared, no, no, not."

Reactionary in her political thinking, according to the standards of her times, a supporter of Franco and Pétain, Gertrude had gradually undergone a change in attitude. The courage of the maquis hiding out in the nearby mountains and forests was one factor in the liberalizing of her outlook, but more important was her comprehension, after long delay, of the rigorous and far from picturesque life of the ordinary French citizen. In the light of this, she came to see that many evidences of corruption in France, apparent in attempts to conserve property and position, were heinous. She took issue with friends who shared the reactionary view that all maquis were political terrorists, since these were the same upper-class Frenchmen who regarded the Fourteenth of July and the fall of the Bastille, as one of them said to her, as *quelle masquerade.*" When the tide of war began to change in favor of the Allies she found herself in personal conflict with at least one of her neighbors. "And then there are the decayed aristocrats," she wrote, "who are always hoping that a new regime will give them a chance . . . and the decayed bourgeoisie, who feel sure that everybody but themselves should be disciplined, I had a row with one of them on the street last night."

373

Travel by train was forbidden for most purposes, but they found they could get permission to see a doctor or a dentist in Aix-les-Bains whenever they asked for it. They made the journey often, to shop and to visit cafés in the hope of running into someone they knew. Otherwise, Gertrude's "island of daily living" was little changed. She still rose late, loitered over the few domestic chores Alice might have implied were necessary, read a play of Shakespeare's every few days, walked her dogs, and went on with her writing and thinking about what language could tell and do. She learned from a servant that the villagers were curious as to what the two strange women were doing in their midst. The previous tenant, the villagers remembered, had spent most of his time counting his money. But the few glimpses they had of the Stein household told them only that Alice was perpetually preparing vegetables while Gertrude, under a portrait of herself (the famous Picasso) in the sunlit living room, reclined with books and dogs on a chaise longue. The impression of ease the villagers gained was entirely true. As Gertrude later said, these were the happiest years of her life. If she no longer had a *salon* audience for her monologues, she had the people of the town with whom to share gossip and forebodings; and across the ocean she had an audience of millions who remembered Gertrude Stein and would like to hear from her. If she cared, she might have said, "I am I because everyone in America knows me." With this warming sense of audience, she wrote, in fourteen large, bound ledgers, a diary-like account of her wartime years. She would end the book, she said, when the first Americans of the conquering army came to her house. Until that event she would go on telling of her domestic life, ruminating at length and leisure on life and death and civilization and wars.

These daily scribblings to which she gave the general title "Civil domestic and foreign wars" were eventually published under the title *Wars I Have Seen*. This book notably lacks reference to name after celebrated name that had made a sort of anecdotal litany of her previous autobiographical pieces, and this makes it seem less self-conscious and more genuine as a personal document. Written in her broken-narrative style, the book is mainly concerned with ordinary people under the pressures of war and the occupation. Stories they

374

tell and stories about them that Gertrude tells have a vitality, and often a poignancy, far richer than the atelier-conscious vignettes which had previously engaged all of her attention. Well received in America, the book became a great popular success and for a time stood high on the best-seller lists. Again, Gertrude Stein out of sibylline character had achieved success for reasons she once would have deplored. As journalism, the book was convincing and full of human interest, and as the documentary record of a national experience had the advantage of both a closely observant eye and a richly participant spirit. At a time when the fabulous adventures of war correspondents around the world were being turned out in one sensational book after another, her intimate, modest record of the realities of life under the occupation was fresh and welcome relief. No other volume had as yet presented such homely details in their true setting; and only the most famous of the war correspondents had the advantage of previous reader acquaintance as wide as hers.

But by and large *Wars I Have Seen* is a dull, long-winded and self-indulgent book which does not outlive its topical interest. Naïve, self-justifying mannerisms that had seemed artlessly fresh in the *Autobiography of Alice B. Toklas* now tended to be tiresome and cute. As the narrative weaves and circles through months and years of large and small events, it becomes interesting or intense only when the events it reports become themselves interesting or intense. The closing pages where, in one epiphanous outburst, Gertrude registers the days of mounting excitement as the American army comes closer and closer to her doorstep, are entirely warming as an insight into the personality she had never before exposed so simply and attractively. But from pages crowded with exclamations, exhortations and simple cries of joy and gratitude, Gertrude Stein, the adroit and revolutionary molder of words has disappeared. In her place, unabashed, stands a flag-waving descendant of Barbara Frietchie who has been rescued from oblivion.

Critics who liked the book, and most of them did, felt that at last Gertrude had found subject matter outside of herself. To a degree, this was true. Yet she had finally won general approval only by meeting the notions of critics who had previously been alien and peevishly antagonistic toward anything she considered important. Praise for *Wars I Have Seen* was by nature implied dispraise for the great body of her work, a recommendation of Stein on terms that, earlier, she would have neither recognized nor accepted. The sharpest negative judgment came from Edwin Berry Burgum, who regarded Gertrude's emotionalism as a sort of indecent exposure: ". . . when the American soldiers came over, she knew the Nazis and even her old friend Bernard Faÿ must have been wrong. Since these brave men and openhearted lads were rescuing her from the uncertainties of the Occupation, there could be no doubt that they were the rescuers of civilization. Thus simple persons, uninterested in politics and unaccustomed to the larger issue, feel the impingements of events in proportion to the violence with which it disturbs the daily chore. A surge of patriotism swept through her. . . . Under the pressure of events, the paradox that had hounded her life dissolved at least for the time being. She could now frankly be herself, frankly indulge her secret craving to be common and ordinary like the bulk of mankind. She had reached the goal that had been closed to her (when years ago she had written 'Melanctha') by both the spirit of the age that had now passed and the demands of her ambition which had long since been satisfied. According to the harsh judgment of criticism, she could no longer be considered a writer of importance, but had become a woman of the people. It lay with the unknown events of tomorrow, whether she would be obliged to resume the protection of the mask."

Months before liberation was a reality, the air in the byways of Culoz and Belley had been changed by general expectation and little portents: Children began openly to make fun of the Germans; every now and then one heard, or thought he heard, someone in the distance singing the *Marseillaise*. The maquis grew bolder, harrying the doomed Germans at every turn from ingenious points of ambush and killing them by truckloads. In the imminence of great events, Gertrude and Alice were more deeply isolated than they had ever been. Without newspapers, telephone or mail, they depended upon a radio, the first they had ever owned, for general news and tried to analyze rumors that might confirm the good things they were promised. When the Germans imposed a six o'clock curfew, threatening to shoot on sight anyone who might be abroad after that time, Gertrude bought a wrist watch so that she could lead Basket II punctually home to safety.

On the Fourth of July, she reported, "everybody is on the broad grin." But suddenly there was a fearful business to deal with. Basket barked one evening, and when Gertrude looked out she saw a German officer and a soldier. "They said in French," she wrote in her journal, "they wanted to sleep and I said have you a paper from the mayor because they are always supposed to have and he said like an old time German officer I must see the house, certainly I said, you go around to the back and they will open, and I called the servants and told them to attend to them. I thought with that kind of German it was just as well to keep our American accents out of it, and then they were at it, the German said he wanted two rooms for officers and mattresses for six men and he did not want any answering back and he did not care how much he upset the ladies of the house, and the servants said very well and he left and as soon as he left the soldiers were amiable and they carried around mattresses and they had three dogs and we locked up as much as we could and took Basket upstairs and went to bed, finally there were fifteen men sleeping on the six mattresses and the two dogs the third one would not come in and in the morning after they all left we could not find my umbrella it turned out that it was used by a poor devil of an Italian whom they kept outside all night in the rain to sit with the horses." Before the Germans concluded their visit, they killed a calf on the terrace and improvised a spit on which to cook it. When they finally left in the afternoon, Alice discovered they had taken away a new pair of slippers, broken a cellar lock, stolen peaches, and then had gone off with the keys of both front and back doors.

Within a few days came the excitement of Bastille Day to foster hopes that were now almost irrepressible. In nearby Belley — already totally free of Germans — French, English and American flags flew boldly from every window and rooftop. By the end of July, things had become "mixed up," as Gertrude recorded. The maquis

377

had taken over in some places; some towns and villages still had Germans, Culoz among them, and some were not quite sure if they were free or not. Still, intimations of freedom came regularly and one night Gertrude heard a man going down the street whistling. "What a sense of freedom," she wrote, "to hear some one at midnight go down the street whistling."

As American forces advanced toward Paris, and news of the landing in southern France made the great day seem closer, Alice began furiously to type the book that Gertrude had always said would end when she saw her first American. The villagers, taking time to make Allied flags even in the midst of harvest, felt that things were moving so fast that it was as if they were watching a cinema. And when the maquis drove the last Germans out of Culoz, liberation was all but final. "What a town," wrote Gertrude, "everybody is out on the streets all the time, and in between time they sing the Marseillaise, everybody feels so easy, it is impossible to make anybody realize what occupation by Germans is who has not had it, here in Culoz it was as easy as it was possible for it to be as most of the population are railroad employees and the Germans did not want to irritate them, but it was like a suffocating cloud under which you could not breathe right, we had lots of food, and no interference on the part of the Germans but there it was a weight that was always there and now everybody feels natural, they feel good and they feel bad but they feel natural, and that was our battle, the maquis are all down there at the bridge they do not think the Germans can come back, but they are watchful, there was firing just now it did not last, so it was probably a false alarm, we like the maquis, *honneur aux maquis.*"

The Americans were at Grenoble, only eighty-five kilometers away when, crackling with excitement, a voice on the radio told them that Paris was free. As she had in the First World War, Gertrude immediately went out into the streets of the village to present little ribbons of the American flag to every youngster she met.

She had fallen in love with the maquis — "*honneur aux maquis,*" she wrote, "one cannot say it too often" — and cherished every contact she could make with any of their number. One day, walking near Culoz, she was driven by a thunderstorm into a roadside café.

There she encountered a group of Spaniards who, they told her, had been fighting for freedom for ten years, first in their own country with the anti-Franco forces and now with the maquis. She found that they knew about Hemingway, and when she told them that she was a close friend of Picasso's, they all stood up and solemnly shook hands with her.

Ingredients for Alice's "Liberation Fruit Cake," hoarded like rubies all through the war, were ready and waiting for the touch of her master hand. Gertrude was busy daily clearing the terrace of weeds so that the American army could sit on it. Everything was set for action, and there was still not an American in sight.

The maquis, meanwhile, had accelerated their activities and assumed a new character with old political overtones. Their aggressions were now directed less against the few Germans still pocketed here and there and more against the collaborators in their midst. They had become Robin Hoods, expropriating the hoarded supplies of the well-fed, particularly those who had remained in the favor of the Germans, to give to those whom the war had dispossessed. Their excuse for taking over stores and distributing them to the needy was merely that they felt the friends of the Germans should be the first to pay for the victims of the Germans. Besides the pro-Nazis among the rich, others were also being called to account for their mistakes. "Today the village is excited terribly excited," wrote Gertrude, "because they are shaving the heads of the girls who kept company with the Germans during the occupation, it is called the coiffure of 1944, and naturally it is terrible because the shaving is done publicly, it is being done today."

"Well that was yesterday and today is the landing," Gertrude wrote, and the strain of five long years of war quickly disappeared in news of swift and spectacular events. "We heard Eisenhower tell us he was here they were here and just yesterday a man sold us ten packages of Camel cigarettes, glory be, and we are singing glory hallelujah, and feeling very nicely, and everybody has been telephoning us congratulatory messages upon my birthday which it isn't but we know what they mean. And I said in turn I hoped their hair was curling nicely, and we all hope it is, and today is the day."

Fired by news of the liberation of Paris, the last of the maquis forces came down from their mountain hide-outs and drove every last man of seven hundred Nazis from the town. "It was glorious, classic, almost Biblical," said Alice Toklas. "We celebrated by taking one of the liberated taxis to Belley. Home-made flags were flying from windows — not only the tricolor but the stars and stripes. . . ."

At last, on August 31, 1944, Gertrude saw the American soldiers for whom she had pined and prayed. Villagers had reported to her that they had heard that the American Seventh Army was advancing toward them from Grenoble. This was a familiar rumor; she was skeptical. But while she was shopping in Belley, other villagers told her that some Americans had come and were now actually in the town. "Lead me to them," she said. With Alice in tow, she marched toward the hotel to which they were directed. She was stopped at the door, but the proprietor intervened when he saw that the intruder was the famous Mlle. Gertrude Stein, and allowed her to proceed into a room filled with maquis who were in conference with the mayor. "Are there any Americans here?" she shouted. Three men stood up. "They were Americans," Gertrude wrote, "God bless them and we were pleased." The three were Lieutenant Walter E. Olson, of the 120th Engineers, and Privates Edward Landry and Walter Hartze, of the Thunderbirds. After bussings and embraces, questions and answers and sighs of joy, Gertrude accepted their offer of a ride in a jeep.

Later, continuing her shopping rounds with Alice, she saw another American. "I'm Gertrude Stein," she announced. "Who are you?" He was Lieutenant Colonel William O. Perry, inspector general of the Forty-fifth, and they took him and his companion, Private John Schmaltz, back to the Dovecote to spend the night. Their servants wept to see the Americans, called them *nos Libérateurs,* and their cook who had refused to cook all through the war, preferring to let Alice deal with the shortage problem, showed her gratitude by preparing her first dinner in years. Gertrude and Alice talked with the visitors for hours, then Gertrude showed them to their beds. "You are going to sleep in beds where German officers slept six weeks ago, wonderful," she said, "my gracious perfectly wonderful."

Next morning, between the time that the Lieutenant Colonel and the Private had departed and luncheon, a chance meeting brought them still other Americans — war correspondents Eric Sevareid and Frank Gervasi. Severeid later reported in his book, *Not So Wild a Dream*, that he had been supplied with the Bilignin address from an American source' and, unaware that Gertrude and Alice had moved to Culoz, he and his companion had been searching the countryside for them when their car broke down. As they tried to get started again, along came Lieutenant Colonel Perry. "Good story down that way," he said to the stymied correspondents. Within a few minutes, they reached Culoz, where the assistant mayor sped them to Gertrude's door.

She and Alice were dining with friends from Belley when the maid rushed in crying, "The American Army, they are at the door!" Gertrude greeted them with shouts and bear hugs and set them down for lunch. Sevareid, who had known Gertrude years before, found her much the same, though heavier in her walk and slightly more bent. Alice, too, seemed a little more stooped, but was "still soft, small, and warmly murmurous," and, of course, as magnificent a cook as she had ever been. They spent hours in gossip of old acquaintances as, hungry for news, Gertrude inquired about one person after another. But the correspondents had other news to dispatch to America, and finally she had to let them go. "When she said goodbye to me in the command car," Sevareid reported, "and we had turned away, Private Bill, our hardheaded driver from Boston said: 'Who'n hell is that old battle-ax?' We said it was Gertrude Stein, and he replied: "That beats the —— out of me," which is G.I. for 'That's beyond me.' "

Two days later the correspondents drove them forty miles to Voiron where Gertrude made a broadcast to America. As Sevareid records the speech, it went like this:

What a day is today that is what a day it was day before yesterday, what a day! I can tell everybody that none of you know what this native land business is until you have been cut off from that same native land completely for years. This native land business gets you all right. Day before yesterday was a wonderful day. First we saw three Americans in a military car and we said are you Americans and they said yes and we choked and we talked, and they took us driving in their car, those long-awaited Americans, how long we have waited for them and there they were Lieutenant Olson and Privates Landry and Hartze and then we saw another car of them and these two came home with us, I had said can't you come home with us we have to have some Americans in our house and they said they guessed the war could get along without them for a few hours and they were Colonel Perry and Private Schmaltz and we talked and patted each other in that pleasant American way and everybody in the village cried out the Americans have come the Americans have come and indeed the Americans have come, they have come, they are here God bless them. Of course I asked each one of them what place they came from and the words New Hampshire and Chicago and Detroit and Denver and Delta Colorado were music in our ears. And then four newspaper men turned up, naturally you don't count newspaper men but how they and we talked we and they and they asked me to come to Voiron with them to broadcast and here I am.

. . . You know I thought I really knew France through and through but I did not realize what it could do and what it did in these glorious days. Yes I knew France in the last war in the days of their victories but in this war in the days of defeat they were much greater. I can never be thankful enough that I stayed with them all these dark days, when we had to walk miles to get a little extra butter a little extra flour when everybody somehow managed to free themselves, when the Maquis under the eyes of the Germans received transported and hid the arms dropped to them by parachutes, we always wanted some of the parachute cloth as a souvenir, one girl in the village made herself a blouse of it.

It was a wonderful time it was long and it was heart-breaking but every day made it longer and shorter and now thanks to the land of my birth and the land of my adoption we are free, long live France, long live America, long live the United Nations and above all long live' liberty, I can tell you that liberty is the most important thing in the world more important than food and clothes more important than anything on this mortal earth, I who spent four years with the French under the German yoke will tell you so.

I am so happy to be talking to America today so happy.

Ambitious to make the Dovecote the welcoming post for the whole American Army, Gertrude wrote to Lieutenant General A. M. Patch, Seventh Army Headquarters, inviting him to dinner. Happy developments prevented his acceptance. "I have regretted deeply," he wrote back, "that our rapid advance has prevented me from visiting the area of the Lac du Bourget and Aix les Bains of which I hold so many happy memories of a delightful, if short, vacation during the last war. The opportunity of meeting the lady whose literary works and humanitarian achievements I have long admired, together with the tempting offer of a chicken dinner, have convinced me that I cannot long postpone a trip to your delightful countryside. I shall make every effort, as soon as the military situation permits, to accept and thank you in person for your thoughtful invitation." General Patch never came to the Dovecote but, to thank him for his courteous reply, Alice singled him out as the recipient of her "Liberation Fruit Cake" weighing twelve pounds.

It was "pretty wonderful and pretty awful to have been intimate and friendly and proud of two American armies in France apart only by twenty-seven years," Gertrude felt. Her fascination with the new soldiers as compared with the old eventually led her to writing a whole book of new-soldier dialogues, *Brewsie and Willie*. "Write about us they all said a little sadly, and write about them I will," she promised in the concluding pages of her journal. "They all said good-bye Gerty as the train pulled out and then they said, well we will see you in America. . . ."

The main thing about the new army, she felt, was the fact that "it talked, it listened," whereas "the older Americans always told stories that was about all there was to their talking but these don't tell stories they converse and what they say is interesting and what they hear interests them and that does make them different not really different God bless them but just the same they are not quite the same."

She could never get enough of American faces and soon began to watch for the arrival of every troop train. The G.I.'s knew her as soon as she came in sight, and extended envelopes and note-pads and franc notes for her autograph. "I came away meditating yes they were American boys but they had a poise and completely lacked the provincialism which did characterize the last American army, they talked and they listened and they had a sureness, they were quite certain of themselves, they had no doubts and uncertainties and they had not to make any explanations . . . the G.I. Joes have this language that is theirs, they do not have to worry about it, they dominate their language and in dominating their language which is now all theirs they have ceased to be adolescents and have become men."

CHAPTER 25

Come one and come one at a time but really
I expect and I receive a great many.
Thank you for hurrying through.
— GERTRUDE STEIN

"SO busy just being excited and being liber-
ated that we did not think of Paris," Gertrude and Alice remained
where they were through the autumn months. Reports from the city
had warned them that they would find neither light, food nor gas;
and they dreaded to have to see for themselves what might have
happened to their apartment and their masterpieces during the occupation. Gertrude had been so fearful and superstitious all through
the war years that she had allowed no one even to mention the apartment or anything in it. It was less painful to pretend that it did not
exist.

In mid-November of 1944, they learned with enormous relief that
all was well, in a letter they received from their neighbor Katherine
Dudley, who had already set the Russian exile Svidko, who used to be
their cleaning man, to work in preparation for their expected return. "Ferren came to see me yesterday with news of you," Miss Dudley wrote. "He thinks perhaps you may not return to Paris immedi-

ately. So I have told Svidko to finish cleaning the kitchen and your bedroom & bath and to verify the gas & test the radiators and to await your word before continuing the cleaning. . . . I went with him the first day and saw the condition things were in. Fortunately as far as I could see all the pictures on the walls were unhurt though several of the small Picasso heads had been thrown on the floor. We put them back in their places & none are harmed. . . . But it's a miracle that your collection is still there for about 2 weeks before the Boches left 4 men of the Gestapo came, demanded the key of the concierge who protested in vain that you were Americans. The young girl who is secretary in the Bureau Weil heard steps overhead, rushed up, banged on the door until they opened it, pushed in past them and asked by what right they were there — that the proprietor was American, that she had charge of the house. They tried to put her out but she stayed. They were lashing themselves into a fury over the Picassos saying they would cut them to pieces and burn them. *'De la saloperie juive, bon à brûler.'* The big pink nude *'cette vache.'* They recognized your Rose portrait — they had a photo of you with them — and the other Rose heads in the long gallery. *'Tous les juifs et bon à brûler.'* The girl rushed downstairs to her office, telephoned the police and in 10 minutes there was the Commissaire & 30 agents before the door much to the excitement of the street. By this time they — the G.'s — were trying on your Chinese coats in your bedroom. The Commissaire asked them for their order of perquisition which they had neglected to bring with them and they had to go but taking the key with them. So she waited before the door until a menuisier could be found to change the lock. They opened the coffer with the rugs & tore the papers but Svidko doesn't remember how many packages he did up in '39. Also they opened one or two other boxes of ornaments. But I doubt if much is missing. . . ."

By mid-December, Gertrude and Alice had decided to return. For the journey to Paris, they hired a wood-burning taxi (Gertrude had sold her car to a friend in the Red Cross at Lyon) and a *camion* to follow with their household goods. Taking with them a Savoyarde servant girl, they started at midnight on a cold journey made hazardous by recent floods that forced them off the main roads. The ersatz tires of the taxi blew out one after another, time and again they started up icy hill roads only to have to back down and begin over. Throughout the journey, Gertrude cheered herself up with American K-rations — crackers, sugar, candy, and a touch of lemon — which she found "very comforting." On the second night they were stopped by three unarmed F.F.I. men and an armed woman. Their papers were examined and found to be satisfactory. Then one of the men asked what was in the bundle they were transporting. "Oh those," said Gertrude, "are meat and butter and eggs. Now don't touch them they are all carefully packed, and enough to keep us a week in Paris."

"Ah yes," said the F.F.I. man. "And this big thing?"

"That," said Alice, "is a Picasso painting, don't touch it."

"I congratulate you," said the man, and waved them on.

The official stamp of the Gestapo was on the door of V Rue Christine, but their chill at sight of this was momentary. Within minutes of their arrival neighbors came pouring in — the concierge, the landlord's secretary, the bookbinder from the courtyard, even the husband of the laundress downstairs. Contrary to Katherine Dudley's belief, the apartment had earlier been looted of linen, dresses, shoes, kitchen utensils, dishes, bedcovers and pillows. But in general its appearance was quite as they had remembered it five years before. Two groups of marauders had visited the flat. The first, who had taken only household and personal effects, were apparently unaware of the value of the paintings.

Picasso came to see them the very next morning. They embraced one another as survivors of still another war, marveling that they could meet once again in the presence of "all the treasures which had made our youth," as Gertrude put it, "the pictures, the drawings, the objects. . . ."

Resettled, Gertrude began to take long daily walks with Basket II. Rediscovering her own Paris bit by bit, she found it miraculously the same. "I began to think the whole thing was a nightmare," she wrote, "it wasn't true, we had just been away for a summer vacation and we had come back. Every little shop was there with its same proprietor, the shops that had been dirty were still dirty, the shops

387

that had been clean before the war were still clean, all the little an-tiquity shops were still there, each with the same kind of things in it that there used to be, because each little antiquity shop runs to its own kind of antiquities. It was a miracle, it was a miracle."

Old friends — many of whom, all through the war, had sent letters that never reached Bilignin or Culoz — were at last heard from, and some of them turned up in Paris on governmental or other assign-ments. Guthrie McClintic and his wife Katharine Cornell, touring for the USO with *The Barretts of Wimpole Street*, came to lunch; Francis Rose came to Paris to be on hand for an exhibition of his paintings; Carl Van Vechten wrote about the deaths of Alexander Woollcott and Florine Stettheimer, and said he was sending "the whole American Army as far as I know it STRAIGHT to 5 Rue Christine!" Cecil Beaton was back from the Far East; Bravig Imbs, after wartime service in radio work for the Office of War Informa-tion, was back in France; Bennett Cerf reported a fine critical press and good sales for *Wars I Have Seen*.

The old sense of Paris had at last returned, the old sense of daily adventure and the imminence of new friends. Gertrude discovered an unknown painter, Riba-Rovera, and wrote an introduction to the catalogue of his first exhibition:

It is inevitable that when one has great need of something one finds it. What you need you attract like a lover.

I returned to Paris, after these long years passed in a little countryside and I needed a young painter who would awake me . . . I walked a great deal, I looked around, in all the painting shops, but the young painter was not there. Yes, I walked a great deal, a great deal along the Seine where they fish, where they paint, where they walk the dogs (I am one of those who walk their dogs). No young painter.

One day, at a turning in the street in one of those little streets of my neighborhood, I saw a man making a picture. I looked at him and his picture, as I always look at everyone who does something — I have an insatiable curiosity to look — and I was moved. Yes, a young painter!

We began to talk for one talks easily, as easily as in the country byways, in the little streets of the neighborhood.

His history was the sad history of the young of our time. A young Spaniard who studied at the Beaux-Arts at Barcelona; the civil war, exile, concentration camp, escape, Gestapo, prison again, escape again . . .

Eight lost years. Were they lost, who knows? And now a little hardship, but even so painting.

Why did I find that he was he the young painter, why? I went to see his sketches, his paintings; we talked.

I explained that for me, all modern painting is based on that which Cézanne failed to do instead of being based on that which he almost succeeded in doing. . . .

And now, I found a young painter who was not following the tendency to play with that which Cézanne was not able to do, but who attacked directly the things which he had tried to do, to create objects which must exist, for, and in themselves, and not in relation to anything else. . . .

The continuity of many things seemed almost unbroken. When young Pierre Balmain, with whom she had become friendly in war days, came to Paris to establish himself as "The young designer of Liberated France," Gertrude took influential friends to his showings and wrote an article about them for *Vogue*. Yet, as she had often said, "Everything is the same and everything is different." Bernard Faÿ, who had been appointed Director of the Bibliothèque Nationale under Vichy, had recently been sentenced to prison and *indignité nationale* after his trial on charges of collaboration. Gertrude felt he was a victim of grievous injustice, that his criminal conviction did not take into account his patriotism or the complications of living in an occupied country. For the candy and messages and vitamin pills she and Alice sent to him in jail, he wrote grateful notes.

V Rue Christine, like 27 Rue de Fleurus of another age, another section of the *arrondissement*, was about to become a shrine toward which would come the first pilgrims of the postwar era. This time, the visitors were not the great and famous or the *jeunesse dorée*, but earnest young American soldiers, lettered and unlettered; and they came endlessly and at all hours. But before they came in droves, they came alone and by invitation as acquaintances Gertrude had picked up in the streets. "And then there are the soldiers," she wrote in her first impressions of Paris regained, "who wander eternally, wander about the streets, they do funny things. The other day I was watching one look at the reflection of the Louvre in a glass shop window. He said he seemed to get it better that way. I talk to them all, they seem to like it, and I certainly do. At first I hesitated a bit, it's all right, everybody seems to have plenty of time, of course, when you have to walk so much you must have plenty of time."

Barely fifteen years before, Gertrude Stein was a self-published author of obscure books who walked miles to catch a glimpse of some title of hers luckily placed in some bookstore window. She was now greeted by "Hi' ya, Gert," or "There goes Gerty Stein!" It had always been the easiest thing in the world for her to strike up random acquaintances, and now as she went about on errands or walked her dog, always she was followed by an entourage that was apt to increase in number as it progressed. Once more, it seemed, she could in her own special way appropriate a segment of a generation of the young. Her personal magnetism was unquestioned, but the nature of her response to her new heroes was something for conjecture. As the American critic Robert Warshow wrote of her relation to American soldiers, "she endowed them with her own innocence . . . and in giving her innocence to the soldiers, whom she had made quite responsible and *public* . . . she fell in love, and she allowed herself to be taken in by the myth of a special American decency and good-heartedness."

Her favorite walk was along the promenade of the Seine embankment. With Basket II's leash being handed from one G.I. to another, Gertrude would lead her disciples down the steps to the water's edge, discoursing as she went. "And so she led them," wrote her friend Natalie Barney, "as a sort of *vivandière de l'esprit,* from war into peace, and to realize their own, instead of their collective, existence." She may never have been quite the Rhine-maiden of the G.I.'s, but no one could doubt that her personal magic had survived a war and become the delight of still another generation of the young. The siren in brown cotton stockings and a flower-embroidered waistcoat, her Lorelei's voice was even more gently mellowed, yet strong and comforting. She had become one of the things to "do," in Paris, like the Place Pigalle or the *Folies Bergères,* and many a soldier and sailor came long distances by train or jeep to spend a good part of his brief furlough time in her company.

She accepted invitations to Army mess, spoke to a school of G.I.'s at the Cité Universitaire, and lectured for gatherings organized by the Red Cross, "telling them how to smile at the French and fight the depression." She was such a hit with the soldiers that on one occasion at least, they walked her home fifty strong, forcing automobiles into side streets and causing the puzzled gendarmerie to investigate the nature of the procession of which she was the Pied Piper. In bull-sessions that took place after some of these events, as well as in her own home, she listened to the rhythms of American speech that gave impetus to her last book, *Brewsie and Willie*. This was not only her last but probably her least, in spite of the pleasure she took in writing it. When the manuscript was finished, she wrote to W. G. Rogers: "Alas the U.S. Army is dwindling and dwindling and what there is left has not really the authentic G.I. flavor, but I do think that I did get into Brewsie and Willie . . . that authentic flavor, I think in a kind of way it is one of the best things I have ever done. You know how much I have always meditated about narration, how to tell what one has to tell, well this time I have written it, narration as the 20th century sees it."

She did not, as she had hoped, capture the rhythms of G.I. speech, and the subjects her soldiers discuss in arcs and circles of endlessly tentative beginnings and re-beginnings are not only commonplace but beside the mark of any but the most marginal of G.I. interests. She herself figures in the book as a kind of *rentier* mama who knows best. In the epilogue, assuming her own voice, she mounts a platform. In this position, Gertrude Stein as a political prophet could only disappoint those who remembered her on the platform as a writer whose superb and ingratiating intelligence commanded the respect of everyone within earshot. This, many of her admirers were sad to say, was her final word to Americans in general:

G.I.s and G.I.s and G.I.s and they have made me come all over patriotic. I was always patriotic, I was always in my way a Civil War veteran, but in between, there were other things, but now there are no other things. And I am sure that this particular moment in our history is more important than anything since the Civil War. We are there where we have to have to fight a spiritual pioneer fight or we will go poor as England and other industrial countries have gone poor, and dont think that communism or socialism will save you, you just have to find a new way, you have to find out how you can go ahead without running away with yourselves, you have to learn to produce without exhausting your country's wealth, you have to learn to be individual and not just mass job workers, you have to get courage enough to know what you feel and not just be all yes or no men, but you have to really learn to express complication, go easy and if you can't go easy go as easy as you can. Remember the depression, dont be afraid to look it in the face and find out the reason why, dont be afraid of the reason why, if you dont find out the reason why you'll go poor and my God how I would hate to have my native land go poor. Find out the reason why, look facts in the face, not just what they all say, the leaders, but every darn one of you so that a government by the people for the people shall not perish from the face of the earth, it wont, somebody else will do it if we lie down on the job, but of all things dont stop, find out the reason why of the depression, find it out each and every one of you and then look the facts in the face. We are Americans.

When the United States Army asked her to make an official tour of bases in occupied Germany, she and Alice set out, in June, 1945, on a whirlwind five-day junket by air. Traveling "like an Oriental pasha and his tail," accompanied by three lieutenants and nine enlisted men for whom billets and mess and transport had to be quickly arranged everywhere, she was flown in an army plane first to Frankfurt. They were wandering through a bombed area there when Gertrude noticed that the German townspeople were all staring at her and Alice: ". . . some went quite pale and others looked furious," she reported in an article published in *Life*; and she realized that she and Alice were the first foreign civilian women the Germans had seen in years. Having earlier observed this same reaction to strangers in France, she concluded: "Civilians are more permanent and appalling than any army. . . ."

She talked openly and vehemently wherever she went in Germany, delighted for the chance to air old convictions. When the question of what was to be done with the Germans in the future came up, she had a ready answer: ". . . teach them disobedience . . . Make every German child know that it is its duty at least once every day to do its good deed and not believe something its father or its teacher tells them, confuse their minds . . . and perhaps they will be disobedient and the world will be at peace."

They went on to Cologne, Coblenz, Salzburg. At Berchtesgaden they saw Hermann Goering's collection of art works which, Gertrude observed, gave evidence of having been chosen under professional guidance but which showed no sign of personal taste. Their visit to Hitler's home was a lark: ". . . there we were in that big window where Hitler dominated the world a bunch of GI's just gay and happy. It really was the first time I saw our boys really gay and careless, really forgetting their burdens and just being foolish kids, climbing up and around and on top, while Miss Toklas and I sat comfortably and at home on garden chairs on Hitler's balcony."

In a speech she delivered in Heidelberg, she was shaken first by her own eloquence and soon afterwards by official reactions to what she said. "Sergeant Santiani who had asked me to come complained that I confused the minds of his men," she wrote, "but why shouldn't their minds be confused, gracious goodness, are we going to be like the Germans, only believe in the Aryans that is our own race, a mixed race if you like but all having the same point of view. I got very angry with them, they admitted they liked the Germans better than the other Europeans. Of course you do, I said, they flatter you and they obey you, when the other countries don't like you and say so, and personally you have not been awfully ready to meet them halfway, well naturally if they don't like you they show it, the Germans don't like you but they flatter you, doggone it, I said I bet you Fourth of July they will all be putting up our flag, and all you big babies will just be flattered to death, literally to death, I said bitterly because you will have to fight again. Well said one of them after all we are on top. Yes I said and is there any spot on earth more dangerous than on top. You don't like the Latins, or the Arabs or the Wops, or the British, well don't you forget a country can't live without friends, I want you all to get to know other countries so that you can be friends, make a little effort, try to find out what it is all about. We all got very excited, they passed me cognac, but I don't drink so they found me some grapefruit juice, and they patted me and sat me down, and there it all was."

Close association with soldiers in these travels pleased her, yet she was not always pleased with what she observed. "You know," she told a reporter, "these G.I.'s kept pinup girls all over. The walls of their barracks — like religious icons. They idealized women, but, when they walked the streets of Paris, many of them would be drunk and would leer at and insult almost every woman they met. American boys are virginal, for only virgins would act that way. They liked the German women. When they made love to the German women, the German women did all the work, like the cows they did all the work."

She and Alice were glad to come back to the city for the summer. They felt they had had enough of country life for a while and in the continuing excitement of their return were pleased with Paris and with "lots of it." Gertrude's life continued to be centered largely in entertaining her soldier acquaintances simply because the new generation of American painters and writers, as a consequence of postwar restrictions, was beyond her pale. Few civilians could get to Paris in the years immediately after the war, and only a very few tried to break the barriers of red tape and priority. An American writer who did get through was Richard Wright, an old devotee of her work, who came to the Rue Christine with expectations as buoyant as any that had, a generation before, carried Hemingway and Fitzgerald, Hart Crane and Paul Bowles to the threshold of "27," and he was not disappointed. His initial embrace of Paris was so wholehearted and enthusiastic that Gertrude, wise with the experience of four decades of Parisian life, felt she should try to curb his excitement. In spite of his first impressions, she warned him, he would as a Negro find prejudice. "But," she added, "you won't find a problem." A good friend of Gertrude's during her remaining lifetime, Wright settled permanently in Paris with his family two years after her death.

But outside of such exceptions as Richard Wright, the war had ended a procession of artists which, earlier, the depression had reduced to a trickle. "The tables, literally the tables, have turned," wrote art critic Alfred M. Frankfurter. "Where Iowa poets and Boston painters used to be served on the terrace of the Dome and occasionally inside Foyot's, nowadays the French intelligentsia along with the French *émigration dorée* is likely to be drinking post-prandial *fines* at the little places in the East Fifties. No matter how strong the youthful urge to protest the banality of Gopher Prairie or the advertising business, it is going to be hard if not impossible for a new generation to do it from a studio on the Left Bank or a beach at Palma de Mallorca. . . . The best that post-war Europe can offer an American hungry for an unmixed diet of aesthetic pleasure is a meagre bunch of the decade-before-yesterday's hyacinths for his soul."

Nevertheless, some of the old Paris hands were returning, and among them was Caresse Crosby who, with her husband Harry, had published avant-garde writings under the imprint of their Black Sun Press. "I was one of the first Americans to return," wrote Caresse Crosby in *The Passionate Years*. "I did not bring coffee and rice to my friends but I had brought them drawings by the American artists Pietro Lazzari and Romare Bearden, and I arranged to show these at John Devolny's minute gallery in the rue Furstemberg. I had invited friends and artists by telephone; Paris was starving for contact with the American world of art and everyone flocked. Gertrude Stein came stalking in with her white poodle at her heels. She sat in the center of the tiny room and almost stole the show, my show, but even when she walked off with the best-looking G.I. in the place, I forgave her."

Life was never busier for Gertrude than it was during the first year of her return to Paris. Working toward completion of *Brewsie and Willie*, beginning the script of a new opera for Virgil Thomson, *The Mother of Us All*, continually occupied with arrangements for her books and the entertainment of the American army, she was all but overwhelmed. "Dear me," she wrote to a friend, "we who used to think we were rushed when we had two engagements a week, now the door bell just rings and the telephone just rings, and I have to answer that I don't make appointments more than 2 days ahead.

"I've never seen anything like it, I said to Alice, we can't sell any more books because we have no more to sell, sold 4 to Italy the other day, editions in Sweden, Geneva, and now Darantière wants to do my other child's book To Do, the First Reader is sold to England, to think how hard it used to be to get anybody to do anything, anyway it's nice to be glorious and productive in your old age."

The nature of Gertrude's *salon* had changed, and her old genius as a hostess now seemed less important than her simple patience and power to endure. She would receive the first unannounced visit of any G.I. warmly — she seemed, as one of them said and many of them probably felt, "like everybody's grandmother." Yet, except in rare cases, she managed to let the first-time visitor know that he was not invited to a second meeting. This was a necessary limitation if she were not to be continually overwhelmed by callers, and its application was seldom interpreted as rudeness. She was never rude, even on the many occasions when she had to put up with the banalities and suffer the unrelieved boredom she must have felt with some of the curiosity-seeking soldiers who came for the show. One of her defenses was her artistry in maintaining a monologue, and the talk at her evening gatherings was seldom conversation. She would silence any attempt at abstract talk or theorizing, and tended to draw from her visitors facets and simple reactions upon which she might theorize. Hundreds of young men were asked, "What does your father do?" and thus led quickly into the stories of their lives. Alice, who had become somewhat hard of hearing, often broke into these interviews with irrelevancies that showed she had not been following the train of thought. This sometimes annoyed Gertrude, but she was always noticeably deferential to Alice, inviting her participation and worrying over her comfort. When she wanted corroboration on some matter or other, she would turn to Alice. "Don't you think so, Pussy?" she would ask, and Alice would nod.

Thousands of soldiers stationed in Paris had never heard of Gertrude Stein and never would hear of her, in spite of the well-publicized postwar legend that she stood in their midst like a surrogate Statue of Liberty. But among the great numbers of G.I.'s who were taking courses at the Sorbonne awaiting accumulation of points necessary for discharge, she was a famous and respected figure. Thousands of them had heard her lecture in America, and many had chatted for a few moments with her during the American tour. Some of them brought manuscripts to the Rue Christine and she read

396

hese with great patience and repeated to hopeful young writers advice she had given to the writers of a generation old enough now to be their fathers. "Either the phrase must come or it must not be written at all," she told them. "I have never understood how people could labor over a manuscript, write and re-write it many times, for to me, if you have something to say, the words are always there. And they are the exact words and the words that should be used. If the story does not come whole, *tant pis*, it has been spoiled, and that is the most difficult thing in writing, to be true enough to yourself, and to know yourself enough so that there is no obstacle to the story's coming through complete. You see how you have faltered, and halted, and fallen down in your story, all because you have not solved this problem of communication for yourself. It is the fundamental problem in writing and has nothing to do with metier, or with sentence building or with rhythm. In my own writing, as you know, I have destroyed sentences and rhythm and literary overtones and all the rest of that nonsense, to get to the very core of this problem of the communication of the intuition. If the communication is perfect, the words have life, and that is all there is to good writing, putting down on paper words which dance and weep and make love and fight and kiss and perform miracles."

Such advice had proved salutary to many writers who listened to her, and now, in 1946, she had further pronouncements. If these contradicted her earlier concern for sound patterns, especially in her own large collection of word-portraits, she seemed unaware of the fact and spoke with her unflagging sense of authority. "A writer does not write with his ears or his mouth, he writes with his eyes," she said. "It is his eyes that make his writing, sound is not of any interest to him, ears and mouth useless from the standpoint of writing, all he needs are his eyes and his hand, that is all, he can hear and talk all he wants but he writes with his eyes and his hand."

Her method for arriving at some point of judgment any young writer might carry away was unusual but highly practical. She would "make a book," as she put it, of selections from the manuscript she felt particularly worthy. It was a relative method of criticism, but according to George W. John of Milwaukee, who was twenty-two

397

when he became one of Gertrude's last "discoveries," its advantages were clear. Before John left Paris, she gave him the following message to be used as an introduction or blurb for the book she felt he was sure to produce: "A great many soldiers came and one day unexpectedly a poet. He had come and left many little pieces of paper and on each piece of paper was a poem. He like all the soldiers had been in many places, Italy France Belgium Holland Germany England and then later India, as he was a field service man, and everywhere there were landscapes and all the landscapes were poems. He was the only one to whom that happened and he was a poet. I was excited and thought I would never see him again and only have the little pieces of paper with the poems on them and the name George John. At the end of a long week he came again, tall gentle thin and young, and then I told him he was a poet but he knew that and I knew it, and now I am telling it here where the poems are printed. George John." When the poet's first book, A *Garland About Me,* appeared in 1951, it bore the dedication: "In memory of Gertrude Stein: my friend too briefly but my teacher forever."

In December, 1945, Gertrude went by automobile to Brussels to speak to soldiers stationed there and to give a second lecture before the members of the *Cercle Artistique Belge.* During the course of this visit she complained of intestinal trouble which, eight months later, was to be diagnosed as cancer. This was not the first occasion for complaint, but earlier manifestations of distress had been relieved for a time and she persisted in her natural distaste for doctors and medicine. She had never been ill in all her life and, when she had first felt abdominal pains, had gone only so far as to consult a country doctor in Culoz. The best advice this man could give her was to wear her corset differently. Gertrude was impressed, followed his advice and claimed that her pains were less frequently recurrent. But her illness was deep-rooted by this time and, whether or not she cared to recognize the source of her days of profound weariness, she must have been aware that the homely advice in which she most wanted to believe was not enough to return her to health.

She finished the script of *The Mother of Us All* in March, 1946, and sent it to Van Vechten, asking him to read it and turn it over to

Virgil Thomson. The opera had been commissioned by the Alice M. Ditson Fund of Columbia University, and as soon as the libretto was in hand, Thomson wrote her of ideas for the production that was eventually scheduled to be given in Brander Matthews Hall on the University campus early in 1947. ". . . certainly Susan B. comes out a noble one," Thomson wrote. "She is practically St. Paul when she says 'let them marry.' And the whole thing will be easier to dramatize than 4 Saints was, much easier, though the number of characters who talk to the audience about themselves, instead of addressing the other characters, is a little terrifying. Mostly it is very dramatic and very beautiful and very clear and constantly quotable and I think we shall have very little scenery but very fine clothes and they do all the time strike 19th century attitudes. Agnes DeMille will be useful for that; she is after all a granddaughter of Henry George."

Gertrude would not live to see *The Mother of Us All* in performance, or to hear so much as a note of the music which Thomson described as "an evocation of nineteenth century America, with its gospel hymns and cocky marches, its sentimental ballads, waltzes, darn-fool ditties and intoned sermons." But at the very end of her life she had written one of her most powerful and beautiful works. Her libretto, which she composed after long and careful rereading of dozens of works of the period in the American Library in Paris, is a kind of "memory book" of the United States in the lifetime of Susan B. Anthony, a woman whose struggles to gain the vote for women, like Gertrude's own struggle, occupied all of her many years. Like Gertrude, Susan B. Anthony was attended always by a faithful companion; and like Gertrude she suspected and dearly believed that the meaning of her life's work would show most clearly when she could speak from beyond the grave.

In the series of intimate period-piece tableaux that comprise the whole dramatic substance of the opera, Susan B. and her compatriots, along with a wildly various complement of other characters, who exist only for their charm or their dilemmas or their gifts as chirping commentators — Indiana Elliott, Jo the Loiterer, Daniel Webster and Lillian Russell — reiterate their great and small meanings. The opera has no narrative line, yet it is richly alive at every moment, "every moment of the telling," as Gertrude might say. Essentially, it is a discussion in song that finally forms a single lyric in depth, as self-contained as a motto worked in colored wool and framed in mahogany. Gertrude Stein had come out of the depths of the nineteenth century and her last and most eloquent utterance glowed with her pleasure, and even love, for all that she had spent a lifetime escaping.

As she would never see *The Mother of Us All*, neither would she live to see a performance of another of her last works, *Yes Is for a Very Young Man*. But in the case of this work she had at least the satisfaction of knowing that, without benefit of music or dance, one of her plays had reached the public. On March 13, 1946, through the efforts of a young actor, Lamont Johnson, who had come to know Gertrude when he was touring with *Kind Lady* for the USO, *Yes* was performed in California at the Pasadena Playhouse — the first of scores of American productions that would follow. The history of *Yes* had been beset with troubles, in spite of warm support Gertrude had from influential friends who believed in the play and wanted to see it performed. Katharine Cornell and Guthrie McClintic had taken a copy of the script back to New York with them to see what might be done in a commercial way; and the actor Richard Whorf had actually gone ahead with plans for a production at the American Army University at Biarritz. But when details of this production became clear to Gertrude, she canceled the whole project. "It was Gertrude's objection to a workshop production," Alice later wrote to Carl Van Vechten, ". . . that is a production without scenery and to a specially invited audience — that caused her to ask for an immediate return of her manuscript from Biarritz. We did have such a time when Biarritz proposed this — precious Baby blew a fuse — we stayed up till the next morning getting the people at Biarritz on the phone. She wished her play to be produced in an ordinary way, simply, realistically, before ordinary theatre-goers. She considered it a play like any other — except perhaps for its quality — that the characters were portraits of ordinary people, that there was nothing mystical or symbolical about them or their actions."

Ordinary or not, *Yes* is a play of types rather than of individually defined characters, and was the fruit of Gertrude's attempt to recapture in the setting of occupied France the spirit of the Civil War as she remembered it from stories her mother told her as a child, and from the melodramas she had seen in San Francisco. "I loved these stories," she wrote in a program note, "and then when I was in France during the occupation, knowing intimately all the people around me, I was struck with the resemblance to the stories my mother used to tell me, the divided families, the bitterness, the quarrels and sometimes the denunciations, and yet the natural necessity of their all continuing to live their daily life together, because after all that was all the life they had, besides they were after all the same family or their neighbors, and in the country neighbors are neighbors."

As she had done nearly forty years before in *The Making of Americans*, she had put types of people in relation to one another as they undergo the common stresses of life. Her main character, the American — Constance — was modeled on Clare Boothe Luce but, as usual, Gertrude is herself very clearly the dog beneath the skin. What "happens" in the play is, again, not centered in action, but in the slow spiraling of many suggestions, portents, revelations and general comments. The final effect is less the reality of a situation explored and resolved than the reality of a climate of fear and dissension articulated.

Until her very last days, articles about Gertrude Stein, and a number written by her, appeared frequently in American magazines and she was a constant target for interviewers representing periodicals of mass circulation as well as those whose mailing lists were but a few hundred names. When the editors of the *Yale Poetry Journal* approached her for a statement, she took seriously her chance to pronounce on world events, and answered them in words perhaps too naïvely self-concerned to carry much weight. "They asked me what I thought of the atomic bomb," she wrote in a piece entitled *Reflections on the Atomic Bomb*. "I said I had not been able to take any interest in it. I like to read detective and mystery stories, I never get enough of them, but whenever one of them is or was about death rays and atomic bombs I never could read them. . . . And really way down that is the way everybody feels about it. They think they are interested about the atomic bomb, but they really are not any more than I am. Really not. They may be a little scared, I am not so scared, there is so much to be scared of, so what is the use of bothering to be scared, and if you are not scared, the atomic bomb is not interesting. Everybody gets so much information all day long that they lose their common sense. They listen so much that they forget to be natural. This is a nice story."

The pleasures of being constantly attended by the young were real, but Gertrude eventually came to feel that adulation was more of a burden than a comfort. She decided to refuse invitations to speak at the Red Cross center in Paris, and began to cool in her enthusiasm for receiving any young man in uniform who rang her doorbell. Her sessions with the soldiers had come to seem all alike and to weary her out of all proportion to the enjoyment she took from them. There had also been incidents of rudeness she could not tolerate. On one occasion, as a group of English field service men were leaving the apartment, one of them handed her a packet of poems saying he would be happy to have her opinion of their merit. Gertrude agreed to read them, and invited the young man to come back for her report within a few days. When she got around to reading the poems, she found among them a carefully hand-written copy of a poem by John Donne. Members of the field service were suddenly no longer welcome at the Rue Christine.

But her unshakable weariness was caused by more than the constant drain on her attention. The digestive disorder she had complained about in Brussels had returned in the early spring, but by April she felt her health was improving. "I was a little under the weather," she wrote to a friend, "I had some infection of the lower bowel and I was kind of low in my mind, but now it seems definitely on the mend, not entirely well yet but so much better. . . ." Still, she wanted to leave Paris for a rest and, with this in mind, bought a new Simca. Bernard Faÿ loaned her and Alice his house in the country 200 kilometers from Paris and, in mid-July, they set off for what they hoped would be many days of respite. But they had gone only part way toward their destination when Gertrude was taken violently ill and had to be rushed back to Paris. She was received into the American Hospital at Neuilly-sur-Seine on July 19, 1946, and kept under observation for several days. Alice stayed by her side and even succeeded in cheering her by delivering to her copies of *Brewsie and Willie* on July 22, the day on which the book was published in New York.

She made her will on July 23, leaving her manuscripts and correspondence of literary value to Yale, and the bulk of her estate to Alice with the understanding that on Alice's death it would go to Allan Daniel Stein, the son of Michael and Sarah. Besides her paintings and personal property, she held $20,000 in securities and had $6,650 in cash on deposit with the Mercantile Trust Company. Alice Toklas and Allan Stein were nominated as executors of her estate to serve without pay, and in further relation to Alice the will was specific: "In so far as it may become necessary for her proper maintenance and support, I authorize my Executors to make payments to her from the principal of my Estate, and, for that purpose, to reduce to cash any paintings or other personal property belonging to my Estate." The executors were also requested to pay to Carl Van Vechten "such amounts as he deems necessary for publication of my unpublished manuscripts." It was her wish that her will be probated in the state of Maryland; and the administrator was the Baltimore attorney Edgar Allan Poe.

When her physicians found that she was suffering from an abdominal tumor in an advanced state of malignancy as well as from calcification of the uterus, they decided, with little hope of success, upon an operation. This they proceeded to do on Saturday, July 27, and there was nothing to indicate that Gertrude herself knew that the operation was undertaken with only scant hope that she would survive it. When she had come out of the anesthetic her mind was clear enough to formulate for the last time the simple yet inexhaustible problem to which she had addressed the energies of a lifetime of scientific curiosity and aesthetic adventure. "What is the answer?" she asked. There had never been a reply to satisfy her, and finally and again there was none. "In that case," she said, "what is the question?" She had hardly spoken these last words when, late in the afternoon, a cardiac stroke resulted in a coma. Doctors worked for an hour to revive her, but her death at 6:30 ended their efforts. At her bedside were Alice and her niece and nephew, Mr. and Mrs. Dan Raffel.

Her body lay for a brief time in a vault at the American Cathedral and she was buried in the cemetery of Père-Lachaise, only a few yards from the graves of Henri Barbusse and hundreds of Frenchmen killed in the struggle to liberate Paris. Located in the newest section of the ancient burial ground, her grave is marked by a border and a headstone designed by Francis Rose. The legend on one side of the marker reads: GERTRUDE STEIN, SAN FRANCISCO; on the other side is carved, simply, ALICE B. TOKLAS   . The stone is massive and rectangular; the border encloses fresh grass.

"Hearing that Gertrude Stein is dead is like learning that Paul Bunyan has been eaten by his ox Babe," said an editorial in *The Nation*. "Certainly she is not really dead: legends never die, and Miss Stein has made herself into an American legend more lasting than Barnum himself ever created. She sat in Paris as the Pythoness used to sit at Delphi: everybody in the world, from Picasso to a sergeant of the marines, came asking for a sign, and went away happy with some oracular utterance which he could finger as if it were a Chinese puzzle. . . . The world will be a duller place without her; her sins harmed no one; at this moment she is sitting in the Elysian fields talking to Samuel Johnson, the only man who could ever be her match."

But Gertrude had already written her own epitaph. In the concluding scene of *The Mother of Us All* the voice of Susan B. Anthony is overwhelmed by the elegiac rhythms of her own:

We cannot retrace our steps, going forward may be the same as going backwards. We cannot retrace our steps, retrace our steps. All my long life, all my life, we do not retrace our steps, all my long life, but.
(A silence a long silence)
But — we do not retrace our steps, all my long life, and here, here we are here, in marble and gold, did I say gold, yes I said gold, in marble and gold and where —
(A silence)
Where is where. In my long life of effort and strife, dear life, life is strife,

404

in my long life, it will not come and go, I tell you so, it will stay it will pay but

(A long silence)

But do I want what we have got, has it not gone, what made it live, has it not gone because now it is had, in my long life in my long life

(Silence)

Life is strife, I was a martyr all my life not to what I won but to what was done.

(Silence)

Do you know because I tell you so, or do you know, do you know.

(Silence)

My long life, my long life.

Curtain

Epilogue

SINCE I have always responded to the work of Gertrude Stein with instinctive pleasure and without any distracting urge to "understand," this book about her was conceived less by design than promoted by circumstance. In July, 1946, I was living at Yaddo, in Saratoga Springs, and was delighted one afternoon to find in a combined book-and-stationery shop a copy of Gertrude Stein's *Geography and Plays*. Dusty yet otherwise pristine, the book had apparently never been lifted from the shelf where it had stood for nearly twenty-five years. The price of $3.50 stamped on the jacket was, I learned, still in effect. In some amazement at my good luck, I bought the book and returned to Yaddo savoring with enormous pleasure a new aspect of an author who had puzzled and beguiled me ever since, at the age of fifteen, I had first encountered her. That same evening I picked up a newspaper and learned that Gertrude Stein was dead.

Shocked by news that had the particular poignancy of coming just as I was delightedly and newly "discovering" the rhythms of a voice that was now silent, I spent the evening writing a poem that might relieve me of feelings that seemed otherwise inexpressible. The poem was published in *Harper's* some months later, and shortly afterwards I found in my mailbox a letter from Alice B. Toklas. She said that the little elegy had touched her deeply, that she found in it a "tender understanding," and that ever since a friend had sent the poem to her she had been drawn at intervals during each day to reread it. We began to correspond and, soon afterwards, Miss Toklas made me a gift of a carving — small enough to fit into the palm of the hand — of a horse on whose back an octopus is splayed out as if its tentacles were part of some sort of ceremonial gear. "It's a tiny wood carving that Gertrude had already when I came to Paris," wrote Miss Toklas, "she was devoted to it and always had it near her, so it seemed best that you should have it." With this talisman in hand I began, a number of years later, to reconstruct dispassionately a career about which, as the following lines may indicate, my feelings have never been neutral.

Little Elegy for Gertrude Stein

Pass gently, pigeons on the grass,
For where she lies alone, alas,
Is all the wonder ever was.

Deeply she sleeps where everywhere
Grave children make pink marks on air
Or draw one black line . . . here to there.

Because effects were upside down,
Ends by knotty meanings thrown,
Words in her hands grew smooth as stone.

May every bell that says farewell,
Tolling her past all telling tell
What she, all told, knew very well.

If now, somehow, they try to say —
This way, that way, everywhichway —
Goodbye . . . the word is worlds away.

Come softly, all; she lies with those
Whose deepening innocence, God knows,
Is as the rose that is a rose.

Acknowledgments

MY first debts of gratitude for encouragement and specific help in assembling materials for this book are owed to Alice B. Toklas, to Carl Van Vechten, Gertrude Stein's first literary executor, and to Donald Gallup who, in 1958, succeeded him in that capacity. Through Miss Toklas' hospitality, which led to many long conversations with her in the home she shared with Gertrude Stein at V Rue Christine in Paris, my understanding of the world I have attempted to describe was greatly enhanced. Access to the Stein papers in the American Literature Collection of the Yale University Library, and the continually kind services of its curator, Mr. Gallup, and his assistant, Miss Constance Tyson, offered me the opportunity to tell an authentic and comprehensive story.

In a number of interviews that were often the result of happy chance and, for the most part, a matter of casual conversation about the career and personality of Gertrude Stein, I have had the advantage of useful comment and opinion from Frederick Ashton, Joseph Barry, I. Bernard Cohen, the late Muriel Draper, Maurice Grosser, J. R. Isaacs, George John, James Laughlin, Richard Poirier, Basil Rauch, Man Ray, Sir Francis Rose, Dame Edith Sitwell, Sir Osbert Sitwell, Virgil Thomson and Thornton Wilder.

My dependence for information and insight upon others who have written about Gertrude Stein is very likely greater than I realize or would care to admit. Perhaps these writers will accept my thanks and somehow forgive my unconscious thefts when phrases of mine seem to be but echoes of theirs. In this regard, my debt is first to Donald Sutherland — whose Gertrude Stein: A Biography of Her Work — is a performance in the realm of criticism so brilliant as to take on the quality of a lay poem

— and then to Thornton Wilder for his introductions to *The Geographical History of American* and *Four in America;* to Carl Van Vechten for his introduction and notes to *Selected Writings of Gertrude Stein;* to W. G. Rogers for his memoir, *When This You See Remember Me;* to B. L. Reid for his study, *Art by Subtraction — A Dissenting Opinion of Gertrude Stein;* to Elizabeth Sprigge for *Gertrude Stein — Her Life and Work;* to Rosalind S. Miller for *Gertrude Stein: Form and Intelligibility;* to the late Bravig Imbs for his memoir, *Confessions of Another Young Man.*

For faith and for hope and for charity of many kinds directly related to my task, I want to record my gratitude to Elizabeth Ames and the Corporation of Yaddo, Jane Lawson Bavelas, Elizabeth Bishop, Truman Capote, Leonard F. Dean, W. Bernard Fleischmann, Kimon Friar, Victor Glasstone, Lindley Hubbell, Cinna Hynson, Marie Jaffe, Seymour Lawrence, Rollie McKenna, Elias Mengel, Howard Moss, Myron O'Higgins, Theodore M. Purdy, Bill Read, Nancy E. Reynolds, John Robinson, Constance Smith, Holly Stevens, U. T. Summers, John H. Thompson, Ruthven Todd, Edward Weeks and Richard Wilbur.

I am mindful that I have received many kindnesses from persons whose names I do not remember, and I thank them.

JOHN MALCOLM BRINNIN

The author wishes to thank the following for permission to use excerpts from copyrighted material:

ART NEWS for material from Henry McBride's *Memoirs* and for part of an editorial by Alfred M. Frankfurter.

BEACON PRESS and METHUEN & CO., LTD., for *Time and Western Man* by Wyndham Lewis.

THE BOBBS-MERRILL COMPANY, INC., for material from an editor's report on *Three Histories* by Gertrude Stein.

CROWN PUBLISHERS, INC., for material from *Appreciation: Painting, Poetry and Prose* by Leo Stein, copyright 1947 by Leo Stein, used by permission of Crown Publishers, Inc.; and for material from *Journey into the Self* by Leo D. Stein, copyright 1950 by The Estate of Leo D. Stein, used by permission of Crown Publishers, Inc.

THE DIAL PRESS, INC., for *The Passionate Years* by Caresse Crosby, copyright 1953 by Caresse Crosby and used with the permission of the publishers, The Dial Press.

E. P. DUTTON & CO., INC., for *The Writer in America* by Van Wyck Brooks.

DONALD GALLUP, literary executor of Gertrude Stein, for *Picasso* by Gertrude Stein.

DONALD GALLUP, editor of *The Flowers of Friendship* (copyright 1953 by Donald Gallup) and ALFRED A. KNOPF, INC., for permission to quote letters to Gertrude Stein published in this book; and also to the following persons for letters and other material included therein: Janice Biala Brustlein for a letter

(*Acknowledgments, continued*)
from Ford Madox Ford; Katherine Dudley; Mabel Dodge Luhan; Mrs. Ransom B. Matthews for a letter from Grace Davis Street; Henry McBride; Mrs. A. M. Patch for a letter from General A. M. Patch; Jean-Claude Roché for a letter from Henri-Pierre Roché; Ellery Sedgwick; Margaret Sterling Snyder; Daniel M. Stein for a letter from Mrs. Michael Stein; Virgil Thomson; Carl Van Vechten. The author, before his book went to press, tried without success to reach the following authors of letters and other material printed in this volume: Mrs. Harmon C. Bell for a letter from Tillie E. Brown; Paul Bowles; Doris Bry for letters from Alfred Stieglitz; Miss Dorothy Farmer for a letter from Clare Booth Luce; Bernard Faÿ for a letter from Alice B. Toklas; Mrs. Samuel J. Lanahan for two letters from F. Scott Fitzgerald.

GROVE PRESS, INC., for *Apollinaire* by Marcel Adema, translated from the French by Denise Folliot, published by Grove Press, 1955.

CHARLES HAPGOOD for *A Victorian in the Modern World* by Hutchins Hapgood.

HARCOURT, BRACE & CO., INC., for *Movers and Shakers* by Mabel Dodge Luhan; *The Days Before* by Katherine Anne Porter; *The Making of Americans* by Gertrude Stein; and for material reprinted from *The Inmost Leaf* by Alfred Kazin, copyright 1948 by Alfred Kazin, by permission of Harcourt, Brace & Co., Inc.

THE HARVARD ADVOCATE for part of an essay by E. E. Cummings.

HOUGHTON MIFFLIN COMPANY for *American Memoirs* by Henry Seidel Canby.

GEORGE JOHN and CONTEMPORARY POETRY for *A Garland About Me* by George John.

ALFRED A. KNOPF, INC., for *Not So Wild a Dream* by Eric Sevareid.

ALFRED KREYMBORG for *Troubador* by Alfred Kreymborg.

LITTLE, BROWN & CO., INC., for *The Letters of Sherwood Anderson*, edited by Howard Mumford Jones and Walter B. Rideout; for *The Atlantic Book of British and American Poetry*, edited by Dame Edith Sitwell; and for *Laughter in the Next Room* by Sir Osbert Sitwell.

METHUEN & CO., LTD., for *Memoirs of an Aesthete* by Harold Acton.

MARIANNE MOORE for part of a review of Gertrude Stein's *The Making of Americans* which appeared in *The Dial*.

THE NATION for part of an obituary editorial on Gertrude Stein which appeared in 1946.

THE NEWBERRY LIBRARY and DONALD GALLUP, literary executor of Gertrude Stein, for a letter from Gertrude Stein to Sherwood Anderson.

THE NEW REPUBLIC for a review in 1935 by Stark Young.

HAROLD OBER ASSOCIATES, INC., for *An American Artist's Story* by George Biddle, copyright 1939 by George Biddle, reprinted by permission of Harold Ober Associates, Incorporated; and *A Conversation with Gertrude Stein* by John Hyde Preston, copyright 1935 by John Hyde Preston, which appeared in *The Atlantic Monthly*, August, 1935, reprinted by permission of Harold Ober Associates, Incorporated.

OXFORD UNIVERSITY PRESS, INC., for *The Novel and the World's Dilemma* by Edwin B. Burgum.

PANTHEON BOOKS, INC., for *Reflections on the World Today* by Paul Valéry.

PRENTICE–HALL, INC., for *Picasso: An Intimate Portrait* by Jaime Sabartes, copyright 1948 by Jaime Sabartes.

RANDOM HOUSE, INC., for *Not So Long Ago* by Lloyd Morris (copyright 1949 by Lloyd Morris); *The Proud Possessors* by Aline Saarinen (copyright 1958 by the Conde-Nast Publications, Inc., copyright 1958 by Aline Saarinen); *The*

(*Acknowledgments, continued*)

Autobiography of William Carlos Williams (copyright 1948, 1949, 1951 by William Carlos Williams); and the following works by Gertrude Stein: *The Autobiography of Alice B. Toklas* (copyright 1933 by the Atlantic Monthly Company, copyright 1933 by Harcourt, Brace and Company, Inc.); *Brewsie and Willie* (copyright 1946 by Random House, Inc.); *Everybody's Autobiography* (copyright 1937 by Random House, Inc.); *A Geographical History of America* (copyright 1936 by Random House, Inc.); *Selected Writings of Gertrude Stein*, edited by Carl Van Vechten (copyright 1946 by Random House, Inc.); *Portraits and Prayers* (copyright 1934 by the Modern Library, Inc.); and *Wars I Have Seen* (copyright 1945 by Random House, Inc.).

PAUL R. REYNOLDS & SON for the letters of William James.

RINEHART & CO., INC., for *The Painter's Eye* by Maurice Grosser and *When This You See Remember Me* by W. R. Rodgers.

CHARLES SCRIBNER'S SONS for *Axel's Castle* by Edmund Wilson.

MARTIN SECKER AND WARBURG, LTD., for *On Being Geniuses Together* by Robert McAlmon.

LEE SIMONSON for *The Stage Is Set*, copyright 1932 by Lee Simonson.

DAME EDITH SITWELL and PHOENIX HOUSE, LTD., for *Coming to London* by Dame Edith Sitwell, in *Coming to London*.

THE ESTATE OF GERTRUDE STEIN for the following works by Gertrude Stein: *Geography and Plays; A Long Gay Book; Lucy Church Aimiably; Narration.*

TIME, INC., for excerpts from LIFE Magazine August 6, 1945, copyright 1945 Time, Inc.

UNIVERSITY OF OKLAHOMA PRESS for *Art by Subtraction* by B. L. Reid.

CARL VAN VECHTEN for writings by Alice B. Toklas and Gertrude Stein in *Last Operas and Plays* by Gertrude Stein, edited by Carl Van Vechten.

THE VIKING PRESS, INC., for *Exile's Return* by Malcolm Cowley.

GEORGE WEIDENFELD AND NICOLSON, LTD., for *The Sweet and Twenties* by Beverly Nichols.

THE YALE UNIVERSITY LIBRARY OF AMERICAN LITERATURE COLLECTION for photographs.

THE YALE UNIVERSITY LIBRARY and DONALD GALLUP, as literary executor of Gertrude Stein, for the following manuscript material in the Gertrude Stein Collection and elsewhere in the Yale Collection of American Literature, Yale University Library. By Gertrude Stein: *Radcliffe Themes;* "Reflections on the Atomic Bomb" (published in the *Yale Poetry Journal*, 1946); letters to Mabel Dodge Luhan, Mabel Weeks, W. G. Rodgers, and others; and an excerpt from Gertrude Stein's will. By Dr. Arthur Lachman: *Gertrude Stein as I Knew Her* (unpublished manuscript in the Gertrude Stein Collection).

YALE UNIVERSITY PRESS for the following works by Gertrude Stein: *Bee Time Vine; Mrs. Reynolds; Painted Lace; Two and Other Early Portraits;* for *Gertrude Stein: A Biography of Her Work* by Donald Sutherland; and for the introduction by Thornton Wilder to *Four in America*.

In addition, the author was unable to reach the following persons before his book went to press, but wishes here to express his gratitude: Margaret Anderson for excerpts from *My Thirty Years' War* by Margaret Anderson; The Heirs of Muriel Draper for excerpts from *Music at Midnight* by Muriel Draper; The Estate of Claude McKay for an excerpt from *A Long Way from Home* by Claude McKay; Mrs. Wellington M. Watters for excerpts from *Confessions of Another Young Man* by Bravig Imbs.

412

A Selected Bibliography of the Works of Gertrude Stein

Three Lives
  The Grafton Press, New York, 1910
  The Modern Library, Inc., New York, 1933
The Making of Americans
  Contact Editions, Paris, 1925
  Albert and Charles Boni, New York, 1926
  Harcourt, Brace and Co., New York, 1934 (Abridged Edition)
Tender Buttons
  Claire Marie, New York, 1914
  transition No. 14, 1928
Geography and Plays
  The Four Seas Company, Boston, 1922 (With a Foreword by Sherwood Anderson)
Composition as Explanation
  The Hogarth Press, London, 1926
  Doubleday Doran and Co., Inc., New York, 1928
Useful Knowledge
  Payson and Clarke Ltd., New York, 1928
Lucy Church Amiably
  Plain Edition, Paris, 1930

How to Write
  Plain Edition, Paris, 1931
The Autobiography of Alice B. Toklas
  Harcourt, Brace and Co., New York, 1933
  John Lane the Bodley Head, London, 1933
Portraits and Prayers
  Random House, New York, 1934
Lectures in America
  Random House, New York, 1935
Narration
  University of Chicago Press, 1935 (With an Introduction by Thornton Wilder)
The Geographical History of America
  Random House, New York, 1936 (With an Introduction by Thornton Wilder)
Everybody's Autobiography
  Random House, New York, 1937
Picasso
  Charles Scribner's Sons, New York, 1939
The World Is Round
  William R. Scott, Inc., New York, 1939
Paris France
  Charles Scribner's Sons, New York, 1940
What Are Masterpieces
  The Conference Press, Los Angeles, 1940 (Foreword by Robert Bartlett Haas) '
Ida, A Novel
  Random House, New York, 1941
Wars I Have Seen
  Random House, New York, 1944
Brewsie and Willie
  Random House, New York, 1946
Selected Writings of Gertrude Stein
  Random House, New York, 1946 (Edited with an Introduction and Notes by Carl Van Vechten)
Four in America
  Yale University Press, New Haven, 1947 (With an Introduction by Thornton Wilder)
Last Operas and Plays.
  Rinehart and Company, Inc., New York, 1949 (With an Introduction by Carl Van Vechten)
Things As They Are
  The Banyan Press, Pawlet, Vermont, 1951

Two: Gertrude Stein and Her Brother
  Yale University Press, New Haven, 1951 (With a Foreword by Janet Flanner)
Mrs. Reynolds
  Yale University Press, New Haven, 1952 (With a Foreword by Lloyd Frankenberg)
Bee Time Vine
  Yale University Press, New Haven, 1953 (With an Introduction by Virgil Thomson)
As Fine as Melanctha
  Yale University Press, New Haven, 1954 (With a Foreword by Natalie Clifford Barney)
Painted Lace
  Yale University Press, New Haven, 1955 (With an Introduction by Daniel-Henry Kahnweiler)
Stanzas in Meditation
  Yale University Press, New Haven, 1956 (With a Preface by Donald Sutherland)
Alphabets and Birthdays
  Yale University Press, New Haven, 1957 (With an Introduction by Donald Gallup)
A Novel of Thank You
  Yale University Press, New Haven, 1958 (With an Introduction by Carl Van Vechten)

Index

417

Burgos, 152
Burgum, Edwin Berry, 376
Burke, Edmund, 12
Burke, Kenneth, 326
Burlington Review, 189
Burns, Robert, 12
Burroughs, George, 4
Bush Street Theatre, 21
Buss, Kate, 241, 242, 245
Byron, Lord, 82, 169, 262

CAESAR, 34, 353
Cage, John, 297
Caine, Miss Gordon, 190
Calburn, Robbie, 284
Caldwell, Erskine, 263
California, 8, 13, 15, 36, 104, 338, 400
Cambridge, 25, 27, 28, 34, 44, 173, 244, 281-283, 296, 354
Camera Work, 74, 147, 190
Canada, 257
Canby, Henry Seidel, 243, 342
Cape Cod, 202
The Captive, 345
Carlyle, Thomas, 12
Caruso, Enrico, 178, 234
Casa Ricci, 109
Casals, Pablo, 41
Case, Frank, 336
Castagno, Andrea del, 37
Cather, Willa, 124
Cazalis, Henry, 131
Cecil, David, 284
Central Pacific Railroad, 23
Century magazine, 20
Cercle Artistique Belge, 398
Cerf, Bennett, 314, 340, 355, 388
Cézanne, Paul, 50, 52, 56, 60, 61, 62, 63, 69, 77, 91, 122, 127, 134, 136, 174, 177, 183, 184, 192, 194, 197, 207, 257, 302, 312, 363, 365, 366, 370, 389
Chadbourne, Emily Crane, 189
Chambéry, 285, 366
Champlain, S. S., 334, 340
Chang and Eng, 4
Chaplin, Charles, 340
Chastel, André, 146
Chaucer, 164, 337
Chavannes, Puvis de, 181
Chicago, 98, 176, 180, 189, 232, 235, 340, 346

Chicago Tribune, 289
China, 182
Christian Science, 253, 279
Chrysler, Walter P. Jr., 370
Cirque Medrano, 86
Cité Université, 390
Civil War (American), 287, 391, 401
Claire-Marie, 158
Clark, Harriet, 41
Claudel, Paul, 230
Cleopatra, 22
Clermont-Tonnerre, Duchesse de, 287, 312
Cleveland, Ohio, 235
Cluny Museum, 335
Coates, Robert, 238, 280
Cobb, Irvin S., 179
Coblenz, 392
Coburn, Alvin Langdon, 210
Cocteau, Jean, 151, 215, 234, 235, 308, 357, 358
Collins, J. P., 213
Collioure, 215
Cologne, 182, 392
Colon, Panama, 370
Colum, Mary, 250
Columbia University, 399
Columbus, Christopher, 10, 12, 53
Concord, Massachusetts, 332
Cone, Claribel, 75, 76, 77
Cone, Etta, 75, 76, 77, 99, 118, 119
Cone, Frederic, 77
Congressional Record, 12
Contact Editions, 265-267
Cook, John, 17
Cook, Mary, 17
Cook, Thomas, 215
Cook, William, 220
Copley Society, 176
Corbeil, 90
Cornell, Katharine, 388, 400
Cornwall, 354
Correggio, 196
Cortissoz, Royal, 180
Count of Monte Cristo, 21
Cowley, Malcolm, 141, 232, 242, 257
Cox, Kenyon, 180, 319
Crabbe, 12
Crane, Hart, 287, 300, 394
Crane, Stephen, 124
Creevy Papers, 41
Crevel, René, 279

419

421

Wright, Richard, 120, 394
Wright, Wilbur, 315

Yacco, Sadda, 327
Yaddo, 407
Yale, 192, 403

Yale Poetry Journal, 401
Yeats, William Butler, 88, 298-300, 302
Young, Stark, 327

Zangwill, Israel, 40, 189